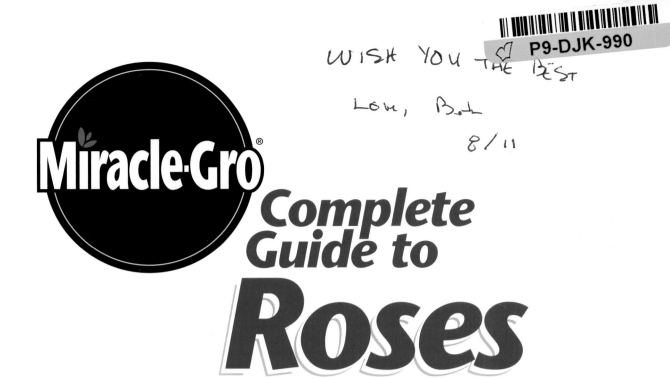

Miracle-Gro®
Complete Guide to
Roses

Meredith® Books
Des Moines, Iowa

Miracle-Gro Complete Guide to Roses
Editor: Michael McKinley
Contributing Editor: Veronica Lorson Fowler
Contributing Designer: Ernie Shelton
Contributing Technical Editor: Steve Jones
Contributing Writers: Erin Hynes, Nancy Rose, Marty Ross.
Copy Chief: Terri Fredrickson
Copy Editor: Kevin Cox
Publishing Operations Manager: Karen Schirm
Senior Editor, Asset and Information Management: Phillip Morgan
Edit and Design Production Coordinator: Mary Lee Gavin
Book Production Managers: Pam Kvitne,
    Marjorie J. Schenkelberg, Mark Weaver
Imaging Center Operator: Jill Reed
Contributing Copy Editors: Sarah Watson
Contributing Proofreaders: Fran Gardner, Sara Henderson, Lynn Steiner
Contributing Indexer: Ellen Sherron
Photo Researcher/Editorial Assistant: Susan Ferguson

**Additional Editorial Contributions from
  Art Rep Services**
Director: Chip Nadeau
Illustrator: Dave Brandon

Meredith® Books
Editor in Chief: Gregory H. Kayko
Executive Director, Design: Matt Strelecki
Managing Editor: Amy Tincher-Durik
Executive Editor: Benjamin W. Allen
Senior Associate Design Director: Tom Wegner
Marketing Product Manager: Brent Wiersma

Executive Director, Marketing and New Business: Kevin Kacere
Director, Marketing and Publicity: Amy Nichols
Executive Director, Sales: Ken Zagor
Director, Operations: George A. Susral
Director, Production: Douglas M. Johnston
Business Director: Janice Croat

Senior Vice President: Karla Jeffries
Vice President and General Manager: Douglas J. Guendel

Meredith Publishing Group
President: Jack Griffin
Executive Vice President: Doug Olson

Meredith Corporation
Chairman of the Board: William T. Kerr
President and Chief Executive Officer: Stephen M. Lacy

In Memoriam: E.T. Meredith III (1933–2003)

Photographers
Photographers credited may retain copyright © to the listed
photographs. L=Left, R=Right, C=Center, B=Bottom, T=Top

Contributing Photographer- Richard Baer
On the cover: Hot Cocoa, a floribunda introduced in 2002
Cover Photographer: Doug Hetherington
Saxon Holt 181TR, 226TR; Jerry Pavia 177TR; Richard Shiell
72B, 183TR.

All of us at Meredith® Books are dedicated to providing
you with the information and ideas you need to enhance your
home and garden. We welcome your comments and suggestions
about this book. Write to us at:
    Meredith Corporation
    Meredith Gardening Books
    1716 Locust St.
    Des Moines, IA 50309–3023

If you would like more information on other Scotts products,
call 800/225-2883 or visit us at: www.scotts.com

Note to the Readers: Due to differing conditions, tools,
and individual skills, Meredith Corporation assumes no
responsibility for any damages, injuries suffered, or losses
incurred as a result of following the information published
in this book. Before beginning any project, review the
instructions carefully, and if any doubts or questions
remain, consult local experts or authorities. Because codes
and regulations vary greatly, you always should check
with authorities to ensure that your project complies
with all applicable local codes and regulations. Always
read and observe all of the safety precautions provided
by manufacturers of any tools, equipment, or supplies,
and follow all accepted safety procedures.

For membership information
to the American Rose Society visit
www.ARS.org

▲ The antique French rose Felicite et Pepetue teams beautifully with this antique vase.

Contents

Understanding roses

Why grow roses?

Some gardeners shy away, unfairly labeling them as fussy, high-maintenance plants.

But roses are a must for nearly any garden. Roses set the bar for floral beauty and excellence through their history, perfect flower form, and intoxicating scent. Queens have honored them and poets have memorialized them. Their image represents the concept of love and perfection. It's no wonder that roses are the most revered flowers on earth.

The versatility of roses

Of all the plants available to grow in your garden, none is more versatile, with more beautiful colors, styles, sizes, shapes, and fragrances, than the rose. What other plant can claim the passionate enthusiasm of millions of gardeners around the world, or a vast number of public and private gardens and festivals around the globe devoted to it? What's more, roses are celebrated as one of the most romantic and thoughtful gifts around.

Rose fans compete in rose shows and garden contests, join societies dedicated to the enjoyment of their hobby, and talk and write about the thousands of varieties available and their characteristics. Even novices can enjoy the pleasures of including roses in the landscape and reap benefits.

▲ Growing roses is addictive. Once you get started, you'll fall in love with their color, fragrance, history, and beauty. They're also ideal for cutting and bringing indoors to enjoy up close.

A palette of color, style, and texture

Rose bushes and the blooms themselves come in all shapes, sizes, and colors. New varieties are introduced every year. Roses can be mixed into the landscape and, with careful selection, can provide color all summer long.

Versatility in size and shape contributes to the rose's popularity. From miniatures that grow 6 inches tall to climbers that will scale a three-story house, roses can provide color and beauty in nearly any sunny location.

Colors to enhance the garden

It's true that most roses are shades of red and pink, but especially with new developments in roses, the color range is becoming breathtaking.

Even a white rose is not just a white rose. It can be dead white, creamy white with just a hint of yellow, or have the slightest suggestion of a pink blush or a delicate beige or apricot that suggests sheets of antique parchment.

Modern roses are now available in the clearest yellows, the deepest purple-mauves, delicious softest apricots, and brilliant clear oranges. There are even greenish roses.

The only colors not truly represented by roses are black and blue, but even then, there are some roses that are such a deep purple-red they are nearly black. And there are some purple-mauve roses that verge on blue.

Bloom form and styles

Roses are also available in a number of flower forms. Though the high-centered swirling flower form of florist roses is the most popular in garden roses, there are many other forms to explore and grow. Single, semidouble, cup-shape, quartered, balled, ruffled, and scalloped flowers are available. The way the flowers bloom also is varied. Roses can grow as single flowers on long stems, on sprays of long stems, or on huge clusters of shorter stems. A single rose petal can offer amazing contrasts of colors on the front and reverse, on stripes down the petal, and on margins contrasting with the middle of the petal or the base.

Fragrance

For some gardeners, fragrance is *the* reason to grow roses. There are almost as many nuances of fragrance in roses as there are colors, especially to the discerning nose. Rose scents can be fruity, spicy, or sweet or redolent of anise or musk or many other fragrances.

Some have no fragrance; some have slight fragrance; some have intense fragrance.

Easier than ever

It's never been easier to grow roses. Thanks to centuries of rose breeding, there are now more roses than ever—for any gardening purpose. They make ideal garden flowers, many types blooming continuously all summer. Roses are excellent landscaping plants too. Many forms grow wide and tall, creating flowering hedges. Low-growing and compact versions can cover up (and dress up) hard-to-landscape areas such as around home foundations.

With roses, beauty does not equal difficulty. Plant roses in your garden, on your patio, and in your landscape with the confidence that they'll reward you with blooms, fragrance, good looks—all the characteristics that have made the rose the so-called queen of flowers for centuries.

▲ Whether they're growing tall (as with this New Dawn climber) or growing low (as with the Ballerina shrub roses), it's not difficult to grow roses in abundance. Just a plant or two can fill the corner of a garden.

New developments in roses

These are exciting times in the world of roses. Gardeners today have far more choices than those of the previous generation, who had two main options: stunning but disease-prone modern roses such as hybrid teas that required weekly pesticide treatments; and tough, old-fashioned rose types with short bloom periods, small flowers, and coarse growth habits.

Thanks to rose breeders who responded to the demand for pest-free, low-maintenance roses that grow well and look fabulous, you can fill your yard with an array of heavy-flowering, durable roses that demand little attention—other than admiration.

A dramatic tradition

The history of roses is fraught with all the elements of a great novel—intrigue, legend, symbolism, love, and war. Roses graced the great ancient civilizations—Rome, Egypt, and China. History records the rose as both an icon and a plant. The rose emblem appeared in the 15th-century War of the Roses—the struggle between the English houses of York and Lancaster. In Greek and Roman mythology, the rose represents characteristics from passion to modesty.

The rose has been a symbol of perfection and wealth for centuries. Depicted in paintings, tapestries, and poetry, the rose has been the muse of artists past to present. Scottish poet Robert Burns captured the metaphorical connection between perfect love and the perfect flower in his lines "my luve's like a red, red rose That's newly sprung in June."

Beyond beauty, the rose also offers medicinal qualities. In physic gardens (the ancient world's answer to modern-day pharmacies) several parts of the rose were used for health care purposes (hence the Apothecary's Rose). Pliny the Elder recorded 32 medicinal uses for the rose in the 1st century. Modern herbalists also find healthful uses for many parts of the rose plant including the petals, leaves, and hips.

Brave new roses

Leading the vanguard of easy-care roses were the English shrub roses of British rose breeder David Austin. In the 1940s, Austin started crossing modern roses with old roses such as albas and gallicas that had fallen far out of fashion. His goal was to combine the fragrance and durability of old roses with the color range and repeating bloom of modern roses in the form of a shrub that would be at home in a cottage garden. He introduced his first repeat-blooming shrub roses in 1969 and started his own nursery to sell them because other rose nurseries weren't interested. Austin's approach to breeding and the roses he created were revolutionary, and more than 150 David Austin English shrub rose cultivars are now on the market.

The rose revolution recently entered a new phase with the introduction of the Knock Out rose in 1998. Knock Out roses are compact enough for small gardens—they grow to about 3 feet tall by 3 feet wide—and bloom from spring into fall. They are winter hardy, tolerate drought, can take part shade, don't need fertilizer, and resist insects and black spot, even in humid regions. And they are self-cleaning—you don't have to deadhead. The first Knock Out rose was named an All-America Rose Selection (AARS) for 2000. Knock Out roses have two drawbacks—they are not fragrant and on the West Coast they are proving to be somewhat susceptible to powdery mildew.

But they've been generally extremely well received nationally and a number of variations are available.

How low can you go?

Another relatively new and popular trend is small, low-care roses, including groundcovers and miniatures.

Groundcover roses are low, sprawling roses. Some cling closely to the ground, while others arch at the center and tumble to the ground. They usually bear small flowers and require little care. Two of the best-known lines are the Meidiland groundcover roses, which came out in the mid-1980s, and the most recent Flower Carpet series.

Another darling is the miniature rose, taking the quest for compactness to an extreme with plants that reach about 1 foot tall. Although a few miniature rose varieties were around in the 1930s, their numbers surged after World War II. In the last decade of the 20th century, 500 new cultivars were registered. It's easy to

ANCIENT TIMES

Rosa glauca

Roses are cultivated in the great gardens of ancient China, Egypt, Rome, and other civilizations.

15TH CENTURY

The White Rose of York

The War of the Roses is fought in England.

1798

Souvenir de la Malmaison

The Empress Josephine creates Chateau de Malmaison, a country house near Paris with a legendary rose garden.

▲ With David Austin roses, it's true that everything old is new again. In the 1940s, the British rose breeder created a type of rose that had many of the best qualities of the wonderful old garden roses but with better disease resistance and much longer bloom time.

19TH CENTURY → **1920S** → **1940S** → **1954** *continued* →

La Reine Victoria

The Bourbon rose is brought to France, sparking a renewed interest in roses and rose breeding and leading to the development of a wide range of roses there and in England known as old garden roses.

Iceberg

The first floribunda rose is hybridized.

Graham Thomas

David Austin begins his breeding work on the so-called English roses.

Queen Elizabeth

The grandiflora class is created specifically for a new rose, Queen Elizabeth.

New developments in roses *(continued)*

▲ Fragrant Cloud has been a triumph of modern rose breeding, which has created a large, gorgeous classic rose with fascinating coloring and intense fragrance.

understand their popularity—they are tiny enough to grow in a pot indoors or out. And although the earliest miniatures were scentless, breeding programs in the past few decades have successfully produced fragrant miniatures.

Gardeners who want bigger flowers than miniatures produce can opt for the minifloras, which are slightly larger plants. They are small enough to grow in a pot on the patio, but with larger flowers are showier.

Another exciting development in miniatures has been that of climbing miniatures. Like their more compact cousins, miniature climbers have delightfully proportioned tiny flowers and foliage, but climb somewhat larger, up to 6 feet. They're perfect to train up a small trellis that a traditional climber would overwhelm.

The future is rosy

Currently, the biggest trend in rose breeding is increasing disease resistance to reduce maintenance even further.

For decades, roses have gotten a bad reputation for being hard to grow, and breeders want to change that image.

It's true that some roses can be difficult to grow, especially if they're not right for the climate. To make sure gardeners have information on the best roses available, the American Rose Society (ARS) now rates roses on a sliding scale in terms of vigor and beauty. (See the Gallery of Roses starting on page 136 for individual listings.)

The ultimate goal of rose breeding, in the mind of many, is to create a rose with the flowers of a hybrid tea that is disease-resistant and highly fragrant.

And the quest for the elusive blue rose that holds its color continues; in the meantime, gardeners can enjoy the lovely lavender "failures" that result.

1970S AND 1980S

Carefree Beauty

Low-maintenance shrub roses become popular as time-strapped and environmentally aware baby boomers settle down and take up gardening.

1990S

Rise 'n' Shine

The popularity of miniature roses surges. Gardeners, especially those with small spaces, are charmed by the tiny foliage and flowers.

2000

Knock Out

Knock Out and other low-maintenance, disease-resistant, long-blooming roses become increasingly popular.

Understanding rose anatomy

Knowing the basic parts of a rose bush will help you understand the plant so you can better provide for its needs.

Roots and foliage

Roses, like many other plants, have two types of roots. Thick, strong, woody anchor roots hold the rose upright and store nutrients for the winter. Attached to these are delicate hair roots or feeder roots, which absorb water and nutrients from the soil.

Rootstock

In a grafted rose, the base (roots) onto which the desired variety is grafted is called the *rootstock*, or the stock. Increasingly, roses are sold without grafts—that is, on their own roots. These are called own-root roses.

Bud (graft) union

On grafted roses, the swollen area where the rootstock meets the grafted stem is called the bud union or graft union. While technically the two terms are slightly different, they are used interchangeably.

Canes

Canes are the main branches of the rose bush. Canes grow from the roots on an own-root rose—one that has not been grafted—and from the bud union on a grafted rose.

Sucker

On a grafted rose, a sucker (not shown) is an undesirable cane that grows up from the rootstock, below the bud union. It can grow right at the base or may sprout through the soil a few to several inches out from the bush. It produces undesirable, different flowers.

Shank

On grafted roses, the shank is the main stem of the rootstock rose. The desired rose is grafted to the top of the shank.

Leaf

The leaves of roses are pinnately compound—that is, each leaf is made up of leaflet pairs that line the leaf stem, or *rachis*, with one leaflet on the end. The stem that holds all the leaflets is the *petiole*. The edge of the leaflet, which is usually serrated, is called the *leaf margin*.

The rose flower

An understanding of the terminology used to describe the parts of rose flowers comes in handy when identifying and understanding roses. Flower anatomy is complex, but you can get by with these basics.

Flower stems

The stems that attach the flower to the plant are called the *pedicel* and the *peduncle*. Although the terms are used interchangeably, they are different. The pedicel is the stem between a *single* flower and the plant. The peduncle is the stem between a *cluster* of flowers and the plant.

Petals and sepals

All roses are based on five petals. On "doubled" roses that look as if they have more petals, the extra petals are really modified forms of the male organs, the stamens. In doubled flowers, the modified stamens are called *petaloids*. Extremely double flowers cannot produce pollen and so are sterile. The female portions, however, may be fertile. The five petals as a unit are called the *corolla*. Below the petals are five leaflike *sepals*, which together form the *calyx*. The calyx covers the bud until it opens. The combination of the corolla and calyx is called the *perianth*.

Male organs

Inside the perianth are many *stamens*, the male portion of the flower. Each stamen has a long, thin stalk called the *filament*. On top of the filament is the *anther*,

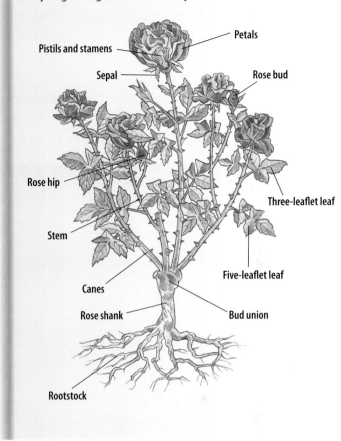

THE ANATOMY OF A ROSE

Knowing the basic parts of this fascinating plant is key to growing roses successfully.

- Pistils and stamens
- Sepal
- Petals
- Rose bud
- Rose hip
- Three-leaflet leaf
- Stem
- Five-leaflet leaf
- Canes
- Rose shank
- Bud union
- Rootstock

which usually is yellow. Pollen is produced inside the anther, which opens and releases the pollen.

Female organs

At the center of the flower is the female portion of the flower, the *gynoecium*. It is made up of many *pistils*. Each pistil has three parts. The sticky *stigma* at the top catches pollen from the male flower, and the long, thin *style* transports the pollen deeper into the flower, to the round *ovary*. Each ovary contains a single egg, or ovule, that becomes a seed when fertilized. The ovary is *inferior*, which means that it develops below the petals and sepals, rather than above.

Rose hips

The fleshy fruit of the rose that swells into the seedpod is called a *hip*. It looks like a small crabapple and can be red, pink, dark purple, yellow, or orange, depending on the rose variety. Inside the hip are seed-bearing structures called *achenes*.

Roses require pollination to produce hips, so species with open-face flowers that pollinating insects can enter are more likely to produce hips. The hips of some rose species are high in vitamin C. Depending on the variety, the hips may persist on the bush into winter, providing winter interest as well as food for birds and other animals.

Understanding rose bloom times

Roses are all about the flowers. So it helps to understand how often and how long different types of roses bloom.

Roses can be divided into two groups based on how often they flower during your region's growing season: once-blooming and repeat-blooming.

Once-blooming roses

These burst into bloom once each growing season, in late spring, about six weeks after growth starts. Once-blooming roses usually belong to the old-rose groups, including damasks, albas, gallicas, and centifolias.

What once-blooming roses lack in flowering frequency, they make up for in volume. For a few weeks, the canes bow down beneath the weight of a breathtaking display of flowers. When blooming ends, prune the plant to the ground and turn your attention to your ever-flowering roses (see page 122 for more about pruning). If the growing season is long enough, some once-blooming roses may bloom again in the autumn.

Once-blooming roses have flowers that start to open as the earlier ones die off, drawing out the duration of flowering. How long they bloom varies with weather—some flower better after a cold winter and some perform better after warm winters. For almost all, a sudden hot spell

ROSE BLOOM TIMES

Different roses bloom in different patterns during the growing season. Below is what the following types of rose might do in climates in the northern two-thirds of the United States.

	June	July	August
Once-Blooming Roses Some roses (primarily old garden roses) bloom very heavily in June then sit out the rest of the season.			
Repeat Blooming Roses Modern roses tend to bloom heavily in June, with intermittent blooming during cooler or wetter spells through the summer and a flush of bloom in fall when temperatures cool off.			
Continuous-Blooming Roses Some of the new low-maintenance roses bloom fairly heavily nearly all growing season.			

usually brings flowering to a quick close.

Some old roses reputed to bloom for a long time include the hybrid Bourbon rose Vivid; the alba roses Felicite Parmentier and Chloris; and the centifolias Chapeau de Napoléon and Gros Choux d' Hollande.

Repeat-blooming roses

These are sometimes called ever-blooming, continuous blooming, free-flowering, or remontant roses. The term "ever-blooming" is a misnomer because most repeat-blooming varieties, more accurately, have flushes of blooms rather than nonstop flowering.

Although some old roses are repeat bloomers (notably hybrid perpetual roses and noisettes), most repeat bloomers are modern roses, including hybrid teas, grandifloras, floribundas, groundcover roses, shrub roses, and miniatures.

Like once-blooming roses, repeat-blooming roses start flowering about six weeks after growth begins, making the first bloom of spring the highlight of the rose season. How often repeat bloomers flower and how long the flowering period lasts depend on the variety and local growing conditions such as temperature and rainfall.

Some cultivars bloom constantly, or nearly constantly. Carefree Beauty blooms steadily all season.

Encouraging bigger and better blooms

Keep in mind that how heavily your rose blooms also has to do with weather, water, pruning, fertilizing, and light.

Roses don't like to bloom in hot weather, that is, repeated days with temperatures above 85°F/30°C. They also bloom as long as they have steady moisture; in times of drought they conserve moisture in any way they can and one of those is to stop blooming.

Pruning also comes into play. Pruning correctly encourages repeat-blooming roses to flower abundantly. Because roses bloom on the parts of the plant that get the most sun, prune for openness and even spacing. Deadhead to remove spent flowers, preventing seed formation that inhibits blooming (see pages 122–128 for more information on pruning).

If your roses aren't blooming well, another possibility is lack of sunlight. Roses love sun—it's hard to give them too much. You may need to move the rose to a brighter place in the garden or remove branches of nearby trees that cast shade.

Another possibility is that the rose plant is starved for nutrients. Roses are heavy feeders. Even if your rose blooms without feeding, you'll be surprised at how many more flowers it will produce if you feed it regularly, as often as every two weeks. (See page 106 for detailed information on feeding roses).

September	October	November

ARS ROSARIAN TIP...

Roses are beautiful companions for other flowers. Try planting them surrounded by larkspur, agapanthus, iris, phlox, and silver-leaved foliage plants such as dusty miller.

Even when the roses aren't in bloom, your garden will look wonderful.

—Marilyn Wellan, Alexandria, Louisiana

Understanding rose color

The color range of roses is remarkable.

The only colors missing in roses are true blue and black. And these days, with the help of genetic engineering, the true blue rose and perhaps even the black rose (some deep red roses verge on it) are not far off. Every other color is represented in roses with reds, pinks, yellows, mauves, whites, oranges, apricots, and even green as well as countless hues and shades of these colors.

A single rose petal can offer amazing contrasts of colors to be found on the front and reverse, stripes down the petal, and margins contrasting with the middle of the petal or the base.

When considering rose colors, it helps to know that most old roses come in cool or pale colors, such as pale pink, soft pink-lilac, or faded yellow. Many modern roses, on the other hand, deliver bright or warm colors, such as vivid yellow, orange, gold, or pure white.

▲ Just in the apricot range alone, roses can vary from softest creamy peach to a deeper orange.

ROSE PETAL PATTERNS

Even on a single petal, the color of a rose can vary. Here are the six classifications for rose petal color variations:

Solid
Gold Medal

Multicolor
Rainbow's End

Bicolor
Duet

Blended
Love & Peace

Striped
Ferdinand Pichard

Handpainted
Brilliant Pink Iceberg

Changing rose colors

When planning your colors, it's important to realize that not all rose colors are stable. Blooms with just a few pigments, such as pink and yellow, generally stay the same color through the season. Those in more complex shades made up of several pigments, such as coral and apricot, tend to change as the rose opens and matures. Reds commonly let blue pigment show through, adding a slight purple tinge to the red as it matures.

Growing conditions, as well as the number of pigments, affect color. Soil fertility, temperatures, intensity of the sun, and rainfall play roles in determining the color of some roses. The coral rose you see in a friend's garden might not be the same color in yours.

For many people, the variability in a rose's color throughout the season and from year to year is part of its charm. It adds interest, like the changing color of tree leaves from spring chartreuse to deep summer green to autumn yellow.

But if it is important to you to have a rose with a stable color, check descriptions of the rose in several sources. Similar descriptions usually indicate a rose that is true to color, while varied descriptions hint at a rose with changing color. You can also check with a local garden center, rose society, or botanical garden.

ROSE COLORS

From the purest white to the deepest, darkest red, rose colors vary significantly.
The American Rose Society (ARS) has a number of different color classifications. Here are some, roughly grouped.

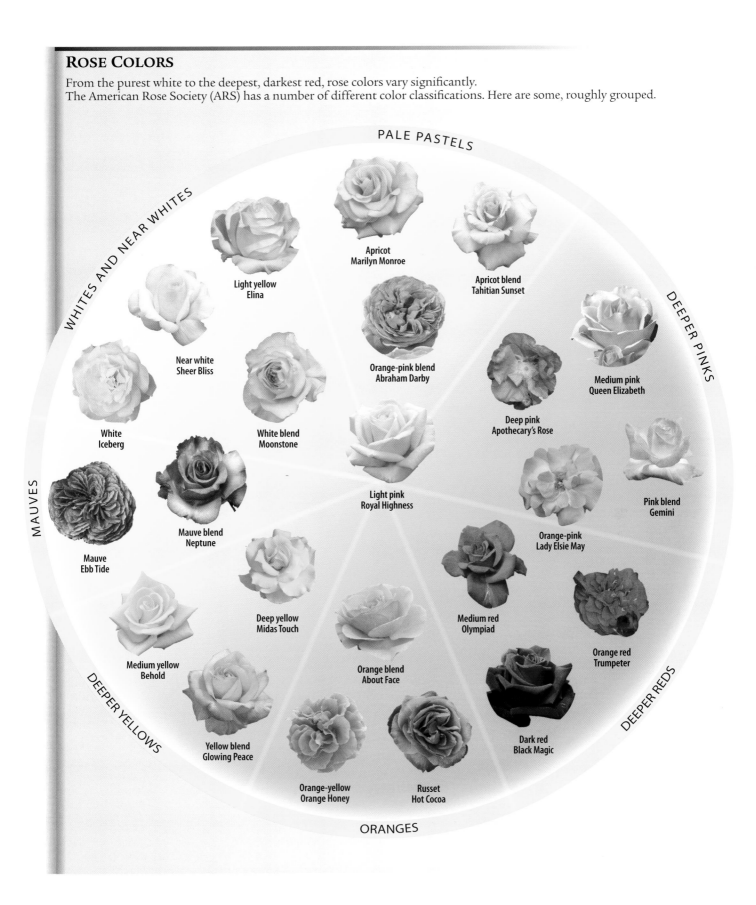

PALE PASTELS

WHITES AND NEAR WHITES

DEEPER PINKS

MAUVES

DEEPER YELLOWS

DEEPER REDS

ORANGES

Light yellow
Elina

Apricot
Marilyn Monroe

Apricot blend
Tahitian Sunset

Near white
Sheer Bliss

Orange-pink blend
Abraham Darby

Medium pink
Queen Elizabeth

White
Iceberg

White blend
Moonstone

Deep pink
Apothecary's Rose

Mauve blend
Neptune

Light pink
Royal Highness

Pink blend
Gemini

Mauve
Ebb Tide

Orange-pink
Lady Elsie May

Deep yellow
Midas Touch

Medium red
Olympiad

Orange red
Trumpeter

Medium yellow
Behold

Orange blend
About Face

Dark red
Black Magic

Yellow blend
Glowing Peace

Orange-yellow
Orange Honey

Russet
Hot Cocoa

Understanding rose plant shapes and sizes

Rose sizes vary to an astounding degree. You can select from a miniature that grows just 1 foot tall and wide or a rambler that reaches 15 feet wide and 60 feet tall.

It all depends on your gardening needs. Remember width as well as height. If you have a small border area 18 inches wide, you may want to plant miniature or minifloras in that space. If your area is 3 feet wide, hybrid teas, grandifloras, or floribundas may be appropriate.

If you have an area 4 to 5 feet wide, sprawling old garden roses may make a good choice. If you want to cover a garage, choose tall climbers, or large shrubs might suffice. If you have unlimited space, you can mix and match various types of roses in groupings that define your environment according to your own design.

STANDARD
These lollipop-shape tree roses grow 2 to 6 feet depending on how they were grafted.

MINIATURE
These roses most often are perfectly scaled-down versions of larger roses with tiny leaves and tiny flowers. They usually range from 1 to 2 feet tall.

PILLAR ROSE
Any rose with moderately long canes can be trained as a pillar rose. Bush-type roses with long canes can be pillars and small climbers can be pillars as well.

CLIMBER
These roses are decidely vertical growers. Choose from climbers that range from 12 to 20 feet or miniature climbers that hit just 6 feet. Climbing versions of many bush-type roses are available.

RAMBLER
These are the giants of the rose world, with rampant growth that can hit 30 or more feet.

SHRUB
A loose category, shrub roses usually grow roughly as wide as they do tall (usually between 3 and 6 feet) and have an attractive, bushy growth habit.

GROUNDCOVER
Nearly any low-growing rose can be used as a groundcover rose, but those roses that are low (3 feet and under) and tend to have long, sprawling canes work best.

HYBRID TEA
The ideal for cut and show flowers, these upright-growing plants can hit up to 6 feet on long, leggy canes.

Rose flower sizes, styles, and textures

When choosing roses for your garden, consider the shapes and sizes of their blooms.

Some gardeners, for example, find they are attracted to the classic high-centered forms found in many hybrid teas. These are the closest to roses sold as cut flowers in flower shops. Conversely, other gardeners prefer the old-fashioned look of a quartered rose or the wild rose look of a single.

BLOOM SHAPE

Bloom shape is the way the petals are arranged on the flower. Rose flowers can range in shape from flat to globular (the so-called cabbage roses) to quartered.

Flat
Sally Holmes

Classic high-centered
Gemini

Fully open
Betty Boop

Globular (cabbage)
Madame Ernest Calvat

Rosette
Sexy Rexy

Quartered
Fair Bianca

PETAL SHAPE

The majority of rose petals are flat and broad with minimal curling. But some are reflexed—that is, their edges roll under. Some are ruffled, with wavy edges, and some are frilled in interesting serrated patterns.

Plain broad, John F. Kennedy

Reflexed, Perfect Moment

Ruffled, Just Joey

Frilled, Abraham Darby

PETAL NUMBER

Petal number can vary greatly from rose to rose, as few as 5 to more than 100. Terminology reflects how many petals are packed into the flower with the ARS breaking them down into the following categories:

Single: 4 to 8 petals
Frau Dagmar Hartopp

Semidouble: 9 to 16 petals
Rosa Mundi

Double: 17 to 25 petals
Showbiz

Full: 26 to 40 petals
Fragrant Cloud

Very full: 41 or more
Gertrude Jekyll

FLOWER SIZE

The flower size on roses varies greatly according to the type of rose and how it is grown. As a rule, hybrid teas, grandifloras, old garden roses, shrub roses, and some climbers have the largest flowers, 3 to 6 inches across.

Rose fanciers who want to show roses tend to favor hybrid teas for their size and form and carefully disbud the roses (see page 129) to make these large roses grow even larger.

Medium-size flowers (2 to 3 inches across) are found on many floribundas.

Miniflora flowers are 1 to 2 inches across. And miniatures are the tiniest with flowers just ½ to 1 inch across.

Below are four rose flowers, shown at their actual size.

FLOWER SUBSTANCE AND TEXTURE

The texture and substance of the petals of each flower are important, especially when taking into account how well it will do in the local climate.

Some roses have very thick petals that are crisp and open slowly in the heat, making them last much longer in hot climates (not to mention in the vase).

In cooler climates, varieties with less substance and fewer petals, such as single roses, do better since the cool conditions prevent heavier petaled blooms (such as fully double) from opening completely.

ARS ROSARIAN TIP...

Growing conditions can significantly affect the size of flowers. Roses that have not had ample water or nutrients tend to produce smaller flowers, so keeping roses well-watered and fertilized is important.

Also, extreme heat can cause roses to produce smaller flowers, if they produce them at all.
—*Connie Vierbicky*
Sarasota, Florida

Very large rose, Glowing Peace

Larger rose, Iceberg

Smaller rose, The Fairy

Miniature rose, Sun Sprinkles

Understanding rose fragrance

What do most people do when handed a rose? They smell it, of course.

Most people expect roses to have that characteristic, nostalgic fragrance associated with old garden roses. That pinnacle of fragrance is probably a byproduct of the efforts of the perfume industry, which has marketed the fragrance of two older roses, *Rosa gallica* centifolia and *Rosa damascena,* in the rose essence used in an array of perfumes. But in the horticultural world, roses in gardens have many types of fragrances—and some have none. To date researchers have identified more than 50 specific fragrances in the genus *Rosa*.

Beyond that each person has a unique sense of smell, which ensures a one-of-a-kind personal experience and interpretation of the fragrance of a particular rose. Because the scent is in the nose of the sniffer, it is often happens that several individuals will describe the fragrance of the exact same rose differently.

Variations in scent

The scent of a rose depends on how mature the rose is, the time of day, and the weather conditions. It's easier to detect the scent of a rose on a warm, still day than on a cool, damp one.

Rose aficionados have smelling a rose down to a science. They have determined that the scent is stronger when a rose is three-quarters open in the early afternoon on a calm day with high relative humidity and temperatures in excess of 70°F degrees.

Variations in the scent of a rose are a little like the variations in the aroma of a glass of wine. Descriptors commonly used include apple, myrrh, citrus, pepper, tea, cinnamon, lemon, grapefruit, licorice, musk, gardenia, honey, spicy, sweet, fruity, and clove.

The key fact remains that for individuals choosing roses, fragrance is an important characteristic.

Fragrance in the garden

Planting fragrant roses not only makes the garden more pleasant for you, but also is a subtle way of inviting others into your environment.

Plant roses next to benches, lawn furniture, gazebos, pergolas, and garden ponds to maximize the pleasure of the garden in terms of sight and smell. Some civic-minded gardeners elect to plant intensely fragrant roses in the curb strip areas in front of their homes or near sidewalks so the passerby is greeted with the sweet aroma.

Plant the most fragrant roses you can find. Better yet, plant a grouping of them for maximum scent.

Fragrance in cut roses

Cut roses are lovely to look at—and smell. In fact, many gardeners snip a single bloom or two to tuck into a bud vase on a nightstand or on an office desk expressly to enjoy the scent.

In larger bouquets, too, it's nice to include fragrant roses, especially when the bouquet is a gift. It takes only one or two fragrant blooms to scent an entire bouquet.

Exercise caution when mixing roses with other highly scented flowers. The pungent scent of yarrow, for example, can overpower and ruin the more delicate scent of roses. Catmint has a distinctive aroma that's not unpleasant, but it doesn't necessarily mix well with the scent of roses.

You'll also want to be careful when using roses in a centerpiece on a dinner table. The scent of roses (the petals of which, in fact, are edible if the rose is grown in a pesticide-free garden) mix nicely with the scent of food as long as the scent is light. If the bouquet is intensely scented, the dining experience could be a rather odd one.

▲ With even a moderately fragrant type of rose, just a few blooms on vase on a nightstand can assure sweetly scented dreams. On a desk, they can transform the mood of your entire work day.

THE MOST FRAGRANT ROSES

Below are some of the most fragrant roses. A bloom or two will fill a room with scent.

Autumn Damask

Fragrant Cloud

Fragrant Plum

Gertude Jekyll

Heritage

Honey Perfume

Just Joey

Louise Odier

Madame Alfred Carrière

Madame Isaac Pereire

Madame Plantier

Mister Lincoln

New Dawn

Radiant Perfume

Roseraie de l'Hay

Sheila's Perfume

Understanding rose foliage and thorns

It's the flowers on roses that get all the attention. But there are other aspects roses that are important in choosing and growing them also. The way the leaves look, and how healthy they are, as well as the type of stems and prickles (also called thorns) also play a role in how you should choose and grow your roses.

Foliage

In most cases, the foliage of the rose plant is taken for granted. This is unfortunate because in many respects the color, texture, sheen, and size of the leaves are vital to the look of the rose. After all, much of the year with a rose the foliage is all you see.

The foliage of rose plants can vary in color from light yellow-green to dark blue-green. It can also change color throughout the growing season. Some plants, for example, have dark red or burgundy foliage on their new growth.

Texture can range from wrinkled (what botanists call "rugose") to smooth. Sheen can vary from matte to glossy.

Foliage ranges in size from small to large. Even the number of leaflets can vary. For example, most of the modern roses have three- and five-leaflet leaves, while the old garden roses can have seven to nine or more leaflets in their leaves.

▲ The foliage and thorns on roses can vary greatly and should be a factor when choosing the best roses for your garden.

Stems and prickles

The stems of rose bushes also vary in color, from green to red to brown.

The thorns on rose bushes have a variety of characteristics, the most obvious being size.

Interestingly, what most of us call thorns on roses are actually prickles. The difference between the two is that thorns are a branch of a plant that has become hard, woody, and pointed, such as those on locust trees, and prickles are spinelike, superficial outgrowths of the stem's outer layer.

The prickles of rose bushes vary not only in size but also in appearance. Some can be quite beautiful. They range in

TYPES OF PRICKLES

The size and, frankly, the nastiness of rose thorns (also called prickles) vary considerably. A select few roses, such as Zephirine Drouhin, are thornless, while most of the rugosas have large thorns. Other roses have small thorns while some have many small, almost hooked thorns that attach themselves tenaciously. And for a few, the prickles are very attractive.

Red, showy thorns
This *Rosa sericea pteracantha* has distinctively large, prominent prickles.

Small prickles
Some roses have many tiny prickles, especially on the lower stems' portions.

Medium to large thorns
Other roses have larger prickles. Thorns are largest on the lower portions of the plant.

ROSE FOLIAGE VARIATIONS

Rose leaves look different not only on different types of roses but also look different during different times of the year.

Many roses boast glossy green, leathery leaves, preferred by many rose growers.

New leaf growth on roses tends to be reddish, slowly turning green over a period of weeks.

Some roses, especially shrub and low-maintenance roses, often have matte, textured, more deeply veined leaves. Some have leaves that appear slighly hairy.

color from red to green to brown and can have many different shapes. Rose prickles can be broad or narrow, hooked or straight, curved upward or downward, and small or large.

Some roses have small, almost insignificant prickles while others have large, jagged ones that can rip a gash in a thumb or forearm. Still others have many smaller prickles that are hard to work with because they cling to clothes and hair with amazing tenacity. A few, such as some species roses (*Rosa banksiae, Rosa blanda*), Veilchenblau, and some nonspecies roses, such as Zephirine Drouhin, are almost thornless.

Veteran rose gardeners have learned to be careful in working with their roses. A good pair of rose gloves, a sturdy long-sleeve shirt, and a pair of long-handled loppers just might become your new best friends.

ROSE BUSH GROWTH HABITS

Whether it's a miniature, groundcover, climber, rambler, or standard bush type, there are variations in how a rose bush grows.

Upright
These roses have stiff, upwardly growing canes and are very vertical looking. Many hybrid tea roses and grandifloras tend to grow upright.

Arching
These roses send out long canes that arch outward like a spray. Many old garden roses have this growth pattern. Roses that tend to sprawl are also a favorite to train up pillars.

Shrubby
These roses tend to be compact and grow densely. Floribundas and many of the so-called shrub roses take on a shrubby form.

Understanding types of roses

Which rose to grow?

With hundreds of varieties available through garden centers and mail-order suppliers, deciding which to grow can be a daunting task. Fortunately, roses have been been divided into classes that help you narrow your choices. These classes are based on roses' growing habits, size of flowers, size of plants, and style of flowers, among other traits. Keep in mind, however, that these categories are fluid. As in most of nature, the rules of grouping roses are broken often, and one group may easily lean toward another. Still, understanding the various categories is a good place to start your rose selection process.

A QUICK GLANCE AT THE DIFFERENT TYPES OF ROSES

Type of Rose	Advantages	Characteristics to Cope With
Hybrid Tea	• Perfect bud and bloom • Many varieties are fragrant • Reliably repeat bloomers • The most popular type of rose • Available in nearly all rose colors	• Dependent on deadheading for repeat bloom • In Zone 5 and colder, require heavy winter protection • Rather bare on lower parts
Grandiflora	• Largest roses • Clusters of blooms • Large-headed flowers • Many varieties are fragrant • Reliably repeat bloomers	• Very tall—need ample space to spread out • In colder climates, require heavy winter protection, especially in Zones 5 and colder
Floribunda	• Nonstop bloom • Floriferous—trusses of blooms • Low-growing, attractively bushy • Extremely hardy • Easy to grow • Suitable for wetter climates	• Smaller blooms than hybrid teas • Some varieties are highly susceptible to black spot • Winter hardiness varies from variety to variety
Polyantha	• Nonstop bloom • Great disease resistance • Low-growing • Excellent container roses • Attractive foliage	• Smaller blooms than hybrid teas • Some varieties have little fragrance • Winter hardiness varies
Shrub/Landscape	• Wide variety of shapes and sizes • Often have old-fashioned blooms • Versatile in landscape garden • Cold hardy and disease resistant • Often used for groundcover	• Lack the traditional, perfect bud found in hybrid teas • Some are poor choices for cutting • Blooms in some are simple
Miniature and Miniflora	• Nonstop bloom • Grown on own roots, so more hardy • Excellent for small-space gardens • Perfect for containers • Compact plants	• Most usually have tiny blooms, which are part of the charm • Little fragrance
Climbing and Rambling	• Vertical color in the landscape • All flower forms and colors • Disguise unattractive structures	• Some bloom only once • Ramblers can grow out of control • Need support • Many varieties not winter hardy in Zones 5 and colder
Species and Old Garden (Antique)	• Versatile landscape roses • Types that suit nearly any hardiness zone • Offer a connection to the past	• Some bloom only once • Some spread problematically through sucker systems • Some varieties are prone to mildew
Groundcover	• Great solution for mass color in problem spots such as slopes • Little deadheading needed • Disease resistant • One plant can cover a large area, depending on the type	• Tend to have smaller flowers • Limited colors • Usually not much fragrance
Standard	• Striking form • Perfect for containers	• Winter hardy without protection only in the warmest climates

ROSE SERIES

Sometimes roses share enough characteristics that they are grouped with similar or related names, creating a "series" of roses.

The popular Knock Out rose, for example, has been further hybridized into variations of color and form, so you will find Blushing Knock Out, Pink Knock Out, Home Run, and others.

Other popular series of roses includes the cold-hardy Explorer and Parkland series. The low-maintenance Romantica and Easy Elegance series are also worth growing.

Still other roses are simply closely related but aren't quite a series. The David Austin roses (also called English roses) are a good example of this. As a group, they share many characteristics—old-fashioned beauty, lovely fragrance, repeat bloom, disease-resistance—but each has its own distinct characteristics that defy easy categorization in a series.

Hybrid teas and grandifloras

Two modern roses offer gardeners beautiful blooms for the garden and table.

Hybrid teas

When you think about the classic rose, you may have an image of a hybrid tea flower in mind.

The hybrid tea bloom starts out as a tight, attractive bud that unfurls into a breathlessly perfect flower.

Hybrid teas, as the name suggests, are a cross between hybrid perpetuals and old-fashioned tea roses. Hybridized in Europe in 1867, this modern rose quickly became the standard for rose beauty throughout the world. But it wasn't until 1945, with the introduction of the Peace rose, that the hybrid tea rose's popularity took off. There are now more than 10,000 varieties of hybrid tea.

In the garden and as a cut flower, the hybrid tea rose never disappoints. The plants have an attractive, upright growth habit. These tall, statuesque bushes reach 5 to 6 feet tall and have a width of 3 to 4 feet. For the cut flower aficionado, the hybrid tea is a favorite. It produces one elegant bloom on each long stem. The high-centered blooms have many petals—from 30 to 65—so they offer a large, full flower that looks as good on the bush as it does in a vase.

Hybrid teas are cherished as a cut flower. They are a standard in the cut-flower and florist industries—the roses you grow in your garden will resemble those you might receive on Valentine's Day. Another reason hybrid tea roses are so popular is that they bloom repeatedly throughout the season. They grow best in Zones 5 to 9.

Grandifloras

The grandiflora is a modern rose and a relative of the hybrid tea; the hybrid tea and floribunda were crossed to create the grandiflora class in 1954. Grandifloras offer large flowers—the term "grandiflora" translates as "large-flowered" in Latin. But where hybrid teas offer one flower per stem, grandifloras offer clusters of three to five perfect flowers per stem. The flower form ranges from high-centered hybrid tealike flowers to cupped flowers that resemble old roses.

The most famous of the grandiflora roses is Queen Elizabeth, a tall, hardy rose that is smothered in pink blooms nearly all summer. This rose is the reason the grandiflora class exists. The cross between a floribunda rose, Floradora, and a hybrid tea rose, Charlotte Armstrong, fit neither class, so the American Rose Society created a new class. This modern rose features characteristics of its parents—the height and rose form of the hybrid tea and the ability to create flower clusters from the floribunda—and offers gardeners a big, hardy rose that blooms all summer.

Grandifloras are big, impressive roses, growing 6 to 8 feet tall. The tallest of all modern roses, grandifloras are useful as a hedge or as back-of-the-border performers. Grandiflora roses offer continuous bloom all summer, making them perfect choices for cutting gardens. Their generous sprays of blooms are long-lasting in the vase. They come in a range of colors. Because grandifloras usually bloom on shorter stems than do hybrid teas, they appear more heavily flowering.

▲ This brilliant Opening Night hybrid tea rose shows all the classic assets of hybrid teas—large size with gorgeous, classic shape atop a long stem perfect for cutting.

Floribundas and polyanthas

▲ One of the most popular polyanthas is The Fairy. It's fairly low-maintenance with a low, spreading habit, large clusters of perfect little blooms, a charming pink color, and a very long bloom time.

For gardeners looking for a flowery flash in the landscape, floribundas and polyanthas deliver bloom after bloom all summer.

Floribundas

As their name suggests, floribundas are floriferous. The Latin translation of floribunda is "many-flowering." Low-growing and relatively hardy, floribundas are beautiful additions to any garden. They are easy to grow and offer diversity of bloom types and colors.

A cross between a hybrid tea and a polyantha, floribundas exhibit the best characteristics of both sides of the family tree. From the hybrid tea side, the floribunda gets its great blooms. From the polyantha side, it gets multiple flowers per stem. The first floribunda was created in 1909 and is still available for purchase. Gruss an Aachen offers white to light pink double blooms on a bushy, upright plant.

Used in landscapes and garden beds, floribundas are covered with trusses of blooms. They grow 3 to 5 feet tall, so they won't overpower the plantings around them. The flowers are the main event on floribundas. Multiple blooms per truss open on the plant, giving the entire bush a rich, floral appearance.

For rose lovers who can't make up their minds about their favorite flower type, floribundas deliver a smorgasbord of options: single, semidouble, double, and rosette flower forms.

Because of their compact form, some floribundas are excellent choices for containers. Floribundas, like hybrid teas, also have a wide range of colors.

Polyanthas

Polyanthas are also known as patio roses because of their compact size, great looks, and versatility. If you have a small garden, polyanthas are a perfect fit—they grow low and maintain a compact form, so you can tuck them in anywhere.

Developed in the 19th century, polyanthas produce bushy 2-foot-tall plants that feature finely textured leaves and clusters of 1-inch blossoms. Roses in this class come from a cross of two Asian roses—*Rosa chinensis* and *Rosa multiflora*.

Polyanthas offer gardeners and landscapers a flower-filled option. In garden beds, polyanthas are small enough to perform as edging plants. But they also have enough presence that they can be planted en masse to create swaths of color. They even make attractive low-growing hedges. Polyanthas such as The Fairy win gardeners over with their bountiful pink blooms, long bloom time, and delicate petal-packed flowers. Polyanthas are an excellent choice for containers because of their compact growth habit and abundant blooms. In pots on patios and terraces, these generous roses add color, charm, and fragrance anywhere you grow them.

Shrub and landscape roses

If you're looking for easy-care roses, shrub roses are the ones for you.

When compared to some other, more traditional varieties, shrub roses are more disease-resistant and do better in harsher conditions of extreme cold, extreme heat, and other less-than-ideal rose conditions. Shrub roses as a group don't need much pruning and yet have a multitude of flowers produced repeatedly over a long growing season.

"Shrub rose" is a loose definition but as a group, shrub roses make up the second largest class of roses.

Further complicating the understanding of what is and is not a shrub rose is the casual way roses sometimes are sold. Many floribundas, for example, might be marketed as shrub roses, as might some antique roses. "Landscape roses" just refers to any type of rose that is fairly disease-resistant and that has a fuller, more shrubby habit (as opposed to the leggy growth habit of hybrid teas) that make the bushes look full and attractive in the garden.

As a group, shrub roses tend to be small (4 foot and under) mounded plants with small flowers growing in large clusters or very large plants (up to 6 foot) with arching canes and varying cluster styles and bloom sizes.

There are various types of roses that can be considered shrub roses:

Rugosa roses

Rugosa roses, which are technically hybrid rugosas, get their name from their characteristic rugged, crinkled leaves. As a group, they are very disease-resistant and can grow in Zones 3 or 4 without winter protection. They actually dislike spraying and pruning—they flower best without it. They do not do well in warmer climates, Zones 8 and southward, and are not very good cut flowers.

They have excellent salt-tolerance and are native to cooler coastal areas. They grow 3 to 6 feet high and as wide.

Hybrid musk roses

These are large, repeat-blooming varieties that can grow up to 20 feet high and wide, though many are much more compact.

David Austin roses

Back in the 1940s, British rose breeder David Austin started crossing old garden roses with modern roses to create beautiful roses that had much of the charming shape and fragrance of old roses with the repeat bloom, vigor, hardiness and color range of modern roses.

Also called English roses, these became highly popular in the 1980s. They're also fairly disease-resistant, but the flowers, while gorgeous, tend to shatter and not to last long in the vase.

House of Meilland roses

The illustrious French House of Meilland has given the United States some wonderful roses, many of which are shrub roses.

One group of shrub roses is the Meidiland series of roses, which are highly durable landscape and groundcover roses. They are vigorous and fast-growing, tolerant of poor growing conditions, very disease-resistant, very winter-hardy, and long and heavy bloomers. They need little or no spraying or pruning. Each has the word Meidiland in its name, such as White Meidiland or Ruby Meidiland. They are favorites for mass plantings since they are so low-maintenance.

Another Meilland rose, Bonica, in 1987 was the first shrub rose to be named an All-America Rose selection.

The House of Meilland also is the originator of the

▲ David Austin roses, such as this Othello, have been extremely popular landscape roses. They have an attractive shrubby habit but also a long bloom time combined with gorgeous, old-fashioned looking flowers and heady fragrances.

Romantica roses. Think of them as the French version of David Austin roses. They are wonderfully fragrant and evocative of old garden ruses, but are very vigorous, highly disease-resistant, and bloom profusely throughout the growing season.

Griffith Buck roses

Iowa State University rose researcher Griffith Buck wasn't given much money for labor to care for his roses, so he developed roses that thrived in the upper Midwest's harsh winters without protection and without much spray or fuss.

His crowning achievement was Carefree Beauty, which is the parent plant for many a low-maintenance rose. It's a rose that flowers nearly nonstop from June until the first frost in fall.

Canadian Explorer/ Morden roses

These roses were developed to survive the Canadian winters by Agriculture and Agri-Food Canada (AAFC), many at the Morden Research Station in Manitoba. The lesser-known Parkland series was also developed there.

Canadian Explorer roses are among the most cold-hardy roses available. They require minimal care and are environmentally friendly, needing minimal sprays. They are hardy down to –31°F without protection.

Each, predictably, is named after a Canadian explorer, such as Henry Hudson and William Baffin.

The Parkland series usually contains the name Morden, such as Morden Blush.

Miniatures and minifloras

With miniatures, small stature doesn't mean less rose. These tiny roses are every bit the rose that their larger cousins are, but in a smaller package. Miniature rose enthusiasts find these plants are more hardy and heavily flowering than regular roses. Miniature roses come in varieties that grow 3 to 18 inches tall. Minifloras, a new classification given to miniature roses by the American Rose Society, offer larger flowers, leaves, and plant size than a miniature rose without exceeding the size of a floribunda. These plants grow about 3 feet tall.

Miniature roses

Miniatures of any kind captivate the imagination, and roses are no exception. There is something mesmerizing about a perfect hybrid tea rose blossom that is the size of a dime. Miniatures come in other flower forms, including single or double flowers. Their equally small canes are delicate and are covered with small, well-formed leaves.

Rosa chinensis var. *minima,* the botanical name for miniature roses, reveals the breeding influence of the miniature. Old garden roses were crossed with repeat-blooming Asian roses to create the modern mini—a compact rose with small flowers that blooms repeatedly all summer.

How to use miniature roses

Miniature roses fit anywhere in a small-space garden. Delivering a blast of color, these hardy little roses produce masses of flowers. They make excellent flower border edging plants and can be tucked in amid an assortment of low-growing perennials in a cottage garden.

But their real talent is in containers, where they excel. Miniature roses may be planted at the base of tree roses in containers for a rose-on-rose display. In a sunny window box, they produce a beautiful view from the outside and an up-close display of the delicate flowers from the inside of the house. Miniature roses are even appropriate for some bonsai creations.

Miniature forms and favorites

Miniature roses come in several forms: Micro-minis are the smallest of the miniatures and grow 6 inches tall or less; climbing miniature roses produce small flowers but can grow to 6 feet tall. Because of their delicate beauty, miniature roses are popular as gifts. They can easily make the move outdoors and be planted in the ground—although some, because they were produced as gift plants, may not survive the winter. For outdoor use, look for miniature roses that were raised to grow outdoors. Indoors, miniature roses require a spot with full sun. Miniature roses are susceptible to spider mites, as are many houseplants.

Minifloras

Bigger than a miniature and smaller than a floribunda, the miniflora offers gardeners a new classification of rose—and more choices for roses in the garden and landscape.

In 1999, the American Rose Society created a new classification of roses—the miniflora. Larger than regular minis, miniflora roses grow about 3 feet tall. Minifloras produce not only bigger bushes than miniatures but also larger flowers and leaves.

How to use minifloras

Minifloras are excellent landscaping roses because of their compact size and recurrent bloom. Plant them as single specimens in mixed gardens or group three to five plants in a bed to create a wave of bloom.

▲ Minatures are, in a word, fun. This Gizmo rose grows only about 2 feet tall and covers itself with flowers in June and continues to bloom sporadically throughout the summer.

Climbers, ramblers, and pillars

▲ It's important to pair the climber and the support carefully, or the rose may overwhelm the structure. This rose will grow no taller than 18 or so feet, just about right for this 12-foot tall arbor.

Climbers rise to the occasion in any garden. Able to scramble up and over arbors and fences, these overachieving roses smother structures in a blanket of bloom.

Climbers

Gardeners looking for vertical appeal can find it in climbing roses. Their long, pliable canes can be trained onto vertical supports such as walls, pillars, and arbors or along ropes or chains, creating rose swags. Planting roses on either side of an arched tunnel creates a fragrant walkway from one part of a garden to another. An invaluable landscaping tool, roses can fill in both vertical and horizontal spaces. Climbing roses can transform an unattractive structural feature, such as a chain link fence, into a wall of bloom.

Climbers come in a wide range of sizes. Although they all feature the same growth habit—long canes—there are several different types of climbing roses.

Miniature climbers offer tiny flowers on canes that grow 3 to 6 feet long. Perfect for containers or small trellises, these diminutive divas offer spectacular flower form for small-space gardens.

Large-flowering climbers can grow 4 to 15 feet tall. Although climbing roses are not considered vines (they don't actively "grab" onto structures), they can be trained to ascend whatever vertical structure is available.

Climbing roses also offer color and form diversity, blooming in the full range of rose colors and in many flower forms—single, semidouble, and fully double.

Many climbing roses are mutations or sports of more bushy roses.

So, for example, you may see for sale climbing versions of many of your favorite low-growing roses, such as climbing hybrid teas (Paul's Lemon Pillar is one example), climbing floribundas (Climbing Iceberg), climbing polyanthas (Climbing Cecile Brunner), and climbing miniature roses (Climbing Lavender Lace).

Rambler roses

Rambler roses are the wild childs of the rose world. Few grow less than 20 feet and some can reach 50 feet.

They very large, very study supports, such as a large pergola. In some cases, they may climb large, mature trees (they overwhelm small trees).

Ramblers bloom just once and their flowers tend to be smaller than those of many other roses, but they are abundant, making a striking sight in June.

Pillar roses

A pillar rose is any rose growing from a few to several feet with long, pliable canes that can be tied to a post, pillar, obelisk, or similar support.

Taller shrub roses and smaller climbing roses are excellent candidates for growing as pillar roses.

▲ When you want a lot of coverage, plant a rambler. Most ramblers hit 20 to 30 feet and this one has engulfed this arbor, charmingly so.

Species and old garden roses

Plant a piece of history: old garden roses and species roses allow you to connect in a hands-on way with a rich tradition of rose gardening. Species roses are the original wild roses. Old garden roses represent a number of rose types that existed before 1867 and offer a wide range of wonderfully romantic blooms.

Species roses

Species roses are wild roses and will grow to true form from seed. Because they are wild, they thrive on neglect and are extremely hardy. You'll find species roses flourishing untended in rural areas. These wild roses are the ancestors and hybrids of the modern roses we love today (hybrid teas, floribundas, polyanthas, and grandifloras). Species roses are single, having just five-petaled blooms. They bloom in the spring and bear rose hips in autumn, providing food for birds.

▲ Belle Amour is an alba rose, but contradictory to its name, is one of the few pink-tinted albas.

Old garden roses

Old garden roses are generally shrub-type roses that usually bloom only once a year though some do repeat. They bear double blooms in red, pink, or white. Old garden roses are classified as follows:

Alba

The term "alba" means "white" in Latin, although alba roses can also bloom in light pink. Albas reach heights of 6 to 9 feet and can be grown as climbers. Hardy albas can grow in the chilly temperatures of Zone 3.

Bourbon

These old-fashioned roses bear large, showy blooms that are heavily scented. Originally from an island called Ile de Bourbon, this rose arrived in France in 1819 and became a revered rose. Plants bloom repeatedly all summer and range from 2 to 15 feet tall. They grow in Zones 6 to 10.

Centifolia

Hailing from 17th-century Holland, this rose is a great choice for those who love full, sensuous blooms. The word "centifolia" means "100-leaved," and each bloom delivers exuberant blooms with more than 100 petals. Also known as cabbage roses, centifolias bear fragrant flowers in colors from white to pink to red. The bushes grow 4 to 8 feet tall in a relaxed growth habit. The canes are thorny. Centifolias grow in Zones 4 to 9.

Hybrid China

Flowering once in the spring and again in the fall, hybrid China roses offer blooms at each end of the gardening season. They exhibit a twiggy growth habit and reach 2 to 3 feet tall. Hybrid Chinas are tender roses, growing best in Zones 7 to 10.

Damask

This is a rose of extremes. It is very thorny (it has been described as "vicious"), and it is famously, intensely fragrant. Most damasks bloom once a season, but there are damasks that bloom repeatedly. Damask roses have tend to have a rangy growth habit and grow 3 to 7 feet tall. They grow best in Zones 6 to 10.

Hybrid Foetida

Tall and vigorous, this rose blooms once in the spring. It is from this rose that all modern yellow roses get their color. Hybrid foetidas grow best in Zones 3 to 9.

Gallica

The gallica rose is reputed to be the oldest rose in cultivation. Extremely fragrant, gallicas are excellent for cutting gardens. Gallicas spread through suckers, which may cause some gardeners problems. They form low, 4-foot-tall shrubs. Gallicas grow in Zones 4 to 9.

Moss

A mossy mutation affecting the stems and sepals of this rose gave it its name. Some varieties of moss rose bloom repeatedly, unlike most old garden roses. Moss rose bushes range in height from 3 to 6 feet tall.

Noisette

Large and sprawling, noisettes grow as high as 20 feet tall. A cross between a china rose and a climbing musk, the noisette rose was cultivated before 1811. Noisettes produce flowers in white, pink, red, and yellow, are good repeat bloomers, and are hardy to Zone 4.

Hybrid Perpetual

Repeat bloom and strong fragrance make perpetuals a favorite. They grow about 6 feet tall and because of that height, are best planted in the back of the border.

Portland

A cross between a China and a damask rose, the portland rose was the first old garden rose to offer consistent repeat flowering. Plants are bushy and upright, growing about 4 feet tall. Portland roses grow best in Zones 6 to 10.

Hybrid Spinosissima

Thorny hybrid spinosissimas are good choices for barrier or hedge plantings. They grow 3 to 5 feet tall and, depending on the variety, may bloom repeatedly throughout the summer. They are extremely hardy and grow best in Zones 3 to 9.

Tea

Tea roses produce large, full blossoms on 4- to 5-foot-tall plants. Tea roses are the ancestors of the modern hybrid tea rose and offer a full summer of repeat bloom. As their name suggests, they have a light tea fragrance. Tea roses are tender and grow in Zones 7 to 11.

Groundcover roses

Some shrub roses, because of their low-growing habit and low maintenance, make excellent groundcover roses, ideal for mass planting.

Knock Out is one of the newer groundcover roses available. Flower Carpet also has been a favorite, growing about 2 feet tall and spreading as much as 4 feet.

The Meidiland series, classified as a floribunda, has a low growth habit that has made it a favorite for groundcover plantings. The Meidiland series includes Alba Meidiland, Ice Meidiland, and White Meidiland, all of which are white. Red roses in this series include Magic Meidiland, La Sevillana, and Red Meidiland.

Rambler roses are sometimes used as groundcover in large areas, especially slopes to help stabilize the soil.

▲ Many roses—even miniatures—can be planted in masses and used as groundcover, but groundcover roses grow low (less than 3 feet tall) and sprawling, often as wide as 5 or more feet. This is a *Rosa wichurana poteriifolia.*

Standard roses

Also called tree roses, standards are regular roses that have been grafted on top of an elongated stem.

A favorite for growing in large pots, they vary in size from 2 to 3 feet, with some specialty standard roses growing as high as 5 feet.

Because of the graft union, standard roses are not very cold hardy and won't survive winters unless heavily protected (usually by burying and covering with soil) in Zones 5 and colder.

Recently, however, own-root standard roses have arrived on the market. They need far less protection in colder climates.

◀ Standard roses are ordinary roses, such as this Gourmet Popcorn, that have been grafted on top of a tall, slender rose trunks for a tree-like effect. Some suppliers have recently begun offering own-root tree roses, which are far more cold-hardy.

Designing with roses

Designing with roses basics

Designing a garden with roses is wonderfully rewarding because roses come in so many forms—and they grow in such versatile ways.

No matter what your gardening need, there's almost certainly a rose that offers a beautiful solution. For example, if you're looking for a low-growing groundcover to plant in a sunny, low-maintenance front yard border, choose a landscape rose such as Scarlet Meidiland. If you want to add height and visual interest, plant a tree rose—they can reach heights of 5 feet. Or opt for a climbing rose, such as the all-white Iceberg, that will fill a vertical space on an arbor or pergola with flowers and fabulous fragrance.

Roses look great from a variety of angles—and in all styles of gardens—so you can plant them in nearly any type of bed, border, or landscape. Here are some factors to think about when using roses in your design.

Pick a garden style

Traditional rose gardens feature many options. You can get the look of a formal rose garden by using squared and rectangular garden beds (both raised and in the ground). Circular beds in the center of a lawn can show off roses from all angles (see page 49 for specific layout ideas).

▲ Roses are versatile plants that can take a design challenge, such as a concrete wall and metal fence.

▶ Roses are attractive on their own and are more interesting when combined with other plants. Purple irises and softly colored verbascum complement this Ballerina rose.

To create a less structured look—like that found in many cottage gardens—you can make irregular, free-form beds filled with roses or a rose/perennial mix. Roses soften hard lines in any landscape and add a touch of romance. If you are interested in harvesting roses all summer for bouquets, be sure to choose those that have a long vase life, such as hybrid teas or grandifloras.

Plant for mass color

Consider creating a dramatic mass of color by planting several roses of the same variety in one spot.

Landscape and groundcover roses, such as Flower Carpet, are excellent choices for this type of planting. Plant them a little closer than recommended on the plant tag to create a solid drift of color. You can also create hedges with roses by

▲ Just a few roses can make a dramatic statement. This simple metal and wire abor is engulfed by several white roses on one side and pink climbing roses on the other.

selecting taller-growing shrub varieties.

Also recognize the value of repetition. If you have a long flowerbed of mixed plantings, consider planting several roses of the same cultivar, evenly spaced, in a long line throughout the bed for an elegant, elongating effect.

If you have a fence that would benefit from a climbing rose, plant a few to several of the same cultivar. As they grow up the fence and bloom simultaneously, the effect will be stunning.

Use roses as architecture

For a showstopping effect, plant tree roses along both sides of a walkway or drive. This parallel planting scheme creates a living architectural element in your garden—an allee of tree roses. To gain the same effect on a terrace or patio, form a line of large potted tree roses.

Fill vertical space

Climbing roses—on posts, pillars, rose towers, arbors, fences, or pergolas—grow up and over structures, filling the vertical space with glossy green foliage and a bounty of blooms. Some roses tolerate light shade and can be used in gardens and landscapes to fill in areas with flower and foliage.

Mini climbers grow just a few feet tall. Climbers tend to climb 6 feet to as much as 15 to 20 feet, while some ramblers can grow 30 feet or more (see page 29 for types of vertical-growing roses).

Plan partner plantings

Although there are certainly enough types of roses to fill any garden—from free-ranging ramblers to controlled miniatures—roses can easily share the stage with other plants. As companion plantings to perennials, roses offer the advantage of a wide range of bloom sizes and forms, from single-petaled, almost wild-looking flowers to petal-packed varieties. Large roses can be used as anchor plants in a bed. Miniatures can be used as edgers interplanted with a low-growing perennial in a complementary color. The all-season, good-looking glossy green leaves of roses are excellent fillers in beds and borders. Roses also mix well together—especially when you pair different growth forms. For example, you can create a unified look by underplanting a tree rose with three or so miniature roses at the base.

Get all-season interest

For gardeners who are looking for color in all seasons, roses can do the job. In early spring, roses produce new foliage growth in fresh shades of green and russet. You can enjoy blooms, fragrance, and cut flowers from May until frost. For fall and winter color, choose varieties that set colorful hips—such as rugosas—that will appear in red, yellow, or orange once leaves fall.

▲ Not all pinks are created equal. This Old Blush rose is of the softest pink, while other pink roses might have such a soft blush they're almost white. Other roses range from lavender-pink to apricot and pink to magenta.

Planning a garden with roses

How you plan your garden depends on your creative process. Some gardeners can see the entire garden in their heads. Others use a sketch pad or borrow a plan from a famous garden they've seen in person or in a magazine. Others like to design a garden by standing on the location and "drawing" it on the ground.

The great thing about garden design is that there is no wrong way to do it. Whatever best works for you and pleases you is the right way. And the same can be said about the results. If it looks good to you, it's a success.

Paper-based planning

If you like to draw plans on paper, in notebooks, or using graph paper, you need to start with some essential information. Keeping a notebook with lots of pockets will help you consolidate ideas into one place.

● **Notebook sketches**
Freehand sketches help you narrow in on a design scenario, starting with garden shape.

● **Magazine tear sheets**
Gardens featured in magazines offer inspiration and help you identify which designs, color combinations, structures, and rose varieties to include in your design.

● **Graph paper renderings**
If you are a stickler for exactness, use graph paper to create a garden plan. Graph paper allows you to create a scale drawing—especially useful if you're hiring out your garden construction. It allows you to provide your landscaper with a to-scale plan.

● **Plant tags** If you're adding to or modifying an existing garden, plant tags are an invaluable tool to help you keep a listing of everything you planted in your garden

▲ Roses lend themselves beautifully to lush, full, casual mixed country gardens. As long as you choose disease- and insect-resistant roses, they'll grow as easily as the perennials that surround them.

(including variety names of each plant). Keeping plant tags also allows you to check the mature heights and widths of the plants in your garden. Some gardeners keep an updated garden plan, adding the variety names of plants to each year's revision. Keeping track of plant names is helpful if you need to replace a plant. For example, if a climbing rose on your arbor dies and you want to replace it, you'll know from

the plant tag whether it was New Dawn or Madamoiselle Cecile Brunner (two similar pink climbing roses).

● **Garden catalogs** Excellent wintertime reading, garden catalogs keep you up to date with the newest plant releases as well as a palette of plants to consider for your garden.

● **Colored pencils/markers**
Get artistic with your drawings and color in the

hues of the plants' flowers and foliage in your plan.

● **Fabric swatches and paint chips** Great gardening is all about color coordination. Keeping swatches of patio furniture, umbrellas, or rugs enables you to match the colors of your garden to your outdoor living accessories. Paint chips of exterior walls, trim, and shutter colors will also help you in your landscaping plans.

On-site, hands-on planning

Some gardeners like to design on the spot. They put together their color combinations in their shopping cart at the garden center—basically creating their garden's color scheme before they've even made a purchase. Then they come home and figure out a planting. If you like designing in the yard, rather than on paper, here's a list of things that will come in handy.

● **Stakes or flags** Wooden stakes or flags allow you to mark boundaries. Stakes are also useful for creating straight lines when you run string or twine between them.

● **Spray paint** Paint is the perfect tool for the artistic gardener because it allows you to "draw" the beds onto the ground. Spray-paint bed boundaries, mark planting spaces, and sketch pathways. Use several colors of paint to

DESIGNING A NEW GARDEN

There are various ways to design a new bed, border, or entire rose garden. Some gardeners feel they can think and design best on graph paper, taking careful measurements and using catalogs and garden books to plot where to place each plant. Others prefer to design in real space, using a hose to mark out a border, then visualizing how to position plants.

Designing on paper

Designing using the actual space

represent various elements (bed edge, planting spots, pathways). Spray paint works well on either lawn or soil.

● **Hose** Flexible and easily visible, a hose makes a great tool for designing curving or freeform garden beds. A hose allows you to create a bed, then reshape it again and again to suit your needs.

● **Bone meal** Sprinkle this white powder fertilizer in a line to draw your beds. This option works best on soil.

● **Plant arrangement** For some gardeners, the easiest way to plan a garden is to set potted plants right into the garden space and move them around—the same way that you would arrange a room with furniture. Before you dig the plants into their spots, arrange them according to their mature heights and widths. This design method also allows you to look at your garden from different vantage points (from the street, for example, or from the inside of your house) so you can enhance your view.

▲ Roses are perfect for formal gardens. White standard Iceberg roses accent the white bench and white gravel for a highly disciplined green and white color scheme.

Using roses in mixed beds and borders

Unless you intend to have a bed of only roses—a practice usually reserved for hybrid teas—you'll want to combine your roses with other plants (such as perennials) to keep them company. Happily, the selection of plants that like the same conditions as roses—sun and well-drained soil—is nearly unlimited.

While there's debate on different companion plants and what they do for—or take away from—roses, the advocates of companion plantings feel that they offer multiple benefits.

COMPANION PLANTS IN FORMAL BEDS

While a hallmark of traditional formal rose beds is that they have few companion plantings, increasingly, formal rose gardeners are working in more companion plants.

Traditional formal beds in the past have usually been outlined with sheared boxwood or santolina and primarily have featured higher-maintenance hybrid tea roses. As a result, they require a good deal of care because both of these plants need regular shearing to look their best.

But it's easy to get a similar look with less effort. For example, instead of hybrid teas, choose small cultivars of disease-resistant roses. And instead of the traditional santolina or sheared boxwoods to outline the bed, consider an easy-care alternative:
'Hermann's Pride' spotted
   deadnettle
'Silver Mound' artemisia
Dusty miller (annual)
French tarragon
Hosta (sun-tolerant type)
Rosemary
Sage
Sesleria (a low, tidy
   ornamental grass)
Threadleaf coreopsis

Companion plants serve as a living mulch, shading the soil to keep it cooler and moister and cutting down on weeds. They also serve as a buffer between plants, slowing or even stopping rose-loving pests and diseases from spreading from plant to plant.

Undeniably, companion plants add a relaxed, more natural look that is difficult to achieve in a planting of roses alone.

Choosing companion plants

Companion plants, as a rule, should have shallow or limited root systems that won't rob the roses of water and nutrients. They shouldn't (with a few notable exceptions, such as smaller

▲ Too often gardeners think formal rose gardens should contain roses only. But this garden beautifully combines hardy geranium and perennial salvia inside a low boxwood hedge.

▲ The larger the rose, the better it wil combine with trees and large shrubs. The climbing rose to the left is taller than some of the trees in this border.

clematis) become entangled with roses or shade them.

But don't let that scare you away from larger companion plants. Let the mature size of your rose help you determine where to plant any surrounding perennials and bulbs. Tall shrub roses and climbing roses are suited to the back of the bed with medium and short plants in front of them. Miniature roses, on the other hand, belong at the front of the planting, along with short perennials. Grow taller perennials, as well as trees and shrubs, behind them.

Keep in mind the foliage and flower of the companion plants. They should complement the foliage and flower of the roses. Plants with many tiny flowers, such as cranesbill, columbine, sweet alyssum, and candytuft, are especially attractive.

Avoid planting perennials that creep or reseed near your roses. Pulling out wandering plants from under and around roses is thorny work—literally—even if you wear gloves and long sleeves.

TREES AND SHRUBS WITH ROSES

Roses require a lot of sun, so they have to keep their distance from large trees and shrubs that might shade them. But you can include small trees and shrubs nearby. Plant them north of the rose so beneficially intense southern sun isn't blocked. Or plant them far enough away that they won't cast a shadow all day.

Also consider tall, upright evergreens, which can form an attractive backdrop when situated where they don't shade the roses all day.

The following are smaller trees and shrubs that work well near roses:
Blue Muffin viburnum
Tiger Eyes sumac
Dwarf false cypress
Dwarf lilacs
Dwarf pines, such as white pine and mugo pine
Peegee hydrangea
Small crabapples, such as Sugar Tyme and Prairifire
Stephanandra
Yellow waxbells (Kirengeshoma)

PERENNIAL AND BULB ROSE COMPANIONS

So many sun-loving perennials are available that your roses need never be lonely. Use perennials to create an ever-changing display of color and flower form to complement your roses. Take advantage of your many choices by planning to have something in bloom all summer.

Plants that grow from bulbs are a special type of perennial. They store food in a fleshy underground onionlike structure during autumn, and then call on those energy reserves to grow in spring. The familiar spring-blooming bulbs that lighten winter-weary hearts—such as hyacinth, tulip, crocus, and daffodil—finish flowering before roses bloom. They are useful for adding color to a formal bed of roses when the roses themselves are just starting to leaf out.

But summer bulbs are often in flower when roses are at their peak, making them excellent companion plants. These include desert candle, the various alliums, and lilies.

Low-growing perennials	Medium-height perennials
Candytuft	Butterfly milkweed
Catmint	Columbine
Cranesbill	Coneflower
Creeping thyme	Coreopsis
Dianthus	Daylily
Lamb's-ears	Delphinium
Lamium	Feather reed grass
Sea thrift	Foxglove
	Iris
Tall perennials	Peony
Blondo or Graziella	Poppy
maiden grass (*Miscanthus*)	Russian sage
Butterfly bush (*Buddleia*)	Salvia May Night
Clematis	Shasta daisy
Hollyhock	
Joe-pye weed (*Eupatorium*)	
Meadow rue	

▲ For spectacular effect, team roses, which flower heaviest in June, with other early summer bloomers such as iris, foxglove, and delphinium.

Roses in mass plantings

When you want to dazzle, plant a mass of roses.

Mass plantings are clusterings of roses of the same sort, such as a half dozen or more Knock Out roses, in the same spot. Mass planting is a great solution for a sunny slope, a stunning way to fill a flowerbed, and a traffic-stopping solution for a problem urban space, such as the strip between the sidewalk and street.

So what constitutes a mass planting? Three roses planted together could be considered a mass planting, though a planting of at least six or seven roses would be more easily defined as a mass.

Masses of roses ideally should be planted at recommended spacing for maximum health and vigor—they'll have good circulation and they won't compete for nutrients and water. However, if the rose cultivar is particularly disease resistant, you may want to plant the roses 20 percent closer than recommended for a lusher, fuller look.

In fact, when choosing roses for mass plantings, you may want to consider only low-maintenance and disease-resistant varieties to minimize upkeep. That's because when planting many roses together (what horticulturists call a monoculture), you increase the chances for problems because one disease or pest could rip through the planting, unencumbered by other types of plants it might not care for.

For this reason you might consider mixing in some groundcovers or other low-growing, low-maintenance perennials.

There are a number of ways to create mass plantings.

Slopes

A mass of roses is an eye-catching way to cover all or part of a sunny slope. You could always plant a rambler

▲ Even with a mixed mass of roses, the planting will have more visual impact if you group three or four of the same rose together.

rose or two to cover a slope—one rambler can cover more than 20 feet. But this kind of planting may look unkempt and is fairly open, leaving ample opportunity for weeds. Also, the root system of one or two plants may be insufficient to anchor soil that might erode.

For a neater appearance, consider a mass planting of better-behaved roses, such as Knock Out or The Fairy. The roots from the several plants will anchor the soil, and the shorter canes will knit together to form a dense mass of foliage and flower.

Hybrid teas and grandifloras, with their upright growth and leggy canes, would not be a good choice for a slope, but any of the groundcover roses would be ideal.

Shrubs, floribundas, polyanthas, and other roses also would be fine choices as long as they grow at least as wide as they do tall. Even miniature roses are beautiful when planted in masses, creating a tight carpet of tiny foliage and flower.

▲ The beautifully rich yellow of tall Amber Queen roses and shorter Behold is even more intense when they are planted in a mass. This long, narrow planting at the base of a stone wall is edged with sidewalk.

▲ A mass planting of low-care shrub roses transforms what otherwise might be a dull stretch of struggling lawn. Landscape roses are especially good for mass planting because they are somewhat self-cleaning; that is, they drop spent blooms so less deadheading is required.

Beds and borders

Mass plantings can also be achieved in traditional beds and borders.

Fill a small bed with nothing but one type of rose for a sweep of uniform color.

You can also fill in portions of a large flower bed with mass plantings of roses. Plant a mass of taller roses in the back of a bed to serve as a backdrop for other flowers, almost as a hedge along the back of other plantings.

Or plant a mass of miniature roses in the front of a bed or border to serve as an partial edging.

Problem spots

Mass plantings of roses can be great problem solvers. If grass is struggling in a spot because of high traffic, slight drought, or poor soil, replacing it with roses may be the answer. They will require less pampering than turf.

Mass plantings of groundcover roses are often ideal for baked urban areas. They're perfect, as mentioned above, in the strip between the sidewalk and street. Also try them along a driveway where grass struggles. Or fill a corner of a lawn where "cattle paths" from children and others cutting through have become an issue.

Creating rose hedges

Rose hedges are a classic in Europe but have been slow to catch on in the United States.

The reason why is a puzzle. Rose hedges provide privacy, foliage, and color. Choose a rose that is low maintenance and fairly disease free, and you'll have a beautiful, casual hedge for years to come.

The site for a rose hedge is crucial. It should be in a spot where you have open space on both sides to provide all-important air circulation for these plants. The site also should be in full sun, with a minimum of 6 hours of direct, unfiltered light a day.

It's not uncommon for an area to receive full sun at one end but be in light shade at the other.

Investing in several or even dozens of roses for a hedge can be daunting if you're at all nervous about growing roses. If possible, plant a hedge with a rose you've already grown and have found to perform well with minimal care.

Alternatively, try planting two or three of the roses you're interested in and live with them for a year or two. If they do well, go ahead and buy dozens. Or, if you have got a bit of a green thumb and are patient, save yourself hundreds of dollars and take cuttings from the established roses to propagate several new plants.

▼ Rose hedges are often quite tall, but this charming hedge of Snow Bride miniature roses is 2 feet high, just tall enough to define a private sitting area.

GOOD ROSES FOR HEDGES

Nearly any low-maintenance, disease-resistant rose with a dense, shrubby growth habit will make a good hedge. Rugosa roses, however, are among the easiest (see page 227 for more information on rugosas) since they are among the most resistant to pests and diseases and don't need pruning.

Other roses that are good choices for hedges include:

Low hedges (under 2 feet)
Behold
Cupcake
Gizmo
Gourmet Popcorn
Pillow Fight
Rise 'n' Shine
Scentsational
Sun Sprinkles

Medium hedges (2 to 5 feet)
All That Jazz
Ballerina
Buff Beauty
Carefree Delight
Country Fair
Graham Thomas
Hansa
Knock Out
Mary Rose

The Meidiland series
Nearly Wild
Royal Bonica
Simplicity
Winchester Cathedral

High hedges (5 feet and taller)
Alba roses
Carefree Wonder
Linda Campbell
Nevada
Penelope
Pink Grootendorst
Roseraie de l'Hay
Shropshire Lass
Sunny June
Therese Bugnet
William Baffin

▲ Roses make great hedges not only because they're beautiful but also because their density and thorns make them impenetrable. They're a good way to keep pets and children in a yard, or out of it, and they add a level of security to a home.

Remember, a hedge doesn't have to be 20 feet long. A hedge can be nothing more than a screen—four or five vigorous roses planted in a row to add privacy or fragrance and color to a crucial area.

Low hedges

One of the easiest ways to create a rose hedge is with miniature roses, which usually grow no more than a foot or two high and wide. This is a charming way to enclose an island bed or an unusual way to edge a flowerbed—essentially using roses as an edging plant.

Using roses, miniature or otherwise, as edging has its practical side. An extensive edging of thorny roses will deter cats and small dogs from digging in your garden.

Medium-height hedges

Hedges 2 to 4 feet tall are used to delineate space, as in dividing your lawn from your neighbors' or planting along a front yard to deter pedestrians from walking across the lawn. Medium-height rose hedges of up to 6 feet provides an unobtrusive sense of enclosure for a front yard or backyard.

A medium-height hedge is also attractive planted along a patio or low deck to enclose it and to provide privacy.

High hedges

High hedges are the classic European hedge. Throughout the British isles, for example, rose hedges 10 feet high and nearly as wide line many a country lane.

Rose hedges such as these are wonderful in open, natural areas where they can sprawl. Wildlife love them, finding secure shelter under the leaves and thorns from larger predators.

Of course, a rose hedge doesn't have to be quite so tall or wide.

Choose more upright-growing rose cultivars that are, say, 6 feet high and 4 feet wide, and your hedge will be well contained.

If you're concerned about sprawling, you could plant the roses along a series of posts connected with wire cable; tie and train the roses along the wire and posts.

Mixed hedges

Most rose hedges are planted all of one type of rose, but you could mix it up with two or more types. A hedge of alternating white Simplicity and pink Simplicity roses would be beautiful. Or plant a mix of roses, the way you might a mix of evergreens in a casual hedge—combining heights, growth habits, and leaf texture and shape for an intriguing effect.

Consider planting two or three rows of hedge with the center taller and the outer roses a shorter type.

▲ This Amber Queen hedge runs along a stone wall, adding color and softness to what otherwise might be a barren-looking expanse.

Using climbing, rambling, and pillar roses

Climbing, rambling, and pillar roses—roses in the air—can pack lots of color into a limited amount of garden space and soften buildings, arbors, and other tall structures. These roses are a lovely way to add vertical elements and romance to the landscape.

Climbing roses

Climbing roses can range in height from 12 to 60 feet, depending on how you choose to grow and prune them. As a rule, you'll find the largest flowers on modern climbing roses.

Climbing roses are not vines and have no tendrils to hold them to vertical surfaces. Therefore, they need supporting devices, such as trellises, to assist them in maintaining their structure and shape.

Use climbing roses to accent structures, plants, or trees. Planting a climber next to the house near a window helps bring nature inside. You can also plant climbers around porches or garden entrances to welcome your guests. You can accent other plants by combining climbing roses and companion plants. Roses go well with almost all other plants, climbing and nonclimbing.

Combine climbing roses and clematis or bush roses for a breathtaking display in the garden. Climbing roses make a great backdrop for all types of plants. For a different effect, you can even have them grow into trees.

Rambler roses

Rambling roses are delightfully rampant, with some, such as the genteelly named Lady Banks Rose, earning the title "house eater." These roses can reach 60 feet and they explode with flowers, which are usually fragrant. They are ideal for covering a large pergola, scrambling up a massive tree or chimney, covering small buildings, engulfing a rustic fence, or basically covering any large space. These are the classic roses associated with the charming English rose-covered cottage.

Their flowers are usually smaller than those of climbers, giving them a wilder, more casual look.

Pillar roses

Pillar roses are small, well-behaved climbers. They don't grow much over 10 feet and are ideal for training onto smaller arbors as well as pillars or posts erected in the middle of flowerbeds for vertical accents.

Many shrub roses or other roses with long canes can be used as pillar roses, such as hybrid musks and noisettes.

▲ Joseph's Coat roses, planted in a narrow bed along the wall of a house, adds romance and style to a simple patio.

FAVORTE VERTICAL ROSES	
Aloha	6 to 10 feet
Altissimo	Up to 10 feet
America	8 to 10 feet
Berries 'n' Cream	10 to 12 feet
Climbing Madamoiselle Cecile Brunner	20 feet
Climbing Rainbow's End	8 feet
Dortmund	10 feet
Dream Weaver	8 feet
Dublin Bay	10 feet
Flutterbye	6 to 8 feet
Golden Showers	10 to 12 feet
High Hopes	10 to 12 feet
New Dawn	12 to 20 feet
Paul's Himalayan Musk	30 feet
Pearly Gates	8 to 12 feet
Rosa banksiae banksiae	30 feet
Sombreuil	6 to 12 feet
Summer Wine	12 feet
William Baffin	10 to 12 feet
Zephirine Drouhin	8 to 12 feet

Six Ways to Support Roses

Tuteur
Taller, sprawling roses such as Golden Celebration benefit from the excellent circulation allowed by a black metal tuteur.

Larger garden structure
A rose that grows 15 or more feet is a good choice for a larger arbor or other larger garden structure.

Fence or hedge
An unsightly fence can be beautifully obliterated by a planting of several New Dawn roses.

Pillar
A pillar or post is a great way to grow a rose such as this Don Juan in a limited space or to add vertical interest to an otherwise flat bed or border.

Large tree
Ramblers, such as this Paul's Himalayan Musk grow 40 or more feet and can be trained up large trees.

Traditional trellis
This Climbing Iceberg rose grows up a wood trellis inserted into the grouping.

Designing with groundcover roses

Groundcover roses are vigorous, low-growing, spreading roses that are amazingly useful in the landscape. They provide another set of rose options for dealing with problem areas in your garden.

Nearly any low-growing, somewhat spreading rose can be used as a groundcover rose, but some definitely lend themselves for use as a groundcover.

Slope solutions

One of the best uses for groundcover roses is in mass plantings. They're excellent on sunny slopes with erosion problems. Their spreading growth habit helps to retain the soil and prevent it from washing away during the rainy season.

Groundcover roses, especially the more compact ones, are an ideal planting for the strips between sidewalks and streets. (With some groundcover roses, the long canes may be a problem in areas where people could come in contact with them. Pruning them hard each spring, however, can prevent this problem.) Groundcover roses tend to be tough and salt-tolerant and are an excellent deterrent to pedestrians who might be tempted to walk over and trample plantings.

Coastal favorites

Because of their salt tolerance, groundcover roses are a favorite of coastal gardeners. Their low profile makes them oblivious to the constant drying, damaging winds found on beachfronts.

Groundcover roses are excellent for rock gardens, where they appreciate the good drainage. And they mix well with alpine plants and herbaceous groundcovers.

Try the more compact groundcover roses, too, in the front of large borders. Like their more upright cousins, these roses blend nicely with the perennials, grasses, annuals, and shrubs found in the mixed border.

Because so many groundcover roses have a loose, sprawling habit and smaller flowers, they are good for naturalistic plantings. Try them along rustic fences or to add color to the base of a windbreak or large hedge.

The miniature alternative

In tighter situations, or a spot where you want a more groomed look, consider planting miniature or miniflora roses in a tightly grouped mass. It will take more roses to fill the area, but the effect will be neater and more uniform.

Groundcover roses are a good solution for disguising the legginess of hybrid teas and some grandifloras. Plant one (as long as it doesn't get taller than 2 feet or so) at the base of a hybrid tea to surround the tall canes with layers of roses.

RECOMMENDED GROUNDCOVER ROSES

Below are some of the best-performing roses that grow with a low, spreading habit, making them good as groundcover.

Aspen	La Sevillana
Baby Boomer	Magic Carrousel
Behold	The Meidiland series
Bonica	Napa Valley
Cape Cod	Natchez
Central Park	Newport
Cliffs of Dover	Pillow Fight
Cupcake	Rainbow's End
First Light	Red Cascade
Flower Carpet	Red Ribbons
Gizmo	Royal Bonica
Gourmet Popcorn	Starry Night
Harm Saville	The Fairy
Iceberg	Yellow Ribbons
The Knock Out series	

▲ Groundcover roses, such as these Starry Night, can also be used in rock gardens and terraces.

► What could be a better way to fill a large space than with these richly colored Carpet of Color roses? As a group, groundcover roses like these are easy to maintain, making them a wise choice for mass plantings.

Designing formal rose gardens

▲ This classically designed formal garden has all the signature touches: Brick paths, neatly clipped box hedges growing in a classic parterre design centered on a statue. Perennials and herbs, especially silver-foliaged ones, are mixed in pleasingly.

Formal rose gardens came into fashion in the Middle Ages, when the church taught that an orderly garden symbolized the order in heaven. In the Renaissance, large and elaborate formal rose gardens became a must-have for the rich to display their wealth.

Today, you can find formal rose gardens in many public gardens and in large private gardens. In a residential setting, they are best used with classic styles of architecture such as colonial houses in the Adams or Georgian style and French provincial, and in palaces of any ilk.

Formal rose gardens require detailed planning and a great deal of upkeep once planted. But if you have the interest and time to devote to them, their orderliness can offer a retreat from the chaos of the world.

The formal layout

Formal gardens have a symmetrical layout made up of one or more beds outlined with a low-growing, clipped evergreen hedge.

Boxwood is most commonly used for the hedge, but yews are an alternative in regions where boxwoods are not hardy or are prone to mite infestations. The hedges form a geometric shape, such as a rectangle, circle, or diamond.

Usually, only one or two geometric shapes repeats throughout the garden, to prevent the design from seeming chaotic. Additional bands of clipped evergreens can subdivide the main bed—for example, a square can be divided into four triangles.

Inside the geometric shapes can be roses, upright evergreens (including topiary), masses of flowering annuals of a uniform height,

perennials, or a combination of all of the above.

The more uniform the plant shape, the more formal the bed. For a slightly more informal formal garden, you can outline the beds with miniature roses, germander, santolina, or blue fescue. See page 36 for more ideas for borders with roses.

Roses for formal gardens

Large-flowered modern roses, such as hybrid teas and grandifloras, are most commonly used in formal beds. Because they are widely spaced, it's easy to admire

▶ A formal garden doesn't have to be fussy. This formal garden is very relaxed-looking, even with the boxwood trim, because of the rustic backdrop and materials.

Designing formal rose gardens *(continued)*

Formal gardens are ideal for showing off statuary, birdbaths, fountains, or other art. Rather than tuck pieces in here or there, locate them at an obvious focal point, such as at the intersection of two paths or the center of a bed. Choose pieces that are in scale with the garden and that keep the formal feel. Avoid using too many pieces, making the garden look cluttered and busy.

For mulching a formal rose bed, it's generally best to use a natural material close to the soil's color, such as darker wood mulch and cocoa hulls. Light-color and dyed wood mulches, pine needles, light colored stone and gravel, and river rock lack subtlety.

▲ This traditional rose garden has brick paths outlined with tightly trimmed dwarf boxwood laid out in geometric patterns. Eden Climber roses fill the fanciful arbor in the back.

their individual shapes and flowers. When properly pruned, they have a well-balanced, open, relatively uniform form. Miniatures are also a good choice, because they are easily shaped into domes. The artificial roundness of tree roses is well suited to the formal effect as well. Climbing roses fit the scheme if trained to a fence or trellis so that the main canes are horizontal. The less-tamed shapes of shrub roses and ramblers are better suited to informal gardens (see page 42).

If you collect roses and want to showcase individual plants, you can plant as many different ones as space allows. This approach encourages a slow stroll through the garden to admire each plant.

Alternatively, to keep the effect soothingly simple, use the same variety throughout, or different varieties of the same color. This uniformity is appealing when viewing the entire garden, especially from above, such as from an upstairs window.

Paths and focal points

Paths in a formal garden accentuate the geometry of the beds. Paths can be made of well-maintained and trimmed lawn, or of a hard material such as brick or crushed gravel. Keep turf paths well edged. For brick paths, a metal or wood edging keeps the bricks from shifting out of place. Edging also is essential for keeping gravel in place—you can use metal or brick edging to corral it.

▲ A formal rose garden need not be fussy. This one is surrounded by a weathered wood fence and has simple wood edging around each bed, keeping the feeling decidedly rustic.

ROSE GARDEN DESIGNS

Below are four rose garden designs, from traditional to contemporary.

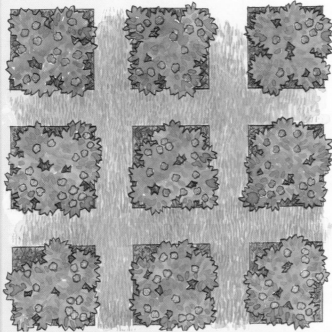

A grid of rose beds can be fun in the right spot, such as a sideyard or even a front yard. It's also a great way to assure excellent air circulation for roses.

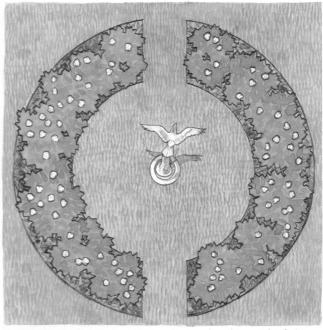

Curved beds with a statuary focal point are classics in formal rose garden design. You could also substitute a fountain or a large pot with a standard rose in it.

This is an extremely traditional formal rose garden, derived from the Middle Ages concept of a garden divided into four portions, modeled after the Christian cross.

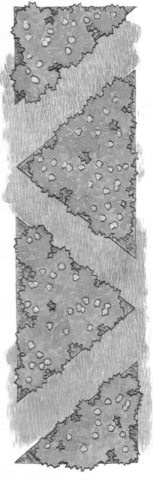

A more modern take on rose garden design, this series of triangles still would be defined as a formal garden because of the symmetry.

Designing roses in containers

▲ Steps are ideal for staging containers of a variety of plants, roses included. They allow you to enjoy the roses up close as you ascend the stairs and view them from a different level. Miniature roses are a great choice for medium-sized pots, but large containers and planters are excellent even for shrub roses.

Bring the color of roses to patios, front steps, windows, decks, porches, balconies, and more by growing them in containers. No matter what your style preference, you'll find a wonderful array of containers available to fit your taste.

Roses are perfect for planter boxes or larger raised beds. Elevating roses in planters or raised beds brings them comfortably in range for closeup viewing and sniffing. On the practical side, planters and raised beds provide an ideal way to give roses the good soil and drainage they need.

If you live in an apartment or in an urban space that doesn't allow for inground planting, try roses in large and small planters and planter boxes. Planters, planter boxes, and containers can give you a rose garden along walkways, the edge of a parking lot, along a driveway, beside a front door, on patios—just about anywhere there is space and sunlight and a ready source to water.

The big chill

In cold regions, Zones 6 and colder, you'll need to plan your rose container plantings in such a way that you can bring the containers into a cool, nonfreezing indoor space to overwinter the plants. Otherwise, they'll freeze solid and die over the winter. Another solution in Zones 5 and warmer is to dig a hole in the ground as deep as the container and slightly wider. In fall, after the first frost, set the container in the hole and cover with packed autumn leaves.

Roses lend themselves beautifully to growing in containers, another reason they're so widely grown. Even gardeners with limited space can enjoy them.

Whether you want a couple of pots by your front door or you want to fill a planter, roses are a smart choice, especially if you choose repeat bloomers. With their pretty foliage and wonderful fragrance, it's a pity to relegate roses solely to inground plantings.

Choosing containers

Containers are available in many materials and a range of sizes. When selecting a container material for roses, consider design aspects such as color and style as well as practical considerations like weight and porosity (how easily water wicks through the material). Container size also has both aesthetic and practical considerations—the container should be in scale with its surroundings, but it's even more important that it be the right size for the rose growing in it.

Drainage a must

No matter what container you choose, one absolute requirement is adequate drainage. Water must be able to move through the potting soil and out the bottom of the container. Soggy soil without drainage can kill roses in a matter of days. If a container does not have a hole, you can drill a drainage hole or two in plastic, resin, or wood containers before planting.

If you have a container that doesn't lend itself to drilling (a large antique iron urn, for example), you can still use the container. Plant your rose in an inexpensive black plastic nursery pot that fits into the outer decorative container. Set the inner pot on bricks, wood blocks, or a layer of gravel to keep the pot above any water that accumulates. You will need, however, to empty water from the outer container if it collects.

Common container materials include clay, wood, concrete, and metal. And

▲ Get creative with your containers. This standard rose has been planted in an old bucket that has been artfully aged further with green and rust-color paint.

while it's easy to find plenty of plastic containers, a new class of interesting and more durable fiberglass and resin containers and so-called cast stone has hit the market. You'll find these materials used in numerous container styles. For example, natural wood containers often have a casual or rustic style, but wood can also be used for more formal containers when crafted into decorative white or green painted planter boxes. Different colors, shapes, and finishes on clay pots create a range of styles from quirky to classic.

Consider weight and weather

The container's material, of course, affects its total weight

and movability. If you know you'll be moving your rose containers frequently, lightweight materials such as plastic, resin, or fiberglass make more sense than, say, clay. Material is also an important factor in how the containers hold up to different climate conditions, especially freezing

▲ Tuck roses planted in containers into beds and borders for a delightful accent. This Red Cascade rose has been set on top of a mortared brick pedestal. You could stack bricks in a bed and top them with a paver for a similar effect.

ARS ROSARIAN TIP...
Use wide containers for growing roses because their roots spread out more than they do down. The half whiskey barrel size is about as small as you would want to go for a hybrid tea rose here, yet its width is good.
—Jan Shannon, Corpus Christi, Texas

temperatures. Clay, ceramic, and plastic containers cannot be left out for the winter in regions where temperatures get much below 20°F for extended periods. Resin, cast stone, fiberglass, and concrete containers shouldn't be left out in regions where it gets much below –10°F.

Your container's material may also affect how often you have to water. Porous materials like unglazed terra-cotta lose water through the container walls. With these containers or in dry or baked situations, consider a potting medium with water-retaining polymers in it, such as Miracle-Gro Moisture Control Pottting Mix.

If you live in a moister climate (the Pacific Northwest or the eastern two-thirds of the U.S.), you may want to use pot feet, bricks, flat stones, or other mechanisms to hold pots up off the concrete or decking material. This prevents stained and rotten wood and deters slugs.

CONTAINERS IN BEDS AND BORDERS

Roses in pots and other containers can be placed right into gardens, tucked into flowerbeds on top of the soil, or seated on a low pedestal.

In colder regions, you can position these pots in spring at planting time. Or do what some seasoned gardeners do: Grow a variety of plants in pots just for a display along front steps or a back door. Then, when a bed develops a bare spot, take a pot and fill the problem spot.

ARS ROSARIAN TIP...

Prevent the soil in rose containers from getting too warm by painting the container a light color.
—*John Mattia,
Orange, Connecticut*

Scale

When choosing container size, keep in mind scale—how an object fits into its surroundings. For example, a small container would look dwarfed and lost on a large patio or next to a cathedral-height entryway. On the other hand, an oversize container might look silly tucked into a flower border just a foot or so wide. Likewise, it might crowd onto a narrow pathway.

But the main factors in determining how big the container needs to be are the size and number of plants you'll be using. A single miniature rose will grow in a container 12 inches wide and deep (the size of a 5-gallon nursery pot). If you want to plant a full-size hybrid tea rose surrounded by annuals, though, you'll need a much bigger container, at least a 20-gallon size. Resist the urge to skimp on container size; roses grown in too-small containers often suffer drought stress, and their growth and flowering decline.

For more information on planting roses, see page 94.

▲ Consider the shape of the rose plant when choosing other plants to include in your planting. A standard rose is naturally spare at the bottom, so trailing plants complement it well.

▲ As long as the window box is fairly large and the rose is fairly small, the two are a pleasant combination. These miniature roses add an elegant touch to a window box filled with English ivy, mosses, lavender, and smooth dark stones.

Growing roses in planters and window boxes

The variety in rose size and shapes means roses can be a delightful choice for window boxes and planters. Whether you plant only roses or combine them with other plants, roses add elegance and color.

Before planting roses, make sure your window box or planter receives full sun, or at least six hours a day. Planter boxes attached to homes may be shaded by eaves or the building itself and may not receive enough sun for roses to grow well. Check planters for drainage before planting; some planters have solid bottoms while others are simply partially buried in the ground and have excellent drainage.

In some climates (Zone 4 and colder) temperatures are too cold to allow roses to survive over winter in all but the largest planters, those several feet across and at least 3 or 4 feet deep. In cold zones you can keep roses in plastic nursery pots, set them into planters for the growing season, then move them to a protected location for winter.

Window boxes and planters elevate blooming roses and increase their visibility. Keep the height of the planter in mind when selecting roses. For example, an entryway planter box that's 4 feet tall should be planted with roses less than 2 feet tall (such as miniature roses), not towering hybrid teas. Mid- to low-height planter boxes placed next to paved walkways make blooming roses accessible to wheelchair users.

Roses in window boxes

Miniature roses also are lovely in window boxes. If you have space for a large window box that holds several gallons of soil, try planting some of the miniature climbing roses for a curtain of bloom.

Make sure the window box is large enough to support your roses. Premade window boxes tend to be small (but should be as wide as the window) so consider a custom-made window box that not only spans the window but also is as deep and wide as is practical. The more soil you have, the less likely the plants are to dry out and overheat.

In window boxes, try Green Ice or Sequoia Gold, two excellent cascading miniature cultivars that trail 2 or 3 feet and don't need as much soil as some roses.

Roses in planters

Planters are often used near entryways or outdoor living areas such as decks and patios. Like raised beds, planters have more soil but lack mobility.

Brick, stone, concrete, and wood are common materials for planter boxes. They can be built in any shape, but square or rectangular is typical. Heights of 24 to 36 inches are common, but this may vary depending on location and purpose of the planter box. Planter boxes may be attached to a building or freestanding. Planter boxes often serve as physical or visual barriers to define spaces. For example, a long, narrow planter box might separate a pool area from the rest of the yard.

Selecting roses

Many different roses can be grown in containers and planters. When selecting roses, you'll note traits like flower color, fragrance, bloom period, and disease resistance. Another important factor is the mature size of the rose plant. For most containers, smaller roses are the best choice. Larger roses, even climbers, can be grown in large planters and raised beds.

Miniature roses for containers

Miniature roses are absolute naturals for planting in containers. Their size—ranging from 1 to 3 feet tall—plus their full, rounded forms and heavily flowering nature make them great choices for container display. Miniatures can be grown singly in small or medium-size containers, or in small groups in larger containers. Miniatures can also be a part of container groupings. For example, a line of five or more miniatures of the same cultivar grown in matching pots makes a simple screen or a barrier at the edge of a deck.

Miniatures can also be used with other roses. For an attractive display, use a set of glazed clay pots in three or more sizes. Grow miniature roses in the smaller one or two pots, then progressively larger roses such as minifloras and floribundas in the larger pots.

Miniature roses also work well in planter boxes and raised beds. In smaller planters they can stand alone or with companion plantings like trailing annuals. In larger planters and raised beds, miniatures make a wonderful edging with larger roses planted in the center or toward the back of the planter or bed.

Floribundas and shrub roses

Floribundas and many modern shrub roses, such as David Austin roses or the relatively new so-called landscape roses, are great choices for medium and large containers. When selecting a cultivar make sure you know its mature size; floribundas range from 2 to 6 feet tall and shrub roses from 2 to more than 10 feet tall. Smaller cultivars are better for container planting. Larger cultivars are fine for large planters and raised beds.

Floribundas are noted for their continuous displays of spectacular flower clusters. This trait makes them especially desirable for outdoor areas like decks and patios that are used constantly through the summer. Floribundas are generally planted singly in containers. A number of floribundas in individual containers could work as a movable hedge to direct foot traffic or to divide outdoor "rooms." Floribundas pair well with larger and smaller roses in containers.

Shrub roses in containers can be used in the same way as floribundas. Select shrub roses that are everblooming for the longest show of color. Many modern shrub roses have excellent disease resistance and require no spraying, making them an even better candidate for pots and planters.

Hybrid teas and other larger roses

Larger roses such as hybrid teas, grandifloras, and large shrub roses can be planted in individual containers as long as the containers have plenty of volume (15 to 20 gallons, about the size of a half-barrel). Large roses with lanky stems can be neatened by placing an attractive pyramidal tuteur in the container and training the rose through the lattice. To produce a vertical sweep of color on a patio or near an entryway, group smaller roses in small and medium-size pots around the sides of tall roses in large containers.

Larger roses are well suited to growing in large planters and raised beds where they'll have plenty of space. Even long-caned climbing roses can be grown in large planters as long as they are trained on a support such as a trellis, arbor, or fence. Climbers grown in paired planters with a central support are especially attractive. For example, climbers in large planters can be trained over a pergola running above the garage doors, making even a utilitarian structure look extremely elegant.

▲ Several pots of roses transform a tiny strip of deck into a haven of flowers.

▲ Choosing a quality planting mix is critical to growing healthy roses. Unlike regular garden soil or lesser quality mixes, good potting medium keeps roses better hydrated and fed.

Choosing planting mix

Roses grown in containers have different planting and maintenance needs than roses grown in the garden. Roses in containers lack the soil ecosystem found in gardens, so they need a specialized growing medium. Containers also have different watering and fertilizing needs than gardens. Planting and refreshing containers is a little different, but it's all easy and with a little knowledge, will lead to great results.

Potting mixes

Container plantings have special requirements of the potting mix used to fill them. The mix needs to drain well but hold enough moisture to keep the rose's roots from drying out. For containers that will be moved around, the weight of the mix is also an important factor.

Regular garden soil from your yard or garden is not a good choice for filling containers. Although regular soil provides nutrients and holds moisture, it also has the disadvantages of being heavy and may harbor fungal spores, other diseases, or insect pests.

For most containers a soilless potting mix such as Miracle-Gro Potting Mix is the best choice. (Consider Miracle-Gro Moisture Control Potting Mix in dry or sunbaked areas.) Soilless mixes are lightweight, have an ideal balance of moisture retention and drainage, and are free of soilborne pathogens. Soilless mixes can be used for new planter boxes or be added to older planters that already have soil in them.

Soilless potting mixes contain a number of components. The main ingredient in most is peat moss, which is partially decayed sphagnum moss harvested from peat bogs. Peat moss holds moisture and supports growing roots. Some soilless mixes use other plant-based material such as composted bark chips and coir (coconut fiber) in addition to peat moss.

Other components of soilless mixes may include perlite (lightweight, expanded volcanic rock, which provides air space and good drainage), ground dolomitic limestone (to balance pH), wetting agents (to make the peat moss easier to moisten), sand (for weight), and starter fertilizers that include trace elements.

RENEWING POTTING MIX

In both soilless and soil-based potting mixes the organic matter breaks down over time. In rose gardens planted directly in the ground, in raised beds, and in some large planters, the organic matter should be refreshed with yearly topdressings of compost and an additional inch or so of organic mulch.

The activity of earthworms and soil-dwelling insects helps move the fresh organic matter into the soil. In containers and planters filled with soilless mix, though, there are no earthworms to incorporate additional organic matter.

For these containers, change the potting mix annually. If your rose needs to be moved to a larger container, you will automatically be adding fresh potting mix to the new container. But if the rose is not potbound, you can simply refresh the mix and replant in the same container.

The best time to refresh the mix is in early spring, when the roses are dormant. Unpot the rose and gently remove as much of the old mix from the root ball as possible, being careful not to damage the rose roots.

Remove any old potting mix left in the container. Refill the container with fresh potting mix that includes slow-release fertilizer, and set the rose in at the appropriate depth as you fill. The roots will soon grow into the new mix.

Read the bag carefully to see what's inside a bag of potting mix. Some mixes are actually soilless, which makes them very lightweight and ideal for windowboxes and many other containers.

Arranging roses

One of the joys of rose gardening is cutting blooms to bring indoors. Many rose gardeners, in fact, grow roses just so they can cut them.

Rose cutting gardens

If you love roses and want lots of them to cut regularly, you may want to consider creating plantings specifically for cutting.

This is particularly practical if you want to cut hybrid teas. With their long stems and large, classic rose shapes, hybrid teas are highly desirable for cutting, though their leggy profile is problematic in ornamental beds and borders. In a cutting garden, however, they can shine in their role solely as a floral crop.

Most cutting gardens are tucked off to the side of the yard or out of sight. The role of the garden isn't to look pretty—it's a place to cut and remove flowers. Still, you can easily create an attractive rose cutting garden if you underplant with companion plants (see pages 36 and 37) that complement the roses in the garden as well as in the vase, such as artemesias, lamb's-ears, peonies, baby's breath, lavender, and irises.

If you want armloads of roses of the same kind, plant generously. Depending on your climate and the plant, you will probably get a maximum of six or so good roses from a hybrid tea at one time, though that plant will continue to bloom all season,

To accommodate large arrangements with as many as two dozen roses at a time, plant at least four of the same cultivar if you want that arrangement to be all the same type of rose.

Cutting from ornamental plantings

Of course, if you have a few rose bushes mixed into other plantings in your garden, you can cut the blooms and bring them indoors, as do most gardeners.

Cutting roses from mixed beds is the most space-efficient way to provide cut flowers for your home. Because you haven't relegated roses for cutting to an area out of sight, you can enjoy the developing flowers (and the ones you decide not to cut) from your garden.

Remember, too, that cutting roses stimulates more bloom. Consider it a form of deadheading. Just be sure to make the cuts in such a way that the rose is encouraged to grow in a healthy pattern (see "How to cut roses" at the bottom of this page).

Good candidates

It's important to realize that not all roses are well suited for cutting. Many rugosa roses, for example, have petals that fall and shatter quickly once the stems are cut. David Austin roses also tend to shatter easily and are short-lived in the vase.

Hybrid teas, on the other hand, are ideal for cutting with long, slender stems and minimal thorns. Floribundas and grandifloras are also excellent for cutting.

Whether a single stem in a bud vase or as part of an ornate floral arrangement, roses add a touch of elegance to any setting. If you enjoy flower arranging, consider planting a cutting garden of annual and perennial flowers to combine with your roses. You can also purchase cut flowers and greenery to complement your roses at florist shops and many grocery stores.

How to cut roses

Cut roses when the plants are well hydrated. This is usually early in the morning, but it's best to wait for the dew to dry so you're not dealing with wet plants. If the plant is looking at all dry, you may want to water the night before cutting.

Bring a clean bucket or large pitcher partially filled with lukewarm water.

Select plump buds that are on the verge of opening—they'll open more fully than tight buds. You can cut opened roses, of course, but they'll have a shorter vase life.

Using clean, sharp pruning shears, floral snips, or a florist's knife, cut the stem at a 45-degree angle right above

◄ One of the simplest ways to arrange roses is to gather them in your hand, arrange them so they are pleasing to you, cut the ends off evenly, and insert them into a vase or jar. Vase-shaped containers often work best because they allow the rose stems to spread out

the first five-leaflet leaf under the flower. You can cut some longer stems if you wish, but avoid taking off too much foliage because the rose bush needs plenty of leaves to produce energy. Immediately place cut stems into the bucket of water.

Once you've cut as many roses as you need, bring the bucket inside, refill it with clean water, and re-cut the rose stems at an angle under water. By cutting the stems under water you'll prevent any air bubbles from entering the rose's water-transporting system, a form of sealing.

Put the bucket of roses in a cool, dark location. This step is known as conditioning; it gives the cut roses time to draw up plenty of water and will make them last longer in the vase. Florists use refrigerated coolers for conditioning.

After the roses have conditioned for at least several hours, they are ready to be placed in vases.

Make a vase solution using warm water and floral preservative, added at the rate recommended on the label. Stir the mixture to dissolve the floral preservative completely, then pour it into the vase.

Carefully remove any leaves that would be below the water line in the vase to prevent decay. Cut stems at an angle to the appropriate length and quickly place in the vase before the pores cut open can close again, diminishing their ability to take up water.

Place cut roses away from sun, heat sources, or drafts. They'll last longer if placed in a cool place at night or when not on display.

Make sure the vase is always full of water, and change the water completely every day or two. Every three days or so, trim off the bottom ¼ inch of the rose stems, if practical, so they can continue to take up water.

Properly cared for, cut roses will provide a full week of enjoyment.

TRICKS OF THE TRADE

You can always just tuck some roses into a vase, but for a more controlled, thought-out look, try some of these tricks florists and others use:

Floral foam is like a firm sponge. Soak it in water until it is thoroughly saturated; then cut it to fit into the container. Insert as much stem as possible to keep the rose as well hydrated as possible.

Floral wire (a fancy version of chicken wire, which you can also use) can be crumpled and stuffed into the rim of a vase or container to encourage the rose to stay upright. Fill in with more roses, foliage, and other flowers.

Frogs come in many different designs. Shown here is a needle type. Place it in the bottom of the vase and insert roses to keep them upright.

Choosing the right rose for your garden and your region

The same rose may perform differently in various locations around the country. Regional conditions are everything when it comes to the beauty, size, and vigor of a rose.

If you live in a moderate or warm climate, you have a longer growing season and your roses, bushes and blooms will tend to be larger than those grown in areas with colder temperatures.

If your area is hot, you may notice that your roses have exceptionally strong fragrance. You may also notice that the colors differ from those you saw when perusing the catalog; they may look softer and more faded. You may have fewer occurrences of fungal diseases.

If you live in a colder climate, your roses may be smaller and perhaps less overpowering in fragrance, but they may have more intense color in the petals.

If your area is damp and humid, you may have roses of great size and color, but you will need to spray with a fungicide early in each growing season to prevent fungal diseases.

The role of local weather

Local weather plays a huge role in how your roses look.

Roses in catalogs have been photographed at their peak and in excellent growing conditions. A rose that looks perfect in the catalog won't necessarily look the same in your garden.

For a better indicator, check out roses in local public or private gardens to discern how those roses will perform in your climate. Take

▲ This rose garden, located on an open plain, is exposed to wind and highly variable temperatures, including extremes of heat and cold, wet and dry. In such conditions, only tough roses thrive with minimal care.

along pencil and paper to keep note of cultivar names.

Take advantage of any lists of recommended roses a public garden might offer. Also check with your local nursery and cooperative extension service for lists of recommended roses for your area. Extension services often post such lists online. Check with your local American Rose Society Chapter as well.

Read catalog and label descriptions carefully. If they state that the rose variety does not open well in cooler climates and you live in such a climate, you would do better to select a comparable rose that will thrive where you live.

Heat and cold tolerance

Heat and cold tolerance refers to how a rose handles a range of temperatures. This does not mean temperature extremes, but average hot and cold temperatures.

Rose catalogs often refer to this tolerance by describing how a rose performs in temperatures. For example, some listings describe varieties as not opening well in cooler temperatures, while others note that the flower opens quickly in warmer temperatures (and may therefore fade quickly).

Regions where summer temperatures may be so cool that roses have difficulty opening include the Pacific Northwest and the higher altitudes of mountainous regions. Regions with summer temperatures so hot as to hamper the ability of roses to bloom well, at least during the height of summer, include much of the southern one-third to one-half of the United States.

Drought and damp tolerance

Drought and damp tolerance describe how much or how little water and humidity a variety can tolerate. This is a relative description of how a rose will perform in either an arid climate, primarily the desert Southwest and arid portions of the West, or a humid environment, essentially the southernmost regions of the South, including Florida.

While no rose will thrive in drought conditions, there are some varieties, such as the rugosas and their hybrids, that do better than others. Most rugosas, however, don't like extreme heat, so they're a better choice for areas with only moderate heat.

Damp tolerance can refer to actual wetness, such as steady rain, or heavy dew—conditions found often in the Pacific Northwest. Damp tolerance also can refer to areas with high humidity, such as much of the South.

If you are in an area where continual dampness and humidity are the norm, you may want to select roses with fewer petals, such as singles, to ensure that they will open properly and display their beauty. Some of the heavier-petaled roses, such as the fully doubles, tend to form into a ball and fail to open well in damp or humid conditions.

Even if an area isn't humid, heavy dew or frequent rainfall can be a problem. In the Pacific Northwest, for example, the single-petaled roses can be more of a sure bet than fully double roses.

▲ This Southern California garden is abundant with roses. The mild, dry climate is ideal for roses as long as they're amply irrigated.

Choosing roses for cold climates

Roses vary widely in their ability to tolerate cold weather. Nearly any rose will be hardy in Zone 6 and warmer (see the map on the opposite page), but farther north, it's trickier.

The term cold hardiness, also called winter hardiness, refers to how well a rose plant adapts to harsh, cold winter weather. In the colder portions of the country, essentially the top one-third

of the United States, many roses die over the winter.

In these colder states, roses will not survive if they are not well-selected and well-protected during the harsy winter months.

Other variables are involved: If the rose hasn't been getting enough water, has been disease-prone or attacked by insects, hasn't been getting enough light, or is otherwise stressed, it's less

likely to make it through the winter.

If the rose has a good insulating blanket of snow all winter long, it's likely to survive. On the other hand, if the winter weather is highly variable, with swings of warmth that bring a rose out of dormancy followed by a cold snap, roses may die.

It's essential in Zones 4 and colder to choose only the most cold-hardy roses. As

groups, climbing roses and hybrid teas are the most likely to die during the winter.

To reduce the risk, choose roses known for their cold hardiness. These include the rugosa roses (see page 30 and 227), the Canadian Explorer series roses (see page 27), roses bred by Iowa's Griffith Buck (see page 27), and, in general, most of the so-called landscape roses.

Understanding roses for cold climates

If your average winter lows reach:

40°F/4.5°C and above (USDA Zone 11) to 20°F/–6.6°C (Zone 9) With mild lows, you do not need to worry about cold tolerance. However, some roses that do well in and are native to cold regions, such as rugosa roses, might not bloom well in your region.

10°F/–12.2°C (Zone 8) to 0°F/–17.7°C (Zone 7) This is the ideal climate for growing a wide variety of roses. Temperatures seldom get cold enough to do any but the slightest damage to roses.

–10°F/–23.3°C (Zone 6) Roses in this region are somewhat susceptible to cold damage but you can choose most roses with confidence. Minimal winter protection is needed.

–20°F/–28.8°C (Zone 5) In this region, rose choices are more limited. Many climbers, for example, won't do well. Heavier winter protection is needed for other roses.

–30°F/–34.4°C (Zone 4) Choose the most cold-tolerant roses you can to minimize the need for substantial winter protection.

–40°F/–39.9°C (Zone 3) A limited number of cold-hardy roses will thrive in this region. Most to all need substantial winter protection.

–50°F/–45°C (Zone 2 and 1) In these regions, only the hardiest roses with substantial winter protection will thrive.

COLD-HARDY ROSES

These are roses that are less likely to be severely damaged or killed by low winter temperatures. Look for any of the rugosa roses, the Canadian Explorer series, the Parkland series, the Griffith Buck roses, or those bearing the word Morden. More specifically, look for the following cultivars:

Ballerina

Bonica

Carefree Beauty

Carefree Delight

Carefree Wonder

Country Dancer

Dortmund

Flower Carpet

Frau Dagmar Hartopp

Henry Hudson

John Cabot

Linda Campbell

Meidiland roses

Morden roses

William Baffin

USDA plant hardiness zone map

This map of climate zones helps you select plants that will survive a typical winter in your region. The United States Department of Agriculture (USDA) developed the map, basing the zones on the lowest recorded temperatures across North America. Zone 1 is the coldest area and Zone 11 is the warmest.

The zone system classifies plants by the coldest temperature and zone they can endure. For example, plants hardy to Zone 6 survive where winter temperatures drop to -10°F. Those hardy only to Zone 8 would die long before it's that cold. Such plants may grow in colder regions but must be replaced each year. Plants rated for a range of hardiness zones can usually survive winter in the coldest region as well as tolerate the summer heat of the warmest one.

To find your hardiness zone, note the approximate location of your community on the map, then match the color marking that area to the key.

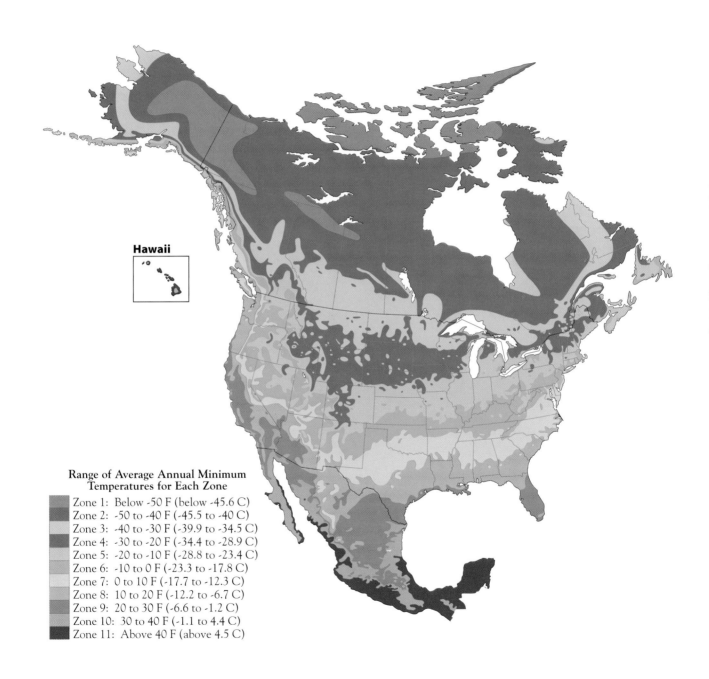

Hawaii

Range of Average Annual Minimum Temperatures for Each Zone

Zone 1: Below -50 F (below -45.6 C)
Zone 2: -50 to -40 F (-45.5 to -40 C)
Zone 3: -40 to -30 F (-39.9 to -34.5 C)
Zone 4: -30 to -20 F (-34.4 to -28.9 C)
Zone 5: -20 to -10 F (-28.8 to -23.4 C)
Zone 6: -10 to 0 F (-23.3 to -17.8 C)
Zone 7: 0 to 10 F (-17.7 to -12.3 C)
Zone 8: 10 to 20 F (-12.2 to -6.7 C)
Zone 9: 20 to 30 F (-6.6 to -1.2 C)
Zone 10: 30 to 40 F (-1.1 to 4.4 C)
Zone 11: Above 40 F (above 4.5 C)

Choosing roses for hot climates

Roses, when well chosen, can do beautifully in hot climates. Many roses, however, when denied the winter dormancy found in colder climates, exhaust themselves and fail.

In the hot, dry climates of the Southwest, roses suited to the region do amazingly well if given ample water. Dry conditions mean roses are less likely to fall prey to a major fungal rose disease—black spot. If you amend the soil well with compost and other soil amendments, mulch deeply (3 or more inches), and water frequently (an irrigation system is almost essential), you'll have roses to brag about.

In the hot, humid climates of the South, it's important to choose roses that can take heat and humidity (see page 78 for recommendations). Heat and humidity create ideal conditions for black spot and a host other fungal rose problems. On the other hand, the long growing season and ample moisture found in the South can result in spectacular roses that reach their maximum height and bloom for months and months on end.

Understanding roses for hot climates

If the average number of days per year above 86°F/30°C in your area is:

150 and more In this, the hottest and often most dry regions of the U.S., roses require watering two or more times a day. Irrigation systems are practically a must. This extensive heat results in smaller flowers that fade or wilt quickly. Some gardeners in this region plant roses in light shade only or use shade cloth over their roses. Also choose the most heat-tolerant roses only.

120-90 Heat can definitely decrease the summer performance of roses in these areas, but the compensating factor is mild winters and a long growing season that allows gardeners to enjoy thriving roses during the other seasons of the year. Still, roses must be kept well watered during the hottest parts of the year. Also, they'll thrive best with very light shade, especially in the afternoon.

45-90 In most of this area, heat comes in waves in late summer. Repeat blooming roses tend to stop blooming during this period but then start blooming again fairly well in the cooler temperatures of fall.

Fewer than 45 Cold, rather than heat, is the challenge in these areas, except in the temperate climate of the Pacific Northwest. See page 60 for a listing of cold-hardy roses.

12
11
10
9
8
7
6
5
4
3
2
1

HEAT-TOLERANT ROSES

These roses continue to bloom better than others even when exposed to high temperatures. They're great for most of the southern third of the United States.

Bonica

Brandy

Crystalline

French Lace

Harison's Yellow

Intrigue

The Knock Out series

Mister Lincoln

Moonstone

Oklahoma

Royal Highness

Showbiz

St. Patrick

Sun Flare

Sunset Celebration

Understanding rose heat tolerance in roses

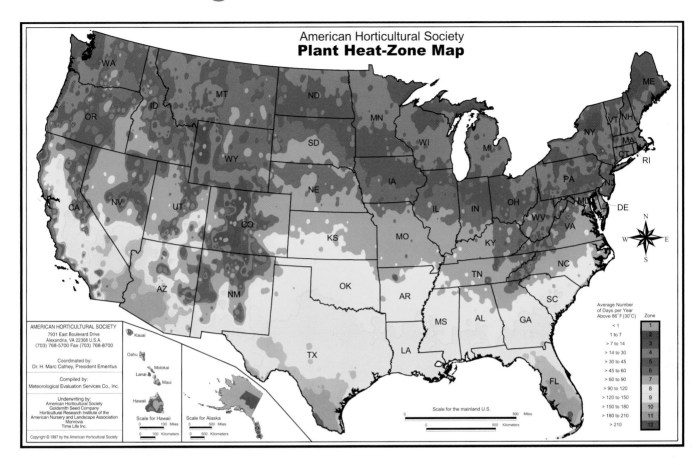

American Horticultural Society
Plant Heat-Zone Map

AMERICAN HORTICULTURAL SOCIETY
7931 East Boulevard Drive
Alexandria, VA 22308 U.S.A.
(703) 768-5700 Fax (703) 768-8700

Coordinated by:
Dr. H. Marc Cathey, President Emeritus

Compiled by:
Meteorological Evaluation Services Co., Inc.

Underwriting by:
American Horticultural Society
Goldsmith Seed Company
Horticultural Research Institute of the
American Nursery and Landscape Association
Monrovia
Time Life Inc.

Copyright © 1997 by the American Horticultural Society

Average Number of Days per Year Above 86°F (30°C)	Zone
< 1	1
1 to 7	2
> 7 to 14	3
> 14 to 30	4
> 30 to 45	5
> 45 to 60	6
> 60 to 90	7
> 90 to 120	8
> 120 to 150	9
> 150 to 180	10
> 180 to 210	11
> 210	12

For decades, the only concrete, national assistance gardeners had in selecting the right plants for their region was the U.S. Department of Agriculture's cold-hardiness map.

This map (see page 61), based on average low temperatures of a region, was created by the U. S. Department of Agriculture and is an excellent way to gauge if a plant will survive cold temperatures in your part of the country.

But if you live in a warm region, roughly the lower third of the U.S., your concern often isn't whether a plant can withstand the cold in your garden but if it can withstand the heat. Roses, especially will refuse to bloom and those flowers they do form tend to fade in just hours when temperatures soar.

The map on this page, created by the American Horticultural Society, will help you compare average highs in your region.

Few labels or catalog descriptions currently carry heat zone information, but some do, especially if they're drought- or heat-tolerant.

Regardless, this map will help you get a better feel for which roses might do best in your landscape, then match with the key.

MINIMIZING HEAT STRESS ON ROSES

You may not be able to control the heat, but you can control some other variables with your roses that will allow them to do their best even when temperatures soar:

● The smartest thing you can do is to choose heat-tolerant roses. Choose from the heat-tolerant list on the opposite page or from the designated EarthKind roses list (see page 76).
● The second most effective thing you can do is to water deeply and well and mulch well—3 or so inches. Well-hydrated roses in cooler soil tolerate extreme heat far better.
● As much as possible, position your roses where they will get light, dappled shade in the afternoon when heat stresses them the most. Some rose growers get creative with this and go so far as to rig contraptions with shade cloth to pamper their roses during the hottest months. Also experiment with planting roses on the east sides of buildings where they're protected from afternoon sun.
● Reduce the fertilization schedule on your roses as they enter the summer months. This reduces their bloom schedule and reduces the amount of new growth put on during the heat of high summer.
● Experiment with lighter-colored roses. Some rose growers swear that red, orange and lavender roses show heat stress more quickly than white, light-pink and pale yellow roses.
● Some rose growers have seen good results with antitranspirants. These waxy polymers reduce the transpiration of moisture through leaves and stems. These spray on and last for several days or even weeks, depending on conditions.

Wet to dry conditions

A key to success with roses is understanding the kind of precipitation you get (rain, snow, humidity, fog, dew, or mist) and the time of year that it occurs.

Precipitation affects roses in three ways:

First, it provides water to the roots, which absorb it and feed it to the rest of the plant. For good health and bloom, roses must receive 1 inch of water a week, whether from rainfall or watering.

Second, precipitation affects the formation of flowers. Humidity, fog, dew, mist, and constant rain can deform flowers, creating a condition called balling. Some roses, either by hybridizing or by petal shape, resist balling better than others.

Third, precipitation affects diseases in roses. Black spot (see page 115), a fungal disease, is the bane of roses. In the eastern half of the United States, there's hardly a rose without it by late summer, and some plants are practically denuded by it.

However, in the dry West, black spot is very seldom a serious problem.

Humid, wet regions experience a host of other fungal problems, including powdery mildew.

As you learn more about the precipitation in your region, you'll be on your way to growing spectacular roses with less effort.

A rain gauge is crucial in determining how much rainfall your garden receives in any given week.

If you're new to a region, talk to experienced gardeners and garden-center staff about precipitation as it relates to growing roses.

The Pacific Northwest, for example, has abundant moisture in spring and winter. Precipitation in summer is moderate and drought is not unusual in autumn.

In the Midwest, with its violent thunderstorms and widely variable weather, a region may get 2 inches of rain one week and none the next. A year of flooding can easily be followed by a year of extreme drought.

ROSES FOR HUMID REGIONS

In areas with high humidity, such as The South and the Pacific Northwest, black spot (see page 115) is a problem. The following roses are resistant to black spot and would be great choices for these regions.

Alba Meidiland	Iceberg
All That Jazz	The Knock Out series
Auguste Renoir	Nearly Wild
Belinda's Dream	New Dawn
Caldwell Pink	Red Cascade
Dortmund	Sea Foam
Else Poulsen	Simplicity
Flower Carpet	Sunsprite
Frederic Mistral	The Fairy
Gruss an Aachen	

▲ In this garden in the arid West, roses thrive along succulents, showing how they can grow well even in drier climates as long as they are amply irrigated.

VERY DRY CONDITIONS

Very to extremely light precipitation: 20 inches or less

In extremely dry conditions, choose roses that are naturally drought tolerant, though with this little rainfall you'll still have to water amply. An irrigation system is a must.

Rugosa roses as a group do well in dry conditions but aren't very tolerant of extreme heat. They are a good choice for dry mountain regions with cooler temperatures rather than low desert where hot weather prevails.

Otherwise, choose from the following roses. They tolerate both heat and drought well.

Austrian Copper	Rosa glauca
(Rosa foetida bicolor)	Rosa hugonis
Banshee	Rosa setigera
Fruhlingsgold	Rosa spinosissima
Harison's Yellow	Rosa xanthina
Lawrence Johnston	Stanwell Perpetual
Persian Yellow	Therese Bugnet
(Rosa foetida persiana)	

DRY CONDITIONS

Somewhat light precipitation: 20 to 30 inches

In dry regions, many roses grow well with good irrigation. Invest in irrigation systems that provide water directly to the roots to minimize water use and to prevent leaves from being sprayed.

Roses thrive in full sun but if you are in the lower half of the United States, where the sun is more direct, try to plant roses where they will receive at least a little afternoon shade. This helps them fight drought.

Conserve what moisture you do have by mulching well, 2 to 4 inches, with an organic mulch such as wood chips, bark, pine needles, or other materials that will break down over time.

Be vigilant for pests and diseases that thrive in dry conditions, such as spider mites. When watering roses, occasionally give the entire plant a spray with the hose to knock off pests and rinse off accumulated dust.

How Much Precipitation Do You Get?

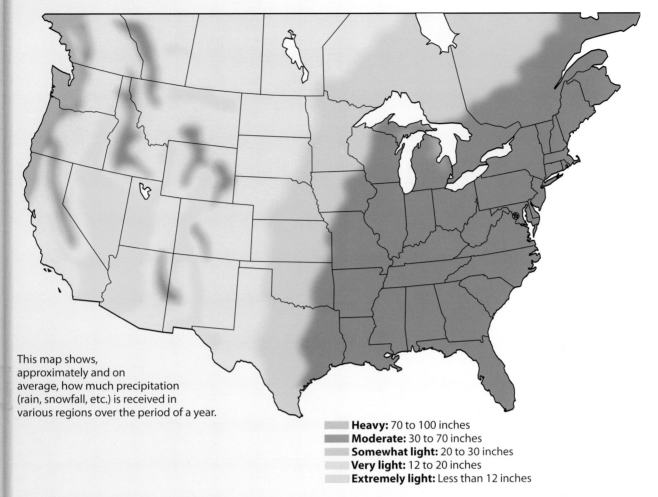

This map shows, approximately and on average, how much precipitation (rain, snowfall, etc.) is received in various regions over the period of a year.

Heavy: 70 to 100 inches
Moderate: 30 to 70 inches
Somewhat light: 20 to 30 inches
Very light: 12 to 20 inches
Extremely light: Less than 12 inches

* Developed from information for 1961 to 1990 from the U.S. National Climatic Data Center and from information for 1931 to 1960 from the Canadian Department of Transport.

Moist Conditions
Moderate precipitation: 30 to 70 inches

This is the ideal range for most roses. Keep track of when your rain falls. In some regions including the Pacific Northwest, most of the moisture occurs in the winter. Others may get heavy spring rains and still others heavy rains in spring and also in fall. And in the Midwest, locked between mountain ranges, anything goes. Entire seasons can be uncommonly wet or dry—even whole years can break records with floods one year, droughts the next.

In this region, wet areas in low spots are common. These are spots where rain water tends to puddle for a few hours (or even days) because of poor drainage. Avoid planting roses in these areas. Any soil that is waterlogged is bad for roses. They can't get oxygen to their roots and then may rot or be susceptible to other diseases.

Wet Conditions
Heavy precipitation: 70 to 100 inches

Much of the coastal Pacific Northwest, some of which is rain forest, receives steady rain. Although much of this region is prime rose growing territory, heavy dew, steady rain, and lack of sun can create a rose-growing challenge. As a rule, look for singles and other roses that don't have lots of packed petals. Moisture evaporates from them more efficiently, minimizing problems. If balling up is a problem in your area, choose the following roses.

Don Juan	Mutabilis
Elina	Pink Pet
Flutterbye	Playboy
Hansa	Seven Sisters
Iceberg	Smith's Parish
The Knock Out series	St. David's
Lady Banks Rose	St. Patrick
Louis Philipe	Veteran's Honor
Memphis King	White Success

Clay to sandy soils

Soil structure is very important. If your soil is too sandy, water and nutrients will trickle through too rapidly, not reaching plants' roots.

If soil is too heavy with clay, it's difficult for water to percolate downward to reach the roots. Water tends to puddle on top of the soil and soak in too slowly, evaporate, or run off. Clay soil also deprives roots of vital oxygen. In wet weather clay becomes soggy, contributing to root rot and other problems.

The ideal is crumbly, dark garden loam. By understanding your soil's structure and conditions, you can grow a wide variety of roses.

The amount of clay and sand in soil tends to be regional, though there are many exceptions to this generalization. Soils in the South tend to be more heavy with clay (as in Georgia red clay), soils in the Northeast and mountain regions tend to be more rocky/sandy, soils along coastlines are usually sandy, and soils in the Midwest tend to have deep deposits of high-quality loam as does the Pacific Northwest.

► Although most roses need moderate water in their root zone, they love having dry conditions when it comes to canes and foliage. Roses are prone to fungal diseases, which bother them far less in more arid regions of the country.

HOW TO COLLECT SOIL FOR TESTING

A soil test gives you a wealth of information about your site. Soil-testing services are offered through the local cooperative extension service in most states. Commercial soil testing services are available in many areas of the country.

To prepare a soil sample for analysis, clear all mulch and vegetation from your sampling area. Mark five spots equally distributed throughout the cleared garden area. Using a small garden trowel, remove a scoop of soil from the top 6 inches of soil at each of the sampling spots and drop it into a clean bucket or pan. Mix the soil thoroughly, then remove about 2 cups of soil and place it in a clean container or plastic bag. This is the sample you'll send to the soil testing lab.

The soil lab will provide analysis of the soil's pH and nutrient levels as well as details about its composition. This information will help you decide what amendments you'll need as well as possible site improvements.

CLAY

Clay soil, when damp, remains in a sticky mass when you poke it with a finger, and it won't break apart. When dry, it's nearly rock hard.

Clay soil can be found anywhere in the country, but it's especially prevalent in the the South. It's also common around houses that were built within the last 20 years. That's because during construction, builders often scrape off high-quality topsoil. Then, as they dig for construction, they unearth poor-quality, clay-laden subsoil and spread that around the yard. When it comes time to lay sod, a thin layer of topsoil is replaced—but often not enough for growing roses and other ornamental plants.

The amount of clay can vary around a yard. One portion of the yard may have clay (often the result of excavation over the years) and another may have good loam.

To remedy clay, work in copious amounts of compost every year. Mulch with 1 to 2 inches each spring and work a spadeful or two into every planting hole. Sphagnum peat moss is also an excellent soil amendment for clay.

Gypsum's effect on breaking up clay is dubious. However, in many clay soils, tilling in sharp sand or gravel is highly effective. Be aware that in some clay soils, working in sand creates a compound akin to cement. Experiment with a small portion of a bed, wait a few months, and proceed with more areas of your garden if the results are good.

DETERMINING YOUR SOIL'S pH

Many gardeners skip testing the soil. But if you know important information about your soil, such as pH and nitrogen levels, you'll get a head start on a successful garden without the time-consuming trial and frustrating error.

Soil pH tests measure the degree of alkalinity or acidity in the soil. On the pH scale, which runs from 0 to 14, a pH of 7.0 is neutral. Above 7.0 is alkaline; below 7.0 is acidic. The real importance of soil pH is that it has a major effect on how well certain nutrients can be taken up by the plant. For example, in alkaline (high pH) soils, iron is less available for plants. Lack of iron can result in yellowing foliage and poor plant growth.

The great majority of landscape plants grow best when the soil pH is between 5.5 and 7.0. Roses generally prefer a soil pH of 6.0 to 6.5, but they'll also grow well if the pH is slightly above or below that range. If the soil is too acidic, the pH can be raised by adding lime. If the soil is too alkaline, the pH can be lowered by adding garden sulfur. Your local cooperative extension service or the soil-testing lab can give you details on how to change soil pH.

The pH of soil tends to be similar in various regions of the country, though there are many exceptions. Soils in the West tend to be more alkaline. Soils in the South and Northeast tend to be more acidic, while soils in the Midwest tend to be neutral.

A pH meter is not expensive (around $20, depending on the design) and gives an instant pH reading in a number of spots. However, the precision of the reading can vary greatly; sending soil samples to a lab is still the most precise method.

LOAM

This is the ideal—very similar to purchased topsoil. It's dark and crumbly and when moist it has a wonderful smell of rich earth. The best loam is dark—a sign that it contains lots of decomposed organic matter, which will attract beneficial earthworms and will naturally feed plants.

Loam is a mixture of sand, clay, and silt. The best loam is a mixture of 30 to 50 percent sand (which makes for good drainage), 30 to 40 percent silt, and 8 to 28 percent clay (which helps retain moisture).

It is loose enough to allow water to percolate down deep but retains enough water to hold the moisture and nutrients until the rose can absorb them well. Good loam is composed of 50 percent solid matter, 25 percent air, and 25 percent water.

SAND

Sand has a number of benefits for roses. It ensures that water will drain freely, giving roses the excellent drainage they need. And that excellent drainage means roses will be relatively free of soil-borne diseases.

The downside is that watering can be a tremendous chore in sandy soils and nutrients quickly wash away. Improve sandy soil for roses and other plants by working in (as with clay) large amounts of compost.

Sphagnum peat moss also is a good amendment for sand because it works like many tiny sponges, holding in water and slowly releasing it.

Also be especially diligent in feeding roses in sandy soils. Combine regular granular, slow-release plant food with foliar feeding to make sure roses, which are heavy feeders, get the nutrients they need.

Choosing the best rose for your region

Sometimes the best rose-growing advice you can get is the over-the-fence-type, from the knowledgeable neighbor or friend who has been growing roses in your part of the country for years and makes the effort to pass that wisdom on to you.

They're the ones who can tell you about the best roses to grow (and not to grow) in your area, pests and diseases to watch for and how to deal with them, what to do to improve your particular soil, and how to have the best roses in the neighborhood.

You may not be lucky enough to have such a font of rose wisdom in your backyards. But on the next several pages some of the best rose growers in various regions of the country will share their hard-won knowledge with you.

Check the map below for the region you live in and the challenges in growing roses in your area. Then turn to the page pertaining to your region and learn in minutes what it takes many rose gardeners years to absorb.

WHICH ROSE-GROWING REGION DO YOU LIVE IN?

This map shows, very roughly, major climate regions in the United States and the most heavily populated portions of Canada.

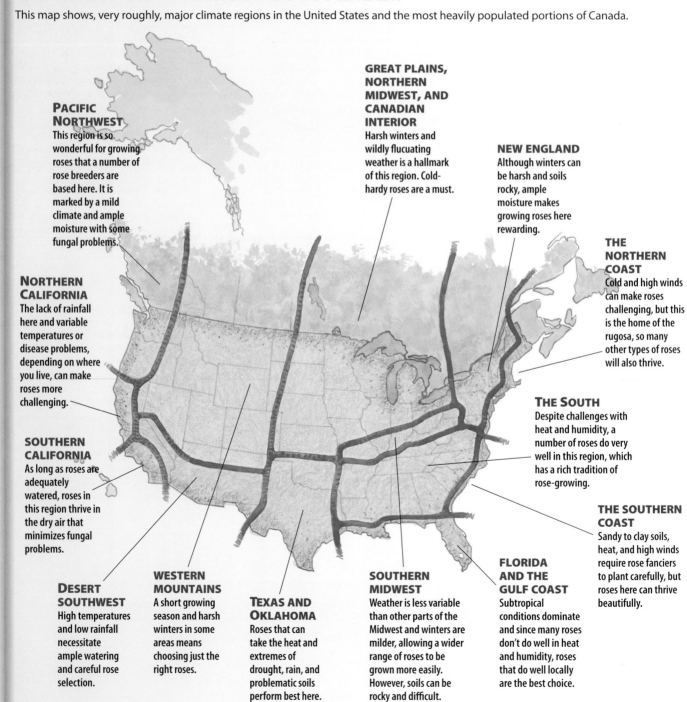

PACIFIC NORTHWEST
This region is so wonderful for growing roses that a number of rose breeders are based here. It is marked by a mild climate and ample moisture with some fungal problems.

GREAT PLAINS, NORTHERN MIDWEST, AND CANADIAN INTERIOR
Harsh winters and wildly fluctuating weather is a hallmark of this region. Cold-hardy roses are a must.

NEW ENGLAND
Although winters can be harsh and soils rocky, ample moisture makes growing roses here rewarding.

THE NORTHERN COAST
Cold and high winds can make roses challenging, but this is the home of the rugosa, so many other types of roses will also thrive.

NORTHERN CALIFORNIA
The lack of rainfall here and variable temperatures or disease problems, depending on where you live, can make roses more challenging.

SOUTHERN CALIFORNIA
As long as roses are adequately watered, roses in this region thrive in the dry air that minimizes fungal problems.

THE SOUTH
Despite challenges with heat and humidity, a number of roses do very well in this region, which has a rich tradition of rose-growing.

THE SOUTHERN COAST
Sandy to clay soils, heat, and high winds require rose fanciers to plant carefully, but roses here can thrive beautifully.

DESERT SOUTHWEST
High temperatures and low rainfall necessitate ample watering and careful rose selection.

WESTERN MOUNTAINS
A short growing season and harsh winters in some areas means choosing just the right roses.

TEXAS AND OKLAHOMA
Roses that can take the heat and extremes of drought, rain, and problematic soils perform best here.

SOUTHERN MIDWEST
Weather is less variable than other parts of the Midwest and winters are milder, allowing a wider range of roses to be grown more easily. However, soils can be rocky and difficult.

FLORIDA AND THE GULF COAST
Subtropical conditions dominate and since many roses don't do well in heat and humidity, roses that do well locally are the best choice.

Choosing roses for the Pacific Northwest

All kinds of roses thrive in the Pacific Northwest, but for the very best blooms, gardeners need to plant varieties that are known to do especially well in the region's generally cool maritime climate, says Jeff Wyckoff, who has been growing roses in the Seattle area for almost 30 years.

Jeff boasts about 300 roses in his garden and specializes in floribundas and old garden roses, which flourish in the Pacific Northwest without too much pampering.

Jeff shows his roses at American Rose Society events, but he and his wife aren't just growing flowers they think finicky judges will approve of; they plant roses that look great in the garden.

When you buy roses, Jeff says, it's essential to get healthy bushes with at least three strong canes. Further, all roses need at least half a day of sun, which can be a challenge in the Seattle area. Shrub roses and rugosas tolerate overcast days well, he says. Vigorous climbers naturally reach for the sun, which makes them a smart choice for gardens with high shade or lots of dappled light. Jeff also looks for varieties known for their resistance to diseases, particularly black spot and mildew.

The Pacific Northwest region includes both the moist climate of the west side of the Cascade Mountains, where Jeff lives, and the dry eastern side of the mountains. In the Seattle area, the average annual rainfall is between 40 and 45 inches; watering is not necessary except in the hottest months of summer. In dry spells and at all times east of the Cascades, he recommends thorough, deep watering twice a week during the growing season. Jeff uses an irrigation system, but soaking roses with a hose near the base of the plants is fine. Deep watering encourages deep roots (see page 101 for further explanation).

New gardeners looking for the best roses for the region should make a list of their priorities, he suggests. Decide what size rose bush you're looking for, what colors you like, and whether fragrance is especially important. Rugosa roses, such as Hansa, are particularly good choices for both fragrance and disease resistance. The so-called "pavement" series are excellent for the Pacific Northwest. David Austin's English roses, hybridized for the cool, moist English climate, are also well-suited to this region.

Making the right choice when you buy will limit problems later and make rose gardening more satisfying.

Jeff recommends planting bare-root or container-grown roses in soil amended with lots of organic matter, such as compost, so it drains well. Organic mulch, also such as compost, helps control weeds and adds to the fertility of the soil. Take care of the soil, Jeff says, and you'll automatically be encouraging healthy, vigorous, beautiful roses for years to come.

▲ Although he lives in an excellent climate for growing roses, Jeff Wyckoff finds the capricious Seattle sun can make it tricky to provide roses with the ample light they demand.

JEFF WYCKOFF'S TOP ROSES FOR THE PACIFIC NORTHWEST

Charles de Mills
Compassion
Easy Going
Elina
Felicia
Folklore
Gemini
Hansa
Lagerfeld
Livin' Easy
Loving Memory
Margaret Merril
Robusta
Savoy Hotel
Sexy Rexy
Stanwell Perpetual
Sunset Celebration
Tournament of Roses
Trumpeter
Westerland

▲ The lush, mild growing conditions of the Pacific Northwest are nearly ideal for growing a wide variety of roses. However, roses love sun and are prone to fungal diseases, so it's essential to plant them where they'll get the most sun possible.

Choosing roses for northern California

**Rose Gilardi
San Francisco, California**

Oak-root fungus is such a formidable problem in the soil of coastal California that Rose Gilardi recommends other gardeners in her region do what she does—grow all roses in pots.

It's a practice this San Francisco gardener recommends for gardeners throughout the region in order to avoid this troublesome native soil fungus. Oak-root fungus causes their roots to rot and kills the plant.

Large, healthy roses may be less susceptible, Rose says, so if you want to risk it, after growing a rose for a year in a pot you can transplant it directly into the ground. But Rose doesn't care to experiment with her roses, so she sticks with 15-gallon pots, which are spacious enough for even her largest types of roses.

Growing roses in pots is an easy compromise, Rose says. Her roses thrive in the pots, and she feels they bloom with all the vigor and exuberance of roses growing in the ground anywhere else.

In San Francisco, where direct sunlight is often reduced by fog, Rose recommends choosing rose varieties with 35 petals or fewer. It is hard for roses packed with with more petals to open fully without enough sunlight, she says.

The coral pink hybrid tea Gemini, which has 25 to 30 petals, is a better choice, for example, than the handsome, dark red Uncle Joe, another hybrid tea, which may have up to 50 petals. Gardeners east of San Francisco Bay, in Oakland, or north in Marin County, can grow roses with more petals.

Most people want plants that bloom prolifically and are not too demanding. Plants with high ratings for disease resistance are important. Knock Out and other shrub roses, like Sally Holmes and Starry Night, which both have delicate blooms, are great choices. Many floribundas and climbing roses also bloom heavily through the long, mild growing season here and are resistant to black spot and other diseases.

Rose uses the *American Rose Society Handbook for Selecting Roses* as a guide. Any rose rated 8.0 or higher usually does very well just about anywhere, she says. (These ratings are listed with roses in the Gallery of Roses starting on page 136).

Most roses resist black spot, powdery mildew, and other diseases (except oak-root fungus) well in this not-too-wet region, especially with proper care.

Fertilizing every other week from March through September and thorough watering twice a week will keep roses in vigorous health through the long growing season, Rose says. Also, she finds that fragrant roses tend to be more susceptible to diseases than those without a fragrance.

The region's climate is so mild that rose gardeners force their plants into dormancy by pruning in January. At pruning time, a good cleanup (removing the oldest canes and refreshing the soil with compost) will help prevent problems in the next blooming season, which in San Francisco is always just around the corner.

▲ Rose Gilardi grows all her roses in her San Francisco garden in pots. Their size and lushness rivals that of many other roses grown in-ground.

ROSE GILARDI'S TOP ROSES FOR NORTHERN CALIFORNIA

Admirable
America
Artistry
Climbing Iceberg
Comte de Chambord
Fame!
Fourth of July
French Lace
Gemini
Gertrude Jekyll
Gourmet Popcorn
Graham Thomas
Hot Cocoa
Julia Child
New Zealand
Olympiad
Perfect Moment
Rainbow's End
Rosa rugosa (the red species and the white, *alba*)
Reba McEntire
Sally Holmes
San Francisco Sunset
Singin' in the Rain
Tournament of Roses

▲ This Marjorie Fair rose in the foreground and the Baronne Prevost rose in the background thrive in this Napa, California, garden. Behind them rises a majestic Atlas cedar.

Choosing roses for southern California

Steve Jones
Valencia, California

Southern California has three distinct climate regions: the sunny coast, with a mild year-round climate; the high desert, known for its extreme temperature swings; and inland areas, which offer a moderate middle ground where winter frosts are rare but summer temperatures can rise above 100 degrees. Steve Jones, who grows about 400 roses in his garden in Valencia, California, says gardeners in all three areas can grow terrific roses.

Steve specializes in old garden roses, shrubs, and polyanthas but also loves miniatures, floribundas, and hybrid teas. Rose de Rescht, one of his favorite old garden roses, blooms throughout the long growing season, from April through November and even into December.

Since so many roses work well for Southern California, the best way to choose one is to think about what you're looking for, Steve says. Avoid buying a large rose for a small space. If you want lots of flowers, make sure the rose is known for its prolific production. The shrub rose Iceberg, for example, is hard to beat. If you're growing roses for bouquets, plant a hybrid tea, like St. Patrick, or try Singin' in the Rain, a floribunda with clusters of flowers on long stems.

Rose gardeners in both coastal and inland areas have problems with rust, a fungus that grows under the leaves, but Moonstone and many other roses tolerate or resist rust damage. Good housekeeping will help prevent problems. Pick up leaves when they fall off, and keep your roses pruned so canes are not crossing and rubbing against one another. Pruning also improves air circulation. Regular weeding will cut down on competition for nutrients. Give roses a good soaking once a week (significantly more often in the heat of summer) to encourage healthy plants and lots of flowers.

Steve fertilizes his roses once a month; he recommends using a balanced fertilizer (such as 10-10-10) from February through the end of May, and again from August through November. Roses will often bloom year-round in Southern California.

Whatever rose you choose, try growing it in a pot before picking a place for it in the garden, Steve suggests. Bare-root roses are available in the region in November, December, and January, and can be planted directly into 5-gallon plastic pots. The roots warm up quickly and the roses get off to a fast start in pots; they need a little more attention to watering than do roses in the ground. While you're caring for your new rose you'll get to know its form, habit, and flowers. Transplant it into the garden in September, when the weather cools.

The fall show of blooms, he says, will encourage you to make room for even more roses in your garden.

▲ Steve Jones, president of the American Rose Society, revels in the excellent rose-growing conditions of Southern California.

STEVE JONES' TOP ROSES FOR SOUTHERN CALIFORNIA

Bees Knees*
Berries 'n' Cream*
Black Magic*
Cal Poly*
Fabulous!
Flower Girl
Fourth of July
Gemini*
Gold Medal
Iceberg
Irresistible
Long Tall Sally
Marilyn Monroe*
Moonstone*
Penelope*
Playgirl
Rosa banksiae banksia
Rose de Rescht
Sally Holmes
Sheila's Perfume
Singin' in the Rain
St. Patrick*
Veteran's Honor*
Watercolors

* Does well in extreme heat

▲ Southern California, blessed with a dry climate that prevents many rose diseases, is a wonderful area to grow roses, as this Del Mar, California, garden illustrates.

Choosing roses for the desert Southwest

Dona and Bob Martin
Gilbert, Arizona

There are two peak seasons for roses in the desert Southwest: early spring and late fall. April's glorious blooms fade by the end of May, when temperatures reach 100°F and higher, and rose gardeners spend the summer keeping their roses as cool, well watered, and healthy as possible so they can unfold their brilliant colors again in November.

Dona and Bob Martin have been growing roses in Gilbert, Arizona, for years. They have almost 400 roses in their garden and all of them receive expert care, including generous watering—four times a week, in fact, through the pistol-hot summer months. The region often has more than 100 days a year with temperatures over 100°F. Furthermore, the desert Southwest receives less than 10 inches of rain a year. Dry winds and low humidity make thorough, regular watering even more important.

Winter doesn't really exist here, and neither does black spot. If you can provide ample moisture, you'll have great roses. To conserve moisture in the soil, the Martins mulch deeply with 4 or 5 inches of pine straw or shredded bark.

Hybrid tea roses thrive in this region when they are grafted onto the rootstock of *Rosa fortuniana*, which is well adapted to the heat. If hybrid teas are your favorite roses, look for varieties with thick petals and glossy foliage, which can stand up to the searing temperatures. Three of the best are the luminous yellow-green St. Patrick; the soft apricot Marilyn Monroe; and Gemini, with creamy buds that open to coral-edged flowers.

It is also important to choose roses with the right number of petals, the Martins say. Blooms with too many petals will not open in the heat. If there are too few, the blooms will open quickly and not last long. Among hybrid teas, for example, the Martins find 30 petals are about right.

Some roses surprise you, Bob Martin says. Polyanthas, which have large clusters of small flowers, are especially beautiful in this region. Dona Martin also loves old garden roses and shrub roses, which grow well on their own roots here. Old roses in the gallica, tea, noisette, and China groups also do well and deserve to be planted more widely in the desert Southwest, they say.

Many people move to the desert Southwest from very different climates. If you are among them, talk with local rosarians and visit local rose gardens; you'll quickly learn which roses will survive this region's astonishing heat, the Martins say. In the winter and spring, the roses' flawless beauty will remind you why you moved here.

▲ For Arizona rose gardeners Dona and Bob Martin, the most glorious roses happen in the cooler temperatures of the winter months when rose gardens farther north are blanketed in snow.

DONA AND BOB MARTIN'S TOP ROSES FOR THE DESERT SOUTHWEST

Baby Grand
Ballerina
Bees Knees
Butter Cream
Fabulous!
Fairhope
Flower Girl
Fourth of July
Golden Celebration
Gemini
Graham Thomas
Hot Princess
Julia Child
Lavaglut
Let Freedom Ring
Lullaby
Marilyn Monroe
Miss Flippins
Peter Cottontail
Pillow Fight
Rose de Rescht
Sexy Rexy
St. Patrick
Verdun
Yolande d'Aragon
St. Patrick
Veterans' Honor

▲ In desert conditions elsewhere, roses flourish as long as they are well-watered. German bearded irises also do well in drier areas and make good rose companions.

Choosing roses for the western mountains

Carol Macon
Colorado Springs, Colorado

Roses grown in the mountains of Colorado have to be cold hardy. In the tough yet variable climate and short growing season of the western mountains, only the hardiest of roses will do.

However, Carol Macon, who grows almost 600 roses in her garden in Colorado Springs, has proved that many roses can be the stars of the garden even in this region. Madame Hardy, Darlow's Enigma, and many old garden roses flourish without pampering. Roses in the Morden or Parkland series (Morden Centennial, Morden Blush, and others),

developed in Manitoba, Canada, and accustomed to cold, practically luxuriate in Colorado, Carol says.

Carol is a high-altitude gardener. She lives at 6,100 feet—800 feet higher than Denver. The growing season is four short months, from mid-May to mid-September. Further, the Rocky Mountain region receives only about 16 inches of rain a year, creating very dry conditions. Summer temperatures can be hot, and gardeners cannot count on a thick blanket of snow to insulate their roses in the wintertime.

Roses for this region should be rated hardy to Zone 4 (see page 61). To help them survive the winter,

grafted bushes should be planted with the graft buried at least 2 inches below the soil and as much as 4 inches deep, depending on the elevation. The higher the elevation, the deeper the graft, Carol says.

Bare-root roses should be planted by the end of April; container-grown roses need to be in the ground by June to make sure the plants have time to develop a vigorous root system before cold weather sets in. Carol creates a wide saucer around her rose bushes, with the graft (sometimes called the bud union) sitting at the base of a saucer. She then mounds soil up 4 inches around the crowns for winter protection. When spring comes, the soil is pulled back to the edge of the saucer. Hybrid tea roses will freeze back to the ground, but new canes will emerge from the deeply planted graft and produce roses through the summer.

In this short-summer climate, repeat-flowering roses should have a fast repeat cycle to give you as many blooms as possible, Carol suggests. Try to find shrub roses that rebloom every four weeks. Among many others, she likes Evelyn and Abraham Darby, two of David Austin's English roses.

Carol stops fertilizing in mid-August—a smart move for any cold-region rose gardener. This helps the roses go dormant and better prepare for winter. She also stops deadheading in early September, removing spent petals but not the hips.

In fact, Carol grows some roses specifically for their winter interest. The species *Rosa canina,* sometimes called the dog rose, grows about 12 feet tall and wide in her front yard. It blooms in late spring, she says, but it's also spectacular in winter, when the bush is covered with bright red hips.

▲ Carol Macon finds that by choosing the most cold-hardy roses, even in her hihg-altitude garden she can enjoy beautiful, luxuriant roses.

CAROL MACON'S TOP ROSES FOR THE WESTERN MOUNTAINS

Abraham Darby
Black Ice
Brother Cadfael
Darlow's Enigma
Double Delight
Escapade
Evelyn
Golden Celebration
Henry Kelsey
Jeanne Lajoie
John Davis
Leonard Dudley Braithwaite
Linda Campbell
Madame Hardy
Marijke Koopman
Morden Blush
Rosa alba semi-plena
Rosa Mundi
Scentimental
St. Cecilia

▲ In this rural Idaho garden, these Ballerina roses thrive partly because they're a very hardy choice but also because they're positioned close to the house, sheltered from winds and making it less tempting for deer to devour them.

Choosing roses for the Great Plains, the northern Midwest, and the Canadian interior

Norma Booty
Apple Valley, Minnesota

The winters are long and harsh and the gardening season is short in the Great Plains, the Northern Midwest, and the Canadian interior. In this tough climate, roses—and the gardeners who grow them—have to be resilient.

Fortunately, truly cold-hardy shrub roses and old garden roses can be grown without pampering in this region, says Norma Booty, who grows 500 roses in her garden in Apple Valley, Minnesota. In the course of a normal winter in Norma's garden, the temperature can drop to –30°F/–34°C.

Half of her roses are hybrid teas, which are less hardy, so she tips them on their sides and buries them completely with soil and other protection. The other half of Norma's roses are cold-hardy, beautiful low-maintenance roses—the roses she recommends most highly for this region.

Only roses that are rated hardy to Zone 4 or colder will survive in this region (see page 61). Rugosa roses, which are known for their distinctly rough foliage, silky flower petals, and bright red hips in the fall and winter, are among the most cold-hardy roses, hardy to Zone 2, where the winter temperature can drop to –50°F/–46°C.

Roses in the Explorer and Parkland series, both developed in Canada, also survive well without special winter protection in the brutally low temperatures of this region. William Baffin, a carefree climber in the Explorer group, is not only cold hardy, Norma says, but it is also "the most disease-resistant plant I've ever seen."

A few well-known roses are conspicuously absent from the list of good choices for this region. The popular Knock Out rose is reliably hardy only to Zone 5. Roses developed for cold climates by the late Griffith Buck at Iowa State University are only marginally hardy in Minnesota and farther north. Carefree Beauty, Buck's best-known rose, is a good choice to at least Zone 4, Norma says, and so is the fragrant Aunt Honey. Of the English roses hybridized by David Austin, Heritage is the toughest and most reliable for northern gardens.

Shrub roses grow on their own roots, but the hybrid tea, grandiflora, and floribunda roses many people love for their large, classic-shape flowers are grafted roses, and the graft must be protected from winter freezing.

Planting the graft 3 to 4 inches deep isn't necessarily good enough in Norma's harsh winters. She wants these fancy roses to be as large and healthy as possible in spring. To protect both grafts and canes, Norma practices "the Minnesota tip," also known as trenching, for these roses. (See page 131.)

She does this in October, when she cuts her big hybrid tea roses back to about 5 feet tall, digs a shallow trench by the rose, ties the canes of each rose into a bundle, loosens the rose in the ground at its base, and bends the bush over so it is lying in the trench. Some of the roots will break, but the rose bush will be all right. The whole rose bush is covered with soil and then insulated with plastic bags of autumn leaves or heavy construction blankets thrown over the top. There the bushes lie, snug under the insulation, until about mid-April, when they're uncovered, straightened up, and given their first pruning.

All the work is worth it, Norma says. During the gardening season, her roses grow to 7 feet tall, and the flowers they produce are nothing short of spectacular.

▲ Extreme cold could deter less determined rose gardeners, but Minnesotan Norma Booty finds that by choosing tough roses, her roses flourish.

NORMA BOOTY'S TOP ROSES FOR THE GREAT PLAINS, NORTHERN MIDWEST, AND CANADIAN INTERIOR

Butter Cream
Elina
Eye Paint
Henry Hudson
Hot Princess
Hot Tamale
Iceberg
Irresistible
John Davis
Leading Lady
Little Artist
Magic Carrousel
Memphis King
Moonstone
Morden Blush
Morden Centennial
Nicole
Peaches 'n' Cream
Playboy
Poulsen's Pearl
Robusta
Secret
Tiffany Lynn
Veteran's Honor

▲ Carefree Beauty is another great choice for nearly any harsh-climate garden. Bred in Iowa, it does well in extreme cold, is very disease-resistant, and blooms nearly nonstop from June until frost.

Choosing roses for the southern Midwest

Phil Schorr
St. Louis, Missouri

The weather in the southern Midwest can fool you. Just when you think spring has arrived, a bitter cold front sweeps through and winter takes its revenge on gardeners who jump the gun. Sudden frosts after a spell of balmy days are particularly hard on roses, says Phil Schorr, who grows about 100 roses in his garden in St. Louis, Missouri.

Spring may be fairly unpredictable, but once you have learned to wait until the danger of frost is past before getting to work in the garden, he says, your roses will reward you through a long growing season. Schorr grows mostly miniature roses. These compact roses, which will tolerate less light than big hybrids, are wonderful for small gardens or for gardens with less than 6 hours of full sun, he says, adding that people shopping for that first rose bush may want something big and showy.

He recommends shrub roses hybridized by the late Griffith Buck, a Midwesterner who developed dozens of hardy and disease-resistant roses at Iowa State University. Many of Buck's roses have country names like Square Dance and Buckaroo. One of Buck's best known and most widely planted roses is Carefree Beauty, which has pale pink flowers and blooms all summer long.

Roses in the Explorer series, hybridized in Canada for their winter hardiness and disease resistance, thrive in the southern Midwest, and the Easy Elegance roses introduced by Bailey Nurseries have also proven to be strong selections for the region, Schorr says. When landscapers ask him for a recommendation, he often suggests Knock Out roses (including Blushing Knock Out, Rainbow Knock Out, and others). They do not need to be sprayed for black spot; they bloom all summer long; and they're widely and easily available.

Hybrid tea roses grow beautifully but are demanding in the Midwest. Elina is one of Schorr's favorites for its creamy yellow flowers and handsome bushy growth. It and other hybrid teas must have mulch or soil mounded about 12 inches around their crowns in late fall or early winter, Schorr says, and the protection should remain in place until the danger of frost is past.

In this region, with its capricious springs, don't let mild spring days tempt you into removing the mulch and pruning away rose canes killed by winter frosts, he says. Wait until the last frost date in your area to prune even hardy roses. Pruning too soon encourages early growth that could die in an unexpected frost.

Climbing roses are popular in southern Midwestern gardens. New Dawn, which has pale shell pink flowers, is one of the best for this region or try the stunning, bright red Altissimo, Schorr suggests. America is also and excellent choice.

Plant climbers by an arbor or run them up a porch pillar or an obelisk for a shower of blooms that can't be beat.

▲ Phil Schorr finds that despite unpredictable springs, his St. Louis roses thrive and he's especially enamored of miniatures.

PHIL SCHORR'S TOP ROSES FOR THE SOUTHERN MIDWEST

America
Betty Boop
Carefree Beauty
Dortmund
Elina
Gemini
Gold Medal
Graham Thomas
Hannah Gordon
   (also called Nicole)
Hot Cocoa
Julia Child
Knock Out
Moonstone
New Dawn
Playboy
Pristine
Sally Holmes
Sunsprite
The Fairy
Touch of Class

▲ Unlike Midwesterners farther to the North, gardeners in the southern Midwest can choose from a wide variety of climbing roses, many of which are not reliably hardy past Zone 6.

Choosing roses for Texas and Oklahoma

**Jan Shannon
Corpus Christi, Texas**

Even the roses seem bigger and brighter in Texas. Fire-engine red, bold orange, and flashy yellow roses are many new rose gardeners' first choices here, says long-time rose grower Jan Shannon.

Jan has been growing roses in Corpus Christi, Texas, where the summers are steamy and the winters are mild, for 32 years. Granted, Texas and Oklahoma encompass a lot of very different growing regions, but what Jan has learned can benefit nearly all rose gardeners in this area.

Most of her roses are hybrid teas, but she also grows floribundas, miniatures, and a few old garden roses. They're all great choices for less experienced gardeners, she says.

Black spot-resistant roses are essential here; the region's long growing season and hot weather are incubators for the fungus disease that causes leaves to develop black spots and fall off. You'll get black spot no matter which rose you plant, Jan says, and if you do not spray a fungicide to prevent or eradicate it, the rose will lose many leaves. Black spot probably won't kill the rose, but a stressed plant will not produce as many flowers as a healthy rose and the roses it produces will not be as robust. If you do not intend to spray, choose tough shrub roses, she says, such as Knock Out, or roses with thick foliage, like the hybrid tea Veteran's Honor.

Floribundas and shrub roses are the best choices for good landscaping plants that provide lots of blooms during the gardening season, Jan says. However, if you're growing roses for bouquets, plant hybrid teas and grandifloras.

Roses that have lots of petals, like the big, deep red hybrid tea Uncle Joe, do extremely well in this climate, she says. Uncle Joe produces blue-ribbon roses, especially in spring and fall.

David Austin English roses do not perform well in Texas, Jan says. Many of them have a wonderful fragrance but English natives that they are, they hate the hot summer climate, and as a result do not bloom well.

Jan recommends that Texans wanting to grow miniature roses buy them from a mail-order specialist who sells roses grafted to the roots of *Rosa fortuniana,* a particularly vigorous rootstock. The diminutive plants are easier to care for when they're in containers, she says, such as 5-gallon pots. Add compost to the top of the pot every year, and the rose will flourish for four or five years. In even bigger containers, you may never have to repot in this climate.

Jan gets up to seven bloom cycles a year in her garden, from the first fresh flush of flowers in April through the last especially colorful and fragrant blooms at the end of November. The rose gardening season, it seems, is bigger in Texas, too.

▲ Jan Shannon has more than three decades of experience growing hundreds of roses in the challenging Texas climate.

JAN SHANNON'S TOP ROSES FOR TEXAS

America
Bonbon
Cajun Moon
Charlotte Anne
Crystalline
Distant Drums
Gemini
George Burns
Heart of Gold
Joyfulness
Knock Out
Lime Sublime
Moonstone
Playgirl
Sexy Rexy
Simplicity
St. Patrick
Stainless Steel
Touch of Class
Veteran's Honor

EARTHKIND ROSES

Any Texan should be aware of EarthKind roses. These are roses have been designated by Texas A&M University as doing especially well in the difficult conditions of Texas. They use minimal water and take minimal maintenance. They include:

Belinda's Dream
Caldwell Pink
Carefree Beauty
Climbing Pinkie
Duchesse de Brabant
Else Poulsen
Knock Out
Marie Daly
Mutabilis
Perle d'Or
Sea Foam
Spice
The Fairy

▲ These pink shrub roses have been growing in this spot in Texas long enough that their name has long been forgotten, but they are perfectly suited to their site and and thrived for as long as many people can remember.

Choosing roses for Florida and the Gulf Coast

Connie Vierbicky
Sarasota, Florida

Many gardeners are irresistibly drawn to the beauty and perfection of long-stemmed hybrid tea roses and want to grow them in their own gardens—and Connie Vierbicky, who grows about 130 roses in her garden in Sarasota is one of those hybrid tea fans.

Hybrid teas produce large, attractive flowers perfect for cutting and showing, but they are demanding, she says. "In Florida you should grow hybrid teas only if you're a devoted rose gardener" who is willing to spray and tend carefully to your roses. Otherwise, she says, there are many other roses that do fine with far less care, primarily shrub roses. With a shrub rose, Connie finds, she has a bush that is easy to care for and blooms from April through February.

Florida rose gardeners have to contend with root-knot nematodes that infest the roots of plants and kill them; fortunately, roses grafted onto the rootstock of *Rosa fortuniana* (sometimes known as Double Cherokee rose) are resistant to nematodes and thrive in the region's mild climate and luxuriously long growing season. Roses grafted onto the roots of Dr. Huey also perform well in Florida; Connie does not recommend planting roses growing on their own roots, unless you'll be content to have that bush for only a couple of seasons. Own-root roses decline and die in her region, she says.

Once you know which rootstocks to look for, you're on your way to successful rose gardening in Florida. Connie especially recommends English roses hybridized by David Austin. These modern roses trace their heritage to the old garden roses. They are beautiful, fragrant, and disease resistant, and she finds that they will grow into large and prolific shrubs in Florida gardens.

Roses get so big in this region that they should be planted 4 feet apart on center. The English rose Abraham Darby, which has fragrant, apricot-pink cupped double flowers, grows as much as 8 feet tall and wide in Connie's garden—once a year she prunes it to 4 feet.

Bugs and blights, particularly black spot, take their toll on roses in this region. Even the highly pest-resistant Knock Out rose is susceptible to spider mites in Florida, she says. English roses are highly disease- and pest-resistant, although even they benefit from spraying with a fungicide during the growing season.

Florida's generous rainfall would seem to provide ample water for roses, but high temperatures exhaust rose bushes. The region's sandy soils drain so well that supplemental watering is essential. Connie waters her roses three times a week from April through October, and weekly from November through March. Invest in an irrigation system, she suggests, and turn on the water for 15 minutes three times a week. Spread 2 or 3 inches of organic mulch, such as shredded wood bark, around your plants to conserve moisture in the soil, and your roses will reward you with countless blooms.

▲ Accomplished rose grower Connie Vierbicky swears by shrub roses for her Florida garden.

CONNIE VIERBICKY'S TOP ROSES FOR FLORIDA

Abraham Darby
Apricot Nectar
Belinda's Dream
Butter Cream
Camden
Eugene Marlitt
   (also called Maggie)
Europeana
Fairhope
Gemini
Hot Princess
Kristin
Kronprincessin Viktoria
Louise Estes
Louisville Lady
Miss Flippins
Moonstone
Paul Neyron
Pierrine
Playgirl
St. Patrick
Souvenir de la Malmaison
Sunsprite
The Dark Lady
Veteran's Honor

▲ This Florida home is surrounded by a mix of plantings, including drought- and heat-tolerant roses, red porterweed, coreopsis, and scarlet milkweed.

Choosing roses for the South

Marilyn Wellan
Alexandria, Louisiana

Rose gardeners in the South have it pretty good, Marilyn Wellan admits. She is able to have lots of flowers over a long growing season, and, because so many roses perform well in this climate, she has a tremendous selection of roses from which to choose.

Marilyn grows about 250 roses in her garden in Alexandria, Louisiana. She is particularly interested in fragrant varieties, and she loves old garden roses for their heady, old-time fragrance, their vigor, and their history (they are, by definition, those roses introduced before 1867). One of her favorite old roses, Duchesse de Brabant, is a classic that has won a place among the exclusive list, developed by Texas A&M University, of EarthKind roses (see page 76) known for top garden performance and excellent resistance to insect pests and diseases.

EarthKind roses are good choices for southern gardeners—not just Texans, Marilyn says. In Texas A&M's program, roses are tested for their ability to thrive with little or no special care. The EarthKind program also encourages gardeners to learn to tolerate minor problems and to turn to chemical remedies only when necessary. Knock Out and Carefree Beauty, two popular shrub roses, are among the low-maintenance stars of the program. The charming and free-blooming polyantha rose Perle d'Or, another EarthKind rose, is one of Wellan's favorites.

Wellan's shrub roses, which are not finicky, grow on their own roots. For more temperamental roses, such as hybrid teas, bred for their blooms and not their toughness, she recommends buying roses grafted onto the roots of *Rosa fortuniana*. While some gardeners rely on the vigorous *R. fortuniana* rootstock's resistance to root-knot nematode, nematodes are not a problem in Wellan's area. She likes *R. fortuniana* rootstock because these roses thrive better in the extremely hot Southern summers.

Roses need plenty of room to grow in the South, Marilyn says, because with the long growing season and mild winters (which mean minimal winter dieback) they can get quite large.

As a bonus, in the mild winters, roses can be practically evergreen. Some of the best blooms of the year come in the cooler months of October and November. Give extra attention to pruning and fertilizing at the end of August or in early September for a spectacular fall show.

Marilyn doesn't find that insects are a problem in her garden. When she does find spider mites, she gives them a spray with a water wand, making sure she reaches the undersides of the leaves.

Choose roses based on how you want to place them in your garden, their size, and the colors you prefer, Marilyn says. Plant them in raised beds, if possible, for drainage, and water them deeply twice a week during the growing season. Your roses will respond beautifully to the care you give them.

▲ A long growing season in her Louisiana garden has made rose growing a joy for Marilyn Wellan.

MARILYN WELLAN'S TOP ROSES FOR THE SOUTH

Belinda's Dream*
Carefree Beauty*
Celine Forestier
Champneys' Pink Cluster
Duchesse de Brabant*
Earth Song
Etoile de Lyon
Excellenz von Schubert
Felicia
Knock Out*
Lady Banks Rose
Martha's Vineyard
Madamoiselle Cécile Brünner
Mollineaux
Monsieur Tillier
Mrs. B. R. Cant
Mutabilis*
Old Blush
Penelope
Perle d'Or*
Pink Pet* (also sold as Caldwell Pink)
Seven Sisters
Souvenir de la Malmaison
The Swamp Rose (*Rosa palustris*)
Tess of the d'Urbervilles
Zephirine Drouhin

* Does well in extreme heat

▲ Many other gardeners in The South share Marilyn Wellan's passion for roses. This Atlanta front yard is filled with almost nothing but.

Choosing roses for New England

John Mattia
Orange, Connecticut

Don't let all the talk about roses being difficult to grow keep you from trying them in your own garden, says John Mattia, who describes himself as a "rose nut who lives and breathes roses." If you buy strong, healthy rose bushes and plant them where they'll get plenty of sun and protection from harsh winds, you're going to have good roses, he says.

John shows his blue-ribbon flowers at rose shows all around the country. He loves the high, pointed buds and large, perfect flowers of hybrid tea roses, but he thinks they're not the best choices for gardeners new to rose growing. Shrub roses are easier to grow, he says, describing them as the roses of the future. John is especially impressed with Knock Out and its offspring, Home Run. Like so many other rose gardeners around the country, he finds these to be cold-hardy and disease-resistant shrub roses that produce abundant flowers all summer.

One of Mattia's favorite all-around successful roses is the climber Fourth of July, which has red-and-white-spangled flowers, climbs to 14 feet tall, and blooms from spring through frost. To grow well in New England, it needs plenty of sunlight (at least 6 hours of full sun a day), protection from harsh north winds, and ample water. Too many gardeners, says Mattia, plant their new roses in shady spots under mature trees or in the shade of the house or garage and forget to water them; then they blame the roses when they don't bloom. Pay attention to the basic needs of your plant and you and the rose will get along famously, John says.

The biggest mistake people make when they shop for roses is buying a bargain-priced bush that is already struggling because of poor care. Rose bushes stressed by neglect may never recover to become the plant of your dreams, or even healthy.

Bare-root roses are available early in the season, John says, and should be planted by mid-April in New England.

Container roses (those already planted in a pot and available through the gardening season), are fine as long as you purchase only those plants that have been well cared for. No matter what color or kind of rose you buy, look for No. 1 grade bushes (see page 83), with three sturdy canes as thick as your thumb. Avoid buying rose bushes with black spot—you'll risk introducing more black spot spores into your garden.

Taking care of your roses should be as simple as taking a walk in the garden every day, John says. When you check on your roses each day, you'll learn when they need water or fertilizer. You can pick off bugs before they become a nuisance. And when they bloom, you'll be right there to smell the roses every time.

▲ John Mattia says that roses unjustly have reputations as fussy flowers. Despite harsh winters, he enjoys growing award-winning roses in his Connecticut garden.

JOHN MATTIA'S TOP ROSES FOR NEW ENGLAND

Betty Prior
Day Breaker
Distant Drums
Double Delight
Dublin
Earth Song
Elina
Flower Girl
Fourth of July
Gemini
Gertrude Jekyll
Graham Thomas
Home Run
Julia Child
Knock Out
Madame Hardy
Pretty Lady
Rosa mundi
Touch of Class

▲ Major challenges of rose growing in New England include harsh winters and variable soils. Work in plenty of compost and plant quality roses in a protected spot and they're almost certain to do well.

Choosing roses for the southern coast

Sandy Lundberg
Bluffton, South Carolina

The key to growing roses successfully along the southern coast of the United States is hidden in the roots, according to Sandy Lundberg, who grows nearly 500 rose bushes in her 1½-acre garden in Bluffton, South Carolina.

Many roses on the market are grafted onto a hardy rootstock of a different type of rose, which then supports the grafted rose on a vigorous, healthy root system (see page 82). The most popular rootstock choices nationally, however, are susceptible to root-knot nematode, which is prevalent in the soil along the southeast coast. Sandy says she has found that hybrid tea roses, especially, decline within a few years unless they are grown on nematode-resistant rootstock—the

rootstock of *Rosa fortuniana*.

Sandy is lucky. Her husband does rose grafting for their extensive rose garden. But you don't have to learn grafting techniques to grow roses successfully in this region. Southern rose suppliers and a few mail-order specialists offer roses grafted onto *R. fortuniana* roots. In the Southeast, these roses will be healthier, produce more and larger flowers, and live longer than roses grafted onto other rootstocks.

Shrub roses and old garden roses growing on their own roots (also called own-root roses), also do fine, Sandy says. But since her preference is for roses that are almost always sold on grafted rootstock, such as hybrid teas, floribundas, and miniature roses (because of their abundant blooms in the region's long growing season

and the fact that they don't need special winter care), she has to be careful about rootstock and looks for roses grafted onto *R. fortuniana*.

To improve the sandy soils so often found along the Southern coast, Sandy recommends amending rose beds with plenty of organic matter. Loose, sandy soils have the advantage of naturally draining well, but they often lack the nutrients and micronutrients roses need. Add plenty of compost, well-aged manure, and other organic soil amendments to boost nutrients and help the soil retain moisture.

Soil testing is also vital along the Southern coast, Sandy says. Roses prefer a slightly acidic soil, with a pH between 6.2 and 6.8, but soils in her region are typically alkaline. To learn your soil's pH, use a home pH test kit from a garden center or send soil samples to your county extension office (check how to do it first online or by phoning your local office), which will make recommendations for adjusting the pH, if necessary. (See page 67 for a further explanation of soil pH.)

Wind is another consideration along this coast. High winds along the Atlantic coast whip and pull on even well-rooted roses, especially tall types. Sandy stakes her roses with concrete-reinforcing rods, which are available at building supply stores. She covers the stakes with plastic PVC pipe or garden hose to protect the roses from being bruised by the steel.

Exposure to salt winds and salt spray during tropical storms is a minor problem, Sandy says. After a storm, she says, drench your plants, washing the salt off with a stream of fresh water from a hose. Sandy finds that roses, like people, with a little help can recover remarkably well from adversity.

▲ Sandy Lundberg's South Carolina garden is resplendent with hundreds of roses, but she says she could never do it if she didn't insist on roses grafted onto *Rosa fortuniana* rootstock.

SANDY LUNDBERG'S TOP ROSES FOR THE SOUTHERN COAST

Ain't She Sweet
Autumn Splendor
Bees Knees
Carolina Lady
Chattooga
Doris Morgan
First Prize
Flutterbye
Gemini
Hot Princess
Lavaglut
Michel Cholet
Moonstone
Nana Mouskouri
Pierrine
Pinnacle
Sheila's Perfume
St. Patrick
Veteran's Honor

▲ This Charleston, South Carolina, garden is a vision of traditional rose growing, complete with delphiniums, poppies, and other cottage flowers.

Choosing roses for the northeastern coast

Clarence Rhodes
Portland, Maine

Clarence Rhodes is crazy about traditional hybrid tea roses and showers his plants with the care and attention they need in his climate. Gardeners looking for beautiful, less-demanding roses, however, should start with some of the great shrub roses now available, he says.

Clarence lives in Portland, Maine, in a climate that is both beautiful and brutal: The northeast Atlantic coast is known for long, pleasant summer days and months of harsh winter weather.

He has found that roses in the Easy Elegance series, introduced by Bailey Nurseries, are good choices for gardeners here.

He especially likes Mystic Fairy, a low-growing shrub in that series that has rich red flowers and blooms for months. My Hero, Paint the Town, and Centennial are some of the other hardy, low-maintenance Easy Elegance roses he likes.

Clarence also likes the popular Knock Out rose, the original in that series, as well as shrub roses in the Canadian Explorer series, developed in Canada, often named after Canadian explorers such as William Baffin and Henry Hudson; they are well adapted to the short growing season and cold winters in this region.

In the coastal North, Clarence recommends planting roses on the southern, southeastern, or southwestern side of buildings and fences so they'll get plenty of light and warmth. In a spot exposed to salt spray, plant rugosa roses, which are known as beach roses in this region because they often grow wild along the coast.

If your heart is set on growing hybrid tea roses, which have been bred for their flowers, not for their hardiness, Clarence recommends his container method. Two hybrid tea roses fit into each of his 20-gallon pots. He grows them in a professional potting mix of 75 percent sphagnum peat moss that also includes perlite and vermiculite. Rhodes finds the mix lightweight and easy to work with. Casters on the bottoms of the pots make it easy to wheel the plants around to get the best sun and to show off roses when they are at their peak of summer bloom.

Even if you don't intend to grow your roses in large containers permanently, in this climate Rhodes advises growing a new rose in a pot for at least its first season so it can develop a strong root system. Then plant it in the ground in September with the graft just at ground level or a little deeper. Mound soil to 10 inches around the crown of the rose bush for the winter. This will protect the plant from the cold weather and from the harsh, desiccating winter winds. Wash the soil mound off in April, when your rose will be ready to grow.

Whatever type of rose gardeners in the coastal Northeast choose, Clarence says, it should be No. 1. grade (see page 83), with three stout canes, healthy looking shoots, bright green foliage, and perhaps a bud already forming on the end of a shoot—but not too many.

For the best success with roses, plant more than two or three or five, Clarence says. Experiment, take notes, and let your successes guide your choices as your rose collection grows.

▲ After decades of growing roses in Maine, Clarence Rhodes has learned a number of tricks for helping them thrive. He prefers growing hybrid tea roses, for examples, in large containers.

CLARENCE RHODES' RECOMMENDED ROSES FOR THE COASTAL NORTH

Andrea Stelzer
Artistry
Brigadoon
Carefree Delight
Diana, Princess of Wales
The Easy Elegance series (see page 188.)
Elina
Festival Fanfare
Frau Karl Druschki
Gemini
Hannah Gordon (Nicole)
Hot Princess
Irresistible
John Waterer
The Knock Out series
Marijke Koopman
Playboy
Remember Me
Rugosa roses
Robusta
Showbiz
Sunset Celebration
The Canadian Explorer series (see page 27)
The McCartney Rose

▲ Along the Maine coast, only the hardiest roses will survive. This John Cabot rose is part of the superhardy Canadian Explorer series.

Rose growing basics

▲ When shopping for roses, read labels and examine plants carefully for signs of disease or weakness. Whenever possible, buy roses that are not in bloom so that once planted, they can focus their energy on getting established.

Buying roses

Roses, in one form or another, have been around for 5,000 years by some estimates. Originally only a handful were in cultivation. Today there are hundreds if not thousands to choose from.

When to buy roses

As the spring days grow warmer and the garden calls, you can find rose bushes for sale at garden centers, home-improvement megachains, warehouse clubs, supermarkets, and even minimart gas stations.

You can also, of course, buy rose plants at local garden centers and other retail outlets. Buying locally not only is convenient but also gives you the chance to see the plant and to ask questions. It's also conducive to buying on impulse, with its potential pleasures and potential pitfalls.

Mail order and online shopping are options that offer far greater varieties. Roses that are shipped via the mail are sold bare root and require early planting.

Fall is also a good time to plant roses (with the exception of Zones 5 and colder), though there are usually fewer plants in garden centers because of less consumer demand.

Propagation methods

Like all plants, roses can be grown from seed. But because seeds mix the genetic material of the parent plants, there's no guarantee that the rose will look like either parent. Growing from seed is also time-consuming.

Most roses are propagated asexually—that is, created without two parents. In asexual propagation, a part of the rose plant is stimulated into producing a new plant that is genetically identical to the original rose.

Hobbyists experiment with asexually propagating roses by taking cuttings—in other words they cut off a piece of a cane and bury it in a growing medium such as soil so it develops roots.

Another method that is trickier to execute is layering. To layer, nick a cane, then bend it down and bury the nicked section, keeping it attached to the main bush.

Because commercial growers want to produce as many plants as possible in a short time, they rely on two other methods of asexually propagating roses: grafting and own-root cuttings.

Grafted roses

In rose grafting, the top of one rose is cut off and attached to the bottom of another to produce a rose bush that is superior to either parent. The top part, or *scion*, is usually a stem from a rose with especially desirable traits such as beautiful flowers or resistance to disease.

The bottom—called the *rootstock* or simply the stock—comes from a rose that is more hardy or vigorous than the scion or is more resistant to soil-dwelling microscopic worms called nematodes. Grafting ensures the delicate beauty on the top with the tough workhorse on the bottom. The knobby scar where the two parts heal together is called the graft union or bud union.

For most grafted roses—also called budded roses—the scion forms the aboveground canes and the rootstock forms the roots, with the graft union lying just below the soil line. However, in standard or tree roses, the graft union is a few feet above the ground.

The main reason for grafting is to give a beautiful rose the hardiness and vigor it needs to thrive in a particular climate. Hybrid teas, floribundas, and tree roses are usually grafted

GREENHOUSE-GROWN ROSES

A small percentage of rose bushes sold spend part or all of their lives in a greenhouse. A greenhouse lets a grower control the environment so the rose can be prompted to bloom in time to be sold for a key holiday, such as Mother's Day. This method offers beautiful roses for sale before they would start blooming in home gardens.

Most greenhouse roses get the deluxe treatment only for a few months—before that, they grow in the field. Be careful about planting them as soon as you take them home. If it's still cold outside, the rose might not do well— no rose likes frost.

A few mail-order rose producers grow some roses entirely in the greenhouse from cuttings to sell as small rooted plants. Because growing in a greenhouse is more costly, greenhouse rose bushes are sold at a premium.

GRADES OF BARE-ROOT ROSES

Bare-root roses are sold in different grades. The lower the number, the better the quality and vigor.

A Grade 1 rose has at least 3 canes $\frac{5}{8}$ inches in diameter. Grade 1$\frac{1}{2}$ roses have just 2 canes with a minimum diameter of $\frac{5}{8}$ inch. Grade 2 roses (not shown) are less vigorous and are seldom available on the retail market.

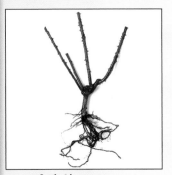
Grade 1 bare-root rose

Grade 1$\frac{1}{2}$ bare-root rose

Grade 1$\frac{1}{2}$ bare-root rose

because they do not grow vigorously on their own roots. Grafting also makes it easier to propagate a cultivar uniformly and reliably.

Another reason to graft is that roses that tend to sucker—to spread by producing new stems from their roots—can be grafted onto nonsuckering rootstocks. On the other hand, sometimes nonsuckering roses are grafted onto vigorous, suckering rootstocks; in that case, suckers that emerge below the bud union must be cut off, because they will produce roses different from those from the scion.

A major disadvantage of grafted roses is that if a hard freeze kills the rose down to the bud union, any new shoots the rootstock produces will look like the plant from which the rootstock was taken, not like the grafted variety.

Because many roses are adapted to temperate climates, rose growers in subtropical areas such as Florida have the best success with grafted roses that are grown on one of the few rootstocks adapted to their climate and soil.

Own-root roses

Because of the problems with cold vulnerability, especially in the northern half of the United States, own-root roses are becoming popular.

Own-root roses are those that grow vigorously on their own roots, including old garden roses, English roses, shrubs, and miniatures. Own-root roses are usually propagated by cuttings.

In cold regions, if the top dies back, canes that come from the roots are true to the original plant. Fans of own-root roses cite other advantages over grafted roses, including fewer viral diseases and a longer lifespan. And own-root roses are less expensive because they require less time and labor to produce than grafted roses.

Field-grown roses

A field-grown rose is one that is grown in a field, dug up once it's dormant (usually in November), and sold either bare root when dormant or potted and actively growing again.

The majority of roses are field grown because this is the most cost-effective means of production. While growing in the field, roses are subject to the same problems with bad weather and pests that any field-grown crop faces. While that means rose growers are subject to the same concerns as farmers, it also means the rose has proven that it can survive and grow with less individual care than it gets in a garden.

To ensure you get the toughest rose, you might want to ask the retailer where it's been grown— especially if you live in a very cold, very hot, or very dry region. If the rose has been locally grown or grown in similar climates, it's already acclimated to the conditions of your garden.

▲ Roses are sold basically in three ways. To the left is a bare-root rose. Roses are sold this way early in the growing season and usually are seen this way when they arrive via mail-order. In the center is a container rose, sold growing and blooming. To the right is a packaged bare-root rose. Bare-root roses are also sometimes sold packed partly into a box.

Understanding sun and shade

A rose bush needs a lot of energy to produce those beautiful, fragrant blooms, and that energy comes from the sun. Without enough light, rose plants have small leaves, spindly canes, fewer flowers, and more diseases. So it's no wonder that when you select a site for your roses, the top priority is sunlight.

Intensity is the key

Common wisdom is that roses require at least six hours of direct sun each day. That guideline is a good starting point, though there are other factors to consider.

The energy in sunlight drives photosynthesis, the complex chemical process a plant uses to produce its food from the water and nutrients it absorbs through its roots.

Two qualities of light affect how much light energy is available for photosynthesis.

The first is brightness, which is what makes you squint on a sunny day. The other is heat. Brightness and heat combined are called solar intensity or the intensity of sunlight.

Location is everything

A matrix of factors determines the intensity of sunlight where you live. For example, light is more intense if you live closer to the equator or at a high elevation where there's less atmosphere to act as a filter. Some factors change with the season, such as the angle of the sun and length of day. And some regions of the country average more cloudy days during the growing season than do others.

Fortunately you don't have to be a meteorologist to grow roses. Use your experience and common sense to adjust the six-hour guideline to your region. If your summers have relatively low light intensity (think Minnesota) or have many cloudy days, choose a planting site that is completely shade free. On the other hand, in regions with intensely sunny, hot summers, plant roses where they are protected from the scorching midafternoon sun.

▲ It can be tricky to grow roses in even light shade, but this arbor situated in a wooded area gets just enough light (at least 6 hours of direct light a day) to keep the plants healthy and blooming well.

UNDERSTANDING FULL SUN TO FULL SHADE

☼ FULL SUN

This is direct, full, unfiltered sun for at least six hours a day in a hot climate, such as that of Texas, and eight hours a day in a cool climate with less-direct sun, such as the conditions Minnesota offers.

Full sun tip: Even sun worshippers such as roses can get too much of a good thing. When the temperature climbs past 90°F on a sunny day, plants shut down the photosynthesis engine. Give roses and other plants—including the lawn—a quick spritz of water from the hose to cool them off. This beneficial practice, called syringing, doesn't violate the rule that plants should only be watered deeply. It has the added benefit of preventing mildew. It's a myth that the droplets can burn the leaves.

◗ PART SUN/PART SHADE

The terms part sun/part shade and partial sun/partial shade are usually used interchangeably.

Technically, part shade describes an area that gets filtered sun for much of the day or is shaded in the morning or afternoon. In northern regions, roses

ROSES FOR PARTIAL SHADE

No rose will flower in full shade, but some are adapted to partial shade. These are some of the most shade-tolerant roses.

Abraham Darby

Fair Bianca

Mary Rose

Sally Holmes

Amber Queen

Iceberg

New Dawn

The Prince

Ballerina

The Knock Out series

Playboy

Zephirine Drouhin

tolerate shade better in the morning if they get plenty of intense afternoon sun. The opposite is true in parts of the West and South where light is more intense.

Part sun technically describes a situation with less light than part shade. It can describe an area that gets direct sun for just a few hours or that is under a tree that filters rather than blocks light, such as a honey locust.

Part sun/shade tip: Light and heat reflecting from light-colored fences, pavement, and buildings can give a boost to the daily light total in partially sunny/shady areas.

● **FULL SHADE**

Full shade comes either from trees with a heavy canopy or from structures that cast a shadow, especially on the north sides of the structures. Roses cannot tolerate full shade.

Full shade tip: You can tell it's full shade when:
● Snow melts there last.
● The lawn is thin.
● Shade-loving plants, such as hostas, lungwort, and impatiens, thrive there.

Understanding microclimates

Every yard and garden is located within a zone, determined by the United States Department of Agriculture (USDA). The USDA Hardiness Zone Map (see page 61) is your system for determining what plants will grow best in your area. The zone map is a general estimation of climatic conditions, largely based on the lowest temperatures that can be expected each year in a given place. There are 10 zones and each represents a winter hardiness area. Within Zones 2–10, there is an "a" and "b" designation: "a" is the warm side of the zone and "b" is the colder side of the zone.

But within every zone there is the possibility of a climatic variance, or microclimate. Microclimates can be as large as a region or city—or as small as one side of a homeowner's yard.

Microclimates can make an area either more temperate or less temperate than the zone in which it is located. This is both good news and bad news for gardeners. A warmer, more temperate microclimate means you can add plant varieties that require warmer conditions than your zone allows. But if you live in a colder microclimate, the plants and trees that you add to your landscape may not survive,

even though the zone designation indicates that they will.

What creates a microclimate?

A microclimate can be created by nature, such as a valley or a hill, or something that a homeowner adds to a landscape, such as a building or a fence. A property with a ravine on one side may have one climate condition at the top and another one at the bottom—yards apart. Another geologic microclimate is the difference in temperature between a south-facing hill and a north-facing hill. A microclimate created by a structure might influence your ability to grow one rose on the south side of a garage, but not the north side.

Regional microclimates

A microclimate can be as large as several miles and affected by a number of weather/climatic factors. Large bodies of water (for example, the Great Lakes) tend to affect air temperatures for the land around them, and winter temperatures are usually less extreme. Even a smaller body of water can cause this effect. Large urban areas also tend to have less extreme winter temperatures and hotter summer temperatures due to accumulated heat buildup from paving and buildings. Buildings also protect from the wind in many areas. According to Cornell University, "urban areas may be a full hardiness zone warmer than rural areas just a few miles away."

Microclimates in your yard

Chances are that you have a microclimate effect in your yard. How can you tell? The surface characteristics of your yard—the flat ground, the slopes, buildings, fences, hedgerows—have the ability to create microclimates.

WHAT CREATES MICROCLIMATES?

Microclimates are created by weather, topographic, and structural factors that include:
Temperature
Humidity
Moisture
Wind
Dew
Frost
Heat
Season
Elevation
Buildings
Fences
Large bodies of water

▲ A rose set out farther from the house will be more exposed to cold and drying winds, but also have excellent sun. The reflected light and heat from the sidewalk and street will help the rose in cooler climates but might stress it in warm climates.

The lay of the land, so to speak, can create a microclimate effect. In the fall, cold air (which is heavier than warm air), can collect in low spots and cause frost sooner than areas on the higher ground around it. The buildings on your property—your house, for example—can create another type of microclimate condition. The north side of your home may be buffeted by cold winds in the winter and you may find that you can't grow the same plants on that side of your house as you could on the opposite, south side of your home.

The microclimates in your yard may be areas that are warmer or colder than other areas in your yard. For example, a patio flower garden that is protected on

one side by a house and trees may experience a different microclimate effect than a vegetable garden in the same yard that is located in a lower or exposed area. Rooftop gardening areas are also influenced by microclimate effects because they are higher than ground level. Fences can protect plants from cold air, or they can collect cold air, depending on the air flow.

Gardening in a microclimate

Being aware of microclimates helps you garden smarter. Knowing the type of microclimates you have in your yard—and matching them with plants that thrive in those conditions—is a little like tricking Mother Nature.

MICROCLIMATES AROUND A HOUSE

Even a small landscape can contain a variety of microclimates, or you can create those microclimates yourself:

Windbreaks These dense plantings of tall trees or shrubs diffuse damaging north winds in winter. Evergreen plantings are especially effective since they're dense all year long. Fencing is less effective but still is helpful.

The strip between sidewalk and street This is often dubbed the hell strip because it can be so hot and baked. Choose drought- and heat-tolerant roses and plantings for this area.

A slope This is ideal because it provides the drainage roses love.

Open sunny lawn This is also an ideal place to situate a rose garden because it gets full sun all day long, which roses love in all but the hottest regions.

A patio The lighter-color the material, the more it bounces back light to roses. It also serves as a passive solar device, slowly releasing heat overnight.

Mature trees Tall trees tend to cast shade, which roses can't tolerate much of. Also, the area underneath mature trees roots sucks moisture from roses, creating an unacceptable environment for roses.

A overhang This prevents rain from falling onto roses. Be sure to water any plantings here well.

The north side This area is shadier than other sides of the house. It's also more exposed to winter winds.

The east side This is ideal for roses since the early sun dries their leaves faster. Also, in hot regions, roses may get relief from the beating west sun in the afternoon.

The south side Roses usually love the full sun in this spot, again, except in very hot regions where they appreciate a little shade in the afternoon.

The west side This side provides roses with plenty of sun, which can sometimes be too much of a good thing in hot regions where they're baked during the hottest parts of the day.

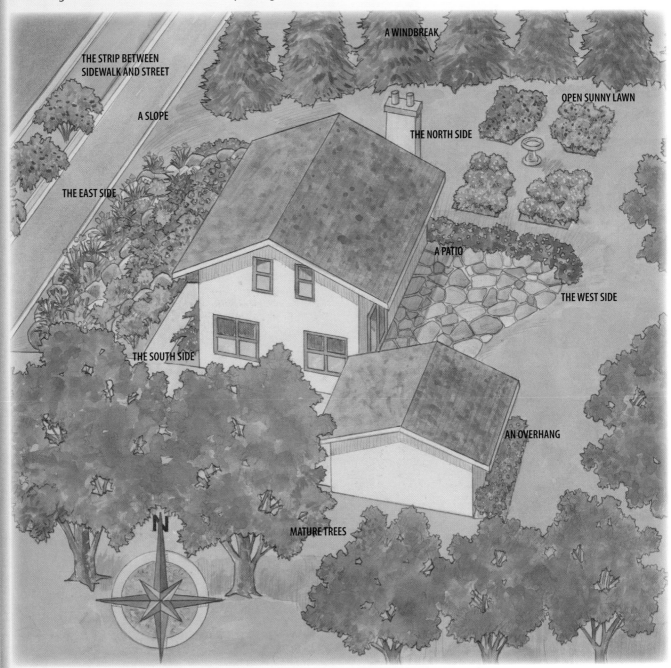

Providing good circulation

One of the biggest enemies of beautiful roses is fungal disease. By late summer, most roses have signs of at least a little black spot. They may also have powdery mildew- and downy mildew-coated leaves, which have the appearance of a gray or white powder over the leaves.

When conditions are right, black spot and mildew mar the appearance of the leaves and can make them fall off altogether. The secret, then, is to do as much as possible to prevent those conditions.

Two powerful weapons in the fight against fungal diseases such as black spot and powdery mildew are plant selection and sun (see page 84). However, because most fungal diseases love dampness, another part of prevention is to ensure that air circulates around the plant to reduce humidity.

ARS ROSARIAN TIP...

A great way to ensure good circulation is to grow really big roses inside an obelisk instead of on a trellis. You can weave the supple new canes in and out of the structure, which supports them gracefully.
—Dona and Bob Martin, Gilbert, Arizona

You don't need a relentless, drying wind. A light breeze will do.

Location

Obviously, roses in humid climates face more risk than those in dry ones. But you can choose a location with good air circulation.

Select a site away from the inner corners of hedges, fences, and buildings. Steal an idea from professional apple farmers by avoiding low

▲ The key to healthy roses is plenty of sun and good circulation. Without these, roses are prone to a host of disfiguring diseases, especially black spot, which can denude a rose by the end of the growing season. This rose is tied on a pillar where air can flow around it freely.

spots where cool air pools; instead, plant roses on the top or side of a slope where air drains.

Spacing

The look of a cottage garden packed with plants is romantic, but if your roses are struggling with leaf diseases, you should thin out the crowd. Cut back or move nearby plants and prune branches from nearby shrubs and trees to allow more air to pass through.

When planting a rose, make sure you're allowing plenty of room for growth. Check the label as well as the growing information in the Gallery of Roses (starting on page 136), for steps to ensure good air flow.

Training

Pruning a rose plant (see page 123) to open up its center improves air circulation, lets more sunlight reach inner leaves, and encourages blooms.

Training climbing roses to grow on a trellis rather than allowing them to sprawl and flop on the ground also improves circulation. Use plant twine or cloth strips to secure the main canes so they grow away from the center of the plant.

▶ Training a rose up an openwork fence is a great way to allow for excellent circulation. This New Dawn rose grows fairly tall, so it's a natural for this technique. As it grows, the gardener ties it loosely to the fence with soft cloth strips.

▲ Although these roses are generously spaced, the perennials growing among them could have impeded circulation if they hadn't been carefully selected. These perennials will fill in around the roses but not overwhelm them.

Soil preparation

Once you've selected a good site for your roses, it's time to prepare the area for planting.

Start by laying out the shape of your new garden using stakes and strings for straight lines or garden hoses for curves. When you're happy with the shape (it's good to give yourself a day to think about it), mark the outline with aerosol marking paint. Then remove stakes, strings, and hoses.

Following the outline, strip off the sod using a sod-cutting machine, or do it by hand using a flat spade or special sod-cutting tool. Shake as much soil as possible back onto the bed, then toss the remaining grass into the compost pile.

Killing weeds

Alternatively, if you have a weed infestation on the spot, use a nonselective herbicide spray—the kind that kills all plants it touches—and allow the plants to die back over a day or two. With Roundup Weed & Grass Killer Ready-To-Use Plus, you can plant after just one day. (You may need to repeat if the weeds are persistent.)

If the plants have not gone to seed , you can then simply till in the dead plant matter.

Another method, which is easy and allows you to capitalize on the organic matter that turf can provide, is to cover the area with several layers of newspaper, wetting them down with a

COMPOSTING BASICS

If you're going to do even a little gardening, it's smart to start a compost heap.

A compost heap gives you a generous, free supply of one of the best soil amendments around. It works almost like an outdoor trash can, collecting leaves, grass clippings, and other yard waste. (Avoid large sticks and branches, which break down slowly.)

Check out the many compost bins and systems available at your local garden center. Then set one up and fill it with yard waste. You can speed the process by turning the pile every few weeks and watering it during dry weather. In a year or so, you'll have a fairly good supply of compost.

Recommended materials for compost include eggshells, coffee grounds, and remnants of fruits and vegetables from the kitchen. Shredded newspaper may also be composted. Sawdust or straw from most livestock, such as chickens or horses, is very good.

Materials to avoid because they attract pests or could spread disease include pet droppings, meat products, bones, and oils or kitchen grease. Also avoid weeds that have gone to seed and diseased plant parts, or you may spread those problems along with the compost.

 An easy way to create a new rose bed is to cover the area with several layers of newspaper and top with a few inches of compost. Allow the paper and grass to break down for a few months, then till the area.

hose as you work to keep them in place. Cover with 3 or more inches of top-quality compost or topsoil. Wait a few months (or over the winter) for the grass to break down, then dig up the area or till it. (This method works best in areas that have been planted with a noninvasive turfgrass, such as Kentucky bluegrass. It works less well in warmer parts of the country where lawns commonly are planted with bermudagrass and other tough, drought-tolerant grasses.)

If you are planting in an existing bed or border, prepare it by raking back any mulch and pulling or treating any weeds. Work in several spadefuls of compost to enrich the soil.

SOIL AMENDMENTS

Compost
One of the best soil amendments there is, compost helps sandy soil retain moisture, breaks up clay, adds nutrients, and encourages beneficial insect and microbial activity.

Sphagnum peat moss
Made from peat bog material, spongelike sphagnum peat moss (never get just "peat") breaks up clay, adds organic matter, and helps sandy soil retain water.

Gravel
In some clay soils, working in gravel helps break up clay. Always experiment in a small area first and see how it reacts over the period of a year. Some gardeners like to put gravel in the bottom of planting holes to improve drainage.

Topsoil
A generic term for darker, more crumbly soil suitable for growing most plants (compared to subsoil or fill dirt). Quality varies radically, so check out the contents of bags and approve any truckloads that you order before they're dumped.

Sand
In some clay soils, sand is excellent for tilling into the soil to break it up. However, in some other soils, it may cause a concretelike effect, so test a small area first and wait several months to a year.

Providing drainage

Roses don't ask for much—sun, water, a little fertilizer, and well-drained soil. The latter is critical because roses do *not* like wet feet. They do best in soil that is loose (not clay) so that the water hydrates, then drains away from their roots. Good drainage is essential for healthy, happy roses.

Improving your soil for better drainage

If you, like so many people, don't have good soil in your yard, you can greatly improve it. Add soil amendments and you will over time create good soil that will produce healthy roses. Adding organic or inorganic materials to your soil enhances its structure—improving drainability, adding nutrients, increasing aeration, and neutralizing acidity or alkalinity.

Amendments that improve the drainage of soil include packaged garden soil mixes, sphagnum peat moss, compost, rotted manure, leaf mold, and gypsum.

Adding raised beds

Raised beds can compensate for poor soil because they essentially include new, drainable soil layered on top of the poor soil.

Elevating plants above the soil line allows them to grow in places where they might not otherwise thrive. Planting

Although roses need ample moisture, they do not like soggy soil. Raised beds help roses thrive with maximum blooms and minimal disease, as this rose in its prime demonstrates.

▲ Raised beds of even a few inches can make a radical difference in the health of your roses, especially if you fill the raised beds with top-quality compost and soil.

Creating drainage

If the area where you want to plant roses is too wet, you can remedy the situation in several ways. Some are fast and simple, but some are more extensive and should be used only in severe cases.

● **Add coarse gravel to planting holes** Improve drainage by digging several feet below the planting depth of the rose and filling the hole with coarse gravel.

● **Add a tile drainage system** A tile system draws water away from the root system of the roses. You can use corrugated drain tiles or 4-inch plastic pipe, which you add before installing the bed.

● **Install a French drain** This type of drainage system is a combination of the first two methods. A French drain is a gravel-filled trench that drains the water away from the rose bed.

● **Be wise about watering** Regulate and monitor your irrigation schedule to avoid overwatering. The best time to water is in the morning so the water on the leaves can dry in the sun during the day. Watering at night may leave excess dampness on the leaves that could result in fungal problems.

TEST DRAINAGE

Poorly drained soil holds too much water and not enough air. Roots don't function properly in soggy soil and they become prone to root diseases. To determine how well your soil drains, do a soil drainage test.

Start by digging a straight-sided hole 12 inches deep. Fill the hole with water and let it drain completely. After it has drained, refill the hole with water. Wait one hour, then use a ruler to measure how far the water level has dropped below the soil line.

● A less-than-½-inch drop indicates poor drainage.
● A ½- to 2-inch drop indicates moderate drainage.
● A 2- to 6-inch drop indicates good drainage.
● A more-than-6 inch drop indicates very rapid drainage.

them higher off the ground allows air to move through the foliage, keeping it dry and disease-free. Another practical benefit of raising the height of the bed is that the roses are easier to prune, water, and harvest. Their fragrance will also be closer for you and guests to enjoy.

Raised beds are built on top of the ground and are constructed from wood, stone, or brick. Popular weather-resistant wood choices are redwood, cedar, and pressure-treated pine. You can also make raised beds with brick or stone sides for planting beds that will last for decades.

You can add a raised bed anywhere. It's easiest, of course, on level ground. But you can also grow roses on a hillside by terracing the slope, adding raised planting beds in stairsteps down a hill. This is an extremely attractive way to tame a slope.

Most raised beds can be about 6 to 8 inches deep; however, in wet areas, beds may need to be up to 12 inches deep to achieve the proper drainage.

Raised beds can be any shape or form (in a variety of materials) to match the overall style of your landscape. For example, if your home is traditional, squared or rectangular raised beds of cut stone or brick continue the theme. If you like the cottage look, you can build more casual or rustic beds using field stones to create curving or round beds.

▲ A wonderful solution for slopes, raised beds and terraces give roses the excellent drainage they love.

Planting roses

Planting a rose is a pretty simple process, but it's worth taking the time to do it right. A properly planted rose will get off to a great start in your garden. Careful planting also helps avoid future problems with root systems, drying out, and graft unions.

Roses are commonly available in two forms: bare root and potted (sometimes called container roses).

Before you plant bare-root roses

Bare-root roses, most commonly sold mail order, are available in spring in colder regions, spring and fall in warmer areas, and even in winter in frost-free areas. Most bare-root roses should not be planted later than your region's last average frost date.

Container roses, by comparison, are widely available. You can purchase and plant them throughout the entire growing season.

Bare-root roses are dug from nursery fields, cleaned, pruned, and packaged for shipping or local sale. The roots are protected in a plastic bag filled with a barely damp packing medium such as wood shavings or sphagnum moss. Some bare-root roses are packed in biodegradable boxes rather than plastic bags.

Check the roots of bagged or boxed roses carefully before purchasing; if the packing medium and roots are dried out, the rose is already too damaged to grow well. Ideally, bare-root roses should have minimal leaf growth. If there's growth, it should be vigorous and healthy looking. Be sure to keep the roots moist, cool, and shaded until you plant.

Before you plant container roses

Container roses—the kind already leafed out and sometimes blooming in pots—are the most available

EXTRA PROTECTION

If larger burrowing animals are a problem in your garden, you may want to consider planting your rose in a cage made of chicken wire. The mesh is large enough to allow rose roots to grow freely but small enough to keep out many critters.

▲ Container-grown (also called potted) roses often have the advantage of being in bloom so you can see what you're getting, but when the weather is exceptionally hot or cold, they may be more tricky than bare-root roses to get established.

and most popular form of roses sold.

They can be planted anytime during the frost-free growing season, although spring or fall usually provides the best weather conditions. The ideal potted rose has a healthy network of roots extending throughout the pot. Some potted roses have been in pots too long and develop a mass of roots circling the bottom of the pot. Others have hardly any

root systems at all and you can practically pull them out of the pot (and, in fact, may, by accident). Avoid purchasing these roses since they are far less likely to establish well in the garden.

The potted plant should be well-hydrated and isn't dull-leafed (unless it's supposed to be) or wilted. If it is, give it a soaking and then wait several hours for the rose to recover before planting.

HOW TO PLANT A BARE-ROOT ROSE

1
Soak
When you are ready to plant a bare-root rose, remove it from the bag and shake off the packing material. Examine the roots and prune off any that are dead or damaged. Don't remove any healthy roots, though—your rose plant needs as many roots as possible to help it get re-established. Soak the roots in a bucket of lukewarm water for an hour or two while you prepare the planting hole. If you're planting several roses, put them in a relatively clean garbage can to soak.

2
Dig and prepare the hole
Use a sharp shovel to dig a wide, shallow hole. The planting hole should be at least twice as wide as the root system; this gives new roots plenty of loosened soil to spread into. The hole should be as deep as the root system, plus as many additional inches as it will take to bury the graft union.

Take this opportunity to work in soil amendments, such as Miracle-Gro Garden Soil, compost, and others.

3
Prune as needed
Trim off any obviously dead or damaged wood or stubs. Also, if any branches are rubbing, trim them. Trim any obviously damaged roots as well.

4
Position and plant in the hole
Position the bare-root rose in the hole, being sure to spread out the roots as evenly as practical. Don't worry if all the roots don't cooperate perfectly— the main goal is to prevent badly tangled roots or roots that all head straight downward. The most important part of this process is to get the bud union at the right height (see page 97).

Start filling the hole with soil, tamping it down with your foot around all the roots to prevent root-drying air pockets from forming. When the hole is about half-filled, water gently to settle the soil. Continue to fill in with soil, tamping it down with your hands as you go.

5
Water
Mound and shape the soil so it makes a moat around the rose. Fill with water and let soak in. Repeat two or three times until you're confident the water has trickled down to the bottom of the roots. Keep the soil moist for the next two weeks or so until the rose becomes established. Keep the rose from wilting.

Planting roses *(continued)*

HOW TO PLANT A POTTED ROSE

Prepare the hole
Make the hole at least twice as wide as the pot and gently slope the sides of the hole (it's easier for roots to penetrate a sloped wall than a straight one).
As with bare-root roses, work in soil amendments, such as Miracle-Gro Garden soil, compost, or others.

Remove the rose
If you can, hold the rose firmly at its base and slide the rose out of the pot. Some roses can be difficult to get out of the pot. Set the pot on its side and press your foot on it to loosen the soil and roots. If that doesn't work, stomp on it with moderate force. If there are a few circling roots at the bottom, loosen them with your fingers.

Postion the rose
For own-root roses that don't have a graft union, make the hole only as deep as the pot. If needed, measure depth accurately by laying a stake or tool handle across the hole, then use a ruler to check the depth from the stake to the bottom of the hole.

For grafted roses, follow the guidelines for determining graft union placement (see opposite page) and dig the hole an appropriate depth.

Mulch the rose
Mound the soil to form a moat around the base of the rose with a mulch such as Scotts Nature Scapes Color Enhanced Mulch. Mulch with at least an inch of mulch. If you prefer, you can mulch after watering.

Water the rose
Water well, allowing the water to puddle in the moat you've made and then soak in. Repeat two or three times until you're confident the water has worked down to the deepest roots. Keep the soil moist for the next two weeks or so until the rose becomes established. Avoid letting the rose wilt.

TRANSPLANTING ROSES

Occasionally you may need to move a rose to another spot. Small to medium-size roses are the best candidates for transplanting. If you have a large rose, consider hiring a professional who will use mechanized transplanting equipment such as a small tree spade to cut a hole large enough to prevent serious root damage and who will be able to move the root ball safely and efficiently.

The best time to transplant roses is when they are dormant (not actively growing) in late winter or early spring. Carefully dig up the rose, leaving as many roots intact as possible. Gently shake off soil, then immediately plant the rose in the new location using the bare-root planting method. Water well, applying a root stimulator to assure that the roots take off faster and better. Keep well watered for the next week or two.

Long-established roses can be moved successfully if you do a little work beforehand. To develop a good root ball for transplanting, root prune the rose several months before you move it. To root prune, use a sharp spade to cut through the soil at a slight inward angle in a circle 12 to 18 inches out from the base of the rose bush. New roots will grow inside the pruning line, and the rose will be ready to be transplanted in a few months.

HOW DEEP TO PLANT THE GRAFT UNION

The graft union is the swollen-looking knobby part of the stem just above the roots. It's where a desirable rose was grafted onto the roots of a more vigorous rose to combine the best of the two plants. (Not all roses have graft unions.)

The graft union is easily damaged by cold, so the best planting depth of the graft union varies with climate. In warm-winter climates the graft union has less need for protection and may be placed at or above the soil line. In progressively colder climates the vital graft union benefits from progressively more protection, which is provided by placing the union below the soil line.

As a rule, plant the graft union 1 to 4 inches below the soil line in cold-winter climates where winter lows hit −10°F or lower. Position it at ground level or slightly above where winter lows are between −10°F and 10°F and warmer.

Plant own-root roses—those that don't have a graft union—with the crown (where roots and stems meet) at soil level. In cold climates, set the crown a few inches below soil level for extra winter protection.

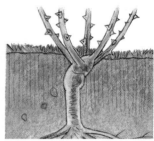

Graft union above the soil line | Graft union at the soil line | Graft union below the soil line

POSITIONING THE GRAFT UNION

If you're finding it difficult to figure out whether the graft union will be at the correct depth when finally planted, lay the spade handle across the hole to determine exactly where the soil level is.

Planting roses in containers

Roses do surprisingly well in containers, as long as you get them off to a good start.

Roses, by their nature, are best grown in the ground because their roots have ample room to spread and the soil stays evenly moist.

In some situations you want a rose in a pot, either because your soil or growing conditions are problematic—or you just like the look of roses in pots. Half whiskey barrels are favorites of many rose gardeners.

Miniatures and minifloras, small roses by nature, do especially well in containers. Medium-size shrub roses, hybrid teas, and other modest-size roses also do well in containers. Avoid very large and climbing roses because it's almost impossible to provide them with enough soil.

Roses in containers are longest-lasting in mild climates. Except in the most temperate parts of the country (the South and the Pacific Northwest), roses in containers will not last for years, even with winter protection (see page 50 for instructions on caring for roses in containers during harsh winter weather).

With some thoughtful planting, you can use containers to showcase your roses right where you can enjoy them best.

See page 50 for information on designing with roses in containers.

ARS ROSARIAN TIP...

Consulting rosarian Carol Macon of Colorado Springs, Colorado, has been growing roses in containers for years and has hard-won knowledge about what works and what doesn't when planting roses in containers. Here's what she recommends.

- Use a 12-inch-wide container for small roses and miniatures. Use 15-inch pots for floribundas and small hybrid teas and 18 inches and larger for tree roses and larger hybrid teas. The container should be at least as deep as it is wide.
- The lighter the container, the easier it will be to move around, especially when it's time to give the rose winter protection. Macon likes to put hers on saucers with wheels made specifically for large pots.
- Only use clay pots if you first put a plastic liner or black plastic nursery pot inside. Clay dries out too quickly.
- Macon likes to put bark chips in the bottom of her pots for good drainage.
- Add an inch of mulch on top of the soil to conserve moisture.
- Hold off fertilizing a newly planted rose for a couple of weeks. Macon says fertilizing too soon is a primary cause of failure to bloom and the death of new plants.

▲ Planting a rose in a container takes minutes and is a great way to grow and enjoy roses. Miniature and miniflora roses (see page 230 in the Gallery of Roses) do especially well as long as the pot is of a generous size.

HOW TO PLANT A ROSE IN A CONTAINER

1

Provide good drainage
Select a large container that has at least one good drainage hole. Put gravel or other loose material at the bottom of the pot to prevent soil from sifting out of the hole and to promote good drainage at the bottom of the container. Clay shards from a broken pot are also a favorite, if you have them.

2

Add potting soil
Choose a top-quality potting mix and partly fill the container. Regular garden soil doesn't work well in containers, where soil needs to have a balance of lightness and ability to retain moisture.

3

Fill in around the rose
Remove the rose from its original container, if it's in one, and position it in the pot. Position the bud union according to your climate (see page 97). Fill in with additional potting soil, tamping it down firmly.

4

Add other plants
If desired, add other plants to the container for color and variety. Choose low-growing plants that won't overwhelm the rose.

5

Water well
Position the pot. (It's easier to move before watering.) Water well, saturating the soil enough that water runs out of the drainage hole. Avoid feeding the rose for at least a couple of weeks after planting, but keep it well-watered.

Watering roses

To grow and bloom beautifully, roses need a steady and ample supply of water. Water is vital to all plant processes, including nutrient uptake, cell development, and temperature regulation. When roses are actively growing, water is continually being taken up by the roots, moving throughout the plant, and exiting as water vapor from tiny pores on the rose leaves.

How much water do roses need? The short answer is that most roses grow well with about one inch of water per week. Variables such as temperature, wind, and soil type, however, can alter the amount of water needed in your garden. In hot regions especially, roses may well need daily water.

On hot days, roses lose lots of water from their leaves, so their roots need to have plenty of water available for uptake. Wind and dry air can also speed up water loss from leaves. The ability of your garden's soil to hold water also affects watering needs. Soils that drain very rapidly may need to be irrigated more often to make sure there's enough water in the roses' root zones.

IRRIGATION SYSTEMS

In the eastern two-thirds of the country where rainfall is more abundant, irrigation systems are seen as a bit of a luxury. In the arid West, however, they're a necessity.

In all regions, irrigation systems are the ideal for roses, which are susceptible to the fungal diseases that are encouraged by wet leaves.

Drip irrigation systems provide precise water delivery to each plant in a garden or container. Individual tubes are inserted where needed in the main hose, then each tube-end is placed on the soil near the base of a plant. Water is delivered slowly, giving the soil a thorough soak over a number of hours. Drip systems provide efficient water use but are more expensive and require more maintenance than other irrigation methods.

Automation can make any of these watering methods even easier. Some sprinklers have built-in timers, or you can use a separate timer that attaches at the faucet. These timers also work well for soaker hoses. Many drip irrigation systems have extensive automation options that allow customization for your garden.

Depending on the complexity of the system, you can install a simple irrigation system or consult a professional.

If you have an irrigation system, check all parts regularly for water-wasting leaks.

Inexpensive rubber gaskets on hose ends and sprinkler connections can save gallons of water and many dollars throughout the growing season.

Microsprinklers
These act like tiny sprinklers, adding water at the base of the rose. They're connected by underground pipe.

Drip Emitters
A long hose connects a series of emitters that dribble water precisely where you want it, such as at the base of a small rose.

Ring Dribbles
A ring dribbles water all around the rose for even distribution.

Bubblers
Bubblers create minifloods, soaking entire areas. They're good for large rose bushes.

Leaky Hoses
Leaky hoses slowly dribble water their entire length and are good for snaking through the planting bed.

An important part of smart watering is smart mulching.

Use an organic mulch, such as pine bark chips, cedar chips, or pine needles, around your rose bushes. A good layer of mulch helps maintain an even soil temperature, conserves moisture in the soil, and suppresses weeds. As it breaks down, the mulch contributes organic matter to the soil. You can't lose.

—*Carol Macon,
Colorado Springs, Colorado*

Pamper newly planted roses

Monitor newly planted roses carefully to make sure they receive enough water. Established roses, with their more extensive root systems, are more tolerant of brief dry periods, but to look their best they should be irrigated when rainfall is scarce at the rate of one inch of water a week. Place a rain gauge in or near your rose garden to get an accurate measure of rainfall.

How you water your garden can determine how well your roses grow. A quick daily sprinkle may perk up wilted roses, but it's not a good watering technique for long-term plant health. Frequent light sprinkling tends to encourage shallow root growth in the top few inches of soil. A shallow root system is more susceptible to drought stress and winter injury. A healthy rose needs a deep, well-developed root system. Less frequent but more thorough waterings encourage deeper root growth that will sustain the plant. When you do water, try to soak the soil slowly to a depth of at least 6 inches.

There are several good ways to water your rose garden. Some gardeners prefer hand watering with a hose. While hand watering can be a pleasantly contemplative experience, it's difficult to provide a truly even, thorough garden watering by hand. Mechanical watering is much easier and more efficient for almost all rose gardens. You'll give your roses a good, deep drink and as a bonus, give yourself more time for just enjoying the garden.

WATER DEEPLY

When watering roses, take the time to apply plenty of water and allow the water to soak in deeply. This encourages the roots to go down deep, which helps keep them moist longer in times of drought, as shown on the right.

On the left, you'll see what happens when plants are watered lightly. Roots tend to stay at the surface, making them less drought-resistant. Follow the adage of watering deeply and less often rather than shallowly and frequently.

▲ Proximity counts. The closer in to the house a rose garden is the more likely you are to keep it watered. That's not only because it's closer to the hydrant but also because you're more likely to see it up close every day and spot the early signs of too little water.

Watering roses *(continued)*

Sprinklers can do the job

Garden sprinklers are available in many forms. Fan, ring, and rotating sprinklers are common. They are simple to use, but may require dragging lengths of hose through the yard. Underground irrigation systems with pop-up sprinklers are also widely available although they're more expensive.

Very early morning—before sunrise, even—is the best time to water with sprinklers; cooler temperatures and lighter winds mean less water loss through evaporation.

Once the sprinkler is set up, adjust the water pressure so the sprinkler delivers an even pattern of water to the garden without wasting water on driveways or streets. Use a rain gauge or empty can to monitor how much water has been applied.

Overhead watering has the disadvantage of wetting rose foliage. Fungal disease problems often develop and spread more quickly when the leaves stay wet for extended periods.

Two other types of irrigation, soaker hoses and drip systems, avoid the problem of wet foliage.

Soaker hoses look like regular garden hoses, but they are made of porous material that allows water to seep out along the entire length of the hose. Lay soaker hoses directly on the soil at the base of the roses. To water, connect a regular hose from the faucet to the soaker hose and turn on the water at fairly low pressure. Soaker hoses deliver water slowly, so be sure to leave the faucet on long enough to thoroughly water the soil. Soaker hoses degrade more quickly when exposed to sunlight, so it's a good idea to cover them with mulch once they are in place. Bring soaker hoses indoors over winter in all but frost-free regions.

▲ To keep roses this lush, healthy, and heavily blooming, it's critical that they receive plenty of water, either through rainfall or irrigation. It's important to water deeply and well at the roots, keeping foliage as dry and therefore healthy as possible.

SMART WATERING TIPS FOR ROSES

● Water regularly. Don't let roses get extremely dry or keep them extremely wet. Roses adapt somewhat to current conditions but taking them between wildly varying moisture levels stresses them

● Water in the morning, rather than the evening. This allows water to evaporate more quickly and makes it more difficult for fungal diseases to gain a foothold.

● Avoid wetting leaves when watering roses, no matter what time of day you're watering. The drier the leaves, the less likely diseases might take hold. However, once in a while, on a clear, breezy day when there's not been much rain and if the roses are looking a little dusty, it's not a bad idea to give roses a quick spray rinse.

● Be diligent about watering roses in the fall. In colder, more arid regions, roses have a much better chance of surviving winter if they go into that difficult season well-hydrated.

● Work to improve your soil. Good, loose, dark soil not only absorbs and holds onto water better, it also allows water to drain away at just the right rate, creating the ideal environment. Good soil also allows water (and fertilizer and other nutrients) to percolate down deep where roses can make best use of it.

See page 90 for tips on creating the best soil possible for roses. But a good rule of thumb is to incorporate as much compost as possible at every chance, including planting time, and mulching with it regularly.

WATERING CONTAINERS

Roses potted in soilless mixes need special attention to watering and fertilizing. A soilless mix doesn't hold water as long as most garden soil does, so it will dry out more quickly. Ideally, soilless mix in containers should be evenly moist at all times so the roses can have uninterrupted water uptake.

Other tips for watering roses in containers:
● Wilting once won't kill a container-grown rose, but repeated drying out kills roots and stresses the plant, making it more susceptible to pests and diseases.
● Standing in water also damages roots. Avoid using saucers under containers, but if you do, always empty excess water within 30 minutes of watering.
● Watering frequency for containers will vary depending on factors such as the size of the container and plants, sunlight, air temperature, rainfall, humidity, and wind. Most containers require watering every day or two if there is no rain. If the potting mix in a container needs to be watered more than twice a day even in moderate weather, you should move the rose into a larger container.
● There are several ways to water container plants. Because containers are often placed in scattered spots, watering by hand, either with a hose or a watering can, is common. Just as with inground plantings, it may be difficult to thoroughly water container plants by hand. If the potting mix has dried out excessively, it tends to pull away from the container wall, leaving a gap. If you quickly apply a large amount of water, much of that water may run through the gap before it can be absorbed by the potting mix.
● Slow, gentle water application is best. A good way to water thoroughly and destress yourself at the same time is to turn the hose on low and let it trickle into each container while you enjoy the roses or relax nearby. If you have large groupings of containers, sprinklers may be a watering option. However, this method may waste water. Drip irrigation can be a solution, especially if you have many containers in a fairly small area. Connector hoses can be routed inconspicuously along baseboards or deck edges, with individual drip tubes placed in each container. You may need to pin the tubes down to keep them in place. Drip irrigation can save time and water, but you'll need to check each container regularly to ensure that water is flowing properly.
● There are several ways to water large planter boxes and raised beds. Sprinklers work well for larger areas. Soaker hoses left in place under mulch are a good option for raised beds and some planters. Drip irrigation can also be installed in most planters and raised beds.

Depending on the number and position of your containers of roses, it might make keeping them watered easier to purchase a lightweight mini hose. Attach a valve with two outlets and you'll never have to drag a heavy hose to water pots again.

WHEN IS IT TIME TO WATER ROSES?

How can you tell if your roses are getting enough water? Look at the leaves.

If the leaves normally have a sheen and lose that, it's time to turn on the water. The leaves should never wilt, even in the heat of the afternoon sun. Wilting stresses the plants and makes them more susceptible to pests and diseases. It also damages any flowers on the plant and reduces future flowering.

Roses are getting too much water if their lower foliage starts to yellow and fall off (without any dark spots, the telltale clue that black spot is the culprit). Yellow leaves mean the plant is starved of oxygen, a result of waterlogged roots that can't get access to air.

Another way to tell if it's time to water roses is to feel the soil. Wiggle your finger down an inch or two into the dirt. If it's dry that far down, it's probably time to water.

Yet another method is to rely on so-called indicator plants. Some annuals, such as impatiens, are even more thirsty than roses. And while they're planted in the shade (roses need sun), impatiens are usually the first plants in the garden to start wilting when it's been dry. If you see the impatiens starting to wilt, it's time to water them—and the roses as well.

Mulching roses

Mulch is indispensable in any rose garden. By shielding the soil from direct sun, mulch helps it retain moisture and maintain moderate temperatures. Mulch can also protect plant roots by reducing soil compaction from foot traffic and heavy rain and by preventing soil erosion. A swath of mulch helps protect rose stems by keeping lawn equipment at a safe distance. Mulch also inhibits weed growth, a real boon for the busy gardener. And from a design perspective, an attractive layer of mulch unifies and defines your garden space.

What is mulch?

Mulch is a layer of organic or inorganic material that completely covers the soil's surface. Many types of organic mulch are available, including wood chips, shredded wood, compost, shredded leaves, pine needles, bark chips, and cocoa-bean hulls. Fine-textured mulches such as pine needles and shredded leaves decompose faster than coarse mulches such as wood chips. Inorganic mulches include landscape fabric, shredded rubber, pea gravel, and crushed rock.

Although organic and inorganic mulches are useful, organic mulches have several advantages in rose gardens. Most important, organic mulches add organic matter to the soil as they decompose. Another advantage of organic mulch is that it's easy to remove if you need to make changes to the garden. Inorganic mulches, especially rock products, are difficult to remove down the road.

Where to get it

Mulch is available from many sources. Garden centers and landscape supply companies often sell bulk mulch by the cubic yard. Bagged mulch, usually 2 or 3 cubic feet per

▲ Mulch provides so many benefits for roses. It conserves moisture, suppresses weeds, prevents soil-borne diseases from splashing onto leaves, it can add organic matter to the soil, and just plain looks good.

bag, is sold everywhere from garden centers to gas stations. Be sure to purchase a quality mulch, such as Scotts Nature Scapes Color Enhanced Mulch. You can purchase pine needles, also called pine straw, in bales, or if you have pine trees in your yard you can rake the needles when they fall. You can also rake and save leaves; they're easier to use as mulch if you shred them and let them compost over winter.

If your mulch has a lot of fine particles, like some wood-product mulches, apply only 1 to 2 inches so the soil underneath gets plenty of air. Coarser mulches can be applied 2 to 3 inches deep. Keep the mulch several inches away from rose stems to reduce the chance of fungal diseases developing on the stem. You'll need to add a fresh layer of organic mulch every year or two as the bottom layer decomposes.

ANOTHER WAY TO WAGE WAR ON WEEDS

Keeping weeds out of your rose garden reduces competition for water, nutrients, and sun. Weeds can also harbor certain disease and insect problems that may be transferred to roses. A consistent layer of mulch will keep most weed seeds from germinating. Those weeds that do sprout are easier to pull out because mulch keeps the soil moist and friable. For extra protection you can apply a preemergent herbicide to the soil's surface before mulching.

A preemergent herbicide kills seeds before they germinate. It's most effective when used in early spring.

Even after your initial site preparation the roots of some perennial weeds such as dandelions or thistle may survive. If persistent weeds keep popping up, spot treat them carefully with a nonselective herbicide.

Be sure that the herbicide doesn't drift onto surrounding plants and potentially damage them. Use a cardboard box with the bottom punched out to create a spray box or put a sheet of cardboard or some folded newspaper between the weeds you're spraying and the plants you value.

CALCULATING MULCH QUANTITIES

How much mulch will you need for your garden? If you're buying in bulk, the supplier can usually tell you how much you'll need to cover a specific area to a specific depth. Otherwise, follow this formula:

1 First, calculate the total square feet of the area you want to mulch. This is easy for square or rectangular beds. Just multiply the length and width (example: 25 ft.×10 ft. = 250 square feet).

For round beds, multiply the radius (the distance from the center to the outer edge of the circle) by itself, then multiply by 3.14 (example: [6 ft.× 6 ft.]×3.14 = 113 square feet).

For beds with irregular shapes, measure squares, rectangles, and/or circles that cover the majority of the area and calculate the square feet. Approximate any additional area and add it (example: curved bed that can be measured as a square [10 ft.×10 ft. = 100 sq. ft.] plus a rectangle [6 ft.×12 ft. = 72 sq. ft], plus approximately 15 extra feet for a total of 187 square feet).

2 Multiply the number of square feet in your garden by the depth in inches of mulch you want to apply (example: 187 sq. ft.×3 inches = 561).

3 Divide this number by 324 to find the number of cubic yards of mulch you'll need (example: 561÷324 = 1.73 cubic yards).

Note that one cubic yard (27 cubic feet) of mulch will cover 324 square feet at a depth of 1 inch. It takes about 14 bags (2 cubic feet per bag) to make 1 cubic yard. It takes 9 bags (3 cubic feet per bag) to make 1 cubic yard.

TYPES OF MULCH

Landscape fabric
Porous dark material is ideal in areas where you won't be moving plants or materials around much. It lets water and air into the soil but doesn't allow weeds to grow. Lay it on top of the soil and top with shredded bark or other mulch to disguise it.

Shredded bark mulch
Shredded bark comes in many colors, but dark, nondyed mulch is the most natural-looking. It will break down over time, feeding the soil.

Bark nuggets
Bark nuggets also come in a variety of colors, but again, darker and nondyed is more natural. It breaks down slowly, so it doesn't need to be replenished as often, but it also doesn't feed soil as well.

Gravel
A good choice for drought-loving plants, gravel helps keep crowns (the area where stems meet roots) dry and prevents rot in this susceptible area.

Pine needles
In areas with extensive pine woods, healthy pine needles make an excellent mulch. (Avoid those with obvious blights or disease.) Gather from under your pine trees. Pine needle mulch can also sometimes be found in stores.

Feeding roses

Ask five different roses experts how they fertilize their roses and you'll probably get five different answers. And then ask them that same question the following year and you'll probably have 10 more different answers.

That's because the there's no one perfect way to fertilize roses. Depending on you and your lifestyle, your roses, your climate, and your expectations for how well your roses should perform, you'll constantly be refining how you feed our roses.

Which definitely need it. Roses are heavy feeders. To thrive, roses need 13 elemental nutrients plus oxygen, carbon, and hydrogen from the air. Three major nutrients —nitrogen, phosphorus, and potassium— are essential for leaf and stem growth, root development, and flower production. You'll find one or more of these nutrients in most fertilizers.

Roses get nutrients from minerals in soil and from organic matter in the soil. Adding organic matter before planting and using organic mulch help provide a supply of nutrients. Roses are heavy feeders, though, and for peak performance you'll need to add more nutrients by fertilizing your garden regularly, perhaps as often as every two weeks if you want to be aggressive.

The two most common types of fertilizer are those applied to the soil as dry granules or pellets and those applied to the soil or the foliage in liquid form.

Dry fertilizers

Dry fertilizers may be either quick release or slow release. Granules of quick-release fertilizer are applied to the soil and dissolve quickly when watered in. The nutrients are immediately available to plants but are soon used up or leached away. Quick-release fertilizers must be applied on a regular schedule throughout the growing season to keep a supply of nutrients available.

Slow-release fertilizer consists of coated pellets that slowly release nutrients over an extended period, usually from three to nine months. Slow-release fertilizer is convenient for most rose gardens because it needs to be applied only once or a few times each year. Slow-release fertilizer pellets should be worked lightly into the soil to work properly. High soil temperatures and high levels of rainfall or irrigation may speed up the rate of nutrient release from this type of fertilizer.

Two quality fertilizers to consider are Osmocote Smart-Release Plant Food or Miracle-Gro Continuous Release Rose Plant Food.

Liquid fertilizers

You'll find liquid fertilizers in two forms: liquid concentrate or fine, water-soluble granules. Both types must be diluted in water before applying. Liquid fertilizers can be applied to the soil or sprayed directly on rose foliage, where the nutrients will be readily absorbed. Many liquid fertilizers can be applied with convenient hose-end sprayers. Liquid fertilizers can also be used with drip irrigation systems. Liquid fertilizers are especially useful for newly planted roses, container plantings, and roses that need a quick boost. Liquid fertilizers must be applied frequently, often every week or two, so for large rose

gardens slow-release fertilizers may be more practical and time-saving.

Two quality fertilizers to consider are Miracle-Gro Water Soluble Rose Plant Food or Miracle-Gro LiquaFeed Plant Food.

Organic Fertilizers

Gardeners can also choose from a number of organic fertilizers for roses. Most organic fertilizers come from plant or animal products. They release nutrients slowly as they decompose and have lower nutrient amounts by weight than inorganic fertilizers. Composted manure or manure tea (dry manure steeped in water, then strained) provides nitrogen and other nutrients; amounts vary depending on the source. Other organic fertilizers include alfalfa meal, feather meal, cottonseed meal, blood meal, bone meal, fish meal, greensand, rock phosphate, and liquids such as fish emulsion and seaweed extract.

Whichever fertilizer you use, be sure to follow the directions on the label. The label provides important information about how much fertilizer to apply and what application method to use. Adding too much fertilizer can cause problems for roses. For example, excess nitrogen makes roses produce few flowers but lots of succulent foliage that insects find inviting. Apply the right amount of fertilizer and you'll help your roses develop a healthy root system, sturdy stems, and beautiful blooms.

▶ Roses are heavy feeders and while the shrub roses shown tend to bloom well regardless, they'll bloom even better with larger flowers if they're well-fertilized regularly.

Feeding roses *(continued)*

FOUR WAYS TO FEED ROSES

Most serious rose growers use a variety of feeding methods to make sure their roses are well-nourished throughout the season.

Foliar Feeding
Foliar fertilizer is applied using a hose with a canister attached. The nutrients are absorbed through the plants' leaves. Foliar feeding is popular as a "snack" for roses from early summer onward.

Slow-Release Feeding
Most granular fertilizers are slow-release, and some even have insecticides as part of their formulation. They are quick and easy to use and are applied as seldom as once or twice during the growing season or as often as every six to nine weeks. Check package directions for instructions.

Compost
Compost is a wonderfully complex rose food, but is simple to apply. Just work it into the top inch or two of soil or spread an inch of it on top of the soil around the rose. Unlike chemical formulations, compost causes beneficial microbial and structural changes in the soil.

Liquid Fertilizer
Another easy way to fertilize roses is to add a powder or liquid fertilizer to the water in a watering can and apply it directly to the soil. Again, follow package directions exactly.

FERTILIZING ROSES IN POTS AND OTHER CONTAINERS

Watering and fertilizing go hand in hand when it comes to container plantings. Because they lack the nutrients typically found in mineral soils, soilless mixes require regular fertilizer applications. There are several good ways to provide roses in containers with the nutrients they need. Whatever method you choose, follow label directions. Too little fertilizer can limit the growth and reduce flowering, but too much fertilizer can burn roots or encourage foliar growth at the expense of flowers.

Slow-release fertilizers provide an excellent way to feed container plants. The coated granules of fertilizer slowly exude nutrients over a number of months each time water moves through the potting medium. Look for various formulations that provide from three to nine months of fertilization. Some formulas include systemic pesticides. Many soilless mixes contain only a small amount of starter fertilizer, but you can add a slow release fertilizer such as Osmocote to the mix before planting the container. Better yet, select a potting mix that already contains slow-release fertilizer, such as Miracle-Gro Potting Mix.

Slow-release fertilizers work best when incorporated into the potting mix before planting, but you can also use them on already planted containers. Work the granules into the top several inches of the mix if possible. If fine roots are holding the mix together, use a pencil to poke holes 2 to 3 inches deep across the surface of the potting mix, then distribute the fertilizer so most of it falls into the holes. Water thoroughly to start fertilizer release. Container roses may use up slow-release fertilizers at a faster pace because of frequent watering and higher temperatures.

Liquid fertilizer is another good way to provide nutrients to roses in containers. For a convenient way to provide a steady supply of nutrients, dilute liquid or water-soluble fertilizer, such as Miracle-Gro Water Soluble Rose Plant Food, to an appropriate rate for once-a-week feeding. Then fertilize on the same day of the week through the growing season. Use a 1-gallon watering can for easy fertilizer application. If you have several containers to fertilize, mix the fertilizer solution in larger quantities (5-gallon plastic buckets are convenient), then transfer to a more manageable container to apply.

Dry granular fertilizer is generally a poor choice for smaller containers because of the risk of fertilizer burn if the potting mix dries out. It will work well for most raised beds, though. Work dry fertilizer lightly into the soil's surface, then water it in with a long, slow soak. Reapply the fertilizer as needed through the growing season.

HOW TO READ A FERTILIZER LABEL

Fertilizers are available in many formulations.

If you have several roses, it's worth your while to buy a fertilizer made specifically for roses and follow the package directions exactly.

Some fertilizers contain just one nutrient, such as phosphorus, but those are less useful for roses. Instead, look for a complete fertilizer, one that contains all three of the major nutrients needed by roses and other garden plants. Complete fertilizers contain nitrogen (N), phosphorus (P), and potassium (K).

When you look at a fertilizer label, you'll see three numbers (18-24-16, for example). These numbers indicate the percent of N, P, and K (in that order) contained in the fertilizer. Common formulations for rose fertilizers include 9-18-9 and 18-24-16. Many rose fertilizers contain small amounts of minor nutrients in addition to nitrogen, phosphorus, and potassium.

Choosing pest- and disease-resistant roses

Many people shy away from growing roses, mistakenly thinking that roses require regular applications of pesticides to control insects and diseases. Though some types of roses are high maintenance—notably hybrid teas—not all are prone to pests. After all, people grew roses long before fungicides existed. And the trend in rose breeding for the past two decades has been to develop roses that not only are beautiful but also resist insects and diseases.

With today's wide selection of roses, there's no reason to settle for weak roses with straggly blooms or those that have recurring problems with pests and diseases.

Vigor in roses

In rose gardening the term vigor refers to strength and health. Look for strong, healthy rose plants.

How can you tell if a rose plant is vigorous? Vigor isn't something you can see, though at the nursery the plant must look healthy. You'll need to rely on other methods for determining the potential vigor of the plant. Read the hybridizer's or nursery's description of the plant carefully. If possible, observe the plant as it's growing in a public or private garden. Ask the garden center clerk—or better yet, manager—which roses are the most vigorous. And consult individuals who are experts in the area of rose growing, such as the American Rose Society's consulting rosarians. (Check with local garden clubs to locate a consulting rosarian.)

Your chances of finding vigorous roses are excellent. Hybridizers of today's modern roses strive to produce the most vigorous plants they can.

There may be instances, however, when you purposely choose to grow a less-vigorous rose. Perhaps you remember a rose that your

▲ One of the best ways to avoid disease and pest problems is to choose roses carefully. Read labels at the garden center and ask staff to direct you to the most problem-free roses the center has.

mother or grandmother grew, though it may have been bred in earlier years and is not as vigorous as you would like. Perhaps a particular rose, besides having sentimental value, is an outstanding bloom, or you have one that just happens to grow on a less-than-vigorous bush.

Disease and pest resistance

Though hybridizers strive to produce disease-resistant roses, the genus *Rosa* is susceptible to a variety of pests and diseases.

The best way to avoid these problems is to select the most

pest- and disease-resistant roses you can. (See "Top Roses for Pest and Disease Resistance", opposite.) Roses can vary widely in resistance, with the newer landscape and shrub roses leading the pack.

If you want to find the most pest- and disease-resistant roses in your area, visit a local rose garden in August or early September. Note which cultivars have the fewest spots and nibbles on their leaves. If they still have only minimal problems by late summer, they're resistant.

And, of course, read the label or catalog description carefully. Look for words

such as "easy-care," "carefree," "low-maintenance," and "landscape rose." These are indicators of a tough rose.

But even the most care-free roses aren't perfect. Nearly all roses will have some black spot by summer's end, for example. And east of the Mississippi, most rose gardeners struggle with Japanese beetles. Still, you can minimize even these pests and diseases.

See pages 114–119 for more details on ways to prevent rose pest and disease problems. See pages 113-121 for a listing of rose diseases and pests.

TOP ROSES FOR PEST- AND DISEASE-RESISTANCE

No rose is problem-proof, but these roses come close. They are among the lowest-maintenance roses with the fewest pests and diseases.

Blueberry Hill

Bonica

Carefree Beauty

Carefree Delight

Gemini

Gizmo

Gourmet Popcorn

Iceberg

Ingrid Bergman

The Knock Out series

Meidiland roses, any

Moonstone

New Zealand

Playboy

The Fairy

William Baffin

Choosing low-maintenance roses

Bred to excel in a variety of conditions, low-maintenance roses require little care and will reward you with blooms year after year.

Roses have earned the reputation for being fussy. This is because some roses are susceptible to pests such as Japanese beetles or diseases such as black spot. In addition, some rose varieties are not winter hardy, to the disappointment of gardeners in cold regions.

Many home gardeners lack the time to nurture their roses. That's why rose hybridizers have developed a host of varieties that are low maintenance, beautiful, prolific bloomers that don't need excess attention.

The characteristics of an easy rose

Easy-care roses are popular these days. Here is what to look for in a low-maintenance rose:

● **Disease resistance.** Although no rose is totally immune to diseases in all situations, many roses have been bred to stand up to some common rose ailments. These roses resist black spot and powdery mildew and require no spraying of fungicide to stay healthy and unaffected.

● **Pest-resistance** Many of the new carefree roses are less likely to attract Japanese beetles and aphids, two common rose pests.

● **Winter-hardiness** Low-maintenance roses don't require a lot of extra care to survive cold temperatures. The most cold hardy are those grown on their own roots and are not grafted—such as Knock Out.

● **Long-flowering** Some older rose varieties bloom only once, which can be disappointing to the gardener expecting a season of blooms. Most low-maintenance roses bloom multiple times or continuously all summer.

● **Self-cleaning** These roses require no deadheading (clipping off the dead blossoms) to rebloom. Generally, these roses will not form hips.

Check plant tags for descriptions such as "disease resistant," "pest resistant," and "hardy" for the most low-maintenance varieties.

Low-care doesn't mean no care

Keep in mind that your rose is a living thing with basic needs such as full sun (most roses require at least 6 hours a day), adequate watering, mulching, well-drained soil, and slow-release fertilizer. A healthy rose will require maintenance on your part. Keep your roses in top shape and they will have a better chance to repel whatever challenge comes their way.

▲ Low-maintenance roses allow you to have fairly extensive plantings of roses with minimal work. This garden is planted primarily in Carefree Beauty roses, which are disease- and pest-resistant and cold hardy, practically taking care of themselves.

TOP LOW-MAINTENANCE ROSES

These roses are among the easiest to grow and will reward you year after year.

Abraham Darby
One of the favorite David Austin roses, Abraham Darby is vigorous and black spot resistant. Gorgeous apricot-yellow-pink heavily petaled blooms. Grows 6 feet tall. Zones 4–9.

Bonica
A modern shrub rose with large clusters of clear pink blooms. Bonica grows 3 to 4 feet tall with long, arching canes. It's great for groundcover plantings. Zones 4–9. AARS winner in 1987.

Blanc Double de Coubert
An extremely hardy shrub rose, this rugosa cross features bright white recurrent blooms and dark green, attractively wrinkled foliage. Plants grow 5 to 7 feet tall. Zones 3-9.

Carefree Beauty
A medium pink shrub rose developed by Griffith Buck. Carefree Beauty has flowers that measure 4 inches across with 10 to 20 petals. It grows 4 to 5 feet tall, produces orange-red hips, and takes some shade. Zones 4-10.

Carefree Delight
Elegant single-petal blooms are borne in small clusters on a 3- to 4-foot-tall plant. Takes some shade. Zones 4-10. AARS winner in 1996.

Carefree Wonder
This long-blooming shrub rose has lovely large pink flowers with a white eye. Each bloom has 20 to 25 petals. It grows 3 to 4 feet tall and 2 to 3 feet wide, and can take some shade. Zones 3- 9. AARS winner in 1991.

Country Dancer
Producing deep pink double blooms, this hardy shrub rose emits a light fragrance. Grows 3 to 4 feet tall. Zones 4–9.

Earth Song
This grand grandiflora features deeply perfumed pink flowers with bright yellow stamens. A Griffith Buck rose, it grows 4 to 6 feet tall in Zones 3- 9.

The Flower Carpet series
A hardy and vigorous shrub, the Flower Carpet roses (available in several colors) are excellent choices for groundcovers. They grow 24 to 32 inches tall and spread out to 4 feet. Zones 4 -11.

Frau Dagmar Hartopp
A hardy rugosa cross, this shrub rose has fragrant pink single flowers. Plants grow 4 feet tall and display red rosehips in the fall. Zones 3-9.

Home Run
A relative of Knock Out, Home Run is slightly darker and more compact than its relative—but just as disease resistant. This shrub rose bears dark single petals that surround bright yellow stamens. Zones 4- 9.

The Knock Out series
This shrub rose offers cherry red blooms from May until frost. Resistant to black spot, this rose sets the bar for low-maintenance roses. Light fragrance. Grows 4 feet tall. Zones 4-10.

Meidiland roses
A hardy groundcover rose, this plant features small, perky blooms and glossy foliage. Meidiland landscape roses come in several colors. This rose will form a compact hedge if planted 12 to 18 inches apart. Zones 5-10.

Sun Flare
A lemon yellow floribunda, Sun Flare features blooms with 20 to 30 petals. It emits a light licorice fragrance and grows 3 to 4 feet tall in Zones 5 -10. AARS winner in 1983.

William Baffin
An extremely hardy climbing rose, William Baffin produces semidouble strawberry pink blooms. This tall, upright plant grows 10 to 12 feet tall and produces flowers in clusters—30 blooms per stems. Zones 2-9.

Zephirine Drouhin
An old garden rose with masses of fragrant raspberry pink blooms, this thornless rose is great for cutting. Grows 8 to 12 feet tall. Zones 5-9.

Controlling pests and diseases

True to their reputation, roses can be bothered by a number of disease and insect problems. But not all roses are susceptible to the same problems, and many are highly resistant to common pest problems (see page 111).

The key when selecting roses is to consider how much pest control you're willing to live with. If you want to grow spotless, exhibition-quality hybrid teas, for example, plan on using pesticides on a regular schedule. But if you don't mind a few spotted or chewed leaves on an otherwise-attractive, blooming rose, you may not need to spray at all. There are many garden and landscape roses that require only minimal pest control.

To solve any pest problem you must first identify the culprit. In this chapter, you'll find information on the most common problems.

Other good sources of diagnostic help include your state extension service, local rose societies, and nurseries specializing in roses.

Read the label carefully before using any pesticide; hold off on using any pesticide unless it's labeled for use on roses. Pesticide labels provide vital information on quantity, timing, and method of application, so follow the directions.

Two excellent products include Ortho Orthenex Insect & Disease Control and Ortho RosePride Rose & Shrub Disease Control.

PREVENTING PROBLEMS

Here are tips for preventing most pest problems and coping with those that appear.

● **Select resistant roses.** Shop around for a cultivar that resists common rose diseases such as black spot and powdery mildew. Because cultivars within the same class—such as grandiflora or floribunda—vary in disease resistance, select by specific cultivar, not by class. See page 136 for specific listings.

● **Keep plants healthy.** A vigorously growing rose is significantly less susceptible to insect attack and disease infestations, so plant the rose in a site with full sun, good air movement, and good soil drainage. Water roses regularly during dry periods and fertilize regularly (see page 106).

● **Clean up.** To get rid of pest hiding places, keep garden beds weeded and nearby lawn mowed. Prune out damaged and diseased branches. Pick up rose leaves that fall from the plant so diseases can't winter over.

● **Use chemicals wisely.** Avoid reaching for the bug spray every time you see a hole in your leaves. Roses can put up with a little damage. By the time you notice a hole or a cluster of aphids lining the stem, odds are good that a natural predator has found the pest and started feeding on it. For example, if you see aphids, you're also likely to see ladybugs, which eat them.

● **Know your enemy and your weapons.** If you see an insect, identify it before you do anything. It might be just an innocent bystander or a beneficial bug. Once you identify a true pest, use the appropriate pesticide as indicated on the label.

▲ When insect problems arise, it's important to treat them early before the bugs can do significant damage. It's smart to keep a spray that treats a wide variety of insects on hand so you can apply it the moment you see signs of their presence.

Dealing with rose pests and diseases

Roses are among the most beautiful of garden plants and unfortunately, some are also among the most prone to a host of pests and disease problems.

Although huge advances have been made in breeding roses that are highly disease- and pest-resistant, the flat out fact is that by late summer, there are few roses that aren't showing some signs of pest or disease problems.

In this section, you'll read about the most common roses problems, their signs, their causes, and their treatments.

You'll get out of your roses what you put into them. If you take time to choose the most disease- and pest-resistant (rather than just grab whatever looks pretty on the garden center shelves that day), you will be repaid many times over in roses that look great and demand little.

And if you do fall in love with a rose that isn't particularly low-maintenance, go into it forewarned and ready to give it the care it needs with generous water, fertilizing, spraying, and being on diligent pest control.

Part of that is looking at your roses every day (a nice thing to do with a cup of coffee or cold drink in hand). It's important to spot problems early and act immediately.

If you can't determine the problem with the information in this disease and pest section, snip off a problem portion of the plant and take it into your local garden center. A well-trained garden staff member should be able to diagnose the problem and prescribe the solution.

If a busy schedule or distance is an issue and it might be difficult to get to a garden center within a day of diagnosing a problem, consider keeping on hand a sort of rose first-aid kit: A general-spectrum rose insecticide. That way, when you spot an insect problem, you can deal with it promptly. It might also be smart to keep a fungicide on hand so in early spring you can jump right into preventing black spot.

Fungal problems

In fact, the vast majority of disease problems in roses are fungal diseases (the reason they need plenty of sun and good circulation) with black spot chief among them.

Most fungal diseases affect the foliage, spotting or coating the leaves. Minor infections may mar some foliage but not otherwise affect the health of the rose. However, severe infections may cause leaves to yellow and fall off prematurely, reducing the health and vigor of the rose. Other parts of the rose plant, including flowers and fruit, may also be affected.

High humidity or wet foliage for prolonged periods help fungal infections start and spread. It's impossible to keep foliage dry during wet weather, but you can forestall fungal disease by avoiding overhead watering during dry weather.

Remove diseased plant parts and fallen leaves to further prevent the spread of fungal infection.

Fungicides are another way to prevent fungal diseases. Fungicides act by *preventing* fungal spores from infecting the leaf—they can't cure an already infected plant or reverse existing fungal problems. Fungicides, then, must be applied at the first sign of disease or even before.

Experienced rose gardeners target the roses on which they have observed fungal diseases as an ongoing problem. Then, in late winter or early spring—before temperatures regularly hit 80°F/26°C in their part of the country—they try to work in two or three fungicide spraying sessions.

With most fungicides, repeat applications every 7 to 10 days are recommended, so gardeners try to start spraying three to four weeks before temperatures are expected to get that warm.

Black spot

Black spot is an extremely common fungal disease. By late summer, most roses have at least a little black spot. Susceptible roses may be riddled with it.

Black spot infects rose foliage, causing dark, rounded fungal spots with feathered margins. Severely infected foliage yellows and drops off prematurely. When rose plants are defoliated by black spot infections the plants lose vigor and flowering is often greatly reduced. Black spot is most noticeable on rose foliage but it can also mar stems, flower petals, and fruit. Spores overwinter on fallen leaves and infected rose stems.

To infect rose foliage, black spot fungal spores must stay wet for about seven hours. A rainy day or wet foliage overnight readily allows infections to start. Black spot can occur in rose gardens anywhere in the country but it's most severe in regions with higher rainfall, including the East, Southeast, and Northwest.

If you want very clean rose foliage you may need a regular fungicide spray schedule, especially if you grow black spot susceptible roses or live in a wet region. Better yet select from the ever-increasing number of roses that have good to excellent resistance to black spot.

Crown gall

Crown gall is easy to diagnose. It appears as a large, corky growth up to several inches in diameter at the base of the plant (the crown) and on stems and roots. Galls seldom kill a rose.

When several galls are on a plant, the overall plant will appear weak and sickly, with slowed growth and yellowing leaves. Entire branches may die back. Plants with only a few smaller galls, however, may not be otherwise affected.

Caused by a bacterium in the soil (which can survive on its own for up to three years), crown gall can affect other plants in the garden and be spread to or from them. It cannot be eliminated from a plant, but to improve the rose's appearance, prune out and dispose of galled stems. Disinfect pruning shears with rubbing alcohol or diluted chlorine bleach after each cut.

Dealing with rose pests and diseases *(continued)*

Downy mildew

Downy mildew is a fungal disease that can cause significant defoliation of roses. Downy mildew appears as dark, angular purple or brown blotches defined by leaf veins on the upper surface of the leaf. Sometimes small white powdery patches can be seen on the underside of the leaf, opposite the blotches. Infected leaves may turn yellow and often drop quickly after the infection appears. Severe defoliation can weaken rose bushes. Downy mildew can also infect the stems of roses.

Downy mildew develops under high humidity (over 85 percent) and cool temperatures. This disease is most prevalent in spring in moist coastal regions of California and the Pacific Northwest.

Powdery mildew

Powdery mildew is a common fungal disease that primarily affects rose foliage. Young stems and flowers may also be affected. This fungal disease appears as powdery white or light gray patches on the leaves. New growth is susceptible to powdery mildew, and severe infections can cause young leaves to distort and twist.

Powdery mildew infections occur during periods of moderate daytime temperatures (65°F/18°C to 80°F/26°C), cooler night temperatures, and high humidity. Powdery mildew fungi do not require constantly wet foliage to develop. Infection is more common on roses that are in too much shade.

You may see powdery mildew on other garden plants such as phlox, zinnias, and lilacs. They are not to blame for the powdery mildew on your roses, though. Though the diseases look similar, each is a plant-specific species of the fungus. The powdery mildew on your lilac is not the same powdery mildew that infects your roses.

Rust

Rust is a fungal disease that shows up as bright orange spore masses on the undersides of rose leaves starting with the lower branches. On the opposite side (upper leaf surface) of the rust mass there's often a yellowish spot. Severely infected foliage may twist or curl, turn brown, and fall off. This can lead to reduced vigor in the plant. Rust can also infect stems. Rust spores overwinter on fallen leaves.

Rust infections occur most often in cooler weather (65°F/18°C to 70°F/21°C) and require wet conditions for two to four hours to infect foliage. Rust is most prevalent in rose gardens along the West Coast, but it can occur on susceptible roses anywhere if the conditions are right.

Stem canker

Stem cankers appear as yellowish, reddish, or brown sunken areas on the cane. They may have a purple margin or be cracked. Leaves on the cane may be spotted, yellow, or wilting. Stems may die back.

Stem canker occurs during wet or humid weather when fungi enter the plant at a wound in the cane or a cut. Roses that are already stressed with a black spot infection or are in otherwise weakened condition are more susceptible to this disease.

To treat, cut off and dispose of cankered canes at least 5 inches below the infected area. Otherwise, treat as you would other fungal diseases.

Viral diseases

Most of the common rose diseases are caused by fungi, but several viruses also affect roses. Rose virus diseases typically result in odd color patterns on the leaves. Common patterns include mottled yellowing, yellow zigzags through the leaf, and vein clearing.

Some roses are able to live with a virus disease and show no obvious decline in health. However, in some roses viral diseases can lead to poor growth and overall lack of vigor.

Viral diseases in many plants are transferred from plant to plant by sucking insects such as leafhoppers. Fortunately, common rose viral diseases are not spread this way. Rose virus diseases are spread when infected plants are used for budding or grafting. When shopping for roses, look for virus symptoms on foliage. Avoid rose plants that look questionable. If you notice viral symptoms on a rose that's already planted in your garden, you can remove it immediately or wait to see if the plant remains healthy.

Insect problems

Insects and their relatives are a fascinating, diverse, and sometimes frustrating group of garden dwellers. The majority of insects in your garden are beneficial or do no harm. Beneficial insects prey on damaging insects and can be helpful in reducing pest populations. For example, lady beetles, adults and larvae, voraciously devour aphids on many plants, including roses. Other beneficial insects include lacewings, praying mantises, and predatory wasps.

Only a small percentage of insects cause damage to roses, so you need to be aware that in dealing with problem pests, you may also harm beneficial insects.

There are several ways to deal with problem. Once you see a pest, monitor your roses to see if the insect population is increasing or is causing more damage. You can often stop minor insect infestations with simple treatments such as daily blasts with a stream of water or handpicking individual insects. Cultural practices, including cleaning up fallen leaves and pruning out infested stems, can limit insect problems.

Severe infestations may require treatment with an insecticide. Lower-impact products such as insecticidal soap and neem oil are effective on a number of insect pests. Broad-spectrum insecticides kill a range of insects. Use these chemicals on a limited basis and only when needed because they kill beneficial insects as well as the pests. Always read and follow insecticide label directions.

Consider using Ortho Orthenix Insect & Disease Control or Ortho RosePride Rose & Shrub Disease Control.

Aphids

Aphids are small, soft-bodied insects that use piercing mouthparts to suck fluids from leaves, stem tips, and flower buds of roses. They multiply rapidly and appear in large numbers, sometimes completely covering buds or stem sections. Severe infestations can ruin flowers and cause curling and browning of foliage. Aphids also excrete a sticky substance called honeydew that attracts ants and may become covered with sooty mold, a black fungus that mars rose foliage.

Small numbers of aphids won't cause serious damage to roses. Beneficial insects such as lady beetles often clean up small aphid infestations and keep numbers in check. You can knock aphids off roses by blasting them with a stream of water from a hose (a few of the aphids will make it back to the plant). Do this once or twice a day until the aphid population is reduced. For heavy infestations treat with insecticidal soap or an insecticide and repeat if necessary.

Borers

Borers become apparent when several or all of a rose's larger canes wilt and die. If the dying stems are sliced open, they reveal white to yellowish worms or grubs up to ¾-inch long. Affected stems may be swollen at the base.

Many kinds of insects bore into rose stems. Some prefer weakened plants but some others attack healthy plants as well.

To treat a borer problem, cut out and dispose of infested rose stems, making the cut several inches below the point where the stem is wilted or swollen.

Caterpillars

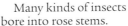

Caterpillars can be spotted on plants, often at night. They leave behind round or irregular holes in the leaves and buds of roses and may chew off entire leaves or buds.

To treat, spray infested plants with insecticide (one that specifies caterpillars) or use Bacillus thuringiensis (Bt). If you find more caterpillars or spot fresh damage, spray again seven or more days later or according to package directions. Repeat as specified on package.

Dealing with rose pests and diseases *(continued)*

Japanese beetles

With their flashy dark green and copper coloring, Japanese beetles are rather attractive. Their damage is less attractive, though. Japanese beetles eat the foliage of many ornamental plants, and roses are a favorite. They often skeletonize leaves, eating everything except the thicker leaf midrib and veins. They also damage buds and flowers.

Japanese beetles do not occur in all states but they are widely distributed in the eastern U.S. and in scattered areas in other regions. They continue to spread to new areas.

Japanese beetles can be treated in their larval stage (a white grub that damages lawns) or as adults. Several biological controls including a bacterium and beneficial nematodes (tiny wormlike soil dwellers) can be used on Japanese beetle larvae. You can handpick adult beetles and drop them into a bucket of soapy water to kill them. Treat severe infestations with insecticides if necessary. Several other beetles infest roses, but they are red, green-spotted, or brownish. Treatment is the same as for Japanese beetles.

Leaf rollers

Leaf rollers appear as tightly rolled leaves tied together with webbing. The leaves may also be chewed, and the plant may be dropping many leaves. When the rolled leaf is opened, a green caterpillar is inside, surrounded by silky webbing. Flower buds may also be chewed.

Treat by applying an insecticide, preferably one that specifies leaf rollers, or Bacillus thuringiensis (Bt) as soon as you notice damage from the feeding larvae—before the leaf rolling stage occurs, if possible.

Rose midges

Rose midges are tiny, inconspicuous flies that lay eggs on the flower buds, stem tips, and new foliage of roses. When the eggs hatch, the midge larvae start feeding on the rose tissues. This feeding causes distortion and darkening of the buds and other affected tissues. Severe infestations can kill many stem tips and flower buds.

Rose midges are most prevalent in the Southeast and Southwest and on the West Coast. Where they occur, rose midges are active in mid- to late summer. Prune out and destroy infested stem tips and flower buds. When adult midges or larvae are present, spray with an insecticide labeled for rose midges, repeating if necessary.

Leafhoppers

Leafhoppers are whitish insects, up to 1/2-inch long, that appear in late spring or summer and hop and fly away quickly when the plant is touched. Leaves are stippled white, usually starting in the spring. Severely infested plants may die.

Treat leafhoppers with a spray-type insect killer (one that specifies leafhoppers) as soon as you notice the damage. Be sure to cover the undersides of the leaves, where young leafhoppers like to settle.

Leafhoppers produce two generations a year, so consider treating the plant a second time in fall, especially if stippling (a sign that young leafhoppers are actively sucking on the underside of the leaves) occurs again at that time.

Rose slugs

Rose slugs make themselves apparent by leaving behind leaves that are eaten between the veins. The lacy, translucent layer of tissue that remains turns brown. Later other portions of the leaf, except for the main vein, may be chewed. Green sluglike worms up to ¾ inch long with brown heads may be found feeding on the leaves.

If there is little damage and you can spot the rose slugs, simply pick them off by hand and dispose of them. For more severe infestations, spray with an insecticide containing acephate or carbaryl as soon as you notice damage. Repeat as directed on the package if fresh damage occurs or you spot more pests.

Scale

Scale appears as white, cottony masses or brown or black crusty bumps or somewhat flattened white, yellowish, or brown scaly bumps cover stems and leaves. They can be scraped off. In some cases, a shiny, sticky substance coats leaves and a black, sooty mold may also grow on the sticky substance.

Scale is caused by young scale insects that feed on the plant and develop a shell over their body. Scale must be controlled before the hardened shells develop, so try to treat at the first sign of scale insects. They appear in spring as small (¹⁄₁₀-inch) and soft-bodied insects.

Prevent infestations (especially important once scale has occurred) by spraying roses with a horticultural oil in late winter or early spring.

Spider mites

Spider mites are arachnids, closely related to spiders, but like insects they can be serious garden pests. Spider mites pierce cells on the undersides of leaves and suck out fluids. This results in yellow stippling on the leaf's surface. Severely infested leaves may turn bronze and dry up. Spider mite infestations often start on new foliage but can spread over the entire plant. Another sign of spider mite infestation is the appearance of fine webbing, especially at leaf axils. Hot, dry weather favors spider mite population explosions.

Spider mites are minute and barely visible with the naked eye. If you suspect the presence of spider mites, hold a sheet of white paper under a leaf, tap the leaf sharply several times, then look at the sheet of paper. Spider mites look like bits of finely ground pepper moving across the sheet.

Spraying the undersides of rose leaves with a blast of water daily may reduce spider mite populations. You may also use insecticidal soap, neem oil, or an insecticide. Treating dormant roses with dormant oil may smother overwintering spider mite eggs.

Thrips

Thrips are tiny insects that use rasping mouth parts to feed on plant fluids. Thrips are especially damaging to rosebuds and flowers. Severe thrip infestations may deform buds or cause failure to open. Thrip damage on open flowers appears as brown streaks or spots on petals. Thrips also damage foliage, especially tender new growth.

Thrips feed on many plants including grasses. They tend to move from nearby plants to roses, which can make them hard to catch in action. Like aphids, thrips multiply rapidly, and large populations can build quickly. Monitor your roses frequently for any sign of thrip damage. You can see thrips more clearly if you collect a damaged flower and shake it over a sheet of white paper. Thrips will appear as tiny yellow-brown flecks moving across the paper.

Because thrips hide within buds and flower petals, they are hard to treat. Keep areas in and around your roses clear of weeds and tall grasses to reduce alternate thrip feeding sites. Prune off and destroy thrip-infested flowers and buds. Severe infestations can be treated by spraying with an insecticide labeled as a thrip control; repeat at intervals specified on the packaging as necessary.

Coping with deer, rabbits, and more

Few situations are more frustrating in rose gardening than to wake up in the morning and find plants stripped by rabbits, deer, or other wildlife.

A number of mammals can damage roses in gardens and landscapes. From deer to mice, these garden visitors are not always welcome.

Deer

Despite the sharp thorns on roses, deer love to nibble rose plants. During the winter they will eat stems and bark; during the growing season they add flower buds and foliage to the menu. Deer bites leave jagged or torn ends on stems.

Deer are common in rural, suburban, and even urban areas throughout most of the United States. Damage from deer feeding can vary greatly depending on weather conditions and population pressure. The only way to completely exclude deer is to install an electrified or very tall (6-8 foot) fence, which is not a practical solution for most homeowners. Repellent sprays may be effective if

ARS ROSARIAN TIP...
Deer can be a big problem for rose gardeners; they'll even eat roses armed with plenty of thorns. Some gardeners say they have success with deer repellents, but the surest way to keep deer out of your garden is to put a tall (at least 6 foot) fence around it, and climbing roses look great on fences.

—John Mattia, Orange, Connecticut

reapplied regularly. However, if deer are hungry enough they may eat any plant, with or without repellent.

If deer are a problem in your area, try planting your roses as close to the house as possible—10 feet away rather than 30 or 40 feet. The lights and sounds of people tend to scare deer away and few are bold enough to come right up to windows or higher-traffic areas of the yard.

Another solution is to cover roses with sturdy netting or chicken wire draped and weighted over a frame of some sort. The netting must be fairly taut and not touch the roses, or

▲ One way to deal with larger burrowing animals is to wrap the rose in chicken wire. The mesh is large enough for rose roots to grow through but too small for larger animals to work through.

the deer may nibble right through the netting. This method is best, of course, for protecting roses in small spaces. It also is more practical in the winter and early spring when you're not in the garden and don't have

to look at the rigging.

Home remedies, such as hanging bars of soap from plants, and commercially available deer repellents have not been definitively proved to work.

▲ It is possible to have an attractive garden that also keeps out unwanted visitors. This garden has fencing high enough to keep out deer. To repel rabbits, the base must be outfitted with chicken wire or other tightly meshed wire about 1 foot up and about 4 inches into the soil to prevent burrowing.

▲ Even in urban environments deer can be a problem, especially when a wooded area is nearby. This fence is highly decorative but also tall enough to deter all but the most determined deer. They're less likely still to jump the fence if you also have dense plantings on either side of the fence to make getting a start difficult.

Rabbits

Rabbits tend to be most damaging during winter when they may clip off entire stems or chew off bark at stem bases. Rabbit bites leave clean, slanted ends on stems.

To prevent winter rabbit damage, encircle roses with chicken wire or small-mesh fencing supported with stakes in late fall. If you have a whole bed of roses, encircle the bed (wood raised beds make this especially easy). Bury the lower few inches of fencing in the ground to deter burrowing. Repellent sprays may be effective if reapplied regularly.

Home remedies, such as spreading human or pet hair around plants, and commercially available rabbit repellants have not been definitively proved to work.

Other animals

Small burrowing animals like gophers and moles are not usually major pests of roses, but they can make a mess with soil piles and raised ridges in lawns and gardens. Burrowing may disrupt rose roots. The best way to reduce mole or gopher populations is by trapping.

The larger problem occurs when mice and voles use existing burrows for overwintering. Mice and voles can seriously damage roses by destroying roots and chewing rose stems during the winter. If mice or voles chew around the entire stem, the stem will die. Severe damage to roots can also kill roses.

Keep potential wintering sites such as brush piles and firewood stacks at a distance from your rose garden. Trapping mice and voles in the fall may reduce their populations. Protect rose stems from rodent girdling over winter with a cylinder of wire-mesh hardware cloth.

If larger burrowing animals are a continual problem, consider planting roses in cages made from chicken wire. Use a mesh large enough that feeder roots can extend out beyond the wire.

Understanding pruning

What is it about the word "pruning" that intimidates even experienced gardeners? Perhaps it's the fear of accidentally doing permanent damage. But correct rose pruning is hardly a secret.

Once you understand the reasons for pruning and a few basics about how roses grow, and how you can guide that growth, you're ready.

Remember, too, that this isn't rocket science. There's wiggle room for mistakes because roses are forgiving. The worst that can happen is that the rose won't bloom to its full potential one year or might look a little awkward. In either case, the rose will grow back and you'll gain experience. And next year you can prune it again, doing a better, wiser job.

Why prune?

Understanding what pruning does takes a lot of mystery out of the process.
- To get rid of stems and canes that make the plant ugly—those that are dead, damaged, or diseased; grow from below the bud union of grafted roses; or are too thin to bear flowers.
- To remove old canes—the thick, woody ones—from the base of the plant to make room for younger growth that produces more flowers.
- To stimulate the plant to produce more side branches—called laterals—to make more places for flowers to develop.
- To encourage stems to grow outward, opening the center to sunlight and air.
- To keep the plant from getting too big for your tastes or your garden.

When to prune

For roses that bloom on new wood (the vast majority of roses), do major pruning in early spring, when buds on the roses are just beginning to plump up and turn pink.

In frost-free climates where roses don't go dormant, prune in late fall or early winter, right before cool weather and winter rains push growth.

Keep an eye on the forsythia bushes if any are nearby—when they start to bloom, it's time to prune roses. If you live where winters are so cold that you bury or cover roses, prune after the risk of a hard freeze has passed and you've uncovered the plants.

▲ Roses, especially climbers, do best with a good pruning each spring to keep them in hand and encourage bigger, more bountiful blooms.

OLD WOOD, NEW WOOD

Roses that bear flowers on shoots they produce the same year are said to bloom on new wood. Some roses don't bloom on new growth; instead they bloom on stems they produced the previous year, called old wood. If you don't know which kind you have, leave the rose alone for a year to observe it. Roses that bloom on old wood bloom earlier than those that bloom on new wood.

TIPS FOR BETTER PRUNING

Pruning is part art, part science. Here's how to get the best results possible.
- Cut yourself some slack. The first pruning roses you do may be difficult, but as you gain experience and an eye, you'll quickly figure out how to do it well and in record time.
- Take your time. Make a few cuts; then stand back and consider your work. Then make a few more and walk around the bush to look at it from all angles. Take a break and work on something else, then go back after a few more minutes. This is a great job to do with a cup of coffee or cold drink in hand!
- Recognize that each plant is different. Few rose bushes look as neat and tidy as those in garden books. Different plants, like different people, have quirks and twists and oddities. Work around them as best you can.
- It's a good idea to sterilize your pruning shears between bushes to prevent the spread of diseases. Dip them in a large bowl filled with water and a few tablespoons of chlorine bleach. Or spray them with rubbing alcohol. In either case, wipe off the shears after dousing.
- Miniatures are easy to prune but take special consideration because they're grown on their own rootstock; there's no graft union or suckers. Precise pruning of miniature roses is labor intensive, and if you want to undertake it, use floral snippers for this delicate job.

Otherwise use a hedge clipper or hand shears to cut the whole bush to about 1 foot above ground level. Then remove any twiggy growth and open up the center of the plant somewhat to increase air circulation.
- Dispose of rose canes carefully. Avoid putting them in the compost heap; if they contain rose disease it may spread the problem—and the thorns in the pile are bothersome as well. Create a separate brush pile for rose trimmings, or dispose of them through your waste-management service.

HOW TO PRUNE A ROSE BUSH

The following is the ideal way to prune a rose bush. In real life, of course, things can be different.

In cold regions, for example, much of the bush might be winter-killed so there are few decisions to make—just cut out the dead stuff and hope the remaining live wood does well.

But as much as the bush you're working with allows you, following these steps.

1 Remove any dead or damaged wood. This wood is not only unattractive but it's also a magnet for pests and disease.

2 Cut off any suckers growing up from the root. If the rose is grafted (see page 97), the new growth will not be the same as the rest of the rose bush and will likely be much inferior.

3 Remove any spindly or very old growth. Thin canes, those more slender than a pencil, aren't vigorous enough to support tip-top growth. Very thick, old, woody canes also aren't as vigorous.

4 Cut out canes that are rubbing or close to it. Rubbing canes can create ideal entry points for pests and diseases.

5 Trim remaining canes. Trim the remaining canes, the ones you want to keep, making a 45-degree cut above an outward facing bud (see page 124). This will direct growth outward for a healthy, attractive shape.

How long you cut the canes depends on how much of the wood is live (see page 124). It also depends on how tall you want the bush to grow. Cut it just several inches tall and you'll have a shorter, tidier bush. Cut it 2 or 3 feet tall and you'll havea larger, more sprawling bush.

And the type of bush also dictates the length of the final canes. Shorter, shrubbier bushes that have the capacity to hit 4 feet tops are happiest when trimmed to a foot or so. But tall roses that can hit 8 feet may be most abundant when pruned to 2 or 3 feet tall.

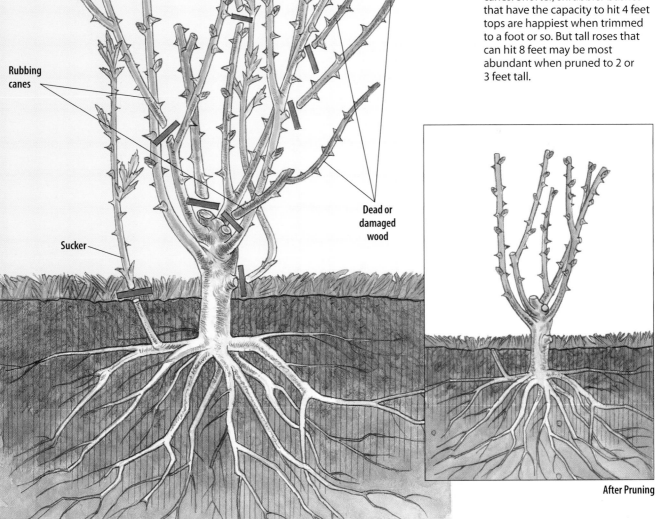

Rubbing canes

Sucker

Dead or damaged wood

Before Pruning

After Pruning

Understanding pruning *(continued)*

MAKING THE CUT

One of the most important principles of pruning roses is making a 45-degree cut just above an outward facing bud.

The ideal shape rose bush has an open center and the canes branch out fairly evenly from the base of the rose. By making a cut right above an outward-facing bud, you direct new growth upward and outward. If you were to make a cut right above a bud that was on the side of the cane facing the center, you would direct growth inward, creating a tangled mess.

The cut should be at a 45-degree angle, sloping inward, to allow water to shed off the cut well and promote fast, healthy healing.

The cut should be right above the bud, as shown. Make it too high and you'll create a dead stump that invites pest and disease. Make it too close and you'll damage the bud.

It can be a little tricky to determine exactly where the buds are, especially early in the season when they're first emerging. (In frost-free regions, of course, roses never go dormant so this isn't an issue.) Buds usually are tiny white or red bumps at first, often not much bigger than a pinhead. As temperatures warm, they emerge as larger, ovoid buds, usually red. After another week or two, they start sending out green or red leaves, as shown in this illustration.

The ideal time to prune, then, is once the bush has a healthy crop of new buds. (Roses tend to develop new buds most vigorously at their base and develop buds later at the tips.) Don't prune too early or it will be difficult to tell where the buds are. And don't let the bush leaf out or you'll allow it to waste a lot of energy on producing new growth that you're only going to cut off.

IS IT DEAD OR ALIVE?

When pruning roses in spring, it may be difficult to tell whether a cane (branch or stem) is dead or alive, or how much of it is dead and how much is alive.

Cut into the tip of the wood. If it looks shriveled and dark, has no growth on it, has an extremely pithy, corky core (below right),

and snaps easily, it's probably dead.

Continue to cut down the stem to see whether you can find live wood, which bends easily and has a firm, white core (left). Some canes, however, may be completely dead, in which case you should remove the entire cane.

Live wood

Dead wood

▲ With a rose garden this extensive, it's critical to prune each plant well in the spring (or in the fall in warm-climate areas) to assure minimal pest and disease problems as the season progresses.

POST-PRUNING CARE

After a severe pruning, roses will thrive with a little pampering.

● Remove debris and weeds from rose beds. This will reduce the potential for insects and fungal diseases to take off. As with all rose plant parts, keep them out of the compost bin. Instead, bag them or create a special rose brush pile in an isolated portion of the landscape.

● Hold off feeding roses for about three or four weeks after pruning. At that time, apply a balanced granular rose food (see page 106) around the base of the plant.

● If you prune early enough in the season, you can apply some pest and disease prevention. As long as there are no bud eyes—the bumps that will eventually turn into new canes and branches—apply a dormant pesticide or fungicide spray immediately after pruning.

● Applying lipstick, petroleum jelly, or fingernail polish to cuts to prevent disease is a myth. The rose should heal fine on its own.

● Immediately after pruning is a good time to lay down fresh mulch, as needed. Roses thrive with 1 to 2 inches of mulch (see page 104), and it will break down over time. Mulch is especially useful during the rainy season of spring because it prevents disease organisms in the soil from splashing onto the plants.

● Fix or replace labels. Rosarians love to keep their roses labeled so they can always remember which is which. But labels fade and disintegrate over time, especially after a rough winter.

Pruning basics: How to prune climbers

Climbing roses look especially romantic when they scale trellises and arch over arbors. Three rose types are considered climbers:

Ramblers are the wildest looking of the climbing roses, forming tangled mats if left to spread on the ground or growing tall enough to cover a cottage if trained upward. They bloom once, in midsummer, on branches that grew the previous season. The flowers are small and form clusters. Their branches are flexible and especially thorny. They train easily over buildings, into trees, and up fences. Dorothy Perkins is the best known of the ramblers.

Large-flowered repeat climbers are less rampant than ramblers. As the name implies, they have large flowers that are either single or in clusters. They bloom in spring and again later in the season. Depending on the variety, they grow to about 10 feet tall. Their stems are more rigid than those of the ramblers but pliable enough to train to a trellis.

Hybrid tea climbers are related to bush hybrid teas. Their canes reach 8 feet long, give or take a couple of feet. They bear flowers on short lateral branches off the canes.

Because the terms are sometimes used interchangeably, and thanks to centuries of rose hybridizing, it can be hard to know which kind of climber you have. If you know what variety you have, you can look up how to prune it. If not, take your best guess based on when and how often it blooms. The worst that can happen is that you'll cut off some flowering wood.

Pruning large-flowering climbers

Pruning large-flowering climbers is surprisingly instinctive because you prune out growth that is going in odd directions or that is obviously too old and woody to flower well. The following is a year-by-year breakdown.

Year 1. Immediately after planting, prune only dead and diseased branches.

Year 2. Before growth starts in spring, choose three to five of the strongest canes to keep, and cut out all the rest. Then cut the remaining ones to about 3 feet tall to encourage side shoots—also called lateral branches. By the end of the season those lateral branches will have grown several feet long.

Year 3. Before spring growth starts, cut back the main canes and lateral branches. How much you cut depends on how you want to control the size. Some gardeners cut back to about 3 feet tall; others cut off 6 to 12 inches.

In addition, apply the usual rules about cutting out branches that are crossing inward, rubbing together, dead, diseased, or spindly.

Year 4 and after. Cut out old woody canes at the base to make room for new growth that flowers more vigorously. Cut back canes and remaining lateral branches as you did in Year 3. Again, cut out any crossed, dead, diseased, or spindly branches.

When you're unsure

If you inherit a neglected climbing rose when you move to a new home, and you're not sure what type the rose is, you can wait until late winter to prune or you can prune it right away (except in extreme heat or cold) if you're willing possibly to lose some bloom for that season.

Either way, first use a long-handled branch pruner to cut the oldest, most woody canes at the base. Loppers also come in handy for tugging those newly cut canes out of the tangle of branches from a safe distance. Next cut out dead, diseased, spindly, and crossed branches. Step back to assess the plant's shape and size. If it looks good, you're done. Otherwise, cut the canes and laterals back to the length you like.

▲ Vigorous roses like this climber are really too large to do much more than trim dead or damaged wood and cut back for size and to thin.

▲ These two climbing roses fit a tight space perfectly with a good hard pruning each spring to keep them in check and to encourage a heavy show of flowers.

HOW TO PRUNE HYBRID TEAS AND OTHER REPEAT-BLOOMING CLIMBERS

Once the canes reach their full height, bend them sideways so they are parallel to the ground and tie them to a trellis or other support. This step stimulates the canes to produce lateral branches (which are, essentially, side shoots.)

Then in late winter or very early spring, when the rose is dormant, cut the laterals to about 6 inches. Climbing hybrid teas seldom produce new canes from the base. Instead of cutting old canes off at the ground—as you'd do on a large-flowered climber—cut them back to the lowest lateral branch.

Also remove any suckers that may have developed.

HOW TO PRUNE RAMBLERS AND ONCE-BLOOMING CLIMBERS

You have two options for pruning ramblers. The easiest is to cut them back to about a foot tall after they finish blooming. The alternative is to cut back the main canes, tie them to a support, then trim their side shoots—called laterals or lateral branches—to about 6 inches long.

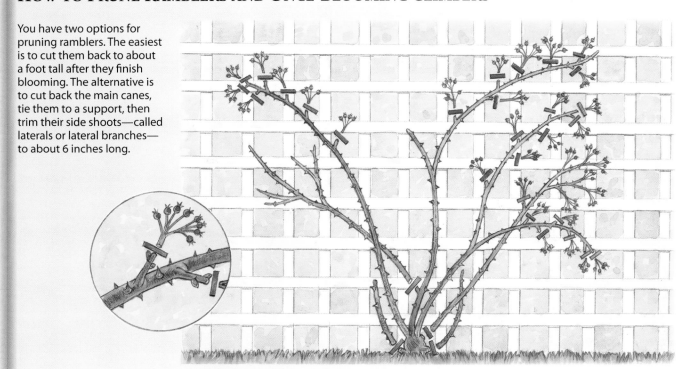

Top tools for pruning roses

Whether you grow manicured hybrid tea roses that need frequent pruning or landscape shrub roses that need only a light annual touch-up, good pruning equipment makes the job easier. No matter how many roses you grow, it's worth investing in high-quality tools that will last and give you pleasure for many years.

Hand shears

You'll reach most often for the hand shears. Pruning shears are for cutting stems up to $\frac{1}{2}$ or even $\frac{3}{4}$ inch in diameter. Choose bypass shears, because this style has a curved blade that slides past a hooked metal plate to make a clean, close cut. Bypass shears are preferable to anvil shears, which crush stems. High-quality bypass shears have removable blades that can be sharpened or replaced. They're available in right-handed and left-handed models. You'll also find models for small hands and ergonomic models for those who do a lot of pruning.

Always clean and sharpen the blade before the first pruning of the season and touch it up a few times if you use it often through the year.

Loppers

To cut larger stems, use lopping shears. Good loppers have bypass blades similar to pruning shears but are larger and heavier. Lopping shears have two long handles, which provide greater leverage. The long handles also make it easier to reach into thorny rose bushes without getting scratched. Most loppers cut stems up to $1\frac{1}{2}$ to $1\frac{3}{4}$ inches in diameter.

Pruning saw

To cut stems greater than $1\frac{3}{4}$ inches in diameter, use a small pruning saw. Folding models with narrow, curved blades 6 to 8 inches long are handy. These pruning saws have sharp, coarse teeth that quickly cut through woody stems.

Rose gloves

Good leather gloves are also essential for pruning roses. Look for special rose gloves with long cuffs that protect forearms as well as hands.

Sharpening stone

A sharpening stone will keep your cutting tools sharp for years to come. Stroke the cutting edge of a tool with the stone held at a 45-degree angle, repeatedly going back and forth. (If you're unsure how to do this, have a knowledgeable clerk show you.) Sharpen cutting tools every few uses.

▲ Rose gardening doesn't require a lot of tools, but if you have the basics, it will make the job much easier and more enjoyable.

Grooming your roses

Once your roses are planted and blooming, they'll need a little primping and grooming to look their best.

Trimming spent blooms—deadheading—and disbudding flowers are enjoyable for many rose gardeners. They are pleasant tasks to do first thing in the morning or last thing at sunset to relax.

During the growing season, try to get out into your garden for just a few minutes a day to perform these tasks. Many gardeners groom their roses during their daily stroll through the garden, checking on the progress and problems occurring in their landscape.

Deadheading

Deadheading is the practice of removing spent flowers. This is a simple but important task since it encourages greater flower production in roses while tidying the plant and reducing petal litter. Deadheading is particularly important for garden roses such as hybrid teas that continuously bloom on new growth. Deadheading also improves flowering in many landscape roses, but it can be difficult to accomplish in mass plantings of shrub roses, for example. If you grow roses that have colorful hips, including many species and shrub roses, you can stop deadheading them in mid- to late summer to ensure an autumn fruit display.

To deadhead most roses, use clean, sharp pruning shears and cut the stem at a 45-degree angle below the faded flower or flower cluster at the point just above the first five-leaflet leaf. This encourages a new flowering stem to grow out from that leaf axil.

When deadheading repeat-blooming climbing roses, you'll do a little extra pruning at the same time. As soon as climbers' flowers fade, cut back the secondary stems that held the flowers to a point that will leave two five-leaflet leaves remaining on that stem. New flowering stems will grow from those leaf axils, soon providing another display of flowers. For climbing roses that bloom only once, prune out the oldest canes when they finish flowering.

Disbudding

Disbudding is a pruning technique that maximizes flower size or, for cluster bloomers, makes an evenly blooming spray of roses. This technique is used for producing specimen quality roses for exhibits and competitions. Even if you don't plan to enter a contest, you may want to try disbudding a few of your roses. The resulting cut flowers will look great in arrangements, whether for a special occasion or just for the family dinner table.

To produce a single, large, exquisite rose bloom, remove all buds on a stem except the terminal bud at the stem tip. This allows all the stem's energy to go toward that one bud. This type of disbudding is used primarily for hybrid teas and grandifloras. To disbud, watch for small, secondary buds to develop in leaf axils below the main terminal bud. Carefully remove the tiny buds as soon as you see them by nipping them out with your fingertips or using a small tool like a knifepoint. By removing the side buds early you'll avoid leaving scars on the stem (rose judges mark down for scars at competitions).

Roses that naturally bloom in sprays, such as floribundas and climbers, can be disbudded in a different way.

The central bud in a spray opens before the other buds, so if that central bud is removed, the whole spray will bloom at the same time.

> **ARS ROSARIAN TIP...**
>
> During a rose's first year, deadhead the flowers as usual but do not prune hard. Newly planted bushes need all their leaves to help them develop healthy, vigorous root systems.
>
> —*Rose Gilardi,*
> *San Francisco, California*

HOW TO DEADHEAD ROSES

When deadheading a single rose, go down to the first leaf that has five leaflets on it and make the cut. Make sure the leaf faces outward so new growth is directed outward away from the center of the bush.

In clusters of roses, one or two blooms often fade before the others. Snip them out.

When an entire cluster has faded, trim off the entire cluster. Again, try to make the cut above the first leaf with five leaflets and make sure it's one that faces outward away from the center of the bush.

Spring pruning and cleanup

In most areas of the country, spring is the time roses awake from dormancy. Follow these guidelines to help get them off to a good start.

Removing winter protection

In late winter or early spring, start gradually removing any winter protection.

Look for any small red leaf buds the rose starts sending out. As soon as these start to swell, remove any burlap or other covering from the rose. Poor air circulation may encourage fungal diseases.

A week or two later, push away any mounding at the base of the plant. This can be done with a gloved hand or with a trowel to get in among thorny canes.

While you're at it, do a little rose cleanup. Rose bushes often collect autumn leaves. Pull as many of them out as you can with a gloved hand. Use a stick or a pair of long-handled kitchen tongs to pull leaves from the very center of larger bushes.

Spring pruning

Pruning is important for several reasons. For one, pruning stimulates growth and subsequent flowering. Pruning also allows you to improve the appearance of roses by removing dead or damaged stems and by shaping the plant. It's also a way to control unwanted growth such as suckers from grafted rootstocks.

Pruning time varies by region. A good rule is to prune in when the plant is dormant or just starting to send out growth. Of course, early spring could be January in the warmest regions or April in cold regions.

Prune as soon as the rose has set plenty of red leaf buds. This allows you to see where to make sloping cuts outward to encourage open growth away from the center of the plant for better shape and air circulation.

If in doubt on timing for your area, check with your local nursery or rose society.

Fertilize, prevent disease

Get a head start on plant diseases by applying a fertilizer and systemic pesticide once the plant starts to send out new growth in earnest; that is, the red leaf buds start to unfurl. Also consider spraying in early

spring with a horticultural oil, such as Ortho Volck Oil Spray, which will suffocate some rose pests.

Once the roses are at least partly leafed out, if you've been having problems with black spot and other fungal diseases, consider applying a fungicide one to three times (every 7 to 10 days) in the season. Fungicides tend to work best if applied in early spring before the fungal damage is apparent, which usually happens in mid- to late summer.

Check the mulch around the roses. Roses do best with at least an inch of mulch around them—just be sure it's an inch or two away from the base of the plant, to prevent disease and rodent problems. Refresh the mulch as needed.

Also keep an eye on the rain gauge. If the weather has been dry, you'll want to keep roses well watered during the crucial fast growth period.

HOW MUCH TO PRUNE IN SPRING?

In most regions you'll be pruning out at least some winter damage on stems. The bark on winter-damaged sections of rose stems may look brown or black, but internal damage often continues down into sections of the stem that still appear green on the outside. The color of the pith (center of the stem) is the real key. Tan or brown indicates that tissue is damaged, but if the pith is white, it is undamaged. (See photo on page 124.) It's important to cut back all the way to undamaged tissue so that new growth arises from a healthy, vigorous part of the stem.

Keep in mind these guidelines for specific types of roses:

Hybrid teas, grandifloras, and floribundas: Leave 3 to 5 large, healthy stems and cut the rest back to the base. In most regions, cut the remaining stems back to 12 to 18 inches tall. In warm regions cut back less, perhaps to 24 to 36 inches. In cold regions, winter damage may determine where to cut back, possibly nearly to the base. For floribundas used as hedges, leave 6 or more stems and cut back to 24 inches.

Polyanthas: Polyanthas require little additional pruning except to even out the height and guide the direction of growth if used as a groundcover.

Species, shrub, and old garden roses: Prune primarily for form; head back excessively long stems, and thin some stems if plant is too dense. Otherwise try to maintain natural form. For one-time bloomers, wait until flowers are gone before doing any major renovation pruning. (Rugosas do best with minimal pruning; just cut out dead or damaged wood.)

While it's ideal to plant wisely to prevent shrubs that are growing too large, if you must control the plant's size, you can cut back rather severely in spring—to just a foot or two.

Climbers: In spring remove only dead, damaged, or weak stems. Cut back stems of one-time blooming climbers after they flower, then select and tie new stems to supports. Cut back laterals of repeat-blooming climbers as you deadhead during the season.

Miniatures: Prune similar to hybrid teas, reducing height by half to two-thirds rather than measuring in inches.

ARS ROSARIAN TIP...

Mild days in spring will tempt you to start pruning your rose bushes, but hold off from starting too early. My feeling is that you should wait until new growth appears and the new canes have grown a couple of inches, then prune. The first new cane that appears may not be the strongest one, and waiting gives you a chance to study the growth.

—*Clarence Rhodes, Portland, Maine*

▲ In the spring, as roses start to leaf out, gently push away any soil or compost you've mounded up around the base. Tiny white shoots may be revealed.

Fall and winter maintenance

In all but the warmest regions in the southernmost United States, fall is the time to start preparing your roses for winter. Even though many roses continue to bloom until October or even later, the plants need to start hardening off to help them survive winter temperatures. Fall is also a good time for garden maintenance such as raking up fallen rose leaves and getting rid of weeds; these tasks can help reduce pest problems next year.

Stop feeding

In the northern half of the United States, stop fertilizing and deadheading roses in late summer or early fall to discourage lush new growth that would not have time to harden off before winter. In warmer regions, stop fertilizing and deadheading by midfall. Watering can taper off as cold weather arrives, but never let roses become drought-stressed since this can increase the chance of winter injury.

Cut back as needed

Prune in early spring, but in some cases a little late fall pruning is also advisable. In cold regions tender roses may need some fall pruning to accommodate methods of winter protection such as tipping or tying up and wrapping in burlap, which are often done in the coldest parts of the northern third of the United States.

In warmer climates in the southern third of the United States, hybrid teas and grandifloras grow quite tall and their stems are susceptible to whipping in strong winter winds. Winds can damage the stems and also cause root and graft-union damage if the crown twists in the soil. If this is a concern in your area, you may reduce these roses in height by about one-half in late fall.

Winter whipping can also be a problem for climbing roses. In warmer climates climbers can be lightly pruned and retied to supports in the fall. Thin out some of the excess untied stems and lateral growth to reduce wind whipping, then tie or retie all remaining stems firmly to the support structure for the winter.

Protect roses

Many roses, including most shrub and old garden roses, require little or no winter protection except in very cold regions. However, tender roses such as hybrid teas and grandifloras benefit from winter protection in all but the warmest regions (Zone 9 and higher). In Zones 5 through 8, tender roses primarily need to have the graft union and roots protected from fluctuating winter temperatures. When soil alternately freezes and thaws, it can twist the graft union and break feeder roots. Winter protection also helps keep soil evenly cool in late winter and early spring. This is important in many regions because early warm soil temperatures can cause roses to break dormancy. This makes the plant susceptible to severe cold injury if temperatures suddenly drop.

You can provide basic winter protection for tender roses by mounding soil over the crown and lower stems to a depth of 8 to 12 inches. The sloping mound of soil will also protect much of the surrounding root system. Protect roses with soil mounds in mid- to late fall after one or more freezes. Bring the soil in from another part of the yard, or purchase it; don't scrape soil up from around the rose plant since this will damage the roots. For additional protection in Zone 5 to 6, pile straw or dry leaves around the roses. To keep mulch in place, form a corral around the rose plant using chicken wire or other mesh fencing secured with stakes. Then fill in the corral with loose mulch. In spring, remove mulch and soil gradually as the weather warms up.

In Zone 7 to 8, a thick layer (12 to 18 inches) of mulch such as clean straw, pine needles, or dry leaves can be substituted for the soil. One advantage is that mulch is easier to remove than soil in the spring, though it won't provide quite as much temperature insulation as soil. Form a corral as described above to keep mulch in place if you wish.

WRAPPING A ROSE FOR A HARSH WINTER

Depending on how cold hardy the rose is and how cold your winters get, you may need to provide significant cold protection for your roses. This rose has been mounded with soil at the base, with its canes tied up; wrapped with straw or leaves; then wrapped in burlap.

THE MINNESOTA TIP

To ensure survival, cold-climate gardeners, especially those in Zone 3 and colder, can tip and completely cover tender roses, a procedure commonly called the Minnesota tip. It also works well with tree roses.

To do this, dig a trench extending from the rose. Prune stems to 3 feet and gently tie stems together. Loosen the soil around the roots on the side opposite the trench, then carefully tip the rose over into the trench, being careful not to damage the graft union. Mound entire trench and root area with 12 inches of soil, then cover mound with 12 to 18 inches of straw or bags of dry leaves. Remove the layers gradually in spring as the plant starts to show signs of breaking dormancy. Reset the rose in an upright position and water thoroughly.

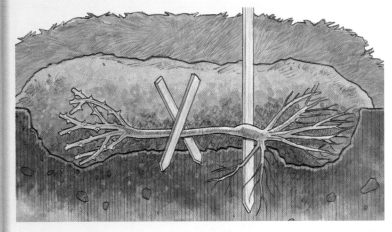

ROSE CARE CALENDAR
MONTH BY MONTH

	Pacific Northwest	Northern California	Southern California	Desert Southwest	Western Mountains	Great Plains / Northern Midwest / Canadian Interior	Southern Midwest	Texas and Oklahoma	The South	Florida/Gulf Coast	New England	The Southern Coast	The Northern Coast
JANUARY													
Review nursery catalogs; order roses	■	■	■	■	■	■	■	■	■	■	■	■	■
Sharpen tools	■	■	■	■	■	■	■	■	■	■	■	■	■
Test soil pH	■	■	■	■				■	■	■		■	
Plant container roses	■	■	■	■					■			■	
Plant bare-root roses	■	■	■	■					■			■	
Transplant roses	■	■	■	■					■			■	
Prune roses	■	■	■	■						■		■	
Fertilize	■	■	■						■				
Start watering as needed	■	■	■	■				■	■	■			
Check for and treat pests and diseases	■	■	■	■				■	■	■		■	
FEBRUARY													
Review nursery catalogs; order roses	■	■	■	■	■	■	■	■	■	■	■	■	■
Sharpen tools	■	■	■	■	■	■	■	■	■	■	■	■	■
Test soil pH	■	■	■	■				■	■	■		■	
Plant container roses	■	■	■	■					■	■			
Plant bare-root roses	■	■	■	■				■	■			■	
Transplant roses	■	■	■	■					■	■		■	
Prune roses	■	■	■	■				■	■	■		■	
Fertilize	■	■	■	■				■	■	■		■	
Start watering as needed	■	■	■	■				■	■	■		■	
Check for and treat pests and diseases	■	■	■	■				■	■	■		■	
Add new mulch	■	■	■	■				■	■	■		■	

Rose Care Calendar Month by Month

	Pacific Northwest	Northern California	Southern California	Desert Southwest	Western Mountains	Great Plains / Northern Midwest / Canadian Interior	Southern Midwest	Texas and Oklahoma	The South	Florida/Gulf Coast	New England	The Southern Coast	The Northern Coast
MARCH													
Review nursery catalogs; order roses					■	■	■				■		■
Sharpen tools					■	■	■				■		■
Test soil pH					■	■	■				■		■
Plant container roses	■	■	■	■				■	■	■	■		■
Plant bare-root roses	■						■	■	■	■	■		■
Transplant roses	■	■	■	■			■	■	■	■	■		■
Prune roses					■			■			■		■
Fertilize					■		■	■	■	■	■		■
Water as needed	■	■	■	■				■	■	■	■		■
Remove winter mulch					■								
Weed rose beds	■	■	■	■		■		■	■	■	■		■
Check for and treat pests and diseases	■	■		■				■	■		■		
Add new mulch	■	■	■	■				■	■	■	■		■
Disbud for larger flowers	■	■	■					■	■				
Deadhead	■	■	■	■				■					
APRIL													
Plant container roses	■	■	■	■	■		■	■	■		■	■	■
Plant bare-root roses	■	■	■		■	■	■				■	■	■
Transplant roses					■	■					■		■
Prune roses					■	■	■				■		■
Fertilize					■	■	■		■	■	■		■
Water as needed	■	■	■	■			■	■	■	■	■		
Remove winter mulch					■	■	■				■		■
Weed rose beds	■	■	■	■				■	■	■	■		■
Check for and treat pests and diseases	■	■	■	■	■		■	■	■	■	■		■
Add new mulch							■		■				■
Disbud for larger flowers						■	■	■					■
Deadhead	■	■	■	■				■	■	■		■	

Rose care calendar (continued)

ROSE CARE CALENDAR MONTH BY MONTH

	Pacific Northwest	Northern California	Southern California	Desert Southwest	Western Mountains	Great Plains / Northern Midwest / Canadian Interior	Southern Midwest	Texas and Oklahoma	The South	Florida/Gulf Coast	New England	The Southern Coast	The Northern Coast
MAY													
Plant container roses	■	■	■		■	■	■	■	■	■	■	■	■
Plant bare-root roses					■	■	■				■	■	■
Transplant roses					■	■	■					■	■
Fertilize	■	■	■	■	■	■	■	■	■	■	■	■	■
Water as needed	■	■	■	■	■	■	■	■	■	■	■	■	■
Weed rose beds	■	■	■	■	■	■	■	■	■	■	■	■	■
Check for and treat pests and diseases	■	■	■	■	■	■	■	■	■	■	■	■	■
Disbud for larger flowers	■	■	■	■	■	■	■	■	■	■	■	■	■
Deadhead	■	■	■	■	■	■	■	■	■	■	■	■	■
JUNE													
Plant container roses	■	■	■		■	■	■	■	■	■	■	■	■
Plant bare-root roses					■							■	■
Transplant roses					■		■						■
Fertilize	■	■	■	■	■	■	■	■	■	■	■	■	■
Water as needed	■	■	■	■	■	■	■	■	■	■	■	■	■
Weed rose beds	■	■	■	■	■	■	■	■	■	■	■	■	■
Check for and treat pests and diseases	■	■	■	■	■	■	■	■	■	■	■	■	■
Disbud for larger flowers	■	■	■	■	■	■	■	■	■	■	■	■	■
Deadhead	■	■	■	■	■	■	■	■	■	■	■	■	■
JULY													
Plant container roses	■	■	■		■	■	■	■		■	■	■	■
Fertilize	■	■	■	■	■	■	■	■	■	■	■	■	■
Water as needed	■	■	■	■	■	■	■	■	■	■	■	■	■
Weed rose beds	■	■	■	■	■	■	■	■	■	■	■	■	■
Check for and treat pests and diseases	■	■	■	■	■	■	■	■	■	■	■	■	■
Disbud for larger flowers	■	■	■	■	■	■	■	■	■	■	■	■	■
Deadhead	■	■	■	■	■	■	■	■	■	■	■	■	■
AUGUST													
Plant container roses	■	■	■		■	■	■	■		■	■	■	■
Fertilize	■	■	■	■	■	■	■	■	■	■	■	■	■
Water as needed	■	■	■	■	■	■	■	■	■	■	■	■	■
Weed rose beds	■	■	■	■	■	■	■	■	■	■	■	■	■
Check for and treat pests and diseases	■	■	■	■	■	■	■	■	■	■	■	■	■
Disbud for larger flowers	■	■	■	■	■	■	■	■	■	■	■	■	■
Deadhead	■	■	■	■	■	■	■	■	■	■	■	■	■
Order roses for fall planting	■	■	■	■			■	■	■	■	■		

Rose Care Calendar
Month by Month

	Pacific Northwest	Northern California	Southern California	Desert Southwest	Western Mountains	Great Plains / Northern Midwest / Canadian Interior	Southern Midwest	Texas and Oklahoma	The South	Florida/Gulf Coast	New England	The Southern Coast	The Northern Coast
SEPTEMBER													
Order roses for fall planting	■	■	■					■	■	■		■	
Plant container roses	■	■	■	■				■	■	■		■	
Fertilize	■	■	■	■				■	■	■		■	
Water as needed	■	■	■	■	■	■	■	■	■	■		■	■
Weed rose beds	■	■	■	■	■	■	■	■	■	■		■	■
Check for and treat pests and diseases	■	■	■	■	■	■	■	■	■	■		■	■
Stop deadheading for hips	■	■	■	■	■	■	■	■	■	■		■	■
OCTOBER													
Order roses for fall planting	■	■	■	■					■	■		■	
Prepare soil for spring planting					■	■	■	■					■
Apply winter protection					■	■				■			■
Plant container roses	■	■	■	■				■	■	■	■	■	■
Water as needed	■	■	■	■	■		■	■	■	■	■	■	■
Weed rose beds	■	■	■	■	■		■	■	■	■	■	■	■
Check for and treat pests and diseases	■	■	■	■	■		■	■	■	■	■	■	■
Stop deadheading for hips	■	■	■	■	■		■	■	■	■	■	■	■
Plant container roses	■	■	■	■				■	■	■		■	
Fertilize roses			■	■						■			
NOVEMBER													
Order roses for spring planting	■	■	■	■	■	■	■	■	■	■	■	■	■
Prepare soil for spring planting	■	■	■	■	■	■	■	■	■	■	■	■	■
Plant container roses	■	■	■	■				■	■	■		■	
Plant bare-root roses	■	■	■	■				■	■	■		■	
Transplant roses	■	■	■	■				■	■	■		■	
Water as needed	■	■	■	■	■		■	■	■	■	■	■	■
Check for and treat pests and diseases	■	■	■	■	■		■	■	■	■	■	■	■
DECEMBER													
Order roses for spring planting	■	■	■	■	■	■	■	■	■	■	■	■	■
Prepare soil for spring planting	■	■	■	■				■	■	■		■	
Plant container roses	■	■	■	■				■	■	■		■	
Plant bare-root roses			■	■						■			
Transplant roses	■	■	■	■				■	■	■		■	
Water as needed	■	■	■	■				■	■	■		■	■
Check for and treat pests and diseases	■	■	■	■				■	■	■		■	■

Gallery of roses

Choosing the best

Even the most modest offering of roses at a garden center can be overwhelming. What colors to choose? What scents?

What size? And which roses will bloom the longest and take the least fuss?

This gallery of roses is designed to help you understand and find the best roses for your garden. In it, you'll find clear, concise information that will set you on your way to choosing and cultivating the healthiest, most free-flowering roses.

Understanding the awards

One of the best ways to choose a high-performing rose is to check and see what awards, if any, it has received. There are dozens of different rose awards from around the world. When choosing a rose, it's a good sign if it's won any award at all. But as with all prizes some are more, well, prized than others. Some of the most prestigious rose awards include:

● **All-America Rose Selections Award**

The All-America Rose Selection, Inc., (AARS) is an association of United States rose producers and marketers who evaluate the new rose varieties and select the most outstanding prior to their introduction into the marketplace.

The organization was established in 1938 to assist amateur gardeners in selecting the best of the newest rose varieties. The first award was made in 1940 and today the AARS designation is one of the most prestigious honors that a new rose variety can receive. The process for conferring the award is two years in duration and the trial occurs in 26 public test gardens located throughout the country.

The locations of the test gardens have been chosen to ensure that there is diversity in climates, soil, growing seasons and other factors that impact growth. The rose plants in the trials are evaluated at four different times per year during the two-year evaluation process.

The criteria that are used in the evaluation are: Vigor, growth habit, hardiness, disease-resistance, foliage, flower production, bud and flower form, opening and finishing color, fragrance, stem strength, overall value, and novelty. Once the evaluation period has concluded, the selections are made.

▲ For nearly every need in the landscape, there's a great rose. In this bed, white Bolero plays off the peach, burgundy, and pinks, including a Love & Peace rose off to the left.

● **Award of Excellence**

The American Rose Society (ARS) Award of Excellence evaluations are conducted by a nation-wide test panel of individuals with expertise in growing miniature and miniflora roses. Like the AARS group, they also evaluate the new varieties in the trial for two years in designated test gardens across the country.

They also conduct four periodic evaluations during the course of the growing season in each of the two years. The criteria that are used in their evaluations are quite similar to those used to evaluate the rose plants in the AARS trial.

Those criteria include: Novelty, bud form, flower form, color opening, color finishing, substance, habit, quality of flowers, vigor/repeat bloom, foliage, and disease/insect resistance. The chairman of the test panel assembles all of the data and announces the winners.

● **Rose Hills Trials**

The Rose Hills Memorial Garden in Whittier, California boasts a beautiful rose garden and test garden. Each October, an international jury of rose enthusiasts converges on the garden to evaluate the new roses there.

There is also a permanent jury of rose professionals who evaluate these roses over the entire growing season. The combination of their scores and the one-day guest jury's will choose the best roses in the Rose Hills Trials and the top rose will be honored as the "Golden Rose of Rose Hills."

● **Portland Gold Medal Award**

The Portland Gold Medal was instituted by the City of Portland in 1919 under the visionary guidance of Jesse Currey, the curator of the Washington Park Gardens. All new roses may be entered into the test gardens and are eligible for the Portland Gold Medal Award.

Six judges evaluate the roses by assigning them points four times a year for at least a two-year period. Their criteria include such traits as bud/flower form, color, substance, bloom habit, bush habit, disease resistance, foliage, finishing color, and any special characteristics.

Only those varieties achieving a certain scoring average are eligible to receive the Portland Gold Medal, a preeminent prize that is coveted by rose nurseries, hybridizers, and others in the rose-growing industry.

Rose shows

Another way to determine the best of the best is to attend a rose show. At these events you can see what teams of expert judges determine are the best roses on that day. Even more importantly, you can see the roses just as they have been grown in a home gardener's rose garden, which suggests that you can grow them equally as well.

WORLD ROSE HALL OF FAME WINNERS

Looking for one of the best roses on the planet? Consider the following roses, chosen by a popular vote on a triennial basis by the Member Countries of the World Federation of Rose Societies.

1976 Peace (hybrid tea)
1978 Queen Elizabeth (grandiflora)
1981 Fragrant Cloud (hybrid tea)
1983 Iceberg (floribunda)
1985 Double Delight (hybrid tea)
1988 Papa Meilland (hybrid tea)
1991 Pascali (hybrid tea)
1994 Just Joey (hybrid tea)
1997 New Dawn (large-flowered climber)
2000 Ingrid Bergman (hybrid tea)
2003 Bonica (shrub)
2006 Elina (hybrid tea) and Pierre de Ronsard (large-flowered climber)

THE WORLD OF ROSE BREEDERS

The rose you fall in love with at the garden center may well be the work of decades or even a lifetime, of breeding efforts. Indeed, entire family dynasties have been built on the work of breeding the best and most captivating roses in the world. Most of the roses available to North American gardeners have been bred by American, British, French, or German hybridizers, though there are rose breeders elsewhere who have made major contributions to the array of roses available.

Some of the best known rose breeders include:

David Austin. This English breeder has blended the qualities of old roses with the ease of growing and repeat bloom of modern roses.

Tom Carruth of Weeks Roses. These American roses tend to have unique coloration and stripes and often combine the best of old and new roses.

Philip and Robert Harkness. These British breeders are known for their roses' ease of growing, such as groundcover roses, as well as interesting colors in the amber and orange range.

Wilhelm Kordes. This German breeder has introduced roses known for hardiness, health, color, form, and fragrance.

Ping Lim of Bailey Nurseries. This American has created roses noted for easy care, fragrance, form, and repeat bloom.

Alain Meilland and Jacque Mouchat. These French breeders have introduced roses with wide appeal that are excellent for mass plantings.

William Radler. This American has bred a long line of exceptionally low-maintenance long blooming roses.

Keith Zary of Jackson & Perkins. This American breeder has developed strong, high-quality plants that are easy to grow and maintain.

CHOOSING ROSES BY THE BOOK

The American Rose Society "Handbook for Selecting Roses" is an annual compilation of the evaluations of the members of the Society of new rose introductions who test new roses in their own gardens. It contains more than 3,000 roses that have been evaluated annually over the years through the ARS's Roses in Review program.

Additionally, members use a specified set of criteria to evaluate recently introduced roses for three consecutive years beginning with the rose's second year in commerce.

The roses are rated using a scale of from 0 to 10 on each of the criteria. The points are then totaled and averaged. The result is a score that indicates how well the rose has performed in home gardens throughout the country. (Some roses have not been rated or have not yet been rated. Wherever possible in this gallery, the rose rating is listed.)

The scoring system that is used is as follows:

9.3-10: One of the best roses ever. Scores in this range are seldom awarded.

8.8-9.2: An outstanding rose. One with major positive features and essentially no negatives. These roses make up the top one percent of all roses.

8.3-8.7: A very good to excellent rose, one recommended without hesitation.

7.8-8.2: A solid to very good rose. Its good features easily outweigh any problems; well above average.

7.3-7.7: A good rose; a little to somewhat above average.

6.8-7.2: An average rose.

6.1-6.7: A below-average rose.

6.0 and below: Not recommended.

Hybrid teas and grandifloras

By far the most popular and widely grown classes of roses are hybrid teas and grandifloras, which are closely related.

Hybrid teas have evolved over the last 150 years through generations of breeding. All this effort has resulted in a myriad of colors, large flowers atop long stems perfect for cutting, long vase life, long plant life, and foliage that is highly resistant to the diseases and insects that nature bombards it with. However, those long stems can look rather stark and leggy in the garden.

Grandifloras, bred from hybrid teas, tend to be taller with flowers that bloom in clusters rather than the solo bloom on the stem or near-solo bloom of hybrid teas.

Hybrid teas come in a vast range of colors and often have the largest flowers, ranging from three to eight inches in diameter, most with spiral form. Their growth habit is usually tall and upright or spreading, with large foliage and a large terminal bloom at the end of each stem.

Many hybrid teas will produce small side buds that stay below the terminal bloom. These can be removed to create one large single flower at the end of the stem, or can be allowed to grow so that the stem can bear a small cluster of large flowers. Plant heights range from 3 to 7 feet in most cases.

The grandiflora class was created a half-century ago when a hybrid tea was crossed with another rose. Today, this strictly American classification is generally used to describe varieties that have long stems with clusters of flowers at the end.

Hybrid teas and grandifloras are ideal for cutting gardens. In areas where they need significant winter protection, it's ideal to plant them altogether to simplify the process. They are fine as part of an overall garden design if interplanted with companion plants or other more shrubby roses to disguise their legginess.

See page 25 for more detail about hybrid teas and grandifloras.

▲ This planting of hybrid teas shows all the hallmarks of the group: Large, classically shaped flowers; long elegant stems perfect for cutting; and glossy green foliage that looks as pretty in the garden as it does in the vase.

About Face

Type: Grandiflora
Hybridizer/Year: Carruth 2003
Growth habits: Vigorous, upright, bushy, 5–7'
Foliage: Medium, dark green, semiglossy
Blooms: Golden orange on the inside and bronzy red on the outside, 35 petals, 4–6"
Fragrance: Light apple
Awards: AARS 2005
Comments: Blooms in a striking color combination on a lush, green, disease-resistant plant. The colorful blooms make a statement in any landscape design. This prolific bloomer does well in all climates.

Aperitif

Type: Hybrid Tea
Hybridizer/Year: McGredy 1998
Growth habits: Tall, bushy, 5–6'
Foliage: Large, light green, matte, moderate prickles
Blooms: Yellow, 17–25 petals, 4–4½", exhibition form
Fragrance: Light, spice
Comments: This elegant, easy to grow bush is perfect for any landscape project. The bright yellow blooms are long-lasting and hold their color well. They have nice form and look great in the garden or in a vase. Not to be confused with the floribunda rose also named Apertif. Rating: 7.5

Aromatherapy

Type: Hybrid Tea
Hybridizer/Year: Jackson & Perkins 2005
Growth habits: Upright, bushy, 5–6'
Foliage: Medium, dark green, semiglossy
Blooms: Rich pink, 30 petals, 4½"
Fragrance: Intense, fruity
Comments: This vigorous bush produces rich pink blooms that stand out in any setting. It is a prolific bloomer for the duration of the growing season. The blooms are long lasting and great for arrangements. In addition, it has its own bouquet that is quite nice.

Artistry

Type: Hybrid Tea
Hybridizer/Year: Zary 1997
Growth habits: Medium tall, 4'
Foliage: Dark green
Blooms: Large coral with light salmon pink, 40 petals
Fragrance: Slight
Awards: AARS 1997, Portland Gold Medal 1999
Comments: This vigorous bush performs well in the garden bed or as a hedge or border. The large coral and salmon blooms hold their shape and color for a long time and repeat bloom throughout the growing season. Its dark green semiglossy foliage is disease resistant. Rating: 7.9

Barbara Bush

Type: Hybrid Tea
Hybridizer/Year: Warriner 1990
Growth habits: Medium, upright, slightly spreading, 4–5'
Foliage: Medium, medium green, glossy
Blooms: Coral pink and ivory, darker shading where exposed to the sun, 25–30 petals, 5", exhibition form
Fragrance: Moderate, damask
Comments: This vigorous bush is a prolific bloomer throughout the growing season. The blooms range from a blush to rosy coral and are darkest where the sun hits them. This rose is hardy but may be prone to mildew. It was named to honor a First Lady of the United States. Rating: 7.5

Barbra Streisand

Type: Hybrid Tea
Hybridizer/Year: Carruth 1999
Growth habits: 3–4' tall × 2–3' wide
Foliage: Glossy, moss green
Blooms: Two-toned lavender with 35-plus petals
Fragrance: Strong, citrus, rose
Comments: This rose, selected by the star for whom it was named, has luscious large blooms that repeat prolifically throughout the growing season. It also has disease-resistant deep green glossy leaves. Its best characteristic is its alluring fragrance. The flower color and size appear best in mild climates. Rating: 7.1

Hybrid teas and grandifloras *(continued)*

Bewitched

Type: Hybrid Tea
Hybridizer/Year: Lammerts 1967
Growth habits: Vigorous, rounded, bushy, 4–5'
Foliage: Large, red turning apple green, glossy
Blooms: Cotton candy pink, 27–30 petals, 5",
exhibition form
Fragrance: Moderate, damask
Awards: AARS 1967, Portland Gold Medal 1967
Comments: This classic pink rose has remained popular for 40 years. Its large cotton candy pink blooms have perfect form and hold their color even in hot weather. The large foliage begins as a reddish color and turns to a beautiful apple green. Rating: 7.7

Black Magic

Type: Hybrid Tea
Hybridizer/Year: Tantau 1997
Growth habits: 5½' tall with 24–28" stems
Foliage: Glossy, dark green
Blooms: Deepest dark red, 4" blooms with 30 petals
Fragrance: Subtle, sweet
Comments: The buds on this plant begin as almost black and open to a velvety dark red garnet with darker red edges, aptly depicting its name. It grows on long stems with disease-resistant foliage. It is superb for cutting and has long-lasting blooms, which has made it a favorite with florists. It can be tender in colder climates. Rating: 7.7

Brandy

Type: Hybrid Tea
Hybridizer/Year: Swim & Christensen 1981
Growth habits: Vigorous, 4' tall × 3' wide
Foliage: Large, glossy with straight prickles
Blooms: Apricot blend with 28 petals, mostly single stems
Fragrance: Mild, tea
Awards: AARS 1982
Comments: This vigorous plant bears classically formed blooms of blended apricot hues. The blooms do not hold their shape for a long time, but open to a gorgeous large spray of petals with bright gold stamens with dark green foliage. Brandy likes cooler temperatures but needs protection in harsh climates. Rating: 7.4

Bride's Dream

Type: Hybrid Tea
Hybridizer/Year: Kordes 1985
Growth habits: 5–6' tall × 4' wide
Foliage: Medium green with grayish sheen
Blooms: Pale satiny pink with 30–35 petals
Fragrance: Medium, sweet
Comments: This plant has often been referred to as the improved Royal Highness, one of its parents. Its blooms possess the same pastel pink color, but are more prolific and repeat throughout the growing season. The bush is more vigorous and the foliage is more disease resistant. This plant is nice in the garden or vase. Rating: 8.1

Brigadoon

Type: Hybrid Tea
Hybridizer/Year: Warriner 1991
Growth habits: Upright, 4–5′ tall
Foliage: Glossy, dark green
Blooms: White, tinted pink, 26–40 petals, 5″, exhibition form
Fragrance: Moderate, tea
Awards: AARS 1992
Comments: This rose invites visitors to take a second look. The creamy color changes to strawberry red to cerise in an ever changing kaleidoscope of colors. With attractive dark green glossy foliage, this is an outstanding addition to any garden. It has been seen on trophy tables. Rating: 7.8

Butter Cream

Type: Hybrid Tea
Hybridizer/Year: Jackson & Perkins 2003
Growth habits: Upright, 5′ tall
Foliage: Medium, dark green, glossy
Blooms: Light yellow, 40 petals, 5″, exhibition form
Fragrance: Light, licorice
Comments: This vigorous bush produces soft yellow blooms that contrast with other colors in any landscape. The scent is intriguing. This rose is great in the garden, in the vase, or on the trophy table. Rating: 7.8

Cajun Moon

Type: Hybrid Tea
Hybridizer/Year: Carruth 2001
Growth habits: Upright, 4–5′ tall
Foliage: Large, medium green, matte
Blooms: White with a pink tinged edging, 30–35 petals
Fragrance: Slight, tea and rose

Comments: This vigorous upright plant does well in the garden or in a vase. Its pink-edged white blooms are large and lovely. It has classic hybrid tea form and has been seen on many trophy tables. Rating: 7.9

Cajun Sunrise

Type: Hybrid Tea
Hybridizer/Year: Edwards 2000
Growth habits: Upright, 4–5′ tall
Foliage: Large, medium green, flat
Blooms: Pink with yellow bases, 26–40 petals, exhibition form
Fragrance: Slight, tea and rose
Comments: This vigorous plant blooms throughout the growing season. Its blooms have great form and maintain their

color even in the heat. This rose does well in the garden or the vase and has been frequently seen on trophy tables. Rating: 7.7

Hybrid teas and grandifloras *(continued)*

Candelabra

Type: Grandiflora
Hybridizer/Year: Zary 1998
Growth habits: Vigorous, upright, bushy, 5'
Foliage: Medium, dark green, glossy, moderate prickles
Blooms: Coral orange, 20–25 petals, 4"
Fragrance: Slight, tea
Awards: AARS 1999
Comments: This plant produces prolifically throughout the growing season. The coral orange blooms are vivid and eyecatching. They are surrounded by glossy foliage that contrasts nicely with the blooms. This bush provides bouquets of cut flowers all season long. Rating: 7.6

Cherry Parfait

Type: Grandiflora
Hybridizer/Year: Meilland 2002
Growth habits: Tall, upright, 4–5', slightly spreading
Foliage: Medium, dark green, glossy
Blooms: White to cream, edged in red, 30–35 petals, 4"
Fragrance: Slight
Awards: Buenos Aires Gold Medal 2000, AARS 2003
Comments: This vigorous grandiflora has a growth habit reminiscent of many shrubs. It makes a striking color display in any landscape design and is nearly always in bloom. It grows well in all climates and hold its color even in the heat of summer. Rating: 7.8

Chicago Peace

Type: Hybrid Tea
Hybridizer/Year: Johnston 1962
Growth habits: Upright, 4–7' tall
Foliage: Large, dark green, leathery, glossy
Blooms: Pink with a yellow base with 50–60 petals, exhibition form
Fragrance: Slight
Awards: Portland Gold Medal 1962
Comments: This rose is a sport of Peace, a classic favorite, that was discovered by a Chicago breeder. It has many of the outstanding characteristics of its parent. The large blooms are more intense in color but repeat as frequently. This is a great addition to any landscape, but it may need black-spot protection. Rating: 7.7

Crimson Bouquet

Type: Grandiflora
Hybridizer/Year: Kordes 1999
Growth habits: Upright, 4–5'
Foliage: Large, dark green, glossy
Blooms: Dark garnet red, reverse a shiny dark red, 20–25 petals
Fragrance: Slight
Awards: AARS 2000
Comments: This bush seems to have almost everything. It is a

vigorous grower with disease-resistant foliage and produces an abundance of bright velvety red blooms that hold their color for a long time. It blooms prolifically for the duration of the growing season. Rating: 7.9

Crystalline

Type: Hybrid Tea
Hybridizer/Year: Christensen & Carruth 1987
Growth habits: Upright, bushy, 4–6′ tall
Foliage: Medium, medium green, semiglossy
Blooms: Large, pure white with 30–35 petals, exhibition form
Fragrance: Slight

Comments: This is a vigorous bush that produces abundant blooms throughout the growing season. Its blooms have exquisite form and show well in the garden, in the vase, or on the trophy table. It likes warm evenings. It will do well in all types of landscape projects. Rating: 8.0

Dainty Bess

Type: Hybrid Tea
Hybridizer/Year: Archer 1925
Growth habits: Vigorous, 3–4′
Foliage: Leathery, dark green
Blooms: Soft rose pink with maroon stamens, single, 4–11 petals
Fragrance: Slight
Awards: Royal National Rose Society Gold Medal, 1925
Comments: This rose has become a classic and is a perennial favorite. Its large single blooms are creamy pink set off by outstanding maroon stamens that create a unique look. This rose is a hardy plant that

produces prolifically throughout the growing season. The leathery foliage adds to the beauty of this bush. Also available as a climber. Rating: 8.5

Diana, Princess of Wales

Type: Hybrid Tea
Hybridizer/Year: Zary 1998
Growth habits: Tall, upright, 4½–5½′
Foliage: Medium, dark green, semiglossy, moderate prickles
Blooms: Pink and ivory blend, 35–40 petals, 4–5″, exhibition form
Fragrance: Moderate
Comments: Named for Diana, Princess

of Wales, this rose is a vigorous plant that produces a lavish display of blooms for the duration of the growing season. The high centered ivory blooms are overlaid with a clear pink blush that seems to radiate. It is adorned by dark green, semiglossy foliage that enhances its beauty. Rating: 7.5

Dolly Parton

Type: Hybrid Tea
Hybridizer/Year: Winchel 1984
Growth habits: Medium, upright, bushy, 4′
Foliage: Large, medium green, semiglossy
Blooms: Luminous, orange-red, 35–40 petals, 4–5″, exhibition form
Fragrance: Intense, clove and rose
Awards: American Rose Center Trial Gardens Bronze Medal 1982
Comments: This vigorous bush is a prolific bloomer throughout the growing season. The large coppery orange-red blooms have an intense clove and rose scent. This plant loves warm nights and warm climates. It was named for the well-known country and western singer and star. Rating: 7.5

Hybrid teas and grandifloras *(continued)*

Double Delight

Type: Hybrid Tea
Hybridizer/Year: Swim & Ellis 1977
Growth habits: Upright, bushy, 4–5′
Foliage: Large, deep green
Blooms: Creamy white becoming strawberry red, 30–35 petals
Fragrance: Intense, spicy
Awards: AARS 1977, World Federation of Rose Societies Hall of Fame 1985, J.A. Gamble Fragrance Award 1986

Comments: This rose earns the name Double Delight with great color and a terrific fragrance. This vigorous plant blooms abundantly from early spring through autumn. Its lovely creamy color blushes to strawberry red and the fragrance is incredible. Rating: 8.4

Dream Come True

Type: Grandiflora
Hybridizer/Year: Pottschmidt 2006
Growth habits: Tall, upright, 5–7′
Foliage: Large, matte dark green foliage
Blooms: Yellow blend, 4″ plus, 26–40 petals high-centered, yellow flushed with red at edges
Fragrance: Mild
Awards: AARS 2008
Comments: A new award-winner introduced by Weeks Roses, Dream Come True bears flowers in a dramatic multi-hued blend of golden yellow flushed with ruby red at the edges of the petals. The exhibition-quality blooms have a classic high-centered form and are borne in long-stemmed clusters perfect for cutting. Plants are attractive in the garden, although somewhat tall and leggy.

Dublin

Type: Hybrid Tea
Hybridizer/Year: Perry 1982
Growth habits: Upright, 4–5′
Foliage: Large, medium, green matte
Blooms: Large smoky red with 35–40 petals, exhibition form
Fragrance: Intense, raspberry

Comments: This vigorous bush produces well throughout the growing season. Large smoky red blooms are redder in warmer climates. This is an eyecatching addition for any landscape project. Rating: 8.2

Duet

Type: Hybrid Tea
Hybridizer/Year: Swim 1960
Growth habits: Tall, vigorous, upright, 6′ plus
Foliage: Large, dark green, glossy, leathery
Blooms: Light pink with a deeper pink reverse, 25–30 petals, 4″, exhibition form
Fragrance: Slight
Awards: Baden-Baden Gold Medal 1959, AARS 1961
Comments: This tall, vigorous bush is disease resistant and an abundant bloomer. Its two-toned pink blooms are large and have the classic high-centered hybrid tea form. Its foliage harmonizes well with the bloom color. It is popular in warm climates. Rating: 6.8

Earth Song

Type: Grandiflora
Hybridizer/Year: Buck 1975
Growth habits: Vigorous, upright, bushy, 5–6′
Foliage: Medium, dark green, glossy, leathery
Blooms: Deep pink, 25–30 petals, 4–4½″ cupped
Fragrance: Moderate
Comments: This is one of the many Buck roses that are winter hardy and do well in colder climates. The deep pink rose blooms are quite large and attract attention. They are surrounded by foliage that is disease resistant. Rating: 8.2

Electron

Type: Hybrid Tea
Hybridizer/Year: McGredy 1970
Growth habits: Upright, medium, bushy, 4′
Foliage: Large, dark green, glossy
Blooms: Shocking-pink, 32–40 petals, 5″, classic exhibition form
Fragrance: Intense
Awards: Gold Medal Royal National Rose Society 1969, Golden Rose of the Hague 1970, Belfast Gold Medal 1972, AARS 1973, Portland Gold Medal 1973
Comments: This vigorous bush has won several international awards. Its shocking-pink blooms are large and have great form. While this rose is ideal for the garden, vase, or exhibition show table, it is slow to repeat. Rating: 7.8

Elina

Type: Hybrid Tea
Hybridizer/Year: Dickson 1983
Growth habits: Vigorous, tall, 5–6′
Foliage: Large, dark green, glossy, long stems
Blooms: Pale yellow to ivory, 30–35 petals, 5–5½″, exhibition form
Fragrance: Slight
Awards: Anerkannte Deutsche Rose 1987, Gold Star of the South Pacific, Palmerston North 1987, Portland Gold Medal 1996
Comments: This is an ideal bush for any landscape. Disease resistant, it is an abundant producer of large, creamy, light yellow blooms that hold their color well. The blooms have classic hybrid tea form and are excellent in the garden or in a vase. This rose has won many awards and continues to grace exhibition trophy tables. It may be winter tender in some harsher climates. Rating: 8.6

Elizabeth Taylor

Type: Hybrid Tea
Hybridizer/Year: Weddle 1985
Growth habits: Upright, 4–6′
Foliage: Dark green, semiglossy
Blooms: Deep shocking-pink petals with smoky edges, 30–35 petals, exhibition form
Fragrance: Light, spice
Comments: With petals as pink as a movie star's lipstick, this rose is a standout in the landscape. For additional interest, petals feather to a deeper pink at the margins. This rose achieves best flower size in warm climates and its light, spicy fragrance is a treat. It blooms in flushes throughout the season. Rating: 8.4

Elle

Type: Hybrid Tea
Hybridizer/Year: Meilland 2003
Growth habits: Vigorous, upright, bushy, 4–5′
Foliage: Medium, dark green, glossy
Blooms: Shell pink with gold-orange undertones, 50–55 petals, 4–6″
Fragrance: Intense, spicy, citrus
Awards: Bagatelle Gold Medal 1999, Tokyo Fragrance Award 2000, AARS 2005
Comments: If the intense fragrance of this rose does not attract attention, the shell pink blooms with gold-orange overtones will. The blooms have classic hybrid tea form and are surrounded by large, glossy foliage. The blooms tend to be larger in cooler temperatures. This bush was named in honor of Elle, an internationally known fashion magazine.

Falling in Love

Type: Hybrid Tea
Hybridizer/Year: Carruth 2006
Growth habits: Bushy, upright 4–5′
Foliage: Large, glossy, deep green
Blooms: Creamy to medium pink blend, 26–40 petals, almost 5″, full
Fragrance: Strong, fruity rose perfume
Comments: Introduced by Weeks Roses in 2006, Falling in Love bears huge quantities of large, classically formed flowers of warm pink with a creamy white reverse to the petals. Perfect flower form, captivating color, and intense fragrance make this an outstanding subject for the vase. Flowers are largest in cool-summer climates.

Fame!

Type: Grandiflora
Hybridizer/Year: Zary 1998
Growth habits: Shrubby, full bush, tall, 4–5′
Foliage: Large, dark green
Blooms: Deep shocking pink, 30–35 petals, 5″, exhibition form
Fragrance: Slight
Awards: AARS 1998
Comments: This vigorous bush requires little care and performs well in all types of landscapes. The abundant blooms have exquisite form. The foliage is disease resistant. The blooms have better form and size in milder temperatures. Rating: 8.1

Firefighter

Type: Hybrid Tea
Hybridizer/Year: Orard 2003
Growth habits: Upright, bushy, 5–6′
Foliage: Dark, reddish green, matte
Blooms: Red, high centered, 40–45 petals, 4–5″
Fragrance: Intense, old rose
Comments: This vigorous, disease-resistant bush remains true to its name. Its blooms are large, spectacularly rich red, and fantastically fragrant. This rose is terrific in any landscape design. It was named to honor firefighters who perished in the September 11, 2001, tragedy. Part of the proceeds of each sale go to maintaining the three Remember Me Rose Gardens in New York, Washington D.C., and Pennsylvania. Rating: 7.5

Folklore

Type: Hybrid Tea
Hybridizer/Year: Kordes 1977
Growth habits: Very tall, vigorous, upright, bushy, 5–6′
Foliage: Large, medium green, glossy, disease resistant
Blooms: Orange, reverse lighter, 44 petals, 4½″, exhibition form
Fragrance: Intense

Comments: This disease-resistant plant is a prolific bloomer. The blooms are large, salmon-orange with a lighter reverse in a classic hybrid tea form. They hold their color and shape well and have a nice, strong fragrance, making them excellent for cutting for vases or exhibition. Rating: 8.2

Fragrant Cloud

Type: Hybrid Tea
Hybridizer/Year: Tantau 1963
Growth habits: Vigorous, upright, bushy, 4–5′
Foliage: Medium, dark green, glossy
Blooms: Ovoid bud, coral-red, 28–35 petals, 5″, exhibition form
Fragrance: Intense, damask, fruity, spicy, citrus, sharp
Awards: Royal National Rose Society Gold Medal 1963, Portland Gold Medal 1966, World Federation of Rose Societies Hall of Fame 1981, J. A. Gamble Fragrance Award 1969, President's International Trophy, Royal National Rose Society 1964
Comments: The captivating fragrance of this rose is attention getting. This plant is a prolific bloomer and quick to repeat. The unusually colored coral-red to geranium red blooms are large, have classic hybrid tea form, and hold their color well. The foliage contrasts well with the blooms. Deeper colors occur in cooler temperatures. Rating: 8.1

Fragrant Plum

Type: Hybrid Tea
Hybridizer/Year: Christensen 1990
Growth habits: Tall, vigorous, upright, 5–6′
Foliage: Medium, deep green, lush, semiglossy, clean
Blooms: Light lavender blushing smoky purple at the edges, 20–25 petals, 4–4½″, exhibition form
Fragrance: Intense, plummy
Awards: J.A. Gamble Fragrance Award, 2007.

Comments: This bush produces abundant blooms with classic hybrid tea form. The foliage offers excellent contrast to the blooms. The color brightens with heat, but the best form occurs with cooler temperatures. Rating: 7.7

Frederic Mistral

Type: Hybrid Tea
Hybridizer/Year: Meilland 1998
Growth habits: Upright, tall, 6′
Foliage: Large, dark green, semiglossy
Blooms: Venetian pink, reverse suffused rose, full, 26–40 petals, 4½″
Fragrance: Intense
Awards: Baden-Baden Fragrance Award 1993, LeRoeuix Fragrance Award 1994, Monza Fragrance Award 1994, Belfast Fragrance Award 1996
Comments: This rose lives up to its many awards. The vigorous growth habit provides versatility for all types of landscapes. The two-toned pink blooms have classic hybrid tea form and hold their color well. This rose is as good in a vase as it is in the garden. Rating: 7.9

Hybrid teas and grandifloras *(continued)*

Gemini

Type: Hybrid Tea
Hybridizer/Year: Zary 1999
Growth habits: Upright, tall, 4–6', 3' wide
Foliage: Large, deep green, glossy
Blooms: Cream blushing to light pink with coral edges, 25–30 petals, 4–5", exhibition form
Fragrance: Mild, sweet
Awards: AARS 2000, Monza Silver Medal 1999, Portland Gold Medal 2003
Comments: This rose is one of the most popular varieties on the market. It is a terrific rose for any type of landscape. Its blooms, gorgeous cream blushed light pink with coral edges, are prolific and borne on long stems. This outstanding rose is a must-have in any garden. It produces best size and form in moderate temperatures. Rating: 8.2

Gentle Giant

Type: Hybrid Tea
Hybridizer/Year: Carruth 2005
Growth habits: Vigorous, upright, tall, 4–6'
Foliage: Medium, bright light green, semiglossy
Blooms: Bright pink with a heart of gold, 25–30 petals, 5–6", exhibition form
Fragrance: Moderate, fruity
Comments: This rose is attractive in the garden or vase. The large, vibrant pink blooms have an inner glow of golden yellow and a classic hybrid tea form. The long stems on these beauties are perfect for bouquets.

Glowing Peace

Type: Hybrid Tea
Hybridizer/Year: Meilland 1999
Growth habits: Upright and bushy, 2–3' tall and wide
Foliage: Deep glossy green
Blooms: Yellow flushed with orange, red edges, 26–45 petals, 3", cupped, exhibition form
Fragrance: Mild tea
Awards: AARS 2001, Lyon Certificate of Merit and Prestige de la Rose 1999, Monza Silver Medal 1998
Comments: Introduced by the Conard-Pyle Company in 2000, this award-winner is a boldly colored version of the world-famous Peace, with the same growth habit and vigor. Large, round buds open into fully double, high-pointed flowers of exhibition form. Strong petal substance, long stems, and light fragrance make this an excellent rose for arrangements. Plants are very disease resistant. Rating: 7.4

Gold Medal

Type: Grandiflora
Hybridizer/Year: Christensen 1982
Growth habits: Upright, tall, 3–6'
Foliage: Large, dark green
Blooms: Golden yellow flushed with orange, 30–35 petals, 4½–5", exhibition form
Fragrance: Slight, fruity
Awards: New Zealand National Rose Trial Ground Winner and Gold Medal 1983
Comments: This is a must for yellow rose fans. The vigorous bush produces outstanding golden yellow blooms that are edged with orangish red and have perfect form. The foliage is deep green and disease resistant. The blooms deepen in color in moderate climates. Rating: 8.4

Helmut Schmidt

Type: Hybrid Tea
Hybridizer/Year: Kordes 1979
Growth habits: Medium, upright, bushy, 3–4'
Foliage: Medium, dark green, matte, disease resistant
Blooms: Clear, even yellow, 35–40 petals, 4½–5", exhibition form
Fragrance: Moderate
Awards: Belgium Gold Medal 1979, Geneva Gold Medal 1979, Royal National Rose Society Trial Ground Certificate 1979
Comments: This is one of the better yellow hybrid tea roses for holding color and form. This plant will do well in all types of landscapes and is often seen on trophy tables.

Like many yellow roses, it needs extra protection in harsh winter weather. It was named to honor a former chancellor of Germany. Rating: 7.3

Home and Family

Type: Hybrid Tea
Hybridizer/Year: Carruth 2002
Growth habits: Vigorous, upright, 4–6'
Foliage: Medium, dark green, glossy
Blooms: Porcelain white, 30–35 petals, 4–5"
Fragrance: Moderate, licorice
Comments: Large, porcelain white blooms stand out in stark contrast to the almost black-green, glossy leaves. The plant produces larger flowers in cooler temperatures.

This rose was designated to commemorate the 100th anniversary of Meredith Corporation, publisher of *Better Homes and Gardens*. Rating: 7.2

Honey Dijon

Type: Grandiflora
Hybridizer/Year: Sproul 2003
Growth habits: Medium to tall, upright, bushy, 4'
Foliage: Medium, medium green, glossy, disease resistant
Blooms: Warm golden brown shading to a golden beige, 25–30 petals, 4", exhibition form
Fragrance: Intense, fruity
Comments: The

novel color of the blooms on this bush defies description. A vigorous grower, it produces abundant blooms with a sweet scent. The color tends to deepen in cooler temperatures. Rating: 7.6

Honor

Type: Hybrid Tea
Hybridizer/Year: Warriner 1978
Growth habits: Upright, tall 4–5½'
Foliage: Large, dark green, semiglossy
Blooms: Clear white, 23 petals, 5"
Fragrance: Slight, tea
Awards: Portland Gold Medal 1978, AARS 1980
Comments: This rose is one of Warriner's triad of Love, Honor, and Cherish. It is a vigorous, disease-resistant plant that is great in the garden or as a cut flower. Its clear white blooms hold their excellent form and open to reveal golden yellow stamens. The foliage begins as a bronzy red and turns dark green as it ages. Rating: 7.6

Ingrid Bergman

Type: Hybrid Tea
Hybridizer/Year: Poulsen 1984
Growth habits: Medium, upright, bushy, 4–5′
Foliage: Medium, dark green, glossy, disease resistant
Blooms: Clear bright red, 35–40 petals, 5″, exhibition form
Fragrance: Slight, spice
Awards: Royal National Rose Society Certificate 1983, Rome Silver Medal 1984, Geneva Silver Medal 1984, Belfast Gold Medal 1985, Madrid Gold Medal 1986, Golden Rose of The Hague 1987, New Zealand Rose Trials 1987, World Federation of Rose Societies Hall of Fame 2000
Comments: This is a compact but vigorous, hardy plant. The clear velvety red blooms have classic hybrid tea form and perform better with a little heat. The foliage adds a luxurious backdrop for this stunning beauty. Rating: 7.8

John Paul II

Type: Hybrid Tea
Hybridizer/Year: Zary 2006
Growth habits: Tall, upright, 4–5′ tall
Foliage: Glossy, dark green, medium leaves
Blooms: Pristine white, 50 petals, 5″, exhibition form
Fragrance: Strong, citrus fragrance
Comments: This new rose has earned high marks in test gardens for vigor, disease resistance, generosity of bloom, flower form, and gorgeous fragrance. Pointed, ovoid buds open to large, sparkling white blooms of classic high-centered form. Excellent in the cutting garden.

Joyfulness

Type: Hybrid Tea
Hybridizer/Year: Tantau 1982
Growth habits: Upright, 4–5′, up to 4′ wide
Foliage: Large, dark green, glossy
Blooms: Shades of peach, apricot, and orange; 35 petals; 3½–4″, exhibition form
Fragrance: Slight
Comments: This vigorous plant is good for borders, hedges, and gardens, as well as for cutting and exhibition, despite its shorter stems. The peach, apricot, and orange blended blooms are bright and cheerful. This prolific grower performs well throughout the growing season. Rating: 8.1

Just Joey

Type: Hybrid Tea
Hybridizer/Year: Cants 1972
Growth habits: Moderate, spreading, 3–4′
Foliage: Large, dark green, glossy, leathery
Blooms: Rich apricot to buff orange, 30 petals, 5″, classic form
Fragrance: Intense
Awards: Royal National Rose Society Gold Medal 1986, World Federation of Rose Societies Hall of Fame 1994
Comments: This rose is a perennial favorite. A vigorous, hardy plant, it blooms abundantly throughout the growing season. Its blooms are loose petaled and achieve their best color in moderate, consistent temperatures. Rating: 7.9

Kardinal

Type: Hybrid Tea
Hybridizer/Year: Kordes 1985
Growth habits: Upright, medium, 3–4′
Foliage: Medium, dark green, semiglossy
Blooms: Bright red, 30–35 petals, 4″, exhibition form
Fragrance: Slight
Comments: Originally hybridized for the florist industry, this rose has exhibition form, is great as a cut flower, and has a long vase life. Its rich cardinal red blooms hold their color. This prolific bloomer has leathery foliage that is disease resistant. Rating: 8.5

Keepsake

Type: Hybrid Tea
Hybridizer/Year: Kordes 1981
Growth habits: Vigorous, bushy, 4–5″
Foliage: Medium, dark green, semiglossy
Blooms: Deep pink blended with lighter pink, 40 petals
Fragrance: Moderate

Awards: Portland Gold Medal 1987
Comments: This is a terrific two-toned pink rose that wins trophies and the hearts of gardeners everywhere. It is a prolific bloomer throughout the growing season. Its leathery foliage is disease resistant and offers contrast to the large blooms. It may need extra winter protection in harsher climates. Rating: 8.0

Lasting Love

Type: Hybrid Tea
Hybridizer/Year: Adam 1993
Growth habits: Vigorous, upright, 3–5′
Foliage: Medium, dark green with a glorious red tint in new growth, glossy
Blooms: Dusky red, 25 petals, 4½–5″, exhibition form
Fragrance: Intense, rose
Awards: Plus Belle Rose de France 1991, Nantes Fragrance Award 1991
Comments: This plant has terrific foliage and blooms. The foliage starts as a burgundy red and ages to a dark glossy green that is superb. The blooms have an enticing scent and become a deeper red in milder temperatures.

Let Freedom Ring

Type: Hybrid Tea
Hybridizer/Year: Earman 2004
Growth habits: Vigorous, upright, 4–5′
Foliage: Medium, medium green, glossy
Blooms: Strawberry red, 25 petals, 4–5″, exhibition form
Fragrance: Slight
Comments: It is appropriate that a World War II veteran hybridized this beauty. This bush produces

blooms with great form and a long vase life as cut flowers. The large, strawberry red blooms have classic hybrid tea form and contrast well with the glossy foliage. This bush does well in all types of landscape designs.

Hybrid teas and grandifloras *(continued)*

Liebeszauber

Type: Hybrid Tea
Hybridizer/Year: Kordes 1990
Growth habits: Upright, tall, 4–6'
Foliage: Large, dark green, leathery
Blooms: Velvety red, 30–35 petals, exhibition form
Fragrance: Slight
Comments: This is a vigorous, tall-growing bush that does well in all types of landscape design. The large blooms

produce prolifically throughout the growing season. The foliage begins as a dark red and ages to a dark, glossy green. Rating: 8.0

Louise Estes

Type: Hybrid Tea
Hybridizer/Year: Winchel 1991
Growth habits: Upright, tall, vigorous bush, 5' tall and 4' wide
Foliage: Mildew resistant
Blooms: Pink blend, medium pink with a white reverse, ruffled at edges in cool climates. Full, classic hybrid tea form, 40–45 petals. Large, 4 to 5" across.
Fragrance: Strong and fruity
Comments: One of the top 10 exhibition roses for its large, perfectly formed flowers of an enticing color blend, Louise Estes is also a strong performer in the garden, with medium-size bushes that are disease resistant. An ideal rose for the vase, long-lived and fragrant. Named to honor Louise Estes, a dedicated rosarian and artist. Rating: 8.3

Love & Peace

Type: Hybrid Tea
Hybridizer/Year: Lim and Twomey 2001
Growth habits: Medium, bushy, 4–6'
Foliage: Dark green, glossy
Blooms: Yellow splashed with pink, 40 petals, 4"
Fragrance: Slight
Awards: AARS 2002
Comments: This rose is a progeny of the one of the all-time favorites, Peace, yet is bushier and has longer stems. The large, showy blooms do well as cut flowers. The characteristic dark green, glossy, disease resistant foliage is similar to that of its parent. Rating: 7.8

Maria Shriver

Type: Grandiflora
Hybridizer/Year: Dorieux 2004
Growth habits: Medium, upright, stately, 4–5'
Foliage: Medium, dark green, glossy, clean
Blooms: Pure white, 40 petals, 4–5", neat clusters on long elegant stems
Fragrance: Intense, citrus
Comments: This is a striking bush for any landscape design. The fragrant white blooms and dark green, glossy leaves are reminiscent of gardenias. It was named for the broadcast reporter and First Lady of California.

Marilyn Monroe

Type: Hybrid Tea
Hybridizer/Year: Carruth 2002
Growth habits: Upright, medium-tall, 4–5′
Foliage: Medium green, matte
Blooms: Creamy apricot showing a light wash of green, large to 6″, 30–35 petals
Fragrance: Mild, citrus
Comments: This vigorous, abundant bloomer was named for the Hollywood

legend. Its large, sultry blooms have classic hybrid tea form and are outstanding in the garden, in the vase, or on the show table. This rose enjoys the heat and reveals its best bloom color in hot conditions. It is a must-have for any rose lover. Rating: 7.9

Mellow Yellow

Type: Hybrid Tea
Hybridizer/Year: Carruth 2001
Growth habits: Medium to tall, upright, 4–5′
Foliage: Medium, dark green, glossy, clean
Blooms: Clear, pure yellow, 30–35 petals, 4½–5½″
Fragrance: Moderate, fruity
Comments: This yellow rose holds its color until the blooms fall off. The plant is a disease-resistant, vigorous bloomer that fits into any landscape design. Its dark green leaves provide contrast for the yellow blooms. Blooms are larger in cooler weather. Rating: 7.8

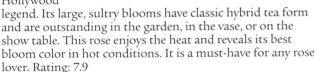

Melodie Parfumee

Type: Grandiflora
Hybridizer/Year: Dorieux 1995
Growth habits: Upright, bushy, medium-tall, 5′
Foliage: Medium, dark green, semiglossy
Blooms: Dark lavender plum with a lighter reverse, 26–40 petals, 4–5″
Fragrance: Intense, damask
Comments: This vigorous bush produces abundant blooms throughout the growing season. The plum-colored blooms are eyecatching and age to a silvery lavender. This bush was hybridized by a Frenchman and has the intense fragrance to prove it. Rating: 7.7

Memorial Day

Type: Hybrid Tea
Hybridizer/Year: Carruth 2004
Growth habits: Upright, bushy, medium-tall, 5–6′
Foliage: Lush, bright green, clean
Blooms: Orchid pink, large, 50 plus petals, 5–6″
Fragrance: Intense, damask
Awards: AARS 2004
Comments: Memorial Day is a time to

remember, and this is a rose to remember. It boasts glorious, large blooms; disease resistant, lush foliage, and intense fragrance. This memorable beauty likes the heat and produces darker blooms in autumn. Rating: 7.6

Michelangelo

Type: Hybrid Tea
Hybridizer/Year: Meilland 1997
Growth habits: 2–5′ tall, 2–4′ wide
Foliage: Deep green, glossy
Blooms: Medium yellow, 40–50 petals, 5″, double
Fragrance: Mild, lemon
Awards: Association des Jounalistes du Jardin et de l'Horticulture 1999, Bagatelle Certificate of Merit 1997, Monza Gold Medal 1997

Comments: One of the Romantica series introduced by the Conard-Pyle Company in 1997, Michelangelo bears loads of butter yellow blossoms with a full, many-petaled, cupped, old-fashioned look. Plants can grow tall, so they are best used toward the back of a bed. Blooms are larger in warmer areas. Rating: 7.6

Midas Touch

Type: Hybrid Tea
Hybridizer/Year: Christensen 1992
Growth habits: Upright, bushy, 4–5′
Foliage: Large, medium green
Blooms: Dark, unfading yellow, urn-shape, 15–25 petals, 3½–4″, exhibition form
Fragrance: Moderate, musk
Awards: AARS 1994
Comments: This vigorous bush is ideal for all types of landscape designs. The bright yellow blooms are quick to repeat and add a spot of color to any garden. The foliage adds great contrast to the blooms. Rating: 7.5

Miss All-American Beauty

Type: Hybrid Tea
Hybridizer/Year: Meilland 1965
Growth habits: Tall, vigorous, upright, bushy, 5–6′
Foliage: Dark green, leathery
Blooms: Deep pink, 55 petals, 4½–5½″, exhibition form
Fragrance: Intense
Awards: Portland Gold Medal 1966, AARS 1968

Comments: This hardy plant is a good choice for the new gardener and performs well in all climates. The large cerise pink blooms hold their color and have a strong rose fragrance. The bushy plant is well endowed with leathery leaves. The blooms are equally attractive in a vase as in the garden. Rating: 7.7

Mister Lincoln

Type: Hybrid Tea
Hybridizer/Year: Swim & Weeks 1964
Growth habits: Upright, tall, 5–7′
Foliage: Dark green, leathery, matte
Blooms: Dark red, 35 petals, 4½–6″, exhibition form
Fragrance: Intense
Awards: AARS 1965
Comments: This rose set a milestone in the history of red roses. It is a vigorous grower that produces gorgeous velvety blooms that tend to acquire a blue tinge as they age. It has a strong damask rose scent that is reminiscent of old garden roses. A stunning bush in the garden, it works well in the back of the border. Rating: 8.3

Moonstone

Type: Hybrid Tea
Hybridizer/Year: Carruth 1998
Growth habits: Upright, medium, 4–6′
Foliage: Large, medium green, leathery
Blooms: White with delicate pink edging, 26–40 petals, 4½–5″, exhibition form
Fragrance: Slight, tea
Comments: This is a gem of a rose. The large, white blooms edged with pink have almost a pearly essence and classic hybrid tea form. The leaves contrast nicely with the blooms. This rose does equally well in the garden, in the vase, or on the show table. It blooms best in a little heat. Rating: 8.2

Nancy Reagan

Type: Hybrid Tea
Hybridizer/Year: Jackson & Perkins 2004
Growth habits: Medium, upright, 5′
Foliage: Medium, dark green, glossy
Blooms: Light apricot aging to a deeper apricot, 30 petals, 5″, exhibition form
Fragrance: Slight, sweet

Comments: This rose was chosen by the former First Lady because of its captivating color. It has long stems and holds its color and shape well, making it great as a cut flower. It is a prolific bloomer throughout the growing season and does well in all types of landscape designs. Rating: 7.3

Neptune

Type: Hybrid Tea
Hybridizer/Year: Carruth 2003
Growth habits: Upright, medium, 4–5′
Foliage: Medium green, glossy, clean
Blooms: Light lavender tinged with purple, 30–40 petals, 4″, exhibition form
Fragrance: Strong, sweet, rose
Comments: This is a vigorous bush with an abundance of vitality. It is a prolific bloomer throughout the growing season. Its large purple-edged, lavender blooms have classic hybrid tea form and are outstanding. It also has disease-resistant foliage. Its fragrance, however, is one of its best characteristics. The best bloom size occurs in cooler temperatures. Rating: 7.4

New Zealand

Type: Hybrid Tea
Hybridizer/Year: McGredy 1989
Growth habits: Upright, medium, 4–5′
Foliage: Large, medium green, semiglossy, disease resistant
Blooms: Large, soft creamy pink, 30–35 petals, 4½–5″, exhibition form
Fragrance: Strong, honeysuckle
Awards: Portland Gold Medal 1996, Rose of the Year, Aukland, New Zealand 1990
Comments: This great rose is another creation of Sam McGredy. It is a vigorous, superbly shaped bush that produces an abundance of blooms throughout the growing season. The soft pink blooms have classic hybrid tea form and a wonderful fragrance. This bush does equally well in the garden, in a vase, or on the trophy table. The best bloom size occurs in cooler temperatures. Rating: 7.9

Hybrid teas and grandifloras *(continued)*

Octoberfest

Type: Grandiflora
Hybridizer/Year: McGredy 1998
Growth habits: Upright, tall, 6′
Foliage: Dark green, glossy, with reddish new growth
Blooms: Large, autumnal colors from cream to orange-red, 35 petals, exhibition form
Fragrance: Slight to moderate, fruity
Awards: Portland Gold Medal 2004
Comments: This bush lives up to its name with blooms that are a blend of autumn colors. It has glossy green leaves that begin as dark red shoots. The color seems to brighten in cool weather. Rating: 7.5

Oklahoma

Type: Hybrid Tea
Hybridizer/Year: Swim & Weeks 1964
Growth habits: Tall, vigorous, upright, bushy, 5–6′
Foliage: Large, dark green, matte, leathery
Blooms: Dark red, 40–45 petals, 4–5½″, exhibition form
Fragrance: Intense
Awards: Japan Gold Medal 1963
Comments: This rose comes from the same parentage as Mister Lincoln and has many of its characteristics. The blooms have the same dusky red color, classic hybrid tea form, and sensational scent. The plant is disease resistant. The darkest color and best bloom performance occur in warmer climates. Rating: 6.9

Olympiad

Type: Hybrid Tea
Hybridizer/Year: McGredy 1982
Growth habits: Upright, medium, bushy, 4–6′
Foliage: Large, medium green, matte, disease resistant
Blooms: Rich, nonfading, medium red, 30–35 petals, 4½–5″, exhibition form
Fragrance: Slight
Awards: AARS 1984, Portland Gold Medal 1985
Comments: This is one of the all-time best red roses for landscape or exhibition use. Its blooms are a brilliant, rich red that does not fade in the heat. The color holds exceptionally well, making it excellent for cutting. The bush is vigorous and disease free. The best size occurs in cool weather. This rose made its debut by lining the streets of Los Angeles in 1984 and awing those attending the Olympic Games. Rating: 8.6

Opening Night

Type: Hybrid Tea
Hybridizer/Year: Zary 1998
Growth habits: Upright, medium, 4–6′, slighty spreading
Foliage: Dark green, semiglossy, disease resistant
Blooms: Medium, bright deep red, 25–30 petals, exhibition form
Fragrance: Slight
Awards: AARS 1998, Portland Gold Medal 2003
Comments: This vigorous bush produces blooms in abundance throughout the growing season. The blooms are a true bright red and hold their color for a long time and are excellent for cutting. The large, velvety blooms have classic hybrid tea form and are surrounded by dark green foliage. It does well in all but the harshest-winter areas with the best flower form and color occur in cooler temperatures. Rating: 7.8

Paradise

Type: Hybrid Tea
Hybridizer/Year: Weeks 1978
Growth habits: Upright, medium, 4–5′
Foliage: Glossy, dark green
Blooms: Silvery lavender with ruby red edging, 25–30 petals, 3½–4½″, exhibition form
Fragrance: Moderate, fruity
Awards: AARS 1979, Portland Gold Medal 1979
Comments: This lavender rose remains one of the most popular today. The bloom colors are exceptional, particularly in warmer temperatures. The bush is adorned by disease-resistant foliage. This rose is great in the garden or the vase, and has graced show trophy tables. Rating: 7.6

Peace

Type: Hybrid Tea
Hybridizer/Year: Meilland 1945
Growth habits: Vigorous, upright, tall, bushy, 5–6′
Foliage: Large, deep green, glossy, leathery, disease resistant
Blooms: Golden yellow with pink edges, 40–45 petals, 5–6″, globular, exhibition form
Fragrance: Slight
Awards: Portland Gold Medal 1944, AARS 1946, Royal National Rose Society Gold Medal 1947, AARS Gold Medal 1947, Golden Rose of The Hague 1965
Comments: This rose set the standard for all modern roses of its century. It is renowned for its vigor, blooms, and foliage. It was one of the first to demonstrate that rose bushes can be beautiful even when not in bloom. A stunning cut flower, it is also available in a climbing form. Rating: 8.1

Perfect Moment

Type: Hybrid Tea
Hybridizer/Year: Kordes 1989
Growth habits: Upright, medium, bushy, 4–5′
Foliage: Medium, medium green, semiglossy
Blooms: Large, yellow with a broad red edge and a yellow reverse, 30–35 petals, 4–4½″, exhibition form
Fragrance: Slight, fruity
Awards: AARS 1991
Comments: This vigorous, disease-resistant bush produces a showy display of blooms throughout the growing season. The bright deep-yellow blooms are edged with a wide band of red, producing amazing contrast. The foliage provides a backdrop for the glowing blooms. The colors appear brighter in moderate temperatures. Rating: 7.8

Peter Mayle

Type: Hybrid Tea
Hybridizer/Year: Meilland 2001
Growth habits: Bushy upright, 4–6′ tall and 3′ wide
Foliage: Semiglossy, deep green
Blooms: Deep pink, 26–40 petals, 4–5″, full cupped
Fragrance: Strong, old rose fragrance
Awards: Monza Silver Medal 1998

Comments: Introduced in the United States in 2003 by Conard-Pyle, Peter Mayle is one of the Romantica series of roses. Borne on long, straight stems, the lovely deep reddish pink blooms with good form and a strong old rose fragrance provide enjoyment indoors as well as in the garden. The flowers are colorfast outdoors even in heat, and are long-lived in the vase, lasting 10 days or more. In the garden this is an extremely vigorous bush that can survive the heat and humidity of summer. It is disease resistant and tolerates more shade than most roses. Zones 6–10. Rating: 7.6

Prima Donna

Type: Grandiflora
Hybridizer/Year: Shirakawa 1984
Growth habits: Vigorous, bushy, spreading, 4'
Foliage: Large, medium green, semiglossy
Blooms: Deep fuchsia-pink, 27 petals, 4", exhibition form
Fragrance: Slight
Awards: AARS 1988, Portland Gold Medal 1992
Comments: This vigorous grandiflora makes quite a statement in the garden. The deep fuchsia-pink blooms have exquisite form and appear in abundance throughout the growing season. Its foliage contrasts well with the blooms. It is occasionally seen on exhibition trophy tables. Rating: 7.4

Pristine

Type: Hybrid Tea
Hybridizer/Year: Warriner 1978
Growth habits: Upright, vigorous, spreading, 5–7'
Foliage: Large, dark green, leathery, disease resistant
Blooms: Large, creamy white with pink blushings, 25–30 petals, 5–6", excellent substance
Fragrance: Slight
Awards: Royal National Rose

Society Edland Fragrance Award 1979, Portland Gold Medal 1979
Comments: This rose is a consistent performer that opens quickly but lasts a long time. It does well in all types of landscape designs. The glorious blooms contrast well with the foliage. The blooms hold their color well in all types of climates. This rose is a must for any rose lover. Rating: 8.6

Queen Elizabeth

Type: Grandiflora
Hybridizer/Year: Lammerts 1954
Growth habits: Upright, vigorous, tall, 5–7'
Foliage: Dark green, glossy, leathery, disease resistant
Blooms: Clear, medium pink, 30–35 petals, 3½–4", small clusters, exhibition form
Fragrance: Moderate
Awards: Portland Gold Medal 1954, AARS 1955, Royal National Rose Society Gold Medal 1955, AARS Gold Medal 1957, World Federation of Rose Societies Hall of Fame 1978
Comments: This is the prototype grandiflora, and it has maintained its popularity for more than 50 years. The large, clear pink blooms have high centers and continue in abundance throughout the growing season. This is a consistent performer in all climates and is appropriately named for the monarch of England. Rating: 7.8

Radiant Perfume

Type: Grandiflora
Hybridizer/Year: Jackson & Perkins 2004
Growth habits: Medium, upright, bushy, 5′
Foliage: Medium, dark green, glossy
Blooms: Golden yellow, 25 petals, 4–5″
Fragrance: Intense, citrus
Comments: This rose has a pleasing fragrance. The vigorous, upright bush has long stems ideal for bouquets. The blooms are a glowing rich yellow. They are surrounded by glossy, dark green foliage that contrasts well with the blooms. Rating: 7.6

Reba McEntire

Type: Grandiflora
Hybridizer/Year: McGredy 1997
Growth habits: Vigorous, upright, medium, bushy, 3–4′
Foliage: Large, dark green, glossy, disease resistant
Blooms: Bright, deep orange-red, 30–35 petals, 4–4½″, small clusters
Fragrance: Slight, tea
Awards: New Zealand Gold Star of the South Pacific 1994, Portland Gold Medal 2000
Comments: This bush adds a splash of color to any landscape. The brilliant orange-red blooms are borne in clusters and seem to glow amid the foliage. This bush shines almost as brightly as the country and western singer and television star for whom it was named. Rating: 7.7

Remember Me

Type: Hybrid Tea
Hybridizer/Year: Cocker 1984
Growth habits: Upright, medium, bushy, spreading, 4–5′
Foliage: Small, dark green, glossy
Blooms: Cinnamon tan blushed to a rusty orange, 20–30 petals, 4–5″, exhibition form
Fragrance: Slight, fruit and spice
Awards: Belfast Gold Medal 1986, Royal National Rose Society James Mason Gold Medal 1995
Comments: The novel color of this rose makes it a memorable garden standout. The blooms have classic hybrid tea form. The plant is vigorous and produces abundant blooms throughout the growing season. It is great in the garden or in a vase. Rating: 7.1

Rina Hugo

Type: Hybrid Tea
Hybridizer/Year: Dorieux 1993
Growth habits: Vigorous, upright, tall, slightly spreading, 5–7′
Foliage: Medium, dark green, glossy, disease resistant
Blooms: Deep pinkish raspberry, 35–40 petals, 5–6″, exhibition form
Fragrance: Slight
Comments: This is a hardy, bushy plant that produces prolific blooms throughout the growing season. The blooms are a deep shocking raspberry pink and are gorgeous in the garden or on the show table. This is an outstanding rose for any landscape project. The rose was named to honor a popular South African singer. Rating: 7.8

Hybrid teas and grandifloras *(continued)*

Rio Samba

Type: Hybrid Tea
Hybridizer/Year: Warriner 1991
Growth habits: Medium, upright, bushy, 4–5′
Foliage: Medium, dark green, matte, some prickles
Blooms: Medium yellow fading to peachy pink, 15–25 petals, 2¾–3″, exhibition form
Fragrance: Slight
Awards: AARS 1993
Comments: The blooms tend to grow in small clusters that make their own statement in the garden. The plant is vigorous and has foliage that contrasts well with the blooms. This bush brightens any landscape project. Rating: 7.4

Ronald Reagan

Type: Hybrid Tea
Hybridizer/Year: Zary 2005
Growth habits: Tall, upright, 4–5′ tall. Vigorous and well-branched.
Foliage: Medium, glossy, dark green
Blooms: Red blend, 4–4¼″ wide, 26–40 petals
Fragrance: Mild, sweet
Awards: Rose Hills Gold Medal
Comments: Introduced by Jackson & Perkins in 2004, this magnificent rose honors the president who declared the rose the national floral emblem of the United States. The two-toned blooms are brilliant red with a white reverse on the petals. Fast repeat to the blooms means the bush is perpetually loaded with flowers all season. Plants are mildew and rust resistant, but protect them from black spot. Rating: 7.6

Royal Highness

Type: Hybrid Tea
Hybridizer/Year: Swim & Weeks 1962
Growth habits: Medium, upright, bushy, 4–5′
Foliage: Medium, dark green, glossy, leathery
Blooms: Soft light pink, 43 petals, 5–5½″, exhibition form
Fragrance: Intense
Awards: Portland Gold Medal 1960, Madrid Gold Medal 1962, AARS 1963, AARS David Fuerstenberg Prize 1964
Comments: This vigorous plant produces abundant blooms throughout the growing season. The soft pastel blooms are large and have a classic hybrid tea form. The foliage provides a pleasant backdrop for the blooms. It does equally well in the garden, in the vase, or on the show table. Rating: 7.7

Secret

Type: Hybrid Tea
Hybridizer/Year: Tracy 1992
Growth habits: Upright, medium-tall, bushy, 4–6′
Foliage: Large, medium green, glossy
Blooms: Creamy pink edged with a deeper pink, 30–35 petals, 4–4½″, exhibition form
Fragrance: Strong, sweet and spicy
Awards: AARS 1994, Portland Gold Medal 1998
Comments: Its creamy pink-edged blooms have hybrid tea form and are as pretty in a vase as they are in the garden. The foliage is a perfect foil for these light colored blooms. This vigorous plant is hardy in harsher climates. Rating: 7.9

Sheer Bliss

Type: Hybrid Tea
Hybridizer/Year: Warriner 1985
Growth habits: Upright, medium, bushy, 5–6'
Foliage: Medium, medium green, matte
Blooms: White with a pink center, 35 petals, 4–4½", exhibition form
Fragrance: Moderate, spicy
Awards: Gold Medal Japan 1984, AARS 1987
Comments: This rose is prized for its use in arrangements and wedding bouquets. The creamy white blooms have a blush pink center and the fragrance is an added bonus. The bush is vigorous and relatively weather resistant and does well in all climates. Rating: 7.8

Signature

Type: Hybrid Tea
Hybridizer/Year: Warriner 1996
Growth habits: Upright, medium-tall, bushy, 4–5'
Foliage: Large, dark green, semiglossy, leathery
Blooms: Deep pink and cream blend with a light pink and cream reverse, 26–40 petals, 5", exhibition form
Fragrance: Moderate
Awards: Jackson & Perkins' Rose of the Year for 1996
Comments: This is another of Bill Warriner's excellent creations. This bushy, upright plant has dark green foliage to show off its opulent blooms. The large blooms are deep pink swirled with cream and have a classic hybrid tea form, which make it an excellent exhibition rose and garden specimen. Rating: 7.6

Silver Lining

Type: Hybrid Tea
Hybridizer/Year: Dickson 1958
Growth habits: Vigorous, upright, 4–5'
Foliage: Medium, medium green, matte
Blooms: Silvery rose, 30 petals, 4–6", exhibition form
Fragrance: Slight
Awards: Royal National Rose Society Gold Medal 1958, Portland Gold Medal 1964
Comments: This is an outstanding rose for any landscape but it can be difficult to find. It is a bushy plant and a prolific producer of excellent blooms. The blooms are a magnificent silvery pink with stunning variations. This is a great rose in the garden or on the show table. Its foliage is disease resistant and completes the display of this beauty.

Spellbound

Type: Hybrid Tea
Hybridizer/Year: Zary 2006
Growth habits: Vigorous, upright, bushy, 5'
Foliage: Medium, dark green, semiglossy
Blooms: Deep coral red to coral pink, 30 petals, 4½", thick petals
Fragrance: Slight, spicy
Awards: Jackson & Perkins' Rose of the Year for 2006

Comments: This rose is a hardy, disease-resistant plant. The blooms have classic hybrid tea form. They are long lasting in a vase and exceptional as cut flowers.

St. Patrick

Type: Hybrid Tea
Hybridizer/Year: Strickland 1996
Growth habits: Vigorous, thornless, 3½–5'
Foliage: Disease-resistant
Blooms: Yellow blend, 30–35 petals, 5–6"
Fragrance: Slight
Awards: AARS 1996
Comments: Chartreuse in bud, the flowers of this novel rose open slowly to a cool yellow with a distinct greenish cast at the base of the petals. Heat brings out the flower color, especially in the Southeast, where the outer petals shade to green. In cool-summer climates the outer petals shade to gold. Plants are highly disease-resistant. It is moderately hardy, loves heat, and is a great cut flower. Rating: 8.0

Strike It Rich

Type: Grandiflora
Hybridizer/Year: Carruth 2007
Growth habits: Upright, medium, bushy, 5–6'
Foliage: Medium, dark green, semiglossy, disease resistant, red stems
Blooms: Deep golden yellow edged with orange and pink, 30 petals, 3½–4"
Fragrance: Intense, sweet, spice
Awards: AARS 2007
Comments: This vigorous bush is loaded with blooms that hold their color and are great for bouquets or in the garden. The intense, spicy fragrance and unusual red stems make it a treasure.

Sunset Celebration

Type: Hybrid Tea
Hybridizer/Year: Fryer 1994
Growth habits: Upright, medium, bushy, 4–6'
Foliage: Large, medium green, semiglossy
Blooms: Creamy apricot and amber blend, 35–40 petals, 4½–5", exhibition form
Fragrance: Mild, fruity
Awards: Belfast Gold Medal 1996, Golden Rose of The Hague 1997, AARS 1998, Portland Gold Medal 2001
Comments: This rose has won many awards and lives up to all of them. It is an outstanding garden plant as well as an exhibition and cut rose. The vigorous, disease-resistant plant produces prolific blooms. The blooms have substance and classic hybrid tea form. This bloom was named in honor of *Sunset* magazine's 100th anniversary. Rating: 7.8

Sunstruck

Type: Hybrid Tea
Hybridizer/Year: Carruth 2004
Growth habits: Tall, vigorous, upright, 5–6'
Foliage: Medium, dark green, glossy, disease resistant
Blooms: Apricot and gold with a darker shading at the edges, 25–30 petals, 5–6", exhibition form
Fragrance: Slight
Comments: This brilliant rose makes a delightful display with large, deep yellow-gold blooms that are blushed and bordered with apricot-orange. The bright yellow-veined fan pattern of the reverse inspired the name. The lush foliage contrasts well with the blooms.

Tahitian Sunset

Type: Hybrid Tea
Hybridizer/Year: Zary 2006
Growth habits: Vigorous, upright, bushy, 5′
Foliage: Medium, dark green, semiglossy, disease resistant
Blooms: Peachy apricot-pink with yellow highlights, 25–30 petals, 5″
Fragrance: Intense, sweet
Awards: AARS 2006
Comments: This plant produces an abundance of blooms. The pink blooms blushed with apricot yellow are quite fragrant. The foliage is disease resistant, dark green and semiglossy.

Tiffany

Type: Hybrid Tea
Hybridizer/Year: Lindquist 1954
Growth habits: Upright, vigorous, medium, 4–5′
Foliage: Medium, dark green, glossy
Blooms: Pink with yellow at the base, 25–30 petals, 4–5″, exhibition form
Fragrance: Intense, fruity
Awards: Portland Gold Medal 1954, AARS 1955, AARS David Fuerstenberg Prize 1957, AARS J. A. Gamble Rose Fragrance Award 1962
Comments: This excellent garden rose has been grown for fragrance and color for decades and remains popular. The bush produces abundant blooms throughout the growing season. The rosy pink to rosy salmon blooms are of classic hybrid tea form. This consistent performer was named for the famous jeweler. Rating: 7.9

Timeless

Type: Hybrid Tea
Hybridizer/Year: Zary 1997
Growth habits: Upright, vigorous, bushy, medium, 4′
Foliage: Medium, dark green, semiglossy
Blooms: Deep pink to light red with deep pink reverse, 17–25 petals, 4″, high-centered, exhibition form
Fragrance: Slight
Awards: AARS 1997

Comments: This is a must-have for fans of dark pink and light red roses. It is an upright bush with dark green, semiglossy foliage. The large, luscious blooms have classic hybrid tea form. Not be be confused with another rose named Timeless, which is white.

Top Notch

Type: Hybrid tea
Hybridizer/Year: McGredy 1998
Growth habits: Medium, vigorous, upright, 3–4′
Foliage: Medium, dark green, glossy, disease resistant
Blooms: Glowing gold, 30–40 petals, 3–4″
Fragrance: Moderate
Awards: Royal National Rose Society Rose of the Year, 2002
Comments: This bush is another disease-resistant product of Sam McGredy. Its glowing gold color is vibrant at any time, but it is especially good when it deepens with warm nights. Rating: 7.6

Touch of Class

Type: Hybrid Tea
Hybridizer/Year: Kriloff 1984
Growth habits: Upright, medium, bushy, 5–6′
Foliage: Large, dark green, semiglossy
Blooms: Large, medium pink shaded cream and coral, 30–35 petals, 4½–5½″, exhibition form
Fragrance: Slight, tea
Awards: AARS 1986, Portland Gold Medal 1988
Comments: The blooms on this plant are elegant, with high centers and unfurling petals. The light, creamy pink blooms are suffused with coral and have classic hybrid tea form. The foliage contrasts nicely with the blooms. This is an essential rose, particularly for gardeners interested in exhibiting. Rating: 8.9

Hybrid teas and grandifloras *(continued)*

Tournament of Roses

Type: Grandiflora
Hybridizer/Year: Warriner 1988
Growth habits: Upright, bushy, medium, 4–5'
Foliage: Large, dark green, semiglossy, disease resistant
Blooms: Light coral with deep pink reverse, 30–35 petals, 4", exhibition form
Fragrance: Slight
Awards: AARS 1989

Comments: Named in honor of the 100th anniversary of the Pasadena Rose Parade, this vigorous, disease-resistant bush is easy to grow. Its two-toned blooms, dark pink on the outside and lighter pink on the inside, grow in abundant clusters. The green leaves and light spicy scent add to this plant's attraction. Color is better in warm temperatures. Rating: 8.2

Ultimate Pink

Type: Hybrid Tea
Hybridizer/Year: Zary 1998
Growth habits: Upright, vigorous, tall, 4–6'
Foliage: Large, medium green, matte
Blooms: Large, light pink, 26–40 petals, 4½–5", full
Fragrance: Slight, sweet
Awards: Jackson & Perkins' Rose of the Year 1999
Comments: This disease-resistant plant produces abundantly throughout the growing season. The blooms are a remarkable clear, true pink borne on long stems that are ideal for cutting. They have high centers and classic hybrid tea form. The foliage contrasts with the blooms. Rating: 7.3

Veterans' Honor

Type: Hybrid Tea
Hybridizer/Year: Zary 1997
Growth habits: Upright, spreading, tall, 5–6'
Foliage: Medium, dark green, semiglossy
Blooms: Large, bright red, 26–40 petals, 5–5½", exhibition form
Fragrance: Slight, raspberry
Awards: Jackson & Perkins' Rose of the Year 2000
Comments: This rose is a terrific selection to honor our veterans. It is a vigorous, bushy, bright red rose.

The blooms have classic hybrid tea form and are borne on long stems. They also have a long vase life. This rose has graced show trophy tables across the country, and 10 percent of the net sales are donated to veterans health care. Rating: 8.1

Voluptuous!

Type: Hybrid Tea
Hybridizer/Year: Zary 2005
Growth habits: Vigorous, upright, bushy, 5'
Foliage: Medium, dark green, glossy
Blooms: Deep fuchsia pink, 30–35 petals, 5", high centered
Fragrance: Slight, sweet
Awards: Jackson & Perkins' Rose of the Year 2005
Comments: This disease resistant bush is a prolific bloomer. The deep fuchsia-pink blooms have classic hybrid tea form and are long-lasting in a vase. The bush does well in all landscapes.

We Salute You

Type: Hybrid Tea
Hybridizer/Year: Carruth 2005
Growth habits: Vigorous, upright, bushy, 4–5'
Foliage: Medium, dark green, glossy
Blooms: Orange buds transition to coral-pink, 30 petals, 5″, exhibition form
Fragrance: Moderate, spicy
Comments: This is the third rose variety named to provide funds for the Remember Me Rose Gardens. This rose honors those who died in the Pentagon on September 11, 2001. It is a statuesque bush with dark green, glossy foliage. The large blooms are warm orange and pink with classic hybrid tea form. This is a special bush with a special purpose.

Whisper

Type: Hybrid Tea
Hybridizer/Year: Dickson 2002
Growth habits: Upright, vigorous, medium, 5–6'
Foliage: Large, dark green, glossy, disease resistant
Blooms: Large, sparkling white with a tint of yellow, 30–35 petals, 4½–5″, exhibition form
Fragrance: Slight

Awards: AARS 2003
Comments: This vigorous, disease-resistant plant is a prolific bloomer throughout the growing season. The white blooms tinged with soft, creamy yellow are among the best in this color class. They have classic hybrid tea form and long stems for cutting and do well in the garden or in a vase. Rating: 7.5

Wild Blue Yonder

Type: Grandiflora
Hybridizer/Year: Carruth 2005
Growth habits: Vigorous, upright, bushy, 4–5'
Foliage: Medium, dark green, glossy, disease resistant
Blooms: Reddish purple, with a lavender eye and bright yellow stamens, 25–30 petals, 4–5″, ruffled
Fragrance: Intense, citrus and rose
Awards: AARS 2006
Comments: These grandiflora blooms are unique in color and style. The ruffled, red-purple blooms have lavender eyes and bright yellow stamens and open similarly to a camellia. The intense citrus and rose fragrance is another distinguishing characteristic. Deeper colors appear in cooler temperatures.

Floribundas and polyanthas

I f you want a lot of color in your garden, floribundas and polyanthas are perfect.

Floribundas range in height from 2 to 6 feet, depending on the variety. They tend to have slightly spreading to full-spreading Growth habits and some mounding Growth habits. But they always bloom in clusters of many flowers.

Many varieties of floribundas have a fairly constant bloom cycle while others bloom first in a large flush and then need some time to repeat. Removing the spent blooms (deadheading) tends to encourage more frequent flushes of flowers in floribundas.

Polyanthas are similar to floribundas but they usually have much smaller flowers borne in large, tight clusters. Their growth habit is usually short to mounded to sprawling and they come in a variety of colors. They go to seed quite readily so diligent deadheading is requried in order to get rebloom.

Most floribundas and polyanthas do well in Zones 5-10 with some doing well even in Zone 4 and Zone 11.

See page 26 for more information about floribundas and polyanthas.

▲ The overall shape of Amber Queen is typical of so many floribundas—attractively compact and shrubby. The lovely apricot hue of the flowers is also typical of floribundas. They come in a wide range of colors and bloom a long time.

Amber Queen

Type: Floribunda
Hybridizer/Year: Harkness 1983
Growth habits: Medium, compact, 3–4'
Foliage: Large, copper red to medium green, semiglossy, reddish prickles, disease resistant
Blooms: Apricot gold, 25–30 petals, 3½", ruffled, cup shape
Fragrance: Intense
Awards: Royal National Rose Society Rose of the Year 1984, Genoa Gold Medal 1986, Orleans Gold Medal 1987, New Zealand Gold Star of the South Pacific 1988, AARS 1988
Comments: This is a hardy, compact bush that produces clusters of blooms for the garden or a vase. The golden amber color and intense fragrance are welcoming. Bushes planted in a group make a striking focal point. Rating: 7.1

Angel Face

Type: Floribunda
Hybridizer/Year: Swim & Weeks 1968
Growth habits: Medium, vigorous, upright, 3'
Foliage: Medium, dark green, glossy, leathery
Blooms: Mauve lavender with ruby blushed edges, 25–30 petals, 3½–4" exhibition form
Fragrance: Intense, fruity
Awards: AARS 1969
Comments: This low-growing, compact bush produces exquisite ruffled blooms all season long. Lavender petals, blushed with ruby red edges, create a dramatic display. Its sweet fragrance makes it a favorite among rose lovers everywhere. It may be tender in harsher climates. Rating: 7.7

Apricot Nectar

Type: Floribunda
Hybridizer/Year: Boerner 1965
Growth habits: Medium, vigorous, upright, bushy, 4–5′
Foliage: Medium, dark green, glossy
Blooms: Pink-apricot with a golden base, 35–40 petals, 5″
Fragrance: Intense, fruity
Awards: AARS 1996
Comments: This is one of the taller-growing floribundas. Its foliage is an ideal background for the pink-apricot blooms. It is relatively disease resistant and produces an abundance of blooms. Rating: 8.0

Betty Boop

Type: Floribunda
Hybridizer/Year: Carruth 1999
Growth habits: Rounded, vigorous, bushy, medium, 3–5′
Foliage: Medium, dark green, glossy, dark red new growth
Blooms: Yellow-ivory edged with red, fades to white, 6–12 petals, 4″, clusters
Fragrance: Moderate, fruity
Awards: AARS 1999, Portland Gold Medal 2001
Comments: This outstanding bush produces long-lasting abundant blooms and reblooms quickly. It performs consistently in all climates and is so striking that it has quickly become a favorite. It was named for the animated cartoon character. Rating: 8.0

Betty Prior

Type: Floribunda
Hybridizer/Year: Prior 1935
Growth habits: Medium, vigorous, upright, bushy, 4–6′
Foliage: Medium, dark green, glossy, disease resistant
Blooms: Carmine pink, 5–7 petals, 4″, single form
Fragrance: Moderate
Awards: Royal National Rose Society of Great Britain Gold Medal 1933
Comments: This versatile bush thrives in harsh climates. The single, carmine-pink roses age to a deeper pink. This longtime favorite brings nostalgic memories for many rose growers. It is ideal for mass plantings. Rating: 8.2

Bill Warriner

Type: Floribunda
Hybridizer/Year: Zary 1997
Growth habits: Medium, compact, 3–4′
Foliage: Medium, dark green, semiglossy, moderate straight prickles
Blooms: Salmon-coral-pink, 26–40 petals, 3½–4″, ruffled edges
Fragrance: Slight
Comments: Named in memory of prolific hybridizer Bill Warriner, this bush epitomizes all that is good in a floribunda. It is a constant bloomer that produces classic hybrid tea form flowers in abundance. Its glossy foliage is a standout in the garden. Rating: 7.8

Black Cherry

Type: Floribunda
Hybridizer/Year: Zary 2006
Growth habits: Vigorous, upright, 3½–5′
Foliage: Medium, medium green, glossy
Blooms: Dark red with blackening, 20–25 petals, 3–3½″
Fragrance: Slight, damask
Awards: Jackson & Perkins' Floribunda of the Year 2006

Comments: It is novel in coloration and true to its name, beginning with a blackening around the tips of the buds and unfurling to a cherry red. It is a compact, abundant-blooming bush with a light fragrance.

Bolero 2004

Type: Floribunda
Hybridizer/Year: Meilland 2004
Growth habits: Medium, rounded, 2–4′ tall
Foliage: Large, glossy, dark green
Blooms: White, full, old garden rose form, 41–100 petals
Fragrance: Strong, traditional rose fragrance
Comments: Bolero exhibits exceptional performance in the garden, producing loads of flowers in quick succession all summer. Short stature makes it ideal for the front of a rose bed or mixed border. While not long-stemmed, the blossoms are beautiful in the vase, long-lived and intensely fragrant.

Blueberry Hill

Type: Floribunda
Hybridizer/Year: Carruth 1997
Growth habits: Upright, medium, rounded, bushy, 3–4′
Foliage: Large, serrated, dark green, glossy
Blooms: Large, clear lilac with golden stamens, 5–11 petals, 4″, exhibition form
Fragrance: Moderate, sweet, apple
Awards: Portland Gold Medal 2002
Comments: Its eyecatching light lavender blooms surrounded by glossy green foliage make it an attractive addition to garden or vase. It is a constant bloomer and does consistently well in all climates. Rating: 7.8

Brass Band

Type: Floribunda
Hybridizer/Year: Christensen 1993
Growth habits: Medium, upright, bushy, 4′
Foliage: Large, dark green, semiglossy, some prickles
Blooms: Melon-orange and yellow, 30–35 petals, 3–3½″
Fragrance: Slight
Awards: AARS 1995
Comments: The compact growth habit of this bush is ideal for the garden or landscape. It is adorned with an abundance of brassy ruffled blooms that stand out. It has better color and bloom size in cooler temperatures. Rating: 7.9

Brilliant Pink Iceberg

Type: Floribunda
Hybridizer/Year: Weatherly 1999
Growth habits: Medium, upright, rounded, 3–4′
Foliage: Large, light green, glossy, few prickles
Blooms: Deep pink with a white reverse, 17–25 petals, 3½–4″
Fragrance: Moderate
Comments: This bush is a sport of Pink Iceberg and has all of its parent's characteristics. The stunning difference is the cerise-pink and cream bloom, which intensifies in cooler weather. It is eyecatching in the garden or vase. Rating: 7.4

Burgundy Iceberg

Type: Floribunda
Hybridizer/Year: Weatherly 2003
Growth habits: Medium, upright, rounded, bushy, 3–4′
Foliage: Large, light green, glossy, few thorns
Blooms: Purple-red with a burgundy and cream reverse, 20–25 petals, 3½–4″
Fragrance: Slight, honey
Comments: This sport of Brilliant Pink Iceberg has all of its growing traits. It differs in its dark reddish-purple blooms, which intensify in cooler weather. It is an outstanding bloomer for all types of landscape uses.

Charles Aznavour

Type: Floribunda
Hybridizer/Year: Meilland 1988
Growth habits: Low, vigorous, bushy, 2–3′ tall, 3–4′ wide
Foliage: Medium, dark green, semiglossy
Blooms: White edged in pink, 15–20 petals, 4″
Fragrance: Slight
Awards: Bagatelle Gold Medal 1987, Courtrai Gold Medal 1987, Baden-Baden Gold Medal 1988
Comments: This low-growing, compact bush produces breathtaking white-edged pink blooms. It seems to bloom continuously and performs well in most climates. It makes a stunning hedge, and looks great in a vase.

Cherish

Type: Floribunda
Hybridizer/Year: Warriner 1980
Growth habits: Medium to tall, compact, spreading, 4′
Foliage: Large, dark green, glossy, leathery
Blooms: Coral-pink, 25–28 petals, 3–4″, exhibition form
Fragrance: Slight
Awards: AARS 1980
Comments: This compact but slightly spreading bush produces soft coral blooms that have a long vase life. Equally attractive in the garden, this rose is one of hybridizer Bill Warriner's award-winning trio of Love, Honor, and Cherish. Rating: 7.6

Chihuly

Type: Floribunda
Hybridizer/Year: Carruth 2003
Growth habits: Medium, upright, bushy, 3–4′
Foliage: Medium, dark green, glossy, leathery, with mahogany red new growth
Blooms: Bold yellow blushing to fiery orange and aging to a deep rich red, 25–30 petals, 3–4″
Fragrance: Slight

Comments: This bush with its great style and flashy colors was named in honor of noted glass artist Dale Chihuly. Its blooms change from apricot yellow to bright yellow edged with glowing red as the sun hits the petals. Foliage changes as well, from mahogany-red to deep dark green. Cooler temperatures bring larger flowers. Rating: 7.7

China Doll

Type: Polyantha
Hybridizer/Year: Lammerts 1946
Growth habits: Vigorous, upright, compact, bushy, 1–1½′
Foliage: Small, medium green, leathery, matte, five leaflets, thornless
Blooms: Rose with a mimosa yellow base, 24 petals, 1–2″, cupped
Fragrance: Slight, tea
Comments: This popular polyantha is a vigorous, compact, low-growing bush that produces large trusses of blooms. This bush seems to be constantly in bloom. The blooms are rose-pink with a mimosa yellow base and only a slight fragrance. This versatile plant can be used in any type of landscape design. Rating: 8.1

City of San Francisco

Type: Floribunda
Hybridizer/Year: Carruth 2000
Growth habits: Vigorous, upright, medium, 3–4′
Foliage: Medium, medium green, glossy
Blooms: Medium red, 17–25 petals, 4″, ruffled
Fragrance: Slight
Comments: Adorned with bountiful medium red

blooms and glossy green foliage, this bush is a welcome addition to any landscape. A vigorous, upright bush produces clusters of ruffled blooms and does well in most climates. Rating: 7.7

Class Act

Type: Floribunda
Hybridizer/Year: Warriner 1988
Growth habits: Medium, upright, bushy, 4–5′
Foliage: Medium, dark green, semiglossy, long narrow prickles
Blooms: Snowy white, 15–20 petals, 4″
Fragrance: Slight
Awards: AARS 1989, Portland Gold Medal 1989, Gold Star of the South Pacific, Palmerston North, New Zealand 1990
Comments: The contrast of the creamy white blooms with the dark green, semiglossy foliage is striking. This bush blooms continuously in sprays throughout the season and is great in borders or gardens. The popularity of this rose continues to grow. Rating: 7.8

Cotillion

Type: Floribunda
Hybridizer/Year: Zary 1999
Growth habits: Low, upright, spreading, 3½'
Foliage: Medium, dark green, glossy, moderate prickles
Blooms: Lavender with a pale lavender reverse, 41 petals, 4"
Fragrance: Intense
Awards: Rome Gold Medal 1998, Australia Gold Medal and Fragrance Award 2001
Comments: This fragrant, low-growing, spreading bush is suitable for borders and hedges. It produces clusters of lavender blooms throughout the growing season. It may be tender in harsher climates. Rating: 7.4

Easy Going

Type: Floribunda
Hybridizer/Year: Harkness 1999
Growth habits: Upright, bushy, medium, 3–3½'
Foliage: Large, bright light green, glossy
Blooms: Large, golden apricot with a peachy overlay, 25–30 petals, 3½–4", clusters
Fragrance: Moderate, fruity
Awards: Dublin Gold Medal 1996, Monza Silver Medal 1997, Royal National Rose Society Trial Ground Certificate 1998, Portland Gold Medal 2001
Comments: This sport of Livin' Easy is as spectacular as its parent. It is disease resistant and does well in all climates. It produces well-spaced clusters of plentiful golden yellow blooms clothed in glossy foliage. A must-have for the garden and great in mass plantings. Rating: 8.0

Day Breaker

Type: Floribunda
Hybridizer/Year: Fryer 2003
Growth habits: Medium, vigorous, bushy, 3–5'
Foliage: Medium, dark green with red edging, glossy, clean
Blooms: Yellow buds changing to shades of pink and apricot, 24–30 petals, 4", exhibition form
Fragrance: Moderate
Awards: AARS 2004, Portland's Best Rose 2004
Comments: This outstanding floribunda performs consistently well in all climates. This flower-laden plant makes a stunning display in the garden. It is equally stunning in a vase or on an exhibitor's table. Its blend of apricot, yellow, and pink is aesthetically pleasing in any landscape. Rating: 7.9

Ebb Tide

Type: Floribunda
Hybridizer/Year: Carruth 2006
Growth habits: Vigorous, upright, medium, 3–4'
Foliage: Medium, dark green, semiglossy
Blooms: Smoky deep plum-purple, 35-plus petals, 3–4"
Fragrance: Intense, clove
Comments: The smoky, deep-plum color is as attention getting as the fragrance. As the blooms open, they reveal bright golden stamens that contrast pleasantly with the plum petals. This bush improves as it becomes more established in the garden.

Floribundas and polyanthas *(continued)*

Escapade

Type: Floribunda
Hybridizer/Year: Harkness 1967
Growth habits: Medium, bushy, 3–4'
Foliage: Medium, light green, glossy, dense
Blooms: Magenta rose with a white center, 12 petals, 3"
Fragrance: Slight
Awards: Baden-Baden Gold Medal 1969, Belfast Gold Medal 1969, Anerkannte Deutsch Rose 1973
Comments: The color combination of this rose is easy to identify even at a distance. The lovely soft magenta petals surround a white eye. Its growth habit is suitable for a hedge or mass planting. Blooms often fade quickly in hot temperatures. Rating: 8.6

Eureka

Type: Floribunda
Hybridizer/Year: Kordes 2003
Growth habits: Low, vigorous, bushy, 3–4'
Foliage: Medium, dark green, glossy, clean
Blooms: Coppery gold and apricot, 35–40 petals, 4"
Fragrance: Light
Awards: AARS 2003
Comments: The bright golden yellow blooms on this plant present a dazzling display. The plant is easy to grow, vigorous, and an abundant bloomer. In warmer temperatures, the colors tend to intensify. Rating: 7.7

Europeana

Type: Floribunda
Hybridizer/Year: de Ruiter 1963
Growth habits: Upright, rounded, vigorous, 3–4'
Foliage: Large, bronze-tinted dark green, semiglossy
Blooms: Dark velvety crimson, 25–30 petals, 3", large, heavy clusters
Fragrance: Slight, tea
Awards: Golden Rose of The Hague 1962, AARS 1968, Portland Gold Medal 1970
Comments: This rose is a proven winner in all climates, although it prefers the heat. The large, bright red, velvety clusters make good color spots in any landscape. This floribunda outpaces many other red floribundas. Rating: 8.6

Excellenz von Schubert

Type: Polyantha
Hybridizer/Year: Lambert 1909
Growth habits: Vigorous, upright, bushy, 3½' tall
Foliage: Small, dark green, matte, some prickles
Blooms: Dark carmine red shading to lilac, 40-plus petals, 1½–2"
Fragrance: Slight
Comments: This tall-growing plant blooms in large clusters. It has long, arching canes and does well as a hedge or a very large shrub. The double blooms have little fragrance. This bush offers an amazing display of color when it is in bloom. Rating: 8.0

Fabulous!

Type: Floribunda
Hybridizer/Year: Zary 1997
Growth habits: Upright, vigorous, bushy, 3½–4′
Foliage: Dark green, glossy
Blooms: Bright, sparkling white blooms, 25–30 petals, 3–3½″, large clusters
Fragrance: Slight, sweet
Awards: Lyon Gold Medal 1997, Jackson & Perkins' Floribunda of the Year 2001
Comments: This plant produces a profusion of pure white blooms that are versatile for the garden or vase. It blooms in large clusters on upright stems. Rating: 7.7

First Kiss

Type: Floribunda
Hybridizer/Year: Warriner 1991
Growth habits: Medium, bushy, compact, 3–4′
Foliage: Medium, medium green, matte
Blooms: Light pink with a light yellow blending at the base, 15–25 petals, 3½″
Fragrance: Slight
Comments: This plant does well in mass plantings. It produces plentiful blooms in small clusters and is a versatile choice for any landscape. It is disease resistant and performs well in most climates. Rating: 8.2

Flirtatious

Type: Floribunda
Hybridizer/Year: Zary 2003
Growth habits: Medium, vigorous, bushy, 3½′
Foliage: Medium, dark green, glossy
Blooms: Cream with light pink-yellow stripes at the base, 25 petals, 3½″
Fragrance: Intense, fruity
Awards: Jackson & Perkins' Floribunda of the Year 2003

Comments: This floribunda has a gracefully spreading growth habit that is perfect for the garden. Its most outstanding feature, however, is the coloration of the blooms. The creamy buds burst open into subtle, lightly striped pink and yellow blooms with an intense fragrance. Rating: 7.5

French Lace

Type: Floribunda
Hybridizer/Year: Warriner 1980
Growth habits: Upright, bushy, 3½–4′
Foliage: Small, dark green, glossy
Blooms: Pastel apricot to creamy ivory, 30–35 petals, 4½″, exhibition form
Fragrance: Slight, fruity
Awards: AARS 1982, Portland Gold Medal 1984
Comments: This rose was one of the first of the pastel-toned blooms that quickly became popular. It is a vigorous bush that is constantly coverd with elegant pale apricot to blushed cream blooms. It is as good in the vase as it is in the garden, though not reliably winter hardy. Rating: 8.1

Floribundas and polyanthas *(continued)*

Gene Boerner

Type: Floribunda
Hybridizer/Year: Boerner 1969
Growth habits: Upright, 3½′
Foliage: Shiny light green
Blooms: Pink, medium, 35-40 petals
Fragrance: Spicy
Comments: Perfect pink blooms have classic high, pointed tea shape in medium to large clusters. Deepest colors occur in spring and fall. Rating: 8.3

George Burns

Type: Floribunda
Hybridizer/Year: Carruth 1996
Growth habits: Medium, vigorous, upright, compact, 3–3½′
Foliage: Large, dark green, glossy, numerous prickles
Blooms: Yellow striped irregularly with red, cream, and pink, 26–40 petals, 3–3½″
Fragrance: Moderate, fruity
Comments: This rose is as gleeful as the comedian for whom it was named, with its novel yellow, pink, scarlet, and cream striped blooms. Its compact growth habit and ruffled blooms fit in almost any landscape. Cooler temperatures bring out more of the yellow in the blooms. Rating: 7.7

Glad Tidings

Type: Floribunda
Hybridizer/Year: Tantau 1988
Growth habits: Medium, vigorous, upright, 3–4′
Foliage: Medium, medium green, semiglossy
Blooms: Bright crimson, cupped, 20 petals, 2–2½″
Fragrance: None
Awards: Durbanville Gold Medal 1991, Royal National Rose Society Rose of the Year 1989
Comments: This bush produces velvety, crimson blooms that are stunning in the garden, in the vase, or on the show table. It is a continuous bloomer throughout the growing season and withstands wet weather. It blooms in showy clusters of medium cupped blooms. It is susceptible to black spot. Rating: 8.1

Goldmarie

Type: Floribunda
Hybridizer/Year: Kordes 1984
Growth habits: Medium, vigorous, bushy, 3–4′
Foliage: Medium, medium green, glossy
Blooms: Deep yellow with a red reverse on the outer petal, 35 petals, 2½–3″
Fragrance: Slight
Comments: This plant does well in all types of landscape designs. It produces large clusters of bright, deep yellow, somewhat ruffled blooms. The blooms are surrounded by foliage that sets off their glowing hue. Rating: 7.5

Gruss an Aachen

Type: Floribunda
Hybridizer/Year: Geduldig 1909
Growth habits: Short, bushy, 3½'
Foliage: Rich, dark green, leathery
Blooms: Light pink fading to white, 40–45 petals, 3–3½"
Fragrance: Slight, sweet
Comments: Though it was hybridized years before the class was created, this plant is considered to be the first floribunda. Its short growth makes it perfect for a hedge or border. It produces an abundance of blooms that are surrounded by dark green foliage. The name means "greetings to Aachen," a town that was the hybridizer's home and also the burial site of Charlemagne. Rating: 8.3

Hannah Gordon *(also often sold as Nicole)*

Type: Floribunda
Hybridizer/Year: Kordes 1984
Growth habits: Upright, tall, 5–7'
Foliage: Large, dark green, semiglossy, disease resistant
Blooms: Medium clear white blooms with a pink to red edge, 25–30 petals, 3½–4"
Fragrance: Slight
Awards: Portland Gold Medal 1995
Comments: This vigorous bush needs plenty of space. Its blooms of white with cerise-red edges and golden stamens are exquisite. It's excellent in mass plantings. Most roses sold as Nicole are actually Hannah Gordon, which, to add to the confusion is also sold as Tabris. Rating: 8.6

Heart 'n' Soul

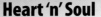

Type: Floribunda
Hybridizer/Year: Orard 2001
Growth habits: Vigorous, upright, 4–5'
Foliage: Medium, reddish dark green, semiglossy
Blooms: White with red ruffled edges, 20–25 petals, 3–4"
Fragrance: Slight
Comments: This rose is a great conversation piece in the garden. The contrasting colors of the white blooms edged with brilliant red nestled among the reddish dark green foliage is spectacular. It is disease resistant and has a tall, growth habit. Rating: 7.7

Honey Perfume

Type: Floribunda
Hybridizer/Year: Warriner 1982
Growth habits: Rounded plants grow 3 to 4' tall
Foliage: Dark green
Blooms: Mauve, 20 petals
Fragrance: Strong, citrus perfume
Awards: AARS 1984
Comments: This classic is still popular after almost a quarter of a century for its unique color and ability to bloom profusely. Buds are a deep purple-red, opening to velvety plum flowers that are quite colorfast even in hot climates.

Floribundas and polyanthas *(continued)*

Hot Cocoa

Type: Floribunda
Hybridizer/Year: Carruth 2002
Growth habits: Rounded, medium-tall, 4–5'
Foliage: Dark green, glossy
Blooms: Deep rust buds open to smoky chocolate-orange with purple tones, 25–30 petals, 3–3½"
Fragrance: Moderate, old rose
Awards: AARS 2003, ARS Members' Choice Award 2007
Comments: It is much easier to grow this floribunda than to describe the color of its blooms, somewhere between rust and chocolate and smoky purple. It is disease resistant and a vigorous grower. Rating: 7.9

Iceberg

Type: Floribunda
Hybridizer/Year: Kordes 1958
Growth habits: Upright, vigorous, bushy, 4–6'
Foliage: Light green, glossy
Blooms: Large, pure white, 20–25 petals, 3–3½", clusters
Fragrance: Moderate
Awards: Roya National Rose Society Gold Medal 1958, Baden-Baden Gold Medal 1958, World Federation of Rose Societies Hall of Fame 1983, Royal National Rose Society Garden of Merit 1993
Comments: This is one of the best of the floribundas and it is as popular today as when it was introduced 50 years ago. It is relatively disease resistant and withstands wet weather well. This prolific bloomer is great in the garden or the vase or in mass plantings. It is a classic. Rating: 8.7

Intrigue

Type: Floribunda
Hybridizer/Year: Warriner 1982
Growth habits: Bushy, 3½'
Foliage: Semiglossy, dark green
Blooms: Mauve, double, clusters, large, 25 petals
Fragrance: Very fragrant
Awards: AARS 1984
Comments: Still popular after a quarter of a century, this rose is beloved for its unusual, purplish color and profuse blooming habit. Rating: 7.1

Johann Strauss

Type: Floribunda
Hybridizer/Year: Meilland 1983
Growth habits: Medium, vigorous, bushy, compact, 4'
Foliage: Medium, dark green, semiglossy, few prickles
Blooms: Pink slightly suffused with yellow, 40-plus petals, 3½–4"
Fragrance: Slight
Comments: This is a plant for all landscaping needs. It is medium in height, vigorous, and bushy. It is relatively disease resistant and suits the garden or the vase. Its blooms are globular and appear in small clusters. Rating: 7.8

Judy Garland

Type: Floribunda
Hybridizer/Year: Harkness 1977
Growth habits: Medium, vigorous, bushy, 3–4′
Foliage: Medium, medium green, semiglossy
Blooms: Yellow edged with orange-red, 35 petals, 3–3½″
Fragrance: Slight
Comments: Plant several of these bushes in a mass planting for a rainbow of color. The blooms are bright yellow edged with orange-red and framed by attractive green foliage. The blooms can fade rapidly in hot sun. Rating: 7.6

Julia Child

Type: Floribunda
Hybridizer/Year: Carruth 2004
Growth habits: Medium, vigorous, rounded, bushy, 3–4′
Foliage: Medium, medium green, glossy, disease resistant
Blooms: Butter gold, 35-plus petals, 4″
Fragrance: Moderate, licorice
Awards: AARS 2006
Comments: Julia Child selected this plant to bear her name. She loved the butter yellow color of the blooms and the licorice fragrance. It is consistent, hardy, and floriferous in all climates.

Katharina Zeimet

Type: Polyantha
Hybridizer/Year: Lambert 1901
Growth habits: Vigorous, compact, 1–1½′
Foliage: Small, rich, medium green, matte

Blooms: Pure white, 25–30 petals, 1–2″
Fragrance: Moderate
Comments: This bush blooms in large clusters of 50 or more flowers that make a magnificent display. It does well as a low hedge or in a container. The blooms are reasonably tolerant of bad weather. It is a continuous bloomer throughout the growing season. Rating: 8.0

La Marne

Type: Polyantha
Hybridizer/Year: Barbier 1915
Growth habits: Vigorous, upright, bushy, 3–6′
Foliage: Medium, dark green, glossy, with few if any prickles
Blooms: Rosy blush with a darker salmon pink at the edges, 12–15 petals, 2″
Fragrance: Slight

Comments: The vigor and charm of this polyantha has maintained its popularity over the years. It is a shrubby plant that blooms in clusters. The double blooms are reminiscent of apple blossoms. This plant does well in borders and containers. It makes a tremendous display of color in the garden. Rating: 8.7

La Sevillana *(also known as Sevillana)*

Type: Floribunda
Hybridizer/Year: Meilland 1978
Growth habits: Medium, vigorous, bushy, 3–5′
Foliage: Medium, reddish green turning to dark green, glossy
Blooms: Vermillion, 13 petals, 2½–3″
Fragrance: Slight
Awards: ADR Germany 1979, Orleans Gold Medal 1980
Comments: This floribunda grows a little taller, bushier, and denser

than most, which makes it perfect for a stunning hedge or border. Its bright red clusters of flowers are borne on long, flexible canes. It is a prolific bloomer throughout the growing season.

Floribundas and polyanthas *(continued)*

Lavaglut

Type: Floribunda
Hybridizer/Year: Kordes 1978
Growth habits: Upright, medium low, bushy, 2–3′
Foliage: Dark green, glossy, disease resistant
Blooms: Deep red, velvety, 25–30 petals, 2½–3″, large clusters
Fragrance: Slight
Comments: This is an ideal plant for borders and hedges because of its even growth

habit. It produces large clusters of long-lasting, intense red blooms. It is a consistent performer in all climates and handles the sun and rain better than most reds. Rating: 8.7

Lime Sublime

Type: Floribunda
Hybridizer/Year: Dickson 2004
Growth habits: Medium, vigorous, upright, 3–4′
Foliage: Medium, dark green, glossy
Blooms: Chartreuse-white, 25 petals, 3–4″
Fragrance: Moderate
Comments: This prolific bloomer is great alone, in mass plantings, or as a border or hedge. Its unique coloration of chartreuse-tinged white framed by glossy, dark green foliage makes a novel addition to the landscape. It does well in all climates and stands up to humid heat.

Livin' Easy

Type: Floribunda
Hybridizer/Year: Harkness 1992
Growth habits: Medium, rounded, 4–5′
Foliage: Medium green, semiglossy, disease resistant
Blooms: Orange-apricot, frilly, 25–30 petals, 4–4½″
Fragrance: Moderate, fruity
Awards: AARS 1996, Royal National Rose Society Gold Medal 1990, Portland Gold Medal 1998
Comments: This is a great bush for any landscape design or mass planting, and is the rose for gardeners who think roses are too much work. It is disease resistant and consistent in all climates. Rating: 8.1

Lovely Fairy

Type: Polyantha
Hybridizer/Year: Vurens-Spek 1990
Growth habits: Somewhat upright but variable, 1½–4′ tall, 2–4′ wide
Foliage: Small leaves are bright apple green
Blooms: Small deep-pink, huge clusters in flushes
Fragrance: Strong, fruity
Comments: This sport of the famed polyantha rose The Fairy is an equally strong performer in the garden, highly disease resistant and more tolerant of shade than most roses. The flowers are a deeper pink than The Fairy and have the added benefit of a delicious fragrance that will bathe the entire garden in a rich, fruity perfume. Like The Fairy, the small button-eye blooms are borne endlessly in great profusion all summer long. Rating: 8.0

Mardi Gras

Type: Floribunda
Hybridizer/Year: Zary 2007
Growth habits: Upright, medium-size, 4' tall
Foliage: Medium-size, semiglossy, dark green
Blooms: Pink blend. Pink, yellow, orange, 3–4″, double (17–25 petals), borne in small clusters in flushes
Fragrance: Slight
Awards: AARS 2008

Comments: Introduced by Jackson & Perkins in 2008, this flamboyant new award-winner can hold its own against the most outrageously colorful costume in a Mardi Gras parade. Bright pink, yellow, and orange hues blend together in each sparkling petal, intensifying as they age and lasting long both on the bush and in the vase. The small clusters are borne on long stems ideal for cutting.

Margaret Merril

Type: Floribunda
Hybridizer/Year: Harkness 1977
Growth habits: Upright, medium-tall, 3–5'
Foliage: Large, dark green, glossy, disease resistant
Blooms: White with a blush of pink in the center, 20–25 petals, 4″
Fragrance: Strong, citrus, spicy
Awards: Geneva Gold Medal 1978, Monza Gold Medal and Fragrance Award 1978, Rome Gold Medal 1978, Royal National Rose Society Edland Fragrance Medal 1978, New Zealand Gold Medal and Fragrance Award 1982, The Hague Fragrance Award 1982, James Mason Medal 1990, Best Floribunda New Zealand Rose Trials 1991

Comments: This proven winner is a prolific bloomer and produces large, high-center blooms surrounded by an abundance of glossy, dark green foliage. It does well in all climates but likes cooler temperatures. It is disease resistant but can get black spot. Rating: 8.2

Marie Pavie

Type: Polyantha
Hybridizer/Year: Alegatiere 1888
Growth habits: Vigorous, upright, bushy, 3–4'
Foliage: Medium, dark green, leathery, few prickles
Blooms: Light pink aging to creamy white with yellow stamens, 35–40 petals, 2″, cupped
Fragrance: Moderate

Comments: This versatile plant can be used in any landscape. The blooms are pinker in shade; fade to white in heat or sun. This bush is outstanding in a border. Rating: 8.9

Marmalade Skies

Type: Floribunda
Hybridizer/Year: Meilland 1999
Growth habits: Medium, vigorous, bushy, 3–4'
Foliage: Medium, dark green, glossy, moderate prickles
Blooms: Clear, orange-red, 17–25 petals, 3–4″
Fragrance: Slight
Awards: AARS 2001
Comments: This is a vigorous, easy-to-grow floribunda. It blooms in large clusters and holds its color. Its performance increases as it becomes more established. Rating: 7.8

Floribundas and polyanthas *(continued)*

Mademoiselle Cecile Brunner

Type: Polyantha
Hybridizer/Year: Ducher 1881
Growth habits: Vigorous, bushy, 1½–3′
Foliage: Small, dark green, matte, 3–5 leaflets, few prickles
Blooms: Light bright pink on a yellow base, 25 petals, 2″
Fragrance: Moderate, sweet
Comments: This is a favorite of many rose growers. It is a prolific, continuous bloomer. The magnificent blooms are perfectly formed, resemble hybrid teas, and occur in clusters. This is a perfect bush for a smaller garden or a container and its climbing version is especially popular. Rating: 8.4

Moondance

Type: Floribunda
Hybridizer/Year: Zary 2007
Growth habits: Upright and ell-branched, vigorous and tall
Foliage: Very glossy, dark green
Blooms: Creamy white, double 25–30 petals, large trusses atop 14–18″ stems, ovoid buds open to flat blooms, 4″
Fragrance: Slight raspberry
Awards: AARS 2007
Comments: Large clusters of luminous, creamy white blooms and strong disease resistance add up an ideal landscape plant. Long-stemmed richly fragrant flowers make gorgeous instant bouquets for arrangements indoors. Highly resistant to black spot, mildew, and rust.

Our Lady of Guadalupe

Type: Floribunda
Hybridizer/Year: Zary 2000
Growth habits: Upright, medium, bushy, 2½–3′
Foliage: Medium, dark green, glossy
Blooms: Silvery pink, 25 petals, 3″
Fragrance: Light, sweet
Comments: This is a quick-repeating floribunda. It is stunning in the garden or the vase. It was named for the Patroness of the Americas, and 5 percent of net sales goes to the Hispanic College Fund. Rating: 8.0

Outrageous

Type: Floribunda
Hybridizer/Year: Zary 1999
Growth habits: Medium, vigorous, bushy, compact, 3–4'
Foliage: Medium, dark green, matte, moderate prickles
Blooms: Bright orange tinged yellow, 26–40 petals, 3–4½"
Fragrance: Citrus
Awards: Lyon Gold Medal 1997
Comments: This bush is great in all types of landscape designs. Its cheery blooms have a long vase life. One of its best features is the lovely citrus fragrance. Rating: 7.4

Passionate Kisses

Type: Floribunda
Hybridizer/Year: Meilland 1998
Growth habits: Bushy, 5'
Foliage: Semiglossy, medium-size
Blooms: Medium flowers, large semidouble clusters
Fragrance: Light
Comments: Considered one of the best roses in its class, this rose has outstanding blooms that are long-lasting and nonfading. The plant is nicely shaped and very disease-resistant. Rating: 7.9

Perle d'Or

Type: Polyantha
Hybridizer/Year: Rambaux 1875
Growth habits: Vigorous, upright, bushy, 2–3'
Foliage: Small, dark green, glossy
Blooms: Golden pink, 20–25 petals, 1½"
Fragrance: Intense
Comments: This variety's name translates to Golden Pearl but it is also known as

Yellow Cecile Brunner. It's highly disease-resistant and is designated as an Earthkind rose. The blooms are ideal for arrangements, corsages, and buttonhole flowers. The blooms, golden pink with honey-apricot overtones, appear in clusters. Rating: 8.5

Phyllis Bide

Type: Polyantha, Climbing
Hybridizer/Year: Bide 1923
Growth habits: Vigorous, upright, bushy, 6–10'
Foliage: Small, dark green, glossy
Blooms: Pale gold shaded pink, 20–25 petals, 1–2"
Fragrance: Slight
Awards: Royal National Rose Society Gold Medal 1924, Royal Horticultural Society Award of Garden Merit 1993

Comments: Lax, arching canes make this rose perfect for fences, pillars, and arches. The prolific small blooms are pale gold-shaded pink rosettes. This bush can be pruned to shrub height for smaller gardens. Rating: 8.5

Playboy

Type: Floribunda
Hybridizer/Year: Cocker 1976
Growth habits: Well-rounded, medium, 3–4'
Foliage: Dark green, glossy, disease resistant
Blooms: Bright orange with scarlet shading and a yellow eye, 7–10 petals, 3½"
Fragrance: Moderate, apple
Awards: New Zealand National Rose Trial Ground Winner 1985, Portland Gold Medal 1989
Comments: This is an outstanding floribunda in every way. It is very floriferous and showy. It is disease resistant and hard pruning encourages bigger sprays. It loves the sun, but blooms will be larger size in cool weather. It is a consistent performer in all climates. Rating: 8.5

Floribundas and polyanthas *(continued)*

Playgirl

Type: Floribunda
Hybridizer/Year: Moore 1986
Growth habits: Upright, medium, bushy, 2–3′
Foliage: Medium, medium green, glossy
Blooms: Large, vivid pink, 5–7 petals, 4″
Fragrance: Slight
Comments: This vigorous grower, like one of its parents, Playboy,

is floriferous and showy. In this case, however, there is an endless display of hot pink, single blooms throughout the growing season. It can be used in all types of landscapes. Rating: 8.4

Pleasure

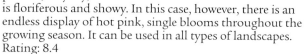

Type: Floribunda
Hybridizer/Year: Warriner 1988
Growth habits: Low, vigorous, compact, 2–3′
Foliage: Medium, dark green, semiglossy, prickles reddish brown and hooked slightly downward
Blooms: Coral pink with a lighter reverse, 33 petals, 3″
Fragrance: Slight
Awards: AARS 1990
Comments: A vigorous, compact growing habit is the norm for this bush. The coral-pink blooms are borne in sprays that repeat throughout the growing season. The blooms have a cupped, ruffled, almost old-fashioned rose appearance. It makes a great border plant or hedge. Rating: 8.0

Preference

Type: Floribunda
Hybridizer/Year: Meilland 2005
Growth habits: Compact rounded plants grow 3′ wide and tall
Foliage: Dark green, glossy
Blooms: Brilliant deep scarlet-red, medium-size, double, 17–25 petals, blooms continuously throughout summer
Fragrance: None
Comments: This small rose has a big impact in the garden because of its intense color, making it ideal for containers and small spaces. It is easy to care for, free-flowering and self-cleaning throughout the season, with above-average disease resistance and excellent heat tolerance. Flowers will not fade or burn in summer heat.

Pretty Lady

Type: Floribunda
Hybridizer/Year: Scrivens 1997
Growth habits: Medium, vigorous, upright, 3–4′
Foliage: Medium, dark green, semiglossy, many prickles
Blooms: Creamy white blushed light pink, 20–25 petals, 3½″
Fragrance: Slight
Comments: This bush makes an attractive display in the garden. The soft white blushed pink blooms are large and contrast pleasantly with the dark green, semiglossy foliage. It blooms well throughout the growing season.

Rainbow Sorbet

Type: Floribunda
Hybridizer/Year: Lim 2006
Growth habits: Vigorous, upright, 4–5′
Foliage: Medium, dark green, glossy, disease resistant
Blooms: Deep yellow edged with red changing to delicate yellow and pink with age, 16–18 petals, 3–4″
Fragrance: Slight, apple
Awards: AARS 2006
Comments: This

is an early blooming floribunda that repeats throughout the growing season. It sends forth blooms with a glorious display of colors ranging from yellow through orange and red. Its glossy dark green leaves provide the perfect backdrop for the glowing blooms. It prefers moderate temperatures.

Regensberg

Type: Floribunda
Hybridizer/Year: McGredy 1979
Growth habits: Low, compact, bushy, 3′
Foliage: Medium, medium green, semiglossy
Blooms: Hot pink with a white reverse, white eye, yellow stamens, 21 petals, 4½″, cupped
Fragrance: Moderate
Awards: Baden-Baden Gold Medal 1980
Comments: This compact, low-growing floribunda is terrific for borders and containers. The hot pink and white blooms are striking and abundant. This is one of the best of the "handpainted" series from Sam McGredy. Rating: 7.9

Salsa

Type: Floribunda
Hybridizer/Year: Zary 2001
Growth habits: Medium, vigorous, upright, 3′
Foliage: Medium, dark green, glossy
Blooms: Bright red, 20 petals, 3½″
Fragrance: Slight
Comments: This bush is vivid in a mass planting. The blooms

provide lively color throughout the growing season. Its moderate growth habit makes it an excellent choice for a hedge or border. Rating: 7.5

Scentimental

Type: Floribunda
Hybridizer/Year: Carruth 1997
Growth habits: Medium, compact, rounded, 3–4′
Foliage: Large, medium green, quilted, matte, moderate prickles
Blooms: Burgundy and white or cream striped, 25–30 petals, 4–4½″, exhibition form
Fragrance: Intense, spicy
Awards: AARS 1997
Comments: This rose combines novelty and beauty. It has old-fashioned form and bears blooms uniquely striped with creamy white and burgundy. While the color display is gorgeous, the real attraction is its fragrance. Definitely a must-have for any landscape design. Rating: 7.7

Floribundas and polyanthas (continued)

Sexy Rexy

Type: Floribunda
Hybridizer/Year: McGredy 1984
Growth habits: Upright, medium, bushy, 3–4'
Foliage: Small, medium green, glossy
Blooms: Clear medium pink, 30–40 petals, 3½",
large clusters
Fragrance: Slight
Awards: New Zealand Gold Medal and Rose Trial Winner
1984, Portland Gold Medal 1990, Best Floribunda, New
Zealand Rose Trials 1990, Auckland Rose of the Year 1991
Comments: A vigorous, easy-to-grow, nearly disease-free
bush, this is a prolific producer of outstanding clear pink
blooms that repeat quickly throughout the growing season.
It is a consistent performer in all climates. Rating: 8.7

Sheila's Perfume

Type: Floribunda
Hybridizer/Year: Sheridan 1982
Growth habits: Upright, medium, bushy, 3–5'
Foliage: Medium, dark green, glossy, disease resistant
Blooms: Yellow edged in pink to red, 20–25 petals, 4–5"
Fragrance: Strong, sweet
Awards: Royal National Rose Societies Trial Ground
Certificate 1981, Glasgow Tollcross Fragrance Award and
Glasgow Silver Medal 1981, New Zealand National Rose
Trial Ground Winner 1983
Comments: This
floribunda grows more
like a hybrid tea in size and
form. The awesome
blooms are yellow brushed
with deep pink on the
edges and fragrant. It has
an abundance of glossy,
deep green leaves. The best
flower color and size
appear in cooler
temperatures. It is named
for the hybridizer's wife.
Rating: 8.2

Showbiz

Type: Floribunda
Hybridizer/Year: Tantau
1981
Growth habits: Low,
bushy, rounded, 2–3'
Foliage: Medium, dark,
semiglossy
Blooms: Bright scarlet-
red, 20–25 petals, 2½–3"
Fragrance: Slight
Awards: AARS 1985,
RNRS Gold Medal 1985
Comments: This
compact bush is great in

mass plantings or borders. The brilliant red blooms are long-
lasting and abundant. This is a consistent performer in all
climates. Rating: 8.3

Simplicity

Type: Floribunda
Hybridizer/Year:
Warriner 1979
Growth habits:
Upright, 4–5' tall
Foliage: Small,
glossy, dark green
Blooms: Medium-
pink blooms are
semidouble, 18
petals
Fragrance: None
Comments: This is
the first successful
rose developed
specifically for
hedges, with profuse
flowering and fast
repeat bloom on an
upright form that
stays well-branched
clear to the ground.
The result is a
dazzling, solid,
5-foot wall of color
all season long and
its hard to find a
better rose for a
hedge. The original
Simplicity is a
bright medium
pink, but now there
are four other colors
available that are
have a little more
interesting-looking:
Purple Simplicity,
White Simplicity,
Yellow Simplicity,
and Fragrant
Lavender Simplicity.
Rating: 7.6

Simplicity

Fragrant Lavender Simplicity

White Simplicity

Singin' in the Rain

Type: Floribunda
Hybridizer/Year: McGredy 1994
Growth habits: Medium, upright, 3–4′
Foliage: Medium, dark green and bronze, glossy, some prickles, disease resistant
Blooms: Apricot-copper, 25–30 petals, 2–3″
Fragrance: Moderate, sweet
Awards: AARS 1995
Comments: A vibrant bush with blooms of unique coloration, this is a great rose for the garden or vase. The golden apricot blooms

have a coppery-shaded reverse and almost always seem to be in bloom. It is disease resistant and easy to grow. Rating: 7.8

Sixteen Candles

Type: Floribunda
Hybridizer/Year: Harkness 2006
Growth habits: Compact, upright, well-branched, 3–3½′
Foliage: Glossy, dark green

Blooms: Light pink, high-centered form, 20–25 petals, 4″
Fragrance: Strong and sweet
Comments: Although slow to start in spring, plants bloom prolifically, bearing huge candelabras of peachy pink flowers in quick succession all summer. It is exceptionally hardy.

Sun Flare

Type: Floribunda
Hybridizer/Year: Warriner 1991
Growth habits: Low, compact, bushy, 3–4′
Foliage: Small, dark green, glossy, reddish prickles
Blooms: Bright medium yellow, 30 petals, 3″
Fragrance: Light, licorice
Awards: Japan Gold Medal 1981, AARS 1983, Portland Gold Medal 1985
Comments: This bush, also available as a climber, provides rich color on a low-growing, vigorous, spreading, bushy plant. This is a good bush for hedges, borders, or mass plantings. It does well in all climates. Rating: 8.3

Floribundas and polyanthas *(continued)*

Sunsprite

Type: Floribunda
Hybridizer/Year: Kordes 1977
Growth habits: Upright, medium, rounded, bushy, 4–5'
Foliage: Dark green, glossy
Blooms: Deep yellow, 25–30 petals, 3½–4"
Fragrance: Strong
Awards: Baden-Baden Gold Medal 1972, Anerkannte

Deutsche Rose 1973, J. A. Gamble Rose Fragrance Award 1979, Royal National Rose Society Gold Medal 1989, Royal National Rose Society James Mason Medal 1989
Comments: One of the hardier yellow floribundas, this rose is ideal for hedges or mass plantings. The deep yellow blooms retain their color better in cooler temperatures. A climbing version is available. Rating: 8.5

The Fairy

Type: Polyantha
Hybridizer/Year: Bentall 1932
Growth habits: Compact, spreading, short, 3½'×3½'
Foliage: Small, medium green, glossy
Blooms: Small, light rose-pink, 20–25 petals, 1½", clusters
Fragrance: Slight
Comments: The Fairy is a favorite because it is hardy, clean, disease-resistant, vigorous, and a prolific bloomer. The blooms are rosette and occur in glorious sprays throughout the bush, which has equally attractive foliage. This is an ideal plant for a low hedge, to trail over a wall, or containers. Rating: 8.7

Topsy Turvy

Type: Floribunda
Hybridizer/Year: Carruth 2006
Growth habits: Vigorous, upright, medium, 3–4'
Foliage: Medium, medium green, glossy with dark red new growth
Blooms: White buds swirling open to scarlet and yellow-orange with a white reverse, 10–15 petals, 4"
Fragrance: Slight, apple
Comments: This floribunda echoes its name in a swirl of brilliant red, yellow-orange, and cream. It blooms early and produces abundantly for the duration of the growing season. It is versatile in the landscape and does best in drier climates.

Trumpeter

Type: Floribunda
Hybridizer/Year: McGredy 1977
Growth habits: Low, compact, bushy, 3–4′
Foliage: Medium, medium green, glossy
Blooms: Red-orange, 35–45 petals, 3½″, cupped
Fragrance: Slight
Awards: New Zealand Gold Medal 1977, Portland Gold Medal 1977
Comments: This vigorous, low-growing, disease-resistant bush produces long-lasting blooms in showy clusters that repeat throughout the growing season. This is an excellent bush for gardens, hedges, and borders. Its name refers to Louie Armstrong, for whom one of its parents, Satchmo, was named. Rating: 8.2

Tuscan Sun

Type: Floribunda
Hybridizer/Year: Zary 2005
Growth habits: Medium, vigorous, upright, 3–4′
Foliage: Medium, dark green, glossy
Blooms: Deep apricot-orange blushed bronze, finishing coppery pink, 25 petals, 4″
Fragrance: Slight, spicy
Comments: This bush retains the disease resistance and gorgeous dark green glossy foliage of one of its parents, Singin' in the Rain.

The bronzy apricot-orange blooms are unique and striking. This bush was Jackson & Perkins' Floribunda of the Year for 2005.

Vavoom

Type: Floribunda
Hybridizer/Year: Carruth 2007
Growth habits: Rounded, compact, 2′ tall
Foliage: Semiglossy, dark green, quilted; new growth is a deep mahogany red
Blooms: Bright orange, medium, slightly ruffled petals, double, 35-plus petals
Fragrance: Moderate, spicy
Comments: Brilliant, electric-orange blooms are borne in small clusters all summer. Individually long-lived, the flowers hold their gleaming color well over their lifespan; although short-stemmed, the clusters are ideal to cut as instant bouquets for the vase. Excellent in the garden; small plants are good performers for containers and small spaces, and effective when massed in beds.

Wing Ding

Type: Polyantha
Hybridizer/Year: Carruth 2008
Growth habits: Medium-size, 1½–2½′
Foliage: Glossy, deep green
Blooms: Scarlet, semi-double, 7–10 petals, borne constantly in huge pyramidal clusters all summer and into fall
Fragrance: None
Comments: Blazing scarlet color is new to polyanthas, and this new

landscape rose provides it in constant supply from late spring well into fall. Introduced by Weeks Roses in 2008, this progeny of Red Fairy has many of its parent's excellent landscape qualities—good disease resistance and vigor matched with unparalleled flower power. The canes are so loaded with blooms that they tend to arch down, making this an excellent subject for spilling over walls and down terraces. It is superb in containers.

Shrub roses

Shrub roses may be easy to grow, but they aren't easy to define. They encompass a wide variety of roses but generally, they share an overall attractive shape, long bloom time, bloom in clusters, and minimal care or fuss.

They can be sold under a variety of names: landscape rose, pavement roses, or other creative names.

Shrub roses come in all shapes and sizes—from compact 3-foot tall varieties to sprawling 15-foot wide plants. And these roses can usually take what Mother Nature dishes out. Hot summers and cold winters don't faze these roses, which makes them ideal, low-maintenance choices for landscapes and gardens.

Most shrub roses are reliably hardy without protection through Zone 5 and hardy with minimal or no protection in Zone 4. Conversely, they can usually take heat as well, doing well even as far south as Zone 10.

Technically, shrub roses can be divided into two classes: Classic and modern. The casual rose gardener will be hard-pressed to find many of the classics (hybrid rugosa, hybrid kordesii, hybrid musk, hybrid moyesii) readily available at most local garden centers, though hybrid rugosas are the easiest to find. However, with the ease of online buying, the exact rose you want is seldom more than a few clicks away.

Alternatively, gardeners are more likely to find modern shrub roses readily available. These are crosses of old garden roses with new varieties to create a whole new and exciting type of rose. There are a number of rose hybridizers that we can thank for creating this new uber shrub rose.

See page 27 for more information about shrub roses.

▲ Sally Holmes is a typically delightful shrub rose. Like so many shrub roses, it needs minimal care, blooms a long time, and is highly pest- and disease-resistant.

UNDERSTANDING ROSE SERIES

Some roses (primarily in the shrub class) can be grouped together as series of roses. Some will share a common name (like many in the Knock Out series) while others will have a common theme or breeder (such as the Canadian Explorer roses or the Griffith Buck roses).

Some of the best-known series include the following:

David Austin/English roses: Austin pioneered in England a new group of shrub roses in the 1970s that offers home gardeners a piece of the past with all the great characteristics of today's modern roses. By crossing elegant old garden roses with modern roses, such as hybrid teas and floribundas, he was able to create large-headed, fragrant shrub roses with the recurrent blooming ability, vigorous growth, and color range that make modern hybrids so popular. His roses, such as the yellow-flowered Charles Darwin or the deeply crinkled crimson blooms of Fisherman's Friend, look like old garden roses but act like modern roses in the garden.

Buck roses: Hybridizer Griffith Buck of Ames, Iowa, worked in his Zone 4 region to create extra-hardy shrubs that can stand up to cold winters. His roses include the pink-blooming semi-double Carefree Beauty and dwarf shrub and pink flowered Country Dancer.

Romantica roses: From the House of Meilland in France, these are also examples of modern shrub roses. They are known for their voluptuous shapes and rich fragrance. Eden was the first of this series.

The Knock Out series: The newest sensation in modern shrub roses is Knock Out, a disease-resistant (particularly to black spot) rose that was introduced by William Radler in 1999. Since then, he has produced other roses in the Knock Out series that includes Pink Knock Out, Double Knock Out, and Double Pink Knock Out.

Knock Out and many other shrub roses, because of their low-growing habit, make excellent groundcover roses.

EarthKind roses: This is a designation given to select roses by the Texas A&M University Agriculture program. EarthKind Roses have been through statewide testing and evaluation that determined that they meet a standard of low maintenance and disease resistance that makes them environmentally responsible.

Easy Elegance roses: A series of low-maintenance roses offered by Bailey Nurseries, each is grown on its own roots so it has a superior shape, evenness of size, and is free from suckering.

Meidiland roses: A French series of roses known for their low-maintenance and nonstop bloom. The first modern shrub to be the winner of an All-America Rose Society (AARS) award was the House of Meilland's Bonica, a prolific pink rose that blooms its heart out all summer. See page 201 for more information on Meidiland landscape roses.

Morden/Parkland roses: Sometimes also called simply Canadian roses, these were developed in Manitoba and are among the most cold-hardy of roses—down to -30°F/-35°C with only snow as protection. They are highly disease-resistant, flower repeatedly throughout the summer, require only minimal pruning, and come in a variety of colors and sizes.

Explorer roses: This series, developed in Ontario, is named after different Canadian historic explorers and figures. They have similar cold-hardiness to Morden/Parkland roses.

Abraham Darby

Type: Shrub (Austin)
Hybridizer/Year: Austin 1985
Growth habits: Vigorous, bushy, 6 × 4′
Foliage: Dark green, glossy, disease-resistant
Blooms: Medium pink to apricot touched with golden yellow, 100-plus petals, 4-5″
Fragrance: Intense, peachy lemon
Comments: This English rose is one of the best for repeat bloom, vigor, and freedom from black spot—a consistent performer in nearly all climates. The old-fashioned blooms are packed with petals. It was named for one of the founders of the Industrial Revolution. Rating: 8.0

Autumn Sunset

Type: Shrub
Hybridizer/Year: Lowe 1986
Growth habits: Tall, vigorous, bushy, 6′ or taller
Foliage: Medium, medium green, glossy, curved medium red prickles, disease resistant
Blooms: Medium, apricot with touches of orange and gold, 20 petals, 4″, cupped
Fragrance: Intense, fruity
Comments: This shrub is a sport of Westerland and can double as a climber. It maintains all of the characteristics of its parent and adds a little pizzazz of its own in the brightly colored blooms. This is a terrific performer in most climates. Rating: 8.1

Ballerina

Type: Shrub (Hybrid Musk)
Hybridizer/Year: Bentall 1937
Growth habits: Medium, vigorous, bushy, 5′
Foliage: Small, dark green, glossy
Blooms: Light pink with white eyes, 5–7 petals, 2–3″, single, large clusters
Fragrance: Slight
Comments: This hardy rose is ideal for any landscape design or mass planting. The small blooms are shallowly cupped

and appear in large clusters that are reminiscent of hydrangea bushes. Rating: 8.7

Be-Bop

Type: Shrub
Hybridizer/Year: Carruth 2003
Growth habits: Medium, vigorous, somewhat spreading, 3′
Foliage: Medium, dark green, glossy, disease resistant
Blooms: Cerise red, yellow eye, 5–7 petals, 3″
Fragrance: Slight
Comments: This plant is easy to grow and is wonderful in any landscape design or mass planting. Large clusters of single formed blooms with gold stamens are a brilliant contrast to the dark green, glossy foliage. Rating: 8.0

Shrub roses *(continued)*

Belinda's Dream

Type: Shrub
Hybridizer/Year: Basye 1988
Growth habits: Upright, medium, bushy, 5 × 4'
Foliage: Medium, medium green, matte
Blooms: Even, medium, pink, 45-plus petals, 3½–4½"
Fragrance: Moderate, fruity

Comments: This Earthkind rose is relatively free of black spot. Clusters of large blooms with classic hybrid tea form thrive in hot weather and have a tangy, fruity scent. The foliage is a greenish blue. This bush will remain compact if pruned. Rating: 8.5

Belle Story

Type: Shrub (Austin)
Hybridizer/Year: Austin 1984
Growth habits: Vigorous, bushy, 5 × 3½'
Foliage: Medium, medium green, semiglossy
Blooms: Soft light pink with a golden yellow center and stamens, 35–40 petals, 4"
Fragrance: Intense
Comments: This is another Austin rose that makes a great shrub. It is a vigorous grower. The large, cupped blooms are a delicate rose-pink with a lighter pink edge and bright yellow stamens. It is a prolific bloomer with an intense fragrance. The foliage is an attractive accent. The rose was named to honor one of the first nursing sisters to join Britain's Royal Navy in 1864. Rating: 8.6

Blanc Double de Coubert

Type: Shrub (Hybrid Rugosa)
Hybridizer/Year: Cochet-Cochet 1892
Growth habits: Tall, vigorous, upright, bushy, 5–7'
Foliage: Small, light green, leathery, rugose, disease resistant
Blooms: Clear white, 30 petals, 4–5"
Fragrance: Intense
Comments: This shrub has many uses in the landscape. It is typical of the rugosa in every way. The large blooms are pure white, semidouble, often with crumpled petals, and very fragrant. They are somewhat fragile and can be easily marked by rain. The Coubert in the name refers to the developer's home village. Rating: 8.3

Bonica

Type: Shrub
Hybridizer/Year: Meilland 1981
Growth habits: Vigorous, bushy, spreading, 4–5'
Foliage: Small, dark green, semiglossy
Blooms: Small, ruffled, soft pink, 35–40 petals, 2½"
Fragrance: Slight
Awards: Anerkannte Deutsche Rose 1983, AARS 1987, World's Favorite Rose 2003
Comments: This hardy, clean, showy bush was the first shrub to win the prestigious AARS award. It is considered a trailblazing modern shrub— a consistent, proven performer in all climates. The blooms are ruffled and clear, pure pink with the scent of fresh-cut apples. It thrives even in harsh climates. Rating: 8.4

Buff Beauty

Type: Shrub (Hybrid Musk)
Hybridizer/Year: Bentall 1939
Growth habits: Vigorous, upright, bushy, 4–6′
Foliage: Large, medium green, semiglossy
Blooms: Apricot yellow, 50 petals, 4″
Fragrance: Moderate
Comments: This

classic shrub is still popular today. With its rounded growth habit and dark green foliage, it is an outstanding garden attraction even when not in bloom. It blooms in huge clusters of twelve. The blooms stand out against the foliage. The moderate tea rose scent adds to the beauty of this rose. Rating: 8.2

Carefree Beauty

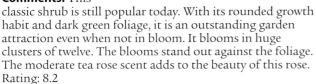

Type: Shrub
Hybridizer/Year: Buck 1977
Growth habits: Medium, vigorous, upright, spreading, 4–5′
Foliage: Medium, bright apple to olive green, glossy, disease-resistant
Blooms: Light rose, 15–20 petals, 4½″
Fragrance: Moderate
Comments: This is another popular carefree winter-hardy variety from Griffith Buck. It performs best in Northern climates. It is a bushy plant that is ideal for hedges or on its own. It always seems to be in bloom. The large blooms are surrounded by unusually colored foliage. This outstanding plant can survive almost any winter. Rating: 8.6

Carefree Delight

Type: Shrub
Hybridizer/Year: Meilland 1991
Growth habits: Vigorous, spreading, bushy, 3–4′
Foliage: Small, dark green, glossy, many prickles
Blooms: Carmine pink with a white eye, 5 petals, 1½–2¾″, single
Fragrance: None
Awards:

Bagatelle Gold Medal 1992, Golden Rose of The Hague 1993, Anerkannte Deutsche Rose 1994, AARS 1996
Comments: This rose is consistent in all climates, has great disease resistance, and may be the ideal landscape rose. It is almost always in bloom. The blooms are small, single, and carmine-pink with bright white eyes and golden stamens. The foliage provides the perfect contrast to the blooms. Rating: 8.2

Carefree Wonder

Type: Shrub
Hybridizer/Year: Meilland 1978
Growth habits: Medium, vigorous, bushy, 3′
Foliage: Medium, medium green, semiglossy, narrow reddish prickles
Blooms: Medium pink with a white eye, light pink reverse, 26 petals, 4″
Fragrance: Slight
Awards: AARS 1991
Comments: This shrub is a consistent performer and relatively carefree. It is hardy and disease resistant and has a rounded growth habit. Its ability to produce prolifically throughout the growing season is truly a "wonder." The large bright blooms complement the glorious, abundant foliage. Rating: 8.0

Shrub roses *(continued)*

Cherries 'n' Cream

Type: Shrub
Hybridizer/Year: Zary 2005
Growth habits: Vigorous, upright, bushy, 5′
Foliage: Medium, dark green, glossy
Blooms: Red and maroon finishing as a deep pink, 20 petals, 3″
Fragrance: Intense, clove
Comments: This shrub gives the appearance of the "handpainted" roses. The large blooms are red and maroon with white highlights, aging to a deep pink. The bush is showy in the garden. It has glossy, dark green foliage to complement the blooms. This rose stands out, even in a back border.

Cornelia

Type: Shrub (Hybrid Musk)
Hybridizer/Year: Pemberton 1925
Growth habits: Tall, vigorous, bushy, 6–8′
Foliage: Medium, dark green tinged bronze, glossy, leathery, nearly pricklefree
Blooms: Strawberry flushed yellow, 40 petals, 2½–3″
Fragrance: Intense
Comments: This rose has remained popular since its introduction. It is a stunning shrub that does well in all types of landscapes. It produces an abundance of blooms that occur in long, arching trusses. The blooms have a perfect rosette shape and a distinctive musky fragrance. Rating: 8.7

Countess Celeste

Type: Shrub
Hybridizer/Year: Poulsen 1998
Growth habits: Medium, compact, rounded, 2–3′
Foliage: Medium, dark green, glossy, moderate prickles
Blooms: Coral pink, 41 petals, 2½–3″
Fragrance: Moderate, apple

Comments: This vigorous, spreading bush does nicely in a mass planting or on its own. It is a prolific bloomer and produces masses of coral-pink blooms that cover the bush. Its compact growth habit and dark green, glossy foliage resemble small, emerald mounds. Rating: 7.9

Country Dancer

Type: Shrub
Hybridizer/Year: Buck 1973
Growth habits: Vigorous, upright, bushy, 2–3′
Foliage: Large, dark green, glossy, leathery
Blooms: Deep pink to rose red, 17–25 petals, 2½–3″, hardy
Fragrance: Moderate
Comments: This bush is from the well-known hybridizer of hardy roses Griffith Buck. This bush has a compact growth habit that makes it perfect for borders. The large blooms are produced abundantly throughout the warm months of the growing season. The large, dark green, glossy foliage is typical of the Buck roses. Rating: 8.6

Darlow's Enigma

Type: Shrub (Hybrid Musk)
Growth habits: Vigorous, upright, bushy, 6–8'
Foliage: Small, dark green, glossy, disease resistant
Blooms: Pure white with golden stamens, 5 petals, 1½"
Fragrance: Intense, honey
Comments: Discovered by Mike Darlow of Oregon in 1993, who helped get it into commercial production, this hardy bush seems to do well in all climates. It is a beautiful plant even without blooms because of the dark green, glossy foliage. However, it is seldom without blooms during the growing season. It produces large clusters of pure white, semidouble blooms highlighted by a sweet fragrance. Rating: 8.3

DayDream

Type: Shrub
Hybridizer/Year: Lim 2005
Growth habits: Vigorous, upright, spreading, 3–6'
Foliage: Small, dark green, glossy, disease resistant
Blooms: Lavender pink, 10–12 petals, 1", hardy
Fragrance: Slight
Awards: AARS 2005
Comments: The arching, spreading canes covered with blossoms on this bush lend it an amazing versatility in any landscape. It produces huge clusters of blooms that are small, lavender jewels. The foliage provides an excellent contrasting support for the blooms.

Distant Drums

Type: Shrub
Hybridizer/Year: Buck 1985
Growth habits: Medium, upright, bushy, 5–6'
Foliage: Medium, dark green, leathery, awl-like brown prickles, hardy
Blooms: Rose-purple, 40 petals, 4"
Fragrance: Intense, myrrh
Comments: This plant blooms in clusters of 2–10 blooms like a floribunda. The unique-color blooms begin as tan buds that change as they open to an arresting rose-purple. Rating: 8.0

Dortmund

Type: Shrub (Hybrid Kordesii)
Hybridizer/Year: Kordes 1955
Growth habits: Vigorous, climbing, 10' or more
Foliage: Dark green, glossy
Blooms: Large, strawberry red, white eye, 5–8 petals, 2½–3"
Fragrance: Moderate
Awards: Anerkannte Deutsch Rose 1954, Portland Gold Medal 1971
Comments: This is a hardy, disease-resistant shrub that also works well as a climber. It produces abundant blooms throughout the growing season. The huge, single, open blooms have bright gold stamens. The bush is resplendent with dark green, glossy foliage. This is a must-have for any gardener. Rating: 9.1

Shrub roses *(continued)*

Evelyn

Type: Shrub (Austin)
Hybridizer/Year: Austin 1991
Growth habits: Vigorous, upright, bushy, 4'
Foliage: Medium, medium green, semiglossy, some prickles
Blooms: Apricot tinged pink fading to light pink, 70-plus petals, 5", cupped, rosette
Fragrance: Intense

Comments: This rose was named on behalf of Crabtree & Evelyn, which used it in a range of rose perfumes. The fragrance is exquisite and reminiscent of the old garden roses. The bush is a prolific bloomer. The blooms are large and have more than 70 petals arrayed in rosette form. The color is soft apricot tinged with a soft pink. Rating: 7.9

Fair Bianca

Type: Shrub (Austin)
Hybridizer/Year: Austin 1982
Growth habits: Vigorous, upright, 3 × 2'
Foliage: Medium, light green, semi-glossy, hardy
Blooms: White with cream overtones, 60-plus petals, 2", cupped
Fragrance: Intense
Comments: This was David Austin's first white rose. He named it for a character in Shakespeare's play "The Taming of the Shrew." It is perfect for a border or a hedge. The blooms are purest white with a hint of cream and open in a saucer shape. It has an intense, old-garden rose fragrance that can be detected 20 feet away. Mass plantings of this variety are spectacular. Rating: 7.8

Felicia

Type: Shrub (Hybrid Musk)
Hybridizer/Year: Pemberton 1928
Growth habits: Vigorous, bushy, 4 × 4'
Foliage: Medium, dark green, matte, disease resistant
Blooms: Soft silver pink fading to white, 17–25 petals, 2–3"
Fragrance: Moderate, musk
Awards: Royal National Rose Society Certificate of Merit 1927, Royal Horticultural Society Award of Garden Merit 1993
Comments: This is a hardy plant that produces most of its blooms in the spring and fall. The blooms are small, range in color from silver-pink to salmon, and have an appealing fragrance. If the spent blooms are not removed in the fall, the plant will produce large hips that remain green for a long time, then slowly turn bright red. Rating: 8.5

Flower Carpet

Type: Shrub
Hybridizer/Year: Noack 1990
Growth habits: Vigorous plants, upright and arching stems, 2–3′ tall, 4′ wide
Foliage: Medium green leaves are small and fine-textured
Blooms: Deep pink blooms are small and variable, from single (5 petals) to double (20 petals). Borne in massive clusters along each stem.
Fragrance: None
Awards: Golden Rose of The Hague 1990
Comments: Flower Carpet is perhaps the most heavily marketed and advertised rose in recent history. Because of its name, it is often recommended as a groundcover, but its rough profile with many upright canes makes it better suited to the mixed border. It performs well in containers. Outstanding vigor, hardiness, disease resistance and prodigious production of self-cleaning blooms make this an excellent low-maintenance choice for any landscape. Now available in a wide range of colors, including Apple Blossom Flower Carpet, Coral Flower Carpet, Red Flower Carpet, White Flower Carpet, and Scarlet Flower Carpet. Rating: 7.6

Flower Girl

Type: Shrub
Hybridizer/Year: Fryer 1999
Growth habits: Medium, bushy, spreading, 4–5′
Foliage: Medium, clean, light green, matte
Blooms: Soft pink fading to light pink centers, 8–15 petals, 1–1½″, large pendulous clusters
Fragrance: Slight, apple
Comments: This is a vigorous, hardy, showy bush. It produces pendulous clusters of blooms that cover the bush. The blooms are soft pink with lighter pink at the center and bright gold stamens. This plant is a proven, consistent performer in all climates. Rating: 8.2

Flutterbye

Type: Shrub
Hybridizer/Year: Carruth 1995
Growth habits: Vigorous, upright, bushy, 5–8′
Foliage: Medium, dark green, glossy, moderate prickles
Blooms: Yellow, coral, orange, tangerine, and pink, 5–9 petals, 1½–2″, single
Fragrance: Moderate, spice
Comments: This tall-growing plant is very hardy. The large, single blooms are deep yellow changing to pinks, golds, and reds as they open. The overall effect of the array of colors is stunning. Dark green, glossy foliage complements the blooms. Rating: 7.7

Shrub roses *(continued)*

Frau Dagmar Hartopp

Type: Shrub (Hybrid Rugosa)
Hybridizer/Year: Unknown 1914
Growth habits: Medium, compact, bushy, 4′
Foliage: Medium, medium green, crinkled, leathery
Blooms: Silvery pink, 5 petals, 4″, single form
Fragrance: Slight
Comments: This is an internationally popular rose. It is hardy, vigorous, bushy, and low growing. It produces wonderful crimson-red hips in the fall. However, it is the blooms that are the real treasure in this plant. The profuse blooms are large, single formed, and silvery pink. This easy-care bush does well in all types of landscapes. Rating: 8.5

Gartendirektor Otto Linne

Type: Shrub
Hybridizer/Year: Lambert 1934
Growth habits: Vigorous, upright-to-arching plants grow 6 to 10′ tall and wide. Can be trained as a climber in mild climates.
Foliage: Apple-green leaves
Blooms: Small, deep-pink, 25 petals, clusters of 30+ flowers.
Fragrance: Mild
Comments: After 75 years this classic shrub rose is still beloved for its massive, solid display of brilliant pink flowers all summer long. Plants are disease resistant, hardy, vigorous, and always in bloom. Rating: 8.8

Gertrude Jekyll

Type: Shrub (Austin)
Hybridizer/Year: Austin 1986
Growth habits: Tall, vigorous, upright, somewhat lanky, 5–6′
Foliage: Medium, medium green, matte
Blooms: Rich, glowing, medium pink, 40 petals, 4–5″
Fragrance: Intense, damask
Awards: Royal National Rose Society James Mason Award 2002

Comments: This popular Austin rose is a disease-resistant, hardy, tall-growing plant that does well in all types of landscapes. The blooms have a rosette shape. Austin refers to its old-rose fragrance as the quintessential rose fragrance. The rose was named for a British garden designer who has had a profound effect on present-day gardens. Rating: 7.6

Golden Celebration

Type: Shrub (Austin)
Hybridizer/Year: Austin 1992
Growth habits: Medium, bushy, 5 × 4′
Foliage: Large, dark green, semiglossy
Blooms: Old-fashioned, deep, rich, golden yellow, 55–75 petals, 3–5″
Fragrance: Intense, citrus
Comments: This is an easy-to-grow, winter-hardy, vigorous plant that has a nicely rounded shape. The blooms are large, deeply cupped, a rich golden yellow, and intensely fragrant. It is a prolific bloomer throughout the growing season and worthy of planting to celebrate any special event. Rating: 8.0

Golden Wings

Type: Shrub
Hybridizer/Year: Sheppard 1956
Growth habits: Medium, vigorous, hardy, bushy, 5–7'
Foliage: Medium, gray-green, matte
Blooms: Large, sulfur yellow, 5 petals, 4–5"
Fragrance: Slight
Awards: ARS Gold Medal 1958
Comments: This bush was one of the first hardy yellow shrubs. It is an upright bush that produces abundant blooms. The large blooms have a single form and are sulfur yellow with darker stamens. The gray-green foliage contrasts well with the blooms. Rating: 8.8

Graham Thomas

Type: Shrub (Austin)
Hybridizer/Year: Austin 1983
Growth habits: Vigorous, upright, bushy, 6 × 4'
Foliage: Small, glossy
Blooms: Rich, deep yellow, 35 petals, 4"
Fragrance: Strong, tea
Comments: This is one of the most popular of the Austin roses. It is a hardy bush that blooms prolifically throughout the growing season. The foliage is disease resistant and glossy. The blooms are cupped, rich, yellow with a fresh tea rose fragrance. It seems to do well in all climates but hot and dry. Rating: 8.2

Henry Hudson

Type: Shrub (Hybrid Rugosa)
Hybridizer/Year: Svejda 1976
Growth habits: Low, vigorous, bushy, 1½–3'
Foliage: Small, medium green, leathery, hardy
Blooms: Pink buds opening to a clear white, 25 petals, 2½–3"
Fragrance: Intense

Comments: This beauty resulted from efforts to develop roses that would withstand harsh Canadian winters. It is perfect as a bedding or border plant. The double white blooms expand to become cupped and reveal golden stamens. Part of the Explorer series, it was named to commemorate the seeker of the Northwest Passage. Rating: 9.0

Heritage

Type: Shrub (Austin)
Hybridizer/Year: Austin 1984
Growth habits: Medium, upright, bushy 4–5'
Foliage: Small, dark green, semiglossy
Blooms: Soft, clear pink at the center with lighter pink outer petals, 50-plus petals, 3", cupped
Fragrance: Intense, sweet
Comments: This is a vigorous, hardy, disease-resistant shrub that does well in all types of landscape design. It has an added bonus in that it is almost thornless. The cupped blooms are of medium size and vary in color from pale pink on the outer petals to a clear rose pink in the center. The foliage contrasts well with the soft pink blooms. Rating: 8.4

Shrub roses *(continued)*

Home Run

Type: Shrub
Hybridizer/Year: Carruth 2004
Growth habits: Vigorous, rounded, bushy, 3 × 3'
Foliage: Medium, dark green, semiglossy, disease resistant
Blooms: Flame red, 5 petals, 4", single
Fragrance: Slight
Comments: An offspring of Knock Out, this bush is even more disease resistant coast to coast. It rarely is without color. The blooms are large, single, and flame red with golden stamens. The color deepens in cooler temperatures. This is a great rose for the novice gardener.

John Cabot

Type: Shrub (Hybrid Kordesii)
Hybridizer/Year: Svejda 1978
Growth habits: Tall, vigorous, upright, bushy, 6' or more
Foliage: Medium, yellow-green, matte, very hardy, numerous prickles
Blooms: Fuchsia, 40 petals, 2½", clusters
Fragrance: Moderate
Awards: Portland Gold Medal 2003
Comments: This super hardy, disease-resistant shrub comes from Canada. It is constantly in bloom. The blooms make a great color display in the garden. The yellow-green foliage is unusual in coloration and contrasts nicely with the blooms. This rose disputes the notion that roses are difficult and time consuming to grow. Rating: 8.8

Jude the Obscure

Type: Shrub (Austin)
Hybridizer/Year: Austin 1997
Growth habits: Vigorous, upright, bushy, 3½ × 4'
Foliage: Medium, medium green, semiglossy, some prickles
Blooms: Pale yellow outside and medium yellow inside, 55–70 petals, 4–5", globular
Fragrance: Intense, fruity
Awards: Monza Fragrance Award 1996

Comments: This hardy, disease resistant shrub is very popular. The blooms are large, incurved, and chalice shape with light yellow on the outside and darker yellow on the inside. They may not open well in damp climates but thrive in dry climates. The intense fragrance has hints of wine and fruit. It was named after the main character in Thomas Hardy's novel. Rating: 8.0

Kaleidoscope

Type: Shrub
Hybridizer/Year: Walden 1998
Growth habits: Medium, vigorous, rounded, spreading, 3–4'
Foliage: Medium, dark green, glossy, numerous prickles
Blooms: Tan mauve blend with a yellow mauve blend reverse, 26–40 petals, 3", clusters

Fragrance: Slight, fruity
Awards: AARS 1999
Comments: This plant produces an abundance of blooms throughout the growing season that are unique and ever-changing. They begin a tan-mauve blend with a yellow-mauve blend reverse and age to an elegant mauve-pink. Rating: 7.3

Kent

Type: Shrub
Hybridizer/Year: Olesen 1988
Growth habits: Vigorous, spreading, bushy, 3–4'
Foliage: Medium, light to medium green, matte
Blooms: Clear white with bright yellow stamens, 15–25 petals, 2"
Fragrance: Slight
Awards: Baden-Baden Gold Medal 1990, Royal National Rose Society President's International Trophy 1990, Royal National Rose Society Certificate of Merit 1992
Comments: This is an excellent rose for any landscape. It is a disease-resistant bush that produces abundant blooms throughout the growing season. The blooms occur in large trusses of small white flowers that open cupped and become flat. They have bright yellow stamens and seem to be clean no matter what the weather. This is a good rose for hedges or borders.

Knock Out

Knock Out

Blushing Knock Out

Pink Knock Out

Rainbow Knock Out

Type: Shrub
Hybridizer/Year: Radler 1999
Growth habits: Rounded bush, 3–4' tall, 3–4' wide
Foliage: Purplish green, semiglossy
Blooms: Red blend, lighter pink in the center deepening to cherry red at the outer edges, single, 5–7 petals, 3", clusters
Fragrance: None
Awards: AARS 2000, ARS Members Choice Award 2004, Portland Gold Medal 2003
Comments: Because of its virtual immunity to the scourge of black spot, Knock Out was an exciting development when it was introduced in 1999, setting the standard for a new generation of carefree shrub roses. It has since become one of the most popular landscape roses in North America. The magenta-red color of the original can be hard to incorporate into the garden, but it is still a stunning rose for massing in large beds. Flowers blanket the plant all summer, repeating quickly. The introduction of new varieties in the series with the same resistance to black spot has expanded the color range of the Knock Out series, including Blushing Knock Out, Pink Knock Out, Double Red Knock Out, Double Pink Knock Out, and Rainbow Knock Out. Rating: 8.6

Shrub roses *(continued)*

Lady Elsie May

Type: Shrub
Hybridizer/Year: Noack 2005
Growth habits: Vigorous, rounded, bushy, 3′
Foliage: Medium, dark green, glossy, some downward hooked prickles, disease resistant
Blooms: Coral pink, 10–14 petals, 3–4″
Fragrance: Slight
Awards: AARS 2005
Comments: This bush is a consistent performer in all climates. It is disease resistant and compact. A prolific bloomer, it seems always to be covered in flowers. The blooms are coral-pink and open to a flat form showing off the bright yellow stamens. This is a good bush for a hedge or border.

Leonard Dudley Braithwaite

Type: Shrub (Austin)
Hybridizer/Year: Austin 1988
Growth habits: Vigorous, upright, bushy, 4½ × 5′
Foliage: Medium, dark green, semiglossy, some prickles
Blooms: Bright crimson red, 45-plus petals, 3–3½″, slightly cupped
Fragrance: Intense, rose

Comments: This rose has the brightest crimson coloring of any of the English type roses. It is a tall, spreading plant that is disease resistant. The blooms open slightly cupped. Their fragrance does not appear until the bloom ages and then they have the old rose fragrance. This rose was named for David Austin's father-in-law. Rating: 7.9

Linda Campbell

Type: Shrub
Hybridizer/Year: Moore 1985
Growth habits: Vigorous, upright, bushy, 5′
Foliage: Large, semiglossy
Blooms: Medium red with a lighter red reverse, 25 petals, 3″, cupped
Fragrance: None

Comments: This is a hardy plant with rugosa heritage. The red velvety blooms occur in large clusters that repeat bloom quickly. The foliage is quilted with some of the typical rugosa characteristics. The rose was named for a former editor of the *American Rose Annual* who died of cancer at an early age. Rating: 8.1

Martha's Vineyard

Type: Shrub
Hybridizer/Year: Olesen, Pernille & Mogens 1995
Growth habits: Vigorous, spreading, bushy, 3 × 4′
Foliage: Small, light green, semiglossy, few prickles
Blooms: Hot pink blending to white at the center, 6–14 petals, 2″
Fragrance: Slight

Comments: This is a disease-resistant, upright plant that makes a good border or hedge. The hot pink blooms are striking in the garden and contrast well with the foliage. This bush produces an abundance of blooms throughout the growing season. Rating: 8.3

Mary Magdalene

Type: Shrub (Austin)
Hybridizer/Year: Austin 1998
Growth habits: $3' \times 3\frac{1}{2}'$
Foliage: Medium matte, green
Blooms: Creamy apricot blend, double, full, cupped, 100-plus
Fragrance: Fragrant
Comments: This English rose shows its old rose heritage with delicate silky petals, smaller at the center, arranged around a button eye. The lovely soft color hints at the scent, which is a particularly nice tea rose scent with a hint of myrrh. This rose also is a strong repeat bloomer. Rating: 7.6

Mary Rose

Type: Shrub (Austin)
Hybridizer/Year: Austin 1983
Growth habits: Vigorous, upright, bushy, medium, $5 \times 3\frac{1}{2}'$
Foliage: Medium, medium green, matte
Blooms: Large, rose-pink, 45–55 petals, 4"
Fragrance: Intense, fruity, myrrh
Awards: Royal National Rose Societies Award of Garden Merit 2001
Comments: This is one of the most popular and widely grown of the English roses. It is a hardy shrub that blooms prolifically throughout the growing season. The blooms have a loose but attractive form. The beauty of the rose is enhanced by its old-rose fragrance. This is an ideal variety for hedges. It is named after Henry VIII of Engand's flagship when it was recovered from the sea more than 400 years after it sank. Rating: 8.3

Meidiland Landscape Roses

Cherry Meidiland

La Sevillana

Alba Meidiland

Type: Shrub
Hybridizer/Year: Meilland, 1978 onward
Growth habits: Low, spreading groundcovers, 1–2' tall, 4–5' wide; mounded shrubs, 4–5' tall, 4–5' wide; hedge varieties, planted 18" apart
Foliage: Small leaves, matte green
Blooms: White, pink, coral, orange, and red. Some are double, some are single blooms with a white eye (see color versions listed below).
Fragrance: None
Comments: Since La Sevillana was introduced in 1978, Meilland of France has populated the world of landscape roses with a wide variety of excellent plants. Wonderfully low maintenance, pest resistant, disease tolerant, and cold hardy, most provide a beautiful show of nonstop, long-lasting, brilliant blooms all summer. A few, most notably La Sevillana (see page 177; it can be classified as either a floribunda or a shrub), provide one massive floral display for several weeks in late spring followed by an outstanding show of red hips in fall and winter. White groundcovers in the Meidiland series include Alba Meidiland (Rating: 8.4), Ice Meidiland, and White Meidiland (Rating: 8.4). Red and orange shrub Meidilands include Magic Meidiland, La Sevillana, Scarlet Meidiland, and Red Meidiland (Rating: 7.4). Pink shrubs include the famous Bonica (see page 190), Royal Bonica, Coral Meidiland, Cherry Meidiland, and Pink Meidiland (Rating: 8.6).

Shrub roses *(continued)*

Midnight Blue

Type: Shrub
Hybridizer/Year: Carruth 2003
Growth habits: Vigorous, compact, bushy, 2–3′
Foliage: Medium, medium green, semiglossy
Blooms: Velvety deep purple, 25–30 petals, 3–5″; cupped
Fragrance: Intense, clove
Comments: This rose provides novel color in the garden or bouquets. It is a velvety, dark purple with bright yellow stamens. It grows in large clusters on a compact bush that is versatile for any landscape design. Rating: 7.6

Morden Roses *(also called the Parkland series)*

Morden Blush

Morden Centennial

Morden Fireglow

Type: Shrub
Hybridizer/Year: Marshall or Collicutt & Marshall, primarily 1977 onward
Growth habits: Heights and width vary, but most are of medium size, 2–4′ × 2–4′
Foliage: Medium, medium green, matte, straight prickles
Blooms: Light pink fading to ivory, 50 petals, 3″, sprays of 1–5 blooms
Fragrance: Slight
Comments: This series of roses is also known as the Parkland series. They are very cold hardy and disease resistant, a great choice for growing roses in the North. Named after the place where these roses were developed— the Morden Experimental Station in Canada—these roses also do well in milder climates. They are a great low maintenance choice for borders and hedges. Most, but not all, have Morden in the name: Morden Blush, Morden Centennial, Morden Fireglow, etc. Others include Adelaide Hoodless and Cuthbert Grant. Rating: 8.0

Noble Antony

Type: Shrub (Austin)
Hybridizer/Year: Austin 1997
Growth habits: Vigorous, upright, bushy, 3 × 2½'
Foliage: Medium, dark green, semiglossy, some prickles, disease resistant
Blooms: Deep magenta-pink, 85–90 petals, 4–5", domed
Fragrance: Moderate
Comments: This compact, hardy bush is shorter than most shrubs, making it ideal for borders or containers. The blooms are full-petaled and deeply domed. The rose was named for a character in Shakespeare's play "Antony and Cleopatra."

Outta the Blue

Type: Shrub
Hybridizer/Year: Carruth 2000
Growth habits: Medium, vigorous, upright, 3–4'
Foliage: Medium, dark green, semiglossy to glossy, moderate prickles
Blooms: Rich magenta to wine spiked with yellow, 25–30 petals, 3", big clusters
Fragrance: Intense, clove and rose
Comments: This bushy plant produces clusters of old-fashioned flowers. The blooms range from rich magenta to deep wine to warm lavender to almost blue, creating a multitoned color display in the garden. Rating: 7.9

Penelope

Type: Shrub (Hybrid Musk)
Hybridizer/Year: Pemberton 1924
Growth habits: Tall, vigorous, bushy, 6'
Foliage: Medium, dark green, matte, leathery
Blooms: Shell pink shading to white with a lemon center, 18–25 petals, 3"
Fragrance: Moderate
Awards: Royal National Rose Society Gold Medal 1925
Comments: This is another of Pemberton's shrub roses that has retained popularity. This disease-resistant plant has large, arching canes perfect for draping over a wall or other structure. It also can create a hedge and has many other potential landscape uses. The eyecatching blooms are sweetly fragrant and appear in large clusters. Rating: 8.8

Shrub roses *(continued)*

Perdita

Type: Shrub (Austin)
Hybridizer/Year: Austin 1992
Growth habits: Medium, upright, bushy, 3–4'
Foliage: Medium, medium green, semiglossy, some prickles
Blooms: Blush apricot, 50-plus petals, 3–3½", clusters
Fragrance: Intense, spicy
Awards: Royal National Rose Society Edland Fragrance Medal 1984
Comments: This plant does well in all landscapes. It is a vigorous, disease-resistant bush that produces clusters of fragrant blooms. The blooms are medium to large, full petaled, rosette shape, and creamy blush-apricot with an intense rose scent. The name means "the abandoned one" and refers to the heroine in Shakespeare's play "A Winter's Tale." Rating: 7.8

Pillow Fight

Type: Shrub
Hybridizer/Year: Carruth 1999
Growth habits: Vigorous, rounded, 3'
Foliage: Medium, dark green, glossy
Blooms: Bright white, 35 petals, 1–2"
Fragrance: Intense, honey, rose
Comments: This plant is a seedling of Gourmet Popcorn and possesses many of its characteristics and more. It is a medium grower that is in constant bloom. These bright white blooms come in large clusters amid glossy, dark green foliage. The bush prefers drier climates. It is ideal for a border or hedge. Rating: 7.9

Prosperity

Type: Shrub
Hybridizer/Year: Pemberton 1919
Growth habits: Vigorous, upright, bushy, 6–8'
Foliage: Small, dark green, glossy
Blooms: Creamy white flushed pale pink, 25–30 petals, 2"
Fragrance: Strong
Comments: This bush blooms in large clusters. The blooms are creamy white and have an intense fragrance. The dark green, glossy foliage offers contrast. The plant is a prolific bloomer, particularly in the early summer. Its growth habit is a little lax, so it may require pruning. Rating: 8.5

Rabble Rouser

Type: Shrub
Hybridizer/Year: Horner 1998
Growth habits: Vigorous, rounded, bushy, 3–4'
Foliage: Small, glossy, moderate prickles
Blooms: Deep yellow with a paler yellow reverse, 8–14 petals, 1½–2"
Fragrance: Slight
Comments: This bush is a seedling of Baby Love and has some similar characteristics. It grows larger in milder climates. The blooms shine against the glossy foliage. As the blooms open, they flatten to reveal beautiful golden stamens. This plant does well as a border or hedge. Rating: 7.4

Rhapsody in Blue

Type: Shrub
Hybridizer/Year: Cowlishaw 1999
Growth habits: Vigorous, upright, semiclimbing, tall, 5–7'
Foliage: Medium, light green, glossy, moderate prickles
Blooms: Dark iridescent purple lightening with age, 16–20 petals, 3″
Fragrance: Intense, sweet, spice
Awards: Royal National Rose Soceity Rose of the Year 1999
Comments: This taller, bushy shrub rose has blooms that are an unusual smoky blue-purple blend that may represent the closest thing to a blue rose to date. Bred in England, it prefers cooler temperatures.

Rockin' Robin

Type: Shrub
Hybridizer/Year: Carruth 1997
Growth habits: Vigorous, rounded, bushy, 4'
Foliage: Medium, dark green, glossy, moderate prickles
Blooms: Red, white, and pink striped and splashed, 40–45 petals, 1½–2″, ruffled
Fragrance: Slight, apple
Comments: This disease resistant plant suits any landscape. The novel, spectacular blooms are ruffled and have pink, red, and white stripes. Rating: 7.5

Roseraie de l'Hay

Type: Shrub (Hybrid Rugosa)
Hybridizer/Year: Cochet-Cochet 1901
Growth habits: Vigorous, upright, bushy, 4–5'
Foliage: Small, medium green, glossy, rugose, many prickles
Blooms: Crimson-red changing to magenta purple, 20–30 petals, 4″
Fragrance: Intense
Awards: Royal Horticultural Society Award of Garden Merit 1993
Comments: This may be the most widely grown and popular of all of the rugosa types of roses. It is disease resistant. The large blooms grow in small clusters of intense crimson to magenta purple with golden stamens. Their rich clove and honey fragrance is memorable. Rating: 8.8

Sally Holmes

Type: Shrub
Hybridizer/Year: Holmes 1976
Growth habits: Very vigorous, upright, bushy, tall, 6–12'
Foliage: Large, dark green, glossy, disease resistant
Blooms: Large, apricot buds opening to creamy white, 5–8 petals, 3½–4″, huge rounded clusters
Fragrance: Slight
Awards: Baden-Baden Gold Medal 1980, Portland Gold Medal 1993
Comments: This rose is rapidly becoming a favorite. It needs plenty of space but can be contained with judicious pruning. The blooms are exquisite and transition from a pink-apricot bud to a creamy white, single bloom with a hint of pink. The foliage is glossy and clean. The blooms occur in large clusters and last even in the heat. This rose is a must-have for any serious gardener or exhibitor. Rating: 8.9

Shrub roses *(continued)*

Sharifa Asma

Type: Shrub (Austin)
Hybridizer/Year: Austin 1989
Growth habits: Medium, vigorous, upright, bushy, 3–4′
Foliage: Medium, dark green, semiglossy, many prickles
Blooms: Pale pink fading to pinkish white, 41-plus petals, 4–5″
Fragrance: Intense, fruity

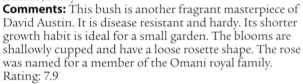

Comments: This bush is another fragrant masterpiece of David Austin. It is disease resistant and hardy. Its shorter growth habit is ideal for a small garden. The blooms are shallowly cupped and have a loose rosette shape. The rose was named for a member of the Omani royal family. Rating: 7.9

Sophy's Rose

Type: Shrub (Austin)
Hybridizer/Year: Austin 1997
Growth habits: Vigorous, 3½–4½′ tall and wide
Foliage: Semiglossy, medium green
Blooms: Reddish purple, dome-shape, double, 80–90 petals, old-fashioned look
Fragrance: Moderate
Comments: Hailed as a new shade of red in the Austin roses, this well-behaved bush makes a fine subject for the mixed border in combination with such plants as baby's breath and rose campion. It also performs well in containers. The old-rose form of the flower is cupped and quartered, as lovely in the garden as in the vase. Rating: 7.7

Starry Night

Type: Shrub
Hybridizer/Year: Orard 2002
Growth habits: Medium, bushy, spreading, 3–5′
Foliage: Medium, medium green, glossy, disease resistant
Blooms: Bright crisp white with golden stamens, 5 petals, 2½″, clusters
Fragrance: Slight
Awards: AARS 2002
Comments: This easy-to-grow shrub needs no deadheading. It is a vigorous, low-growing, somewhat spreading plant that produces huge clusters of abundant blooms. Medium green, glossy leaves contrast well with the single blooms. This shrub makes a great landscape display. Rating: 7.8

Sunrise Sunset

Type: Shrub
Hybridizer/Year: Lim 2004
Growth habits: Arching, spreading, 2–3′ tall, up to 5′ wide, vigorous
Foliage: Slightly blue-green, small leaves with matte texture
Blooms: Bright fuchsia-pink, apricot-yellow centers, semidouble, 13-19 petals, 2-2½″, borne in large clusters.
Fragrance: None
Comments: This is one of the best in the Easy Elegance series of extra-hardy roses from Bailey Nurseries, with glowing pink and apricot flowers borne in profusion all summer long. A dense, arching, spreading habit makes it ideal as a groundcover and for massing in beds. It is extremely hardy, vigorous, and disease-resistant.

Tamora

Type: Shrub (Austin)
Hybridizer/Year: Austin 1987
Growth habits: Thorny, upright, 3–4″ tall, 2–3″ wide
Foliage: Medium green, matte
Blooms: Apricot-yellow, deeply cupped, 40–50 petals
Fragrance: Strong, myrrh
Comments:
Delicate light apricot colors and intense old-fashioned myrrh fragrance make this rose a favorite for the vase. Each bush produces large quantities of flowers for armloads of blooms. This is one of the most disease resistant of the Austin roses. Rating: 7.8

The Countryman

Type: Shrub (Austin)
Hybridizer/Year: Austin 1987
Growth habits: Medium, vigorous, bushy, spreading, 3–4′
Foliage: Medium, medium green, matte, small hooked pale prickles
Blooms: Medium pink, 40 petals, 4″
Fragrance: Intense
Comments: This hardy bush is good for borders and other landscape uses. The blooms are clear rose-pink, heavy petaled, and rosette shaped, with an intense strawberry-rose scent. The blooms are complemented by the soft matte foliage. Rating: 7.8

The Dark Lady

Type: Shrub (Austin)
Hybridizer/Year: Austin 1991
Growth habits: Vigorous, upright, bushy, 3′
Foliage: Medium, dark green, semiglossy, some prickles
Blooms: Dark red, 140 petals, 3″
Fragrance: Intense
Comments: This extra-hardy rose is distantly related to the rugosas. It is a vigorous, rounded, bushy plant. Its rich, dark crimson blooms age to dark purple. The rose was named for the Dark Lady of Shakespeare's sonnets. Rating: 7.8

The Prince

Type: Shrub (Austin)
Hybridizer/Year: Austin 1990
Growth habits: Low, vigorous, upright, bushy, 2–3′
Foliage: Medium, dark green, matte, many prickles, disease-resistant
Blooms: Deep crimson to royal purple, 125 petals, 4″, cupped
Fragrance: Intense, rose
Comments: The best attribute of this bush is its bloom: a full rosette of the deepest crimson that ages to a royal purple. It is striking in any of its color stages. It is best used in landscape designs that highlight the bloom color with harmonizing plants. Rating: 7.7

Shrub roses *(continued)*

The Squire

Type: Shrub (Austin)
Hybridizer/Year: Austin 1976
Growth habits: Rounded, bushy, open, medium, 3–4′
Foliage: Medium, dark green, semiglossy
Blooms: Large, very dark red, rosette form, 120 petals, 3½–4″
Fragrance: Intense
Comments: This rose is a focal point when planted in a group. It is an upright grower that can be leggy. The bloom is superb. It is dark red and deeply cupped, with its petals arranged to create a perfect quartered rose effect as it expands. This variety could grow in a container with extra care. Rating: 8.4

Topaz Jewel

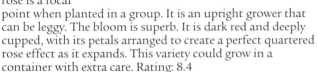

Type: Shrub
Hybridizer/Year: Moore 1987
Growth habits: Vigorous, upright, bushy, 3–5′
Foliage: Large, medium green, matte, rugose, many slender long brown prickles
Blooms: Medium yellow fading to cream, 25 petals, 3½–4″, cupped
Fragrance: Moderate, fruity
Comments: This rose from well-known hybridizer Ralph Moore was one of the first and is perhaps the best of the yellow rugosa type shrub roses. It is a spreading plant that blooms in clusters. It does well as a border or in a mass planting. Rating: 7.4

Watercolors

Type: Shrub
Hybridizer/Year: Carruth 2006
Growth habits: Bushy, spreading, 2½–3′ tall
Foliage: Semiglossy, dark green, medium, new shoots are dark red
Blooms: Glowing yellow petals are brushed with pink, lighter on the reverse, single, 4–8 petals, yellow stamens, 2½″ wide, borne in small clusters
Fragrance: Mild, apple
Comments: Introduced by Weeks Roses in 2008, this elegantly simple, single-petaled rose is adorned with extravagant color. Very disease resistant and hardy, this rose has a delicate appearance that masks its toughness in the garden. Plants can grow taller in cool, mild-winter climates.

Westerland

Type: Shrub
Hybridizer/Year: Kordes 1969
Growth habits: Tall, vigorous, upright, climbing, 10′ or more
Foliage: Large, dark green, glossy, disease resistant
Blooms: Apricot-orange, 20 petals, 3″, cupped
Fragrance: Intense, spicy
Awards: Anerkannte Deutsch Rose 1974
Comments: This shrub has everything, including the ability to grow sufficiently large to classify as a climber. The blooms occur in clusters of blended apricot and orange that are infused with an intense, spicy fragrance. The dark green, glossy foliage complements the blooms. Rating: 8.2

What a Peach

Type: Shrub
Hybridizer/Year: Warner 2001
Growth habits: Vigorous, upright, bushy, 3–4'
Foliage: Medium, medium green, glossy
Blooms: Peachy gold, 25–30 petals, 3"
Fragrance: Moderate, fruity
Comments: This plant does well in all types of landscapes. The blooms have a loose form but hold their color well. The medium green, glossy foliage has red new growth that is especially attractive with the blooms. The clusters of blooms are warm and inviting. Rating: 7.4

William Baffin

Type: Shrub (Hybrid Kordessii)
Hybridizer/Year: Svedja 1983
Growth habits: Upright, slightly arching, 10–12' high
Foliage: Glossy, medium green, highly disease resistant
Blooms: Deep pink, semidouble, clusters of 30-plus, strawberry-pink with a touch of white at the center, brilliant yellow stamens
Fragrance: Little to none
Comments: Extremely cold-hardy plants are smothered in clusters of blooms summer to autumn. When trained as a climber, this is one of the few climbing roses hardy above ground without winter protection Zone 4 or colder. Rating: 8.9

William Shakespeare 2000

Type: Shrub (Austin)
Hybridizer/Year: Austin 2001
Growth habits: Vigorous, upright, bushy, 4 × 3'
Foliage: Medium, dark green, semiglossy
Blooms: Velvety, crimson changing to deep purple, 35 petals, 3–4"
Fragrance: Intense, old rose
Comments: Hybridizer David Austin considers this the best crimson English rose to date. It is a hardy, disease-resistant plant that likes the warmer U.S. summers. The blooms are a rich velvety crimson that gradually changes to a royal purple. The bloom is deeply cupped at first but expands to a shallow quarter cup. This rose should not be confused with the William Shakespeare rose introduced in 1987. Rating: 7.7

Old garden and species roses

What could be more romantic than old garden and species roses, roses that harken back to another era? Old roses also play an important historical role. Many of today's modern roses can be traced to older types of roses still available today in some nurseries. Understanding this critical role of old roses, rosarians around the world have dedicated themselves to preserving these older varieties and styles of roses by supporting and maintaining gardens where old garden and species roses thrive.

As a group, old garden roses, also called antique roses, are renown for their incredible fragrances, huge blossoms or clusters, and can be enormous plants. However, also as a group, they tend not to bloom more than once after their late spring flowering. Types include:

Alba: Albas are very cold hardy and usually grow upright with dense, disease-resistant blue-green foliage. Flowers are fragrant and bloom just once. They are hardy through Zone 3.

Bourbon: These bloom repeatedly and grow 2 to 15 feet tall. They are hardy through Zone 6.

Centifolia: True to their name, these flowers boast an astounding 100 petals each. They bloom just once and do best in Zones 4 to 9.

China: China roses grow just 2 to 3 feet tall. They have clusters of flowers that are repeat-blooming with a spicy scent. They are hardy through Zone 7.

Damask: Most damask roses bloom just once but have a heady fragrance that makes that bloom time memorable. They grow 3 to 7 feet tall and aren't very cold-hardy, growing in Zones 6 to 10.

Gallica: Gallica roses usually don't top 4 feet. They bloom once and are fragrant and known for their brilliant colors. They are hardy through Zone 4.

Hybrid Perpetual: These roses are repeat-blooming, hence the name. They grow up to 6 feet tall and are fragrant. Their hardiness varies depending on the particular rose.

Moss: These are named after the interesting moss-like growth on penduncle and sepals. Some moss roses bloom repeatedly; others bloom just once. Their height ranges between 3 to 6 feet tall and they have fragrant flowers. Moss roses are hardy through Zone 4.

Noisette: These sprawling plants grow up to 20 feet. They are excellent repeat bloomers, are fragrant, and grow in a wide variety of climates, Zones 4 to 11.

Tea: Tea roses are not to be confused with hybrid tea roses, which are more modern version (see page 138). Tea roses are medium-size plants, growing 4 to 5 feet tall. They bloom repeatedly and are very tender, growing only in warmer regions Zones 7 to 11.

See page 30 for more detail about old garden roses.

▲ This Belle Amour, an alba old garden rose, is a vigorous grower that has twined itself through an old pear tree.

Alister Stella Gray

Type: Noisette
Hybridizer/Year: Gray 1894
Growth habits: Tall, vigorous, upright, 15 × 10′
Foliage: Medium, dark green, few prickles, thin canes
Blooms: Pale yellow with a darker yellow center, fading to white, 50-plus petals, 3″
Fragrance: Moderate
Awards: Royal Horticultural Society Award of Garden Merit 1994
Comments: This rose is typical of the noisette class. It is a bushy plant that seems to bloom continuously. The blooms are full and quartered. This bush does well in all landscapes. Rating: 8.0

American Beauty

Type: Hybrid Perpetual
Hybridizer/Year: Ledechaux 1875
Growth habits: Tall, vigorous, bushy 6–8 × 5′
Foliage: Medium, light to medium green, matte
Blooms: Deep pink, 50 petals, 4–5″, cupped
Fragrance: Intense
Comments: When this rose came to the United States with the name Mademoiselle Ferdinand Jamin, it caused a revolution in the cut-flower industry. In 1885 it was

officially renamed American Beauty. It became a favorite florist rose and was officially adopted as the floral symbol of Washington, D.C. It is an upright bush that needs some care to keep it looking its best. It can be hard to find for sale. The blooms are fragrant and glorious. Rating: 7.6

Apothecary's Rose (*Rosa gallica officinalis*)

Type: Species
Hybridizer/Year: Unknown
Growth habits: Medium, upright, lax canes, 3–4′
Foliage: Medium, dark green, leathery
Blooms: Deep pink aging to purple with bright yellow stamens, 18–25 petals, 3–4″
Fragrance: Intense
Comments: This may be the oldest rose grown in Europe. It was initially used for medicinal purposes and was also part of the War of the Roses; it is also known as the Red Rose of Lancaster. This vigorous, disease-resistant plant is often used as a groundcover to stop erosion on steep banks. It is a prolific but one-time bloomer. Rating: 8.7

Old garden roses *(continued)*

Archduke Charles

Type: China
Hybridizer/Year: Laffay prior to 1837
Growth habits: Vigorous, upright, bushy, 6′
Foliage: Medium, medium green, semiglossy, some prickles
Blooms: Rose pink changing to crimson-red in the sun, 25–30 petals, 3″, cupped
Fragrance: Slight, banana
Comments: This rose is a prolific bloomer. This bush does well in any landscape. Rating: 8.5

Austrian Copper

Type: Foetida
Hybridizer/Year: Jacquin & Willmott prior to 1590
Growth habits: Vigorous, upright, bushy, 4–12′
Foliage: Medium, medium green, matte
Blooms: Coppery scarlet with rich yellow reverse, 5 petals, 2″
Fragrance: Slight

Comments: This rose is an improved sport of Austrian Briar, or Austrian Yellow. It is a once-blooming variety. The petals tend to curve inward, creating a colorful display of red and yellow. This bush is known to revert to its parent, so it likely will have branches with solid yellow blooms growing among the scarlet with a yellow reverse. Like all of the *R. foetida* roses, this rose is susceptible to black spot.

Autumn Damask

Type: Damask
Hybridizer/Year: Unknown, prior to 1600
Growth habits: Medium, vigorous, bushy, 3–5 × 5′
Foliage: Medium, medium to olive green, matte, many prickles
Blooms: Medium pink with yellow stamens, 40 petals, 3½″, ruffled
Fragrance: Intense
Comments: This old rose can be traced to the Middle East where its fragrance was used in the perfume industry. It is a robust, repeat-blooming plant that is attractive in the garden even when it is not in bloom. The blooms are ruffled. This plant does well in all types of landscape designs. It has also been known as the Four Seasons Rose. Rating: 8.2

Baronne Prevost

Type: Hybrid perpetual
Hybridizer/Year: Desprez 1842
Growth habits: Vigorous, upright, 6 × 5′
Foliage: Small, medium green, matte
Blooms: Large, deep rose-pink shading to lighter pink, 40-plus petals, 4″
Fragrance: Moderate
Comments: This is one of the the oldest hybrid perpetuals that is still on the market. It maintains its popularity in the

garden, in the vase, and on the exhibition table. This bush does well as a border plant. The blooms maintain the old garden rose form and are quite large. When they open they are full, flat, and quartered. Rating: 8.6

Belle Amour

Type: Alba
Hybridizer/Year: Unknown
Growth habits: Vigorous, upright, bushy, 6 × 4′
Foliage: Large, medium green, matte, many prickles
Blooms: Soft pink with salmon overtones and bright yellow stamens, 25 petals, 3–4″, cupped
Fragrance: Intense, myrrh
Comments: This rose was discovered in 1940 at a convent in Elbeuf, England. It is an easy-to-grow, once-blooming shrub that produces a multitude of small clusters of cushion-shape blooms. The foliage is serrated and coarse. Rating: 8.0

Belle de Crecy

Type: Gallica
Hybridizer/Year: Roeser prior to 1829
Growth habits: Medium, vigorous, bushy, 3–4 × 5′
Foliage: Small to medium, dark gray-green, matte, nearly prickleless
Blooms: Rich pink aging to reddish purple and lilac purple, 100-plus petals, 3″, small greenish eye
Fragrance: Intense
Comments: This rose is a classic gallica. It produces an abundance of blooms that change color with age. It probably was named for Crecy-en-Brie, where the hybridizer had his nursery. Rating: 8.0

Belle Isis

Type: Gallica
Hybridizer/Year: Parmentier 1845
Growth habits: Medium, upright, lax canes, 3–4′
Foliage: Medium, medium green, leathery
Blooms: Pale pink, deep pink center, 18–25 petals, 3″
Fragrance: Intense
Comments: This once-blooming gallica is a parent of Constance Spry, one of David Austin's most popular creations. It is a vigorous, disease-resistant, somewhat lax grower that produces an abundance of blooms. The blooms are quartered and very fragrant. The arrangement of the petals make this rose especially good for arrangements. Rating: 7.7

Blush Damask

Type: Damask
Hybridizer/Year: Unknown 1759
Growth habits: Vigorous, upright, bushy, 3–6'
Foliage: Medium, dark green, matte, short prickles
Blooms: Rose-pink center shading to a pale pink blush on the outer petals, 40-plus petals, 2"
Fragrance: Intense

Comments: This plant has some gallica influence. The fragrant blooms appear in abundance. This plant is easy to grow but needs space to develop.

Blush Noisette

Type: Noisette
Hybridizer/Year: Noisette 1814
Growth habits: Vigorous, upright, 7 × 4'
Foliage: Small, dark green, glossy
Blooms: Blush pink, 20–25 petals, 2–2½"
Fragrance: Moderate, clove
Comments: This was the first noisette on the market for the public. It is a tall-growing bush that does well on pillars or as a hedge. This bush is a prolific bloomer and is somewhat shade tolerant. Some rose experts believe this is a sport of the first noisette introduced from France. Rating: 8.5

Boule de Neige

Type: Bourbon
Hybridizer/Year: Lacharme 1867
Growth habits: Medium, vigorous, bushy, 4–5 × 3–4'
Foliage: Medium, dark green, glossy, leathery, many prickles
Blooms: Milk white, 100-plus petals, 3"
Fragrance: Moderate
Comments: This repeat bloomer is great for hedges and borders. The blooms are milk white, compact, and full. When they open they quickly reflex and form an attractive ball, resulting in its name, which translates to "snowball." This plant is somewhat shade tolerant. Rating: 7.9

Cabbage Rose

Type: Centifolia
Hybridizer/Year: Unknown 1596
Growth habits: Vigorous, upright, bushy, 6 × 4'
Foliage: Medium, gray-green, coarse, some prickles
Blooms: Medium to deep pink, 60-plus petals, 3"
Fragrance: Moderate, old rose
Comments: This once-bloomer is probably the most classic of the old garden roses. It likes the sun and tends not to open well in wet climates. The blooms are shallowly cupped and moderately fragrant. This rose is called The Rose of Painters by the French because it was portrayed in the works of Redoute and the Dutch painters.

Cardinal de Richelieu

Type: Gallica
Hybridizer/Year: Laffay prior to 1847
Growth habits: Medium, upright, bushy, 3–4'
Foliage: Medium, medium green, leathery
Blooms: Dark purple, 40–50 petals, 3–4"
Fragrance: Intense, sweet
Comments: This once-bloomers is one of the most heavily blooming of the gallicas and perhaps the darkest in color. For those reasons, it has maintained its international reputation and popularity. It is a vigorous, neat plant that produces clusters of blooms. The blooms change quickly from a rich dark red to a royal purple. The center petals fold inward to show off the lighter reverse. This rose was named for the well-known minister to Louis XIII. Rating: 8.0

Celestial

Type: Alba
Hybridizer/Year: Unknown 1759
Growth habits: Vigorous, upright, dense, 6'
Foliage: Medium, gray-green, bluish, matte, some prickles
Blooms: Silvery soft blush pink, 25-plus petals, 3"
Fragrance: Moderate, old rose
Comments: Well-known rose enthusiast Peter Beales says this very old garden rose deserves to be in every garden. It does well in all types of landscapes. The fabulous blooms

have been painted by Redouté and Parsons. This rose is once-blooming but the flowers are large, semidouble, loose upon opening, and a glowing soft silvery pink with darker stamens. The blooms contrast well with the blue-gray-green foliage. Rating: 8.5

Celsiana

Type: Damask
Hybridizer/Year: Jacques-Martin Cels prior to 1732
Growth habits: Medium, vigorous, upright, 4–5'
Foliage: Medium, gray-green, smooth
Blooms: Pale pink, 30–40 petals, crinkled, 4", clusters
Fragrance: Moderate
Comments: Many gardeners consider this once-blooming rose the quintessential damask rose. It does well in all climates. The large blooms are double and occur in clusters. The plant has a fairly dense structure for a damask, which makes it ideal for any landscape project. Rating: 8.7

Old garden roses *(continued)*

Champneys' Pink Cluster

Type: Noisette
Hybridizer/Year: Champneys 1811
Growth habits: Vigorous, upright, bushy, 10′
Foliage: Medium, medium green, matte
Blooms: Light pink, 30–35 petals, 2″
Fragrance: Intense
Comments: Many gardeners claim that this is the first noisette and that it originated in South Carolina. The small blooms are double and occur in clusters on purple canes. It is very fragrant and does well on a pillar or as a hedge. In 1986 it was unofficially renamed The Charleston Rose for its birthplace. Rating: 8.4

Charles de Mills

Type: Gallica
Hybridizer/Year: Hardy prior to 1746
Growth habits: Vigorous, upright, 4–6′
Foliage: Small, medium parsley green, matte, almost thornless
Blooms: Large, ranging from dark red to crimson to purple, many petaled, 4½–5″
Fragrance: Slight
Comments: This rose, often depicted as the perfect old-garden rose, has the largest blooms of all of the gallicas and arching canes. It blooms once in late spring and produces magnificent flowers. The petals have the feel of textured velvet but are only lightly scented. The blooms begin cupped and open to saucer shapes. Rating: 8.4

Complicata

Type: Gallica
Hybridizer/Year: Unknown
Growth habits: Tall, upright, spreading, 6′
Foliage: Medium, medium green, leathery
Blooms: Deep pink with a white eye and yellow stamens, 5 petals, 4″, single
Fragrance: Moderate
Comments: This is a proven winner in the gallica class. It is a vigorous plant that grows easily. It is shade tolerant and does well in most landscapes. It is a one-time but prolific bloomer and produces super, single-formed flowers. This is a must-have for any serious gardener. Rating: 8.8

Comte de Chambord

Type: Portland
Hybridizer/Year: Moreau-Robert 1860
Growth habits: Medium, vigorous, upright, 4′
Foliage: Medium, medium green, leathery, disease resistant
Blooms: Pink tinted lilac, 40–50 petals, 4″
Fragrance: Intense
Awards: RHS Award of Garden Merit 1993

Comments: This plant is constantly in bloom and makes a great color display. It has all of the characteristics of the portland class of roses and does well in a group planting or as a hedge. The large blooms are cupped, flat, and quartered. They appear in a great profusion of clusters. Rating: 8.3

Cramoisi Superieur

Type: China
Hybridizer/Year: Coquereau 1832
Growth habits: Vigorous, upright, bushy, 3–6 × 2–3′
Foliage: Small, medium green, matte
Blooms: Clear crimson red, 27–30 petals, 1–2″, in clusters
Fragrance: Moderate, raspberry
Comments: Cramoisi is the French word for crimson. This repeat-bloomer is low growing and suited to borders or containers. The blooms are cupped. Many gardeners know this rose as the Old Bermuda Red Rose because it has naturalized itself to that island. Rating: 8.7

Crested Moss

Type: Moss
Hybridizer/Year: Vibert 1827
Growth habits: Vigorous, upright, bushy, 5 × 3′
Foliage: Small, medium green, matte, broad, coarsely dentate
Blooms: Large, pure pink, 35–40 petals, 3½–4″
Fragrance: Intense
Comments: This once-bloomers is not really a moss rose but is more like the centifolia class of roses. It is a vigorous, rather open-growing rose that is healthy and easy to grow. The blooms are bright medium pink, cupped, and similar to the centifolias. This rose is also known as Cristata and Chapeau de Napoleon. It the name from the fact that as it is developing the calyx and tight sepals form the shape of a tri-cornered hat. Rating: 8.7

Duchesse de Brabant

Type: Tea
Hybridizer/Year: Bernede 1857
Growth habits: Vigorous, spreading, 4′
Foliage: Medium, light green, matte
Blooms: Soft rosy pink, 45 petals, 3–4″, cupped
Fragrance: Intense
Comments: This repeat-blooming rose became popular because President Theodore Roosevelt often wore one. Designated as an EarthKind rose, it does well in nearly any landscape. It's a good cut flower, producing abundant blooms that are large, cupped, and intensely fragrant. It is spectacular when planted in a grouping. Rating: 8.6

Old garden roses *(continued)*

Eugene de Beauharnais

Type: China
Hybridizer/Year: Hardy 1838
Growth habits: Medium, vigorous, bushy, 4 × 3′
Foliage: Medium, medium green, matte
Blooms: Purple-crimson, 70-plus petals, 3″
Fragrance: Intense

Comments: This is a low-growing plant that constantly seems to be in bloom. The blooms vary in color from red to crimson to purple, are cupped, and are slightly reflexed at the edges. It has an intense old-rose fragrance. This rose was named for the brother of Empress Josephine, Prince Eugene, who governed Italy from 1805 to 1814. Rating: 8.0

Fantin-Latour

Type: Centifolia
Hybridizer/Year: Unknown
Growth habits: Vigorous, upright, bushy, 6 × 5′
Foliage: Small, dark green, smooth, matte, hardy
Blooms: Blush pink deepening to shell pink at the center, many petaled, 4½–5″
Fragrance: Strong
Comments: This tall plant blooms only once a season, but the blooms are well worth it. They begin as cupped but quickly reflex to expose button centers that are quite attractive. The scent has been described as overpowering or intoxicating. This rose was named for the well-known French painter of still lifes, many of which were of old garden roses. Rating: 8.4

Felicite Parmentier

Type: Alba
Hybridizer/Year: Parmentier 1834
Growth habits: Vigorous, compact, bushy, 4′
Foliage: Medium, dark gray-green, matte, moderate prickles
Blooms: Soft pink fading to white, 40–50 petals, 2″
Fragrance: Intense, old rose
Comments: This once-blooming disease-resistant plant does well in partial shade and in all types of landscapes or containers. In warmer climates the blooms may be more white than pink. It has an intense old-rose fragrance and provides excellent cut flowers. Rating: 8.7

Ferdinand Pichard

Type: Hybrid Perpetual
Hybridizer/Year: Tanne 1921
Growth habits: Vigorous, upright, bushy, 5 × 4′
Foliage: Medium, light green, smooth
Blooms: Clear pink and scarlet striped, yellow stamens, 25 petals, 3–4″, cupped
Fragrance: Slight
Awards: Royal Horticultural Society Award of Garden Merit 1993
Comments: The novel coloring of this rose makes it one of the better known and loved of the old garden roses. The somewhat repeat-blooming flowers are cupped and clear pink and scarlet striped with yellow stamens. Rating: 7.6

Frau Karl Druschki

Type: Hybrid Perpetual
Hybridizer/Year: Lambert 1901
Growth habits: Tall, vigorous, bushy, 4–6 × 3–4′
Foliage: Medium, light to medium green, leathery, many prickles
Blooms: Snow white, blush pink center, 35 petals, 3–5″
Fragrance: None
Comments: This repeat bloomer was the world's favorite white rose for many years. It is an upright-growing bush that does as well in the garden as it does in the vase. The cupped blooms do not like wet weather. This rose was named for the wife of the president of the German Rose Society. Rating: 8.0

General Jacqueminot

Type: Hybrid Perpetual
Hybridizer/Year: Roussel 1853
Growth habits: Vigorous, upright, bushy, 5 × 4′
Foliage: Medium, rich, green tinged with red, matte, many prickles
Blooms: Dark red with a whitish reverse, 27 petals, 3″
Fragrance: Intense
Awards: First Prize Versailles Exhibition 1854
Comments: This repeat bloomer has produced an incredible number of seedlings and sports. In fact, most of today's red roses can be traced to it. The blooms are dark red with whitish reverse and are intensely fragrant. It is named for a French general of the early 19th century. Rating: 7.4

Gloire de Dijon

Type: Climbing Tea
Hybridizer/Year: Jacotot 1853
Growth habits: Vigorous, upright, tall, bushy 12 × 8′
Foliage: Medium, medium green, matte, reddish canes, hooked prickles
Blooms: Rich buff-pink shading to apricot orange, 40-plus petals, 3½″
Fragrance: Moderate
Awards: First Prize Dijon Horticultural Fair 1852, Paris Gold Medal 1853, Royal Horticultural Society Award of Garden Merit 1993
Comments: This repeat bloomer continues to be one of the most popular roses internationally. It does well climbing on walls or other structures. The blooms are full, globular, quartered, and quilled and always seem to cover the plant. This rose is also known as Old Glory. Rating: 7.8

Old garden roses *(continued)*

Great Maiden's Blush

Type: Alba
Hybridizer/Year: Unknown prior to 1738
Growth habits: Tall, spreading, 4–6'
Foliage: Medium, deep blue-gray-green, leathery
Blooms: White tinged pink, 42 petals, 3", clusters
Fragrance: Intense
Comments: This is a once-blooming variety of old garden rose. It is an upright, bushy grower that produces large arching canes of blooms. The blooms are blush pink, cupped, and quite fragrant. The blue-gray-green foliage contrasts nicely with the light-colored blooms. Rating: 8.9

Honorine de Brabant

Type: Bourbon
Hybridizer/Year: Unknown
Growth habits: Tall, vigorous, upright, 5–6'
Foliage: Medium, light green, matte
Blooms: Pale lilac-pink with mauve and crimson stripes, 40-plus petals, 3"
Fragrance: Intense
Comments: This reblooming variety continues to be one of the most popular internationally. It does well in borders or as a hedge. It produces fragrant blooms that are unique, but subtly so. The bloom is loosely cupped and quartered. The lush foliage contrasts well with the blooms. Rating: 8.2

Harison's Yellow

Type: Hybrid Foetida
Hybridizer/Year: Harison 1830
Growth habits: Tall, vigorous, bushy, 4–6 × 3–5'
Foliage: Small, light to medium green, matte, many prickles
Blooms: Bright yellow with yellow stamens, 20–25 petals, 2–2½"
Fragrance: Moderate, fruity
Comments: This is one of the hardiest roses available. It is an upright, usuall once-blooming variety that produces an abundant display of color in the early spring. The semidouble blooms are bright yellow with yellow stamens and have a moderately fruity fragrance. In the fall it produces bristly ovoid black hips that are unusual and beautiful. Rating: 8.3

Konigin von Danemark

Type: Alba
Hybridizer/Year: Boothe 1816
Growth habits: Tall, vigorous, upright, 5–6′
Foliage: Medium, deep bluish green, matte
Blooms: Medium, pink with a darker pink center, 40-plus petals, 3–4″
Fragrance: Intense
Comments: This is one of the better-performing albas. It is a once-blooming variety that does well in all types of landscapes. The blooms appear in heavy clusters that can weigh the prickly canes down with their fullness. Rating: 8.6

La Belle Sultane

Type: Gallica
Hybridizer/Year: Hardy 1795
Growth habits: Vigorous, upright, bushy, 5 × 4′
Foliage: Medium, medium green, matte, slightly rugose
Blooms: Deep crimson shading to violet with a white base, 12–15 petals, 4″, heart shape, almost single petals

Fragrance: Moderate
Comments: This is a tall once-bloomer that has long, arching canes, suitable for a hedge or border. Its blooms, however, are its major selling point. They are deep crimson shading to violet with a white base and gold stamens. The petals are heart shape and almost single. Rating: 8.3

La Ville de Bruxelles

Type: Damask
Hybridizer/Year: Vibert 1849
Growth habits: Tall, vigorous, upright, 5–6′, lax canes
Foliage: Large, light green, glossy, long, moderate prickles
Blooms: Clear pink, 50 petals, 4″
Fragrance: Intense
Awards: Royal Horticultural Society Award of Garden Merit 1993
Comments: This is a densely growing once-bloomer that produces well-spaced clusters of blooms. The large blooms are consistently clear pink with reflexed petals that show off their button eyes. This bush does well in all types of landscapes and prefers dry weather. Rating: 8.5

Leda

Type: Damask
Hybridizer/Year: Unknown prior to 1827
Growth habits: Medium, compact, 3–4′
Foliage: Medium, dark green, matte
Blooms: White to blush, edged crimson, 40-plus petals, 3″
Fragrance: Moderate
Comments: This once-bloomer, also known as Painted Damask, remains popular with gardeners everywhere. It is a vigorous, upright grower that tends to sprawl. The blooms are creamy white with a crimson edge and are moderately fragrant. The petals reflex to reveal a button eye. The rose was named for the mythological queen who was seduced by Zeus when he appeared in the form of a swan. Rating: 8.3

Old garden roses *(continued)*

Louise Odier

Type: Bourbon
Hybridizer/Year: Margottin 1851
Growth habits: Vigorous, upright, tall, 6 × 4'
Foliage: Small, bright green, matte
Blooms: Rich rose-pink shaded lilac, 60-plus petals, 3–4"
Fragrance: Intense, old rose, sweet
Comments: This rose remains

popular because it is as great in a vase as it is in the garden. While it makes a striking border or hedge, it also has long stems, a great bloom, and a magnificent fragrance that make it wonderful as a cut flower. It is a continuous summer bloomer. The rich rose-pink shaded lilac blooms are cupped at first, then open and become attractively flat and round. The bush has graceful, arching canes that are covered with lush foliage. It is also somewhat shade tolerant. Rating: 8.4

Marchesa Boccella

Type: Hybrid Perpetual
Hybridizer/Year: Desprez 1842
Growth habits: Vigorous, upright, 3–6'
Foliage: Small, jade green, matte, erect stems
Blooms: Compact, light pink with edges shading to blush, many petaled, 3'
Fragrance: Moderate
Comments: This excellent repeat bloomer also blooms profusely, mostly in clusters. It does well as a hedge or in the garden. As the blooms open they become quartered and often have button eyes. This rose is also known as Jacques Cartier. Rating: 9.0

Mermaid

Type: Hybrid Bracteata
Hybridizer/Year: Paul 1918
Growth habits: Tall, vigorous, climbing, 6–9'
Foliage: Medium, dark green, glossy, numerous prickles
Blooms: Creamy yellow with dark gold stamens, 5 petals, 5–6", single
Fragrance: Moderate
Awards: Royal National Rose Society Gold Medal 1917
Comments: This rose is an upright grower and produces wonderfully abundant, repeat blooms. The blooms are huge, single formed, and creamy yellow becoming darker yellow at the center. The dark green, glossy foliage is a perfect complement to the blooms, but it does have large, reddish, hooked prickles. Rating: 8.6

Madame Alfred Carriere

Type: Noisette
Hybridizer/Year: Schwartz 1879
Growth habits: Tall, vigorous, upright, 10–16 × 7–9′
Foliage: Small, light, pale green, serrated edges, flexible canes
Blooms: Pale pinkish white, 40-plus petals, 3½″
Fragrance: Intense, sweet, spice
Awards: Royal Horticultural Society Award of Garden Merit 1993
Comments: This rose was voted the best white climber in 1908 by the Royal National Rose Society of England. This is a healthy, rambling plant that produces a continuous display of blooms. The large blooms are globular and have an intensely sweet old-rose scent. Its flexible canes are ideal for training on a wall, pergola, or other structure. It is somewhat shade tolerant. Rating: 8.9

Madame Ernest Calvat

Type: Bourbon
Hybridizer/Year: Schwartz 1888
Growth habits: Tall, vigorous, bushy, 5–6 × 4–5′
Foliage: Medium, dark green, semiglossy, many prickles, stems are a rich deep purple when young
Blooms: Medium pink shading darker, 40-plus petals, 3–4″, cupped
Fragrance: Intense
Comments: This repeat-bloomer is a sport of Madame Isaac Pereire. It is a vigorous plant with graceful arching canes. The blooms are large, cabbage shape, and very fragrant. This rose was named for the wife of Ernest Calvat, who was a glove manufacturer and amateur horticulturist. Rating: 8.1

Madame Hardy

Type: Damask
Hybridizer/Year: Hardy 1832
Growth habits: Vigorous, upright, 6 × 4′, may tend to droop
Foliage: Small, light green, coarsely dentate
Blooms: Large, creamy to pure white with a green center pip, 60-plus petals, 3–4″
Fragrance: Intense, sweet

Comments: This once-blooming variety produces an abundance of blooms both solitarily and as clusters. The large blooms are consistently pure white with a central green pip. They are cupped at first and open flat to reveal the wonderful array of petals. They are fragrant overall and have feathery pine-scented sepals. This is a classic for any old-garden rose enthusiast. Rating: 8.9

Madame Isaac Pereire

Type: Bourbon
Hybridizer/Year: Garcon 1881
Growth habits: Tall, vigorous, upright, 6–7′
Foliage: Medium, medium green, matte
Blooms: Deep rose shading to purple, 50-plus petals, 4″
Fragrance: Moderate to intense
Comments: The bourbons are very floriferous and are ideal for covering pergolas, fences, or other structures. This rose has all of the qualities of the bourbons, with an extra dash of perfume. Some gardeners consider it the most fragrant rose ever produced. The plant is bushy and produces abundant blooms that become two-toned hot pink as they age. It was named for a member of an influential banking family during the reign of Napoleon III. Rating: 8.4

Old garden roses *(continued)*

Madame Plantier

Type: Hybrid Alba
Hybridizer/Year: Plantier 1835
Growth habits: Vigorous, spreading, 4–6′
Foliage: Small, gray-green, 7 leaflets, matte, few prickles
Blooms: Creamy white changing to pure white, 40-plus petals, 2–4″, green pip in the center
Fragrance: Moderate
Comments: This is a tall, upright shrub that produces large clusters of blooms. The blooms begin as creamy white and age to a pure white with an attractive green pip in the center. They grow on long, arching canes that have few prickles. The gray-green foliage is soft to the touch. This plant makes an attractive hedge or backdrop for other plants. Rating: 8.8

Monsieur Tillier

Type: Tea
Hybridizer/Year: Bernaix 1891
Growth habits: Vigorous, upright, bushy, 4 × 3′
Foliage: Medium, medium green, semiglossy
Blooms: Deep rose to purple, 30–35 petals, 3–4″
Fragrance: Slight
Comments: This is a medium growing plant that can go to greater heights if allowed. It is a prolific bloomer and does well in most landscapes. The blooms are deep rose to purple with intermingled orange and russet shades, creating an attractive array of colors. It can be tender in harsh climates. Rating: 8.4

Mutabilis

Type: China
Hybridizer/Year: Unknown
Growth habits: Vigorous, upright, 6 × 3′, very dense
Foliage: Small, coppery green, matte
Blooms: Small, bright yellow changing to orange, pink, and crimson, 5 petals, 2″
Fragrance: Slight
Comments: This old garden rose blooms continuously. The blooms are single form and resemble butterflies. In fact, it is often called the Butterfly Rose. The blooms are bright yellow changing to orange, pink, and crimson as they age. Since the blooms age differently, there is always an array of colors on this bush. Rating: 8.9

Old Blush

Type: China
Hybridizer/Year: Parsons 1752
Growth habits: Vigorous, upright, 4′, somewhat spreading
Foliage: Small, medium green, matte, thornless

Blooms: Small, soft pink blushing to deeper pink on the edges, 25–30 petals, 2½–3″
Fragrance: Slight
Comments: This is the most common and one of the best of the hybrid china family. It produces blooms throughout the growing season. The blooms are small, soft pink blushing to tp deeper pink on the edges, with a fragrance that is reminiscent of sweet peas. It has been said that this is the "last rose of summer" to which Sir Thomas Moore referred. Rating: 8.7

Paul Neyron

Type: Hybrid Perpetual
Hybridizer/Year: Levet 1869
Growth habits: Medium, vigorous, upright, 4–5′
Foliage: Large, dark green, matte
Blooms: Clear pink to rose-pink, 50-plus petals, 4–5″
Fragrance: Moderate
Comments: This disease-resistant bush produces huge, magnificent blooms. The blooms are clear pink to rose-pink, cupped, and moderately fragrant. Rating: 8.2

Pompon Blanc Parfait

Type: Alba
Hybridizer/Year: Verdier 1876
Growth habits: Vigorous, upright, compact, 4′
Foliage: Medium, gray-green, semiglossy, few prickles
Blooms: Blush white, 40-plus petals, 2–3″
Fragrance: Moderate
Comments: This once-bloomer differs somewhat from the

other classic albas. It is more compact and produces blooms longer into the growing season than do most other varieties in this class. The fragrant blooms are a soft lilac-pink blushed white that appear in bunches along the almost prickleless canes. The gray-green foliage is relatively dense and makes an attractive bush even without the blooms.

Reine des Violettes

Type: Hybrid Perpetual
Hybridizer/Year: Millet-Malet 1860
Growth habits: Vigorous, upright, large, 6 × 4′
Foliage: Small, gray-green, matte, disease resistant, thornless
Blooms: Rich deep violet-purple, 60-plus petals, 4″
Fragrance: Intense
Comments: The vigor of this bush has allowed it to survive and remain popular through the years. It is an upright bush that has almost prickleless canes. The repeat blooms are quilled and quartered, with button eyes. It is fragrant and does well in all types of landscape design—a must for the serious lover of old garden roses. Rating: 8.2

Old garden roses *(continued)*

Reine Victoria

Type: Bourbon
Hybridizer/Year: Schwartz 1872
Growth habits: Medium, slender, upright, 4–5′
Foliage: Medium, medium green, matte
Blooms: Rich rose-pink, 60-plus petals, 3½″
Fragrance: Slight
Comments: This repeat-bloomer often flowers in small clusters. It is vigorous with long, graceful canes, perfect for espaliering on fences, walls, or other structures. The cupped blooms are a rich rose-pink with a hint of mauve. The foliage provides a  textural contrast with the velvety blooms. This rose was named for Queen Victoria. Rating: 8.2

Robert le Diable

Type: Gallica
Hybridizer/Year: Unknown prior to 1850
Growth habits: Medium, vigorous, bushy, 3–4 × 3′
Foliage: Medium, medium green, matte, disease resistant
Blooms: Scarlet-pink aging to deep purple, 30-plus petals, 3″
Fragrance: Intense
Comments: This once-bloomer produces abundant flowers that vary in coloration from scarlet-pink to deep purple and then are mottled with bright red. The blooms are so full of petals that when they are fully open they reflex around the edge in a cushion effect. Rating: 6.9

Rosa banksiae banksiae *(White Lady Banks' rose)*

Type: Species
Hybridizer/Year: Kerr 1807
Growth habits: Tall, vigorous, upright, 15 × 8′
Foliage: Small, light green, elongated, prickleless
Blooms: White, 25–30 petals, 1–2″
Fragrance: Moderate
Comments: This  bush is typical of the banksian class of roses. It is a huge, prickleless grower that produces an abundance of blooms. The blooms are loosely double and have a fragrance reminiscent of violets. This bush provides a spectacular display when it is in bloom. It is also known as Lady Banksia Snowflake. Rating: 9.2

Rosa banksiae lutea *(Yellow Lady Banks' rose)*

Type: Species
Hybridizer/Year: Lindley 1824
Growth habits: Tall, vigorous, upright, 20 × 10′
Foliage: Small, light green, elongated, prickleless
Blooms: Bright yellow, 25–30 petals, 1–2″
Fragrance: Moderate
Comments: This is one of the four banksia roses in cultivation today. It is probably the best known and most widely grown of the banksia class. It is a mammoth grower that produces a proliferation of blooms. The blooms are yellow, fully double, and scented with the violet fragrance that accompanies all of the banksia roses. Rating: 9.1

Rosa Mundi (Rosa gallica versicolor)

Type: Species
Hybridizer/Year: Unknown prior to 1581
Growth habits: Vigorous, compact, medium, 3½ × 4', spreading
Foliage: Small, medium green, matte, disease resistant
Blooms: Pale pink with red and pink stripes accented by golden yellow stamens, 12–18 petals, 3–4"

Fragrance: Moderate
Comments: This rose is probably the oldest of the striped roses and is a sport of Apothecary's Rose. It is a dense, low-growing, once-blooming plant that produces wonderful blooms. This is another must-have for the serious old-garden rose lover. It was named for Rosamund, a mistress of Henry II. The rose is also known as Rosa gallica versicolor. Rating: 9.0

Rosa rugosa alba

Type: Species
Hybridizer/Year: Unknown prior to 1870
Growth habits: Vigorous, upright, tall, 6–8', spreading
Foliage: Small, dark green, semiglossy, rugose, disease resistant

Blooms: Large, pure white accented with golden stamens, 5 petals, 4"
Fragrance: Intense
Comments: This somewhat repeat-bloomer is a sport of Rosa rugosa and maintains all of its splendid characteristics. It will take over any space if allowed. The large blooms are single and intensely fragrant. The bush has beautiful fall foliage and red-orange hips. Rating: 9.1

Rosa rugosa rubra

Type: Species
Hybridizer/Year: Unknown prior to 1854
Growth habits: Vigorous, upright, tall, 6–8', spreading
Foliage: Small, dark green, semiglossy, rugose, disease resistant
Blooms: Large, magenta-purple accented by golden stamens, 5 petals, 4"
Fragrance: Intense
Comments: This is a vigorous, terrific plant that produces an abundance of fragrant repeat blooms. The large blooms are single formed. It does well in all types of landscape designs. Rating: 9.1

Old garden roses *(continued)*

Rose de Rescht

Type: Portland
Hybridizer/Year: Unknown
Growth habits: Vigorous, upright, compact, 3½ × 3'
Foliage: Small, medium green, semiglossy, dense, disease resistant
Blooms: Small, fuchsia-red fading to lilac tints, 50-plus petals, 2½"
Fragrance: Intense
Comments: This outstanding, easy-to-grow variety is great for small gardens. It is a dense, low-growing bush that produces abundant blooms. The blooms come in clusters on short stems close to the foliage. They are fully double, cushion shape, and very fragrant. The foliage is lush and profuse. Rating: 8.8

Salet

Type: Moss
Hybridizer/Year: Lacharme 1854
Growth habits: Medium, vigorous, compact, 4–5'
Foliage: Medium, medium green, semiglossy
Blooms: Rose-pink, 50-plus petals, 2–3"
Fragrance: Intense, sweet, clove
Comments: This moss rose has less moss than most, but it is prized for its blooms. The dense bush produces abundant blooms throughout the growing season. The small blooms are a rich rose-pink with fluted narrow petals and central buttons. It is one of the most floriferous of the moss class. Rating: 8.2

Souvenir de la Malmaison

Type: Bourbon
Hybridizer/Year: Beluze 1843
Growth habits: Vigorous, upright, short, bushy, 2–4', spreading
Foliage: Small, medium green, semiglossy
Blooms: Creamy light pink shading to rose at the center, 35–40 petals, 3"
Fragrance: Intense

Comments: This is perhaps the most famous, if not the most beautiful, of the bourbons. It needs warm weather to open properly. The large, quartered blooms are extremely fragrant. It is an excellent repeat-bloomer It was named for Empress Josephine's chateau near Paris. Rating: 8.7

Stanwell Perpetual

Type: Hybrid spinosissima
Hybridizer/Year: Lee 1838
Growth habits: Moderate, upright, 3–5', spreading
Foliage: Small, gray-green, matte, disease resistant, very thorny
Blooms: Pale blush pink fading to white, 80-plus petals, 3"
Fragrance: Moderate
Comments: This is a vigorous bush that is in continuous bloom throughout the growing season. It has ferny foliage with many nine-leaflet sets reminiscent of the Scots roses. The blooms are flat, quilled, and quartered. Rating: 8.6

Tuscany Superb

Type: Gallica
Hybridizer/Year: Rivers prior to 1837
Growth habits: Medium, upright, 4′
Foliage: Medium, medium green, matte
Blooms: Mauve-purple with bright gold stamens, 30-plus petals, 3½″
Fragrance: Moderate
Comments: This rose was such an improvement over its predecessor Tuscany that it pushed it off the market. This vigorous, once-blooming variety produces bigger blooms and more of them. This bush does well in any landscape. Rating: 8.5

Veilchenblau

Type: Hybrid Multiflora
Hybridizer/Year: Schmidt 1909
Growth habits: Vigorous, upright, tall, 10–15′
Foliage: Large, light green, glossy, pointed, very few prickles
Blooms: Violet streaked with white, white center with gold stamens, 17–20 petals, 1¼″, cupped
Fragrance: Moderate, apple
Awards: Royal Horticultural Society Award of Garden Merit 1993
Comments: This popular rambler blooms in large clusters and is included in many landscapes because of the novel color. It is a vigorous, upright, tall grower that has very few prickles and is a once-bloomer. The flowers are violet streaked with white and have white centers with golden stamens. It has an especially nice fragrance. Rating: 8.4

Zephirine Drouhin

Type: Bourbon
Hybridizer/Year: Bizot 1868
Growth habits: Tall, vigorous, semiclimbing, 8–12′
Foliage: Medium, light green, matte, no prickles
Blooms: Cerise-pink with a white base, 25–30 petals, 3″
Fragrance: Moderate, damask
Comments: This repeat-bloomer produces an extravagant display. The large blooms are double and loosely petaled. This bush does well in all types of landscapes. Rating: 8.1

Variegata di Bologna

Type: Bourbon
Hybridizer/Year: Bonfiglioli 1909
Growth habits: Tall, vigorous, upright, 6–8′
Foliage: Medium, medium green, matte
Blooms: White with purplish red stripes, 40-plus petals, 3–4″
Fragrance: Moderate
Comments: This is perhaps the most famous rose discovered in Italy. It is somewhat lax in growth habit. The fragrant blooms are globular, once-blooming, and form in clusters. Rating: 8.0

Miniatures and minifloras

The minis make up a relatively new class of roses. They have diminutive smaller flowers and generally small plant size—less than three feet. There are hundreds of varieties of miniatures in all rose colors, some growing with single flowers (one row of petals), some with single blooms (one bloom per stem), and some with fully double flowers (many petals), cluster flowering, and climbing varieties.

Even within the category of miniatures there are variations from microminiatures with flowers less than ½ inch across to minifloras that have flowers more than 3 inches across. There are also climbing miniatures, which can grow quite large (for a miniature) but still have small leaves and flowers.

As a group, miniatures are fairly cold-hardy and can survive with heavy projection in Zone 4, minimal protection in Zone 5, and no protection Zone 6 and warmer.

See page 28 for more information on miniatures and minifloras.

▲ This Beauty Secret miniature rose, like most miniature roses, has perfectly down-sized leaves, stems, and flowers that are all charmingly in proportion.

Amy Grant

Type: Miniflora
Hybridizer/Year: Tucker 1998
Growth habits: Vigorous, medium, spreading, 18–24″
Foliage: Medium, dark green, glossy
Blooms: Large, light pink to eggshell white, 17–25 petals, 1½–2″, exhibition form
Fragrance: Slight
Comments: This vigorous, large plant has exquisite exhibition form. The dark green, glossy foliage adds stark contrast to the pale blooms. It does well as a border or in the back of a miniature rose bed. It looks great in the garden, in the vase, or on the show table. Rating: 7.5

Autumn Splendor

Type: Miniflora
Hybridizer/Year: Williams 1999
Growth habits: Vigorous, upright, tall, spreading, 30–40″
Foliage: Large, medium green, semiglossy
Blooms: Large, red with yellow in center and reverse, 26–40 petals, 2″, exhibition form
Fragrance: Slight
Awards: American Rose Society Award of Excellence 1999
Comments: This is a remarkably large miniflora, often growing to 4 feet. The blooms are brilliant red and yellow, echoing the colors of autumn. Its size adds versatility in landscape design. Rating: 8.1

Baby Boomer

Type: Miniature
Hybridizer/Year: Benardella 2001
Growth habits: Medium, vigorous, upright, 2–3′
Foliage: Medium, dark green, semiglossy
Blooms: Clear medium pink, 17–25 petals, 2″, exhibition form
Fragrance: Slight
Awards: American Rose Society Award of Excellence 2003
Comments: This disease-resistant bush is a delight to grow. It is almost always covered with blooms in classic hybrid tea form. The foliage harmonizes with the pink blooms. This bush performs well in all climates. Rating: 7.7

Baby Grand

Type: Miniature
Hybridizer/Year: Poulsen 1994
Growth habits: Low, compact, bushy, rounded, 12–16″
Foliage: Small, medium green, matte, disease resistant, some prickles
Blooms: Clear pink, 25–40 petals, 1½″, clusters
Fragrance: Slight
Comments: This small, compact bush produces an abundance of blooms that have the old-fashioned rose look. The many-petaled blooms open up in the quartered style reminiscent of old garden roses. This plant also does well in containers. Rating: 8.6

Baby Love

Type: Miniature
Hybridizer/Year: Scrivens 1992
Growth habits: Vigorous, upright, bushy, 3′
Foliage: Small, medium green, semiglossy, some prickles
Blooms: Buttercup yellow, 5 petals, 1½″
Awards: Royal National Rose Society Gold Medal 1992
Fragrance: Slight, licorice
Comments: This is a hardy, disease-resistant, bushy, heavy bloomer in all climates. The small yellow single blooms belie its toughness. Its leaves remain clean in all types of weather. It is a prolific bloomer throughout the growing season. Rating: 8.0

Bees Knees

Type: Miniature
Hybridizer/Year: Zary 1998
Growth habits: Tall, vigorous, upright, bushy, 3′
Foliage: Medium, dark green, matte, moderate prickles
Blooms: Yellow-pink blend, 26–40 petals, 2½″, exhibition form, some sprays
Fragrance: Slight
Awards: American Rose Society People's Choice 2005
Comments: This is one of the best miniatures. It produces abundant blooms all growing season. The radiant blooms have classic hybrid tea form and add color to any landscape. These beauties are equally at home in the garden, in the vase, or on the show table. Rating: 8.0

Miniatures and minifloras *(continued)*

Behold

Type: Miniature
Hybridizer/Year: Saville 1997
Growth habits: Vigorous, upright plants, 1–2'
Foliage: Medium-green, matte-textured
Blooms: Medium yellow with a lighter reverse, excellent high-pointed exhibition form, 15–20 petals
Fragrance: None
Comments: Giant clusters of clear yellow, perfectly-formed blossoms appear on long, strong stems all summer. Flowers are colorfast, not fading in heat and strong sunlight unlike many other yellow roses. Protect from mildew in cool coastal climates. Best performance is in warmer areas where mildew is less of a problem.. Rating: 7.8

Black Jade

Type: Miniature
Hybridizer/Year: Benardella 1985
Growth habits: Vigorous, upright, 18–24"
Foliage: Medium, dark green, semiglossy
Blooms: Near black bud, deep red blooms, 35 petals, 1–1½", exhibition form, borne singly
Fragrance: None
Awards: American Rose Society Award of Excellence 1985
Comments: This rose is one of the darkest red roses available in miniatures. It is a

vigorous, upright grower that produces abundant blooms all season long. The blooms are a dark velvety red with classic hybrid tea form that is excellent for exhibiting. The foliage displays the blooms to their best advantage. This bush does well in all landscapes and is particularly suited to containers. Rating: 8.0

Butter Cream

Type: Miniflora
Hybridizer/Year: Martin 2003
Growth habits: Upright, tall, 24–30"
Foliage: Medium green, leathery, very disease resistant
Blooms: Large, creamy butter yellow, 28–32 petals, 2"-plus, exhibition form
Fragrance: None
Comments: The light yellow blooms have classic hybrid tea form and are excellent for the vase and exhibition. This

rose's disease resistant foliage offers excellent contrast to the wonderful blooms. Rating: 7.8

Cal Poly

Type: Miniature
Hybridizer/Year: Moore 1991
Growth habits: Vigorous, upright, bushy, 10–12"
Foliage: Medium, medium green, semiglossy, few prickles
Blooms: Medium yellow, 15–25 petals, 1½–2¾"
Fragrance: Slight
Awards: American Rose Society Award of Excellence 1992
Comments: This disease-resistant plant is a

compact grower that does well in borders. The bright medium yellow blooms have long-lasting color. This rose was named to honor the well-known horticultural school, California Polytechnic State University. Rating: 7.9

Caliente

Type: Miniature
Hybridizer/Year: Benardella 2004
Growth habits: Vigorous, upright, rounded, bushy, 24″
Foliage: Medium, medium green, semiglossy
Blooms: Deep red maturing to bright fire-engine red, 26–40 petals, 2″, exhibition form
Fragrance: Slight
Awards: American Rose Society Award of Excellence 2006
Comments: This is one of the newest winners from hybridizer Frank Benardella. Caliente is Spanish for hot and so is this rose—not only in its vigor and disease resistance, but also in bloom production and color. The deep red buds burst open to fire-engine red blooms with classic hybrid tea form. This is a superb rose in the garden and is a consistent winner on the show table.

Carrot Top

Type: Miniature
Hybridizer/Year: Olesen, Pernille & Mogens 1991
Growth habits: Vigorous, upright, bushy, 16–20″
Foliage: Medium, medium green, matte, few prickles
Blooms: Clear orange-red, 15–25 petals, 1½″, exhibition form, prolific
Fragrance: Slight
Comments: The sizzling orange-red blooms on this disease-resistant bush will stop visitors in their tracks. The blooms are light on petals but strong on substance. They hold their color and form well and are equally good in a vase, on the show table, and in the garden. Rating: 7.7

Child's Play

Type: Miniature
Hybridizer/Year: Saville 1991
Growth habits: Medium, upright, bushy, 1½–2′
Foliage: Medium, dark green, matte
Blooms: Porcelain white with deep pink edges, 30 petals, 1½″, exhibition form
Fragrance: Moderate
Awards: American Rose Society Award of Excellence 1993, AARS 1993
Comments: This award-winning miniature does well wherever it is planted. Its vigorous, compact, rounded growth habit makes it perfect for the garden or in a border. The blooms have classic hybrid tea form and are quick to repeat. This bush blooms continuously during the growing season. Rating: 8.0

Cinderella

Type: Miniature
Hybridizer/Year: de Vink 1953
Growth habits: Upright, compact, bushy, 10–12″
Foliage: Small, medium green, matte
Blooms: Satiny white tinged pale pink, micromini, 55 petals, 1″
Fragrance: Moderate, spicy
Awards: Miniature Rose Hall of Fame 2000
Comments: This rose represents the best of the classic microminiatures. It is a vigorous grower and prolific bloomer. The small blooms have classic hybrid tea form and hold their color, making them useful for arrangements. It also does well in containers. Rating: 8.1

Miniatures and minifloras *(continued)*

Coffee Bean

Type: Miniature
Hybridizer/Year: Bedard 2006
Growth habits: Canes reach 10–12′ long in mild climates
Foliage: Glossy, Medium-size, dark green
Blooms: Russet blooms, 1½″, double, 17–25 petals
Fragrance: Mild, sweet
Comments: With flowers that look like a miniature version of its parent Hot Cocoa (its other parent is the delightful miniature Santa Claus), this 2008 introduction from Weeks Roses finally brings the rare color of russet into the world of miniature roses, with blooms that are smoky chocolate orange on the upper side of the petals, and cinnamon orange on the reverse. The exhibition-quality, high-centered blooms are borne singly in flushes throughout the season. Excellent in combination with Hot Cocoa. Superb in containers with a trellis for support. Cool weather brings out the smoky color.

Cupcake

Type: Miniature
Hybridizer/Year: Spies 1981
Growth habits: Medium, compact, bushy, 1–2′
Foliage: Medium, medium green, glossy, no prickles
Blooms: Clear medium pink, 60 petals, 2″, exhibition form
Fragrance: None
Awards: American Rose Society Award of Excellence 1983
Comments: This rose is as popular today as when it was introduced, making it one of the best-selling miniatures in the U.S. It produces abundant blooms throughout the growing season. The clear, medium pink blooms have classic hybrid tea form and are surrounded by glossy, disease-resistant foliage. This plant does well in any landscape. Rating: 8.0

Dancing Flame

Type: Miniature
Hybridizer/Year: Tucker 2001
Growth habits: Medium size, upright, 2′ tall
Foliage: Glossy, medium green
Blooms: Yellow blend with creamy, glowing yellow center blending to striking red at the edges of the petals, 18–25 petals
Fragrance: None
Comments: While this rose is recognized as one of the top exhibition roses in the country, its magnificent flower color and form will grab plenty of attention in the garden too. The vigorous plants are good growers with good repeat bloom. Rating: 7.7

Doris Morgan

Type: Miniature
Hybridizer/Year: Bridges 2003
Growth habits: Upright and spreading into a vase shape, 2–3′ tall and wide
Foliage: Bright green, shiny
Blooms: Deep pink blooms with a hint of white at the center, classic high-centered form, 20–28 petals
Fragrance: Slight
Comments: Striking cerise-pink blooms glowing with lighter pink highlights and a well-formed exhibition bloom make this rose extraordinary, and it is a fine performer in the garden too—with bright green,  glossy, healthy foliage that sets off the jewellike blooms beautifully. Rating: 7.7

Fairhope

Type: Miniature
Hybridizer/Year: Taylor 1989
Growth habits: Upright, bushy, medium, 24–36″
Foliage: Medium, medium green, semiglossy
Blooms: Soft, light yellow with the same color reverse, 16–28 petals, 1½–2″, exhibition form
Fragrance: Slight
Comments: This miniature is one of the highest-scoring miniatures of all time. It is a vigorous, disease-resistant bush that has strong, straight stems, excellent for cutting and exhibiting. The blooms have exceptional substance and long-lasting form. This beauty does as well in the vase or on the show table as in the garden. Rating: 8.2

Gizmo

Type: Miniature
Hybridizer/Year: Carruth 1998
Growth habits: Medium, vigorous, bushy, 1½–2′
Foliage: Medium, dark green, semiglossy, moderate prickles
Blooms: Scarlet-orange with a white eye, 4–11 petals, 1½–3″, single form
Fragrance: Slight, apple
Comments: This single miniature makes a novel color display in the landscape. The scarlet-orange blooms with white eyes are eyecatching and attractive. This plant seems to bloom continuously and makes a statement in the garden. Rating: 7.9

Gourmet Popcorn

Type: Miniature
Hybridizer/Year: Desamero 1986
Growth habits: Upright, medium, bushy, 18–24″
Foliage: Large, clean, dark green, glossy
Blooms: Medium, pure white with yellow centers, 15–20 petals, ½–1″, large, cascading clusters
Fragrance: Slight

Comments: This rose is one of the all-time favorites of miniature rose growers. It is a sport of Popcorn and is just as disease resistant and hardy. It performs well in all climates and grows equally well in containers and the garden. The pure white blooms have bright yellow stamens and cascade in clusters on the bush. The blooms are set off by the dark green, glossy foliage. It is a consistent performer and a good landscape rose. Rating: 8.7

Green Ice

Type: Miniature
Hybridizer/Year: Moore 1971
Growth habits: Vigorous, upright, bushy, dwarf, 12–16″
Foliage: Small, dark green, glossy, leathery
Blooms: White to soft green, 40-plus petals, 1–1½″
Fragrance: None
Comments: This plant has a somewhat sprawling, spreading growth habit that makes it excellent for hanging baskets and containers. The small, green-tinged, white blooms are full petaled and open in a manner that resembles that of old-garden roses. Rating: 8.0

Hilde

Type: Miniature
Hybridizer/Year: Benardella 2001
Growth habits:
Foliage: Matte, medium green
Blooms: Hint of white deep in the center blending to bright red petals, high-centered, 18–24 petals, 2″
Fragrance: Strong, rose
Comments: Hilde can be slow to start blooming in the spring but once it gets going it turns into a blooming dynamo for the entire summer. The magnificent exhibition-quality blooms have outstanding form and color. Cool weather brings out darker shadings on the outer petals. Rating: 7.6

Miniatures and minifloras *(continued)*

Hot Tamale

Type: Miniature
Hybridizer/Year: Zary 1994
Growth habits: Compact, vigorous, spreading, 15″ tall, 3′ wide
Foliage: Semiglossy, dark green
Blooms: Yellow blend, 18–25 petals
Fragrance: None
Awards: American Rose Society Award of Excellence 1994
Comments: Yellow-orange blooms age dramatically to yellow-pink, even in hot climates. Plants produce single blooms in warm climates, small sprays where summers are cooler. Rating: 8.3

Incognito

Type: Miniature
Hybridizer/Year: Bridges 1995
Growth habits: Upright, tall, bushy 30–34″
Foliage: Medium, semiglossy
Blooms: Mauve blend with yellow reverse, 15–25 petals, 1½″, exhibition form
Fragrance: Slight

Comments: This rose has graced trophy tables almost from the day it was introduced. The vigorous plant produces abundant blooms throughout the growing season. Its large blooms have perfect classic hybrid tea form. They also have substantial substance and hold their color and shape well. The blooms are surrounded by semiglossy foliage that complements them well. Rating: 8.0

Irresistible

Type: Miniature
Hybridizer/Year: Bennett 1989
Growth habits: Upright, tall, 30–36″
Foliage: Medium, medium green, semiglossy
Blooms: Medium, white with pale pink center, greenish in shade, 43 petals, 1–1¾″, exhibition form
Fragrance: Moderate, spicy
Comments: Hybridizer Dee Bennett has produced many excellent miniature roses and this is one of the best. This vigorous bush has long straight stems and is a prolific bloomer. The large clear white blooms often have a pink tinge in the spring and a green tinge at other times during the growing season. They hold their color and shape for a long time and are excellent for cutting or to exhibit. This plant does well in all types of landscape designs. Rating: 9.0

Jean Kenneally

Type: Miniature
Hybridizer/Year: Bennett 1984
Growth habits: Vigorous, upright, bushy, 24–30″
Foliage: Medium, medium green, semiglossy
Blooms: Small, pale to medium apricot, 22 petals, 1½″, exhibition form
Fragrance: Slight
Awards: American Rose Society Award of Excellence 1986

Comments: This is one of the most popular miniature roses in the U.S. and a must-have for any serious exhibitor. It is a vigorous grower, prolific bloomer, and consistent performer. The apricot-blend blooms have classic hybrid tea form and are long lasting. The medium green, semiglossy foliage provides the perfect backdrop for this bloom. The rose was named for a friend of the hybridizer who was an outstanding rosarian from the San Diego Rose Society. Rating: 9.1

Jeanne Lajoie

Type: Miniature, Climbing
Hybridizer/Year: Sima 1975
Growth habits: Upright, bushy, 6–10′
Foliage: Small, dark green, glossy, embossed
Blooms: Small, medium pink, 35–40 petals, 1″
Fragrance: Slight
Awards: American Rose Society Award of Excellence 1977, Miniature Rose Hall of Fame 2001
Comments: This is a vigorous climbing miniature that needs to be anchored to a trellis or fence to support its abundant bloom. It will spread and cover quickly unless pruned. Soft medium pink blooms, set off by glossy dark green foliage, have classic hybrid tea form. This attractive climber continues to be one of the most popular. Rating: 9.1

Jilly Jewel

Type: Miniature
Hybridizer/Year: Benardella 1993
Growth habits: 24–30″ tall, vigorous, tends to spread
Foliage: Medium green, matte
Blooms: Pink, single, clusters, 18-27 petals, 2″
Fragrance: Slight
Comments: This rose blooms in abundance, both singly and in

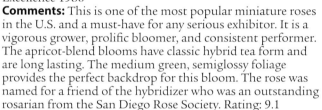

clusters with good form and lovely color all season long. It tends to spread so give it plenty of room at planting time. It is susceptible to rust. Rating: 7.8

Kristin

Type: Miniature
Hybridizer/Year: Benardella 1993
Growth habits: Rounded, 24–30″ tall and wide, vigorous
Foliage: Medium green, matte
Blooms: Red blend, 27–30 petals
Fragrance: Slight
Awards: American Rose Society Award of Excellence 1993
Comments: This is a beautiful selection for warm-summer areas, with an eye-popping color combination of white centers blending to brilliant red that intensifies in the heat. Blooms have good substance for long vase life. In cooler climates the blooms tend not to open fully. Plants are vigorous and generally disease-resistant, but protect from mildew. Rating: 8.1

Miniatures and minifloras *(continued)*

Lavender Jewel

Type: Miniature
Hybridizer/Year: Moore 1978
Growth habits: Vigorous, upright, compact, bushy, 12–18"
Foliage: Medium, dark green, matte
Blooms: Clear lavender-mauve, 38 petals, 1",
exhibition form
Fragrance: Slight
Comments: This plant tends to sprawl. It produces
abundant blooms throughout the growing season. The
blooms are a mauve blend with classic hybrid tea form.
It does best in high humidity. Rating: 7.2

Lavender Lace

Type: Miniature, Climbing
Hybridizer/Year: Rumsey 1971
Growth habits: Medium, vigorous, bushy, 4–6'
Foliage: Medium, medium green, semiglossy
Blooms: Soft lavender, 17–25 petals
Fragrance: Intense
Comments: Lavender-pink blooms open to
reveal golden stamens. Not to be confused with the shrub
rose by the same name. Also, there is a miniature non-
climbing form of Lavender Lace.

Little Artist

Type: Miniature
Hybridizer/Year: McGredy 1982
Growth habits: Vigorous, spreading, bushy, 12–16"
Foliage: Small, medium green, semiglossy, disease resistant
Blooms: Red with white markings that become completely red with age, 14–21 petals, 2½"
Fragrance: Slight

Comments: This miniature, one of Sam McGredy's "handpainted" varieties, makes a novel display in the garden. It is a low-growing, disease-resistant plant that is somewhat spreading. The blooms have bold red splashes and white markings that are quite attractive and disappear with age. Rating: 8.4

Luis Desamero

Type: Miniature
Hybridizer/Year: Bennett 1988
Growth habits: Tall, upright, bushy, 3–4'
Foliage: Medium, medium green, semiglossy
Blooms: Pastel yellow, 28 petals, 2", exhibition form
Fragrance: Slight
Comments: This international favorite is another Bennett creation. The vigorous bush is always covered in blooms. The large, pastel yellow blooms have classic hybrid tea form and are exquisite. They hold their color and shape in any climate. This rose was named for a well-known Southern California rose exhibitor. Rating: 7.9

Magic Carrousel

Type: Miniature
Hybridizer/Year: Moore 1972
Growth habits: Upright, rounded, bushy, 18–22″
Foliage: Medium, dark green, glossy, leathery
Blooms: Small, white with a red edge, 30–35 petals, 1½″
Fragrance: Slight
Awards: American Rose Society Award of Excellence 1975, Miniature Rose Hall of Fame 1999
Comments: This bush brings a bright spot of color to any garden. The creamy white blooms edged with vivid red are eyecatching. They are at their best when they open and show off their bright gold stamens. This rose was popular when it was introduced and it remains so today. It has a place in rose history as it was among the first to receive the American Rose Society's Award of Excellence. Rating: 8.5

Merlot

Type: Miniature
Hybridizer/Year: Benardella 2002
Growth habits: Vigorous, upright, 2–2½″
Foliage: Lush, semiglossy, dark green
Blooms: Dark red blooms with lighter reverse, white eye, single and in small clusters, 18–25 petals
Fragrance: Slight
Awards: American Rose Society Award of Excellence 2002
Comments: Vigorous and highly disease resistant, this outstanding rose is a winner on the show bench and in the garden too. Plants bloom prolifically all summer with fast repeat. Blooms appear on long (6- to 7-inch) stems and last long when cut. Rating: 7.4

Minnie Pearl

Type: Miniature
Hybridizer/Year: Saville 1982
Growth habits: Vigorous, upright, bushy, 14–24″
Foliage: Small, medium green, semiglossy
Blooms: Small, light pink edged with darker pink in the sun, darker pink reverse, 35–40 petals, 1½″, exhibition form
Fragrance: Slight
Comments: This rose has set the standard for other miniature roses. It has above-average disease resistance. It is a consistent performer that has adorned trophy tables across the nation. It holds its color better in less intense heat. It was named for the well-known comedian and country and western singer. Rating: 9.0

Mother's Love

Type: Miniature
Hybridizer/Year: Bennett 1988
Growth habits: Upright, medium, bushy, 24–30″
Foliage: Medium, medium green, semiglossy
Blooms: Pastel pink blending to soft yellow at the base, 23 petals, 1–1½″, exhibition form
Fragrance: Slight, fruity
Comments: This is another exceptional rose from well-known miniature hybridizer Dee Bennett. It is a vigorous grower that produces abundant blooms throughout the growing season. The blooms have classic hybrid tea form and show well. Rating: 8.0

Miniatures and minifloras *(continued)*

My Sunshine

Type: Miniature
Hybridizer/Year: Bennett 1986
Growth habits: Upright, medium, bushy, 14–20″
Foliage: Medium, semiglossy
Blooms: Medium yellow with bright yellow stamens, 5 petals, 1½″
Fragrance: Moderate
Comments: This is a single miniature that adds sparkle to the landscape. It is a vigorous bush that is a prolific bloomer throughout the growing season. The large, vibrant yellow blooms stand out against the semiglossy foliage. Rating: 8.5

Neon Cowboy

Type: Miniature
Hybridizer/Year: Carruth 2002
Growth habits: Vigorous, rounded, compact, bushy, 12–16″
Foliage: Medium, dark green, semiglossy
Blooms: Scarlet red with a yellow eye, 7–11 petals, 2–3″
Fragrance: Slight
Comments: The colors of this bloom are striking. The vigorous bush can far exceed the usual 16 inches, growing up to 3 feet tall in some areas. The blooms are showy scarlet-red with neon yellow eyes and bright gold stamens. The bush is clothed in clean, dark green foliage. This is a proven performer in all types of climates. Rating: 8.1

Nickelodeon

Type: Miniature
Hybridizer/Year: McGredy 1989
Growth habits: Vigorous, upright, bushy, 24–30″
Foliage: Small, dark green, semiglossy
Blooms: Red and white blend, 6–14 petals, 1″
Fragrance: Slight
Comments: This miniature does well in any landscape. Attractive red and white blooms complemented by dark green foliage cover the bush throughout the growing season. This bush will add bright color to any garden.

Over the Rainbow

Type: Miniature
Hybridizer/Year: Moore 1972
Growth habits: Vigorous, upright, bushy, 18–24″
Foliage: Medium, semiglossy, leathery
Blooms: Red with a yellow reverse, 25–30 petals, 1½″, exhibition form
Fragrance: Slight
Awards: American Rose Society Award of Excellence 1975
Comments: This is one of the best bicolor miniatures, and it is striking in the garden. The deep scarlet-red blooms have a stunning yellow underside. The bush produces abundant flowers throughout the growing season. The attractive foliage adds another dimension of contrast to the blooms. This is a good choice for the garden, vase, or show table. Rating: 7.9

Pacesetter

Type: Miniature
Hybridizer/Year: Schwartz 1979
Growth habits: Medium, vigorous, bushy, 1½–2′
Foliage: Medium, dark green, matte, few prickles
Blooms: Pure white, 46 petals, 1½″, exhibition form
Fragrance: Moderate
Awards: American Rose Society Award of Excellence 1981
Comments: This was one of the first pure white miniature roses. It is a vigorous, upright bush and a prolific bloomer. The blooms, which have classic hybrid tea form and hold their color and substance well, are excellent for cutting and exhibiting. The dark green, matte foliage is a dramatic contrast to the glowing white blooms. Rating: 8.1

Rainbow's End

Type: Miniature
Hybridizer/Year: Saville 1984
Growth habits: Upright, bushy, 12–18″
Foliage: Small, dark green, glossy

Blooms: Colors change as blooms age, 35 petals, 1–1½″
Fragrance: None
Awards: American Rose Society Award of Excellence 1986
Comments: This remains one of the most popular miniature roses, primarily for its stunning color changes. The blooms start deep yellow edged with red and age to almost red and then finally fade to pink. The bush is vigorous and compact with abundant flowers. It is also available as a climber. Rating: 8.7

Ralph Moore

Type: Miniature
Hybridizer/Year: Saville 1999
Growth habits: Vigorous, upright, bushy, 16–20″
Foliage: Medium, medium green, semiglossy
Blooms: Rich, vibrant red, 20–24 petals, 1½–2″, exhibition form
Fragrance: Slight
Awards: American Rose Society Award of Excellence 2000
Comments: This welcome addition to the class of red miniature roses is worthy of the name of the well-known hybridizer. It bears glorious blooms with classic hybrid tea form. This rose does well in the garden, in a vase, or on the show table. It is a relatively disease-resistant plant. Rating: 7.6

Red Cascade

Type: Miniature, Climbing
Hybridizer/Year: Moore 1976
Growth habits: Vigorous, upright, bushy, 6–18″
Foliage: Small, deep green, glossy, leathery, many prickles
Blooms: Deep red, 40 petals, 1″, cupped
Fragrance: Slight
Awards: American Rose Society Award of Excellence 1976
Comments: This rose creates a display of color to cover an area, drape a wall, or highlight a container. This vigorous, spreading grower produces abundant blooms. The foliage adds texture and contrast that is outstanding against the velvety blooms. Rating: 7.6

Miniatures and minifloras *(continued)*

Rise 'n' Shine

Type: Miniature
Hybridizer/Year: Moore 1977
Growth habits: Medium, vigorous, upright, bushy 1–2′
Foliage: Medium, medium green, semiglossy
Blooms: Rich yellow, 35 petals, 1½″, exhibition form
Fragrance: Moderate
Awards: American Rose Society Award of Excellence 1978, Miniature Rose Hall of Fame 1999
Comments: This disease-resistant bush does well in any landscape and has been popular for many years. The rich yellow blooms have classic hybrid tea form and do as well in the vase as they do in the garden. They are complemented by dark green foliage that is attractive in its own right. Rating: 8.4

Roller Coaster

Type: Miniature
Hybridizer/Year: McGredy 1987
Growth habits: Medium, vigorous, upright, 1–2′
Foliage: Small, medium green, glossy
Blooms: Red and white striped, 6–14 petals, 1½″, single form
Fragrance: Slight
Comments: This bushy plant tends to spread, making it perfect for containers or borders. The rapidly repeating bloom cycle ensures a continuous display of flowers. The novel, single blooms are a delightful mixture of red and white. No two blooms are alike, and they are most beautiful when they are open and the stamens show. This rose was introduced in Australia, where it was popular under the name of Minnie Mouse. Rating: 8.2

Ruby Pendant

Type: Miniature, Climbing
Hybridizer/Year: Strawn 1979
Growth habits: Tall, vigorous, upright, 4–5′
Foliage: Medium, dark reddish green, semiglossy, needle-shape prickles
Blooms: Red-purple, 28 petals, 2″, exhibition form
Fragrance: Slight
Comments: This is a tall-growing, vigorous bush that produces abundant blooms and red-green foliage. The reddish purple blooms with classic hybrid tea form perform equally well in the garden, in the vase, or on the show table. This climbing miniature is great near a fence or other structure. Rating: 8.4

Ruby Ruby

Type: Miniature
Hybridizer/Year: Carruth 2003
Growth habits: Vigorous, upright, bushy, 12–18″
Foliage: Medium, dark green, glossy
Blooms: Cherry red, 25-plus petals, 1½–2″
Fragrance: Slight
Comments: This medium-growing, rounded bush is a prolific bloomer that does well in all climates. The cherry red blooms hold their color for a long time and do well in a vase and in the garden. They are accented by a multitude of dark green, glossy foliage that contributes to an overall stunning effect. Rating: 7.8

Sachet

Type: Miniature
Hybridizer/Year: Saville 1986
Growth habits: Vigorous, upright, bushy, 16–20″
Foliage: Small, dark green, semiglossy, thin medium prickles
Blooms: Lavender with yellow stamens, 30 petals, 1–1½″
Fragrance: Intense, damask
Comments: This rose provides such fragrance that a single bloom can perfume an entire room. This medium-growing bush produces abundant blooms with delicate, slightly ruffled petals. Rating: 7.4

Santa Claus

Type: Miniature
Hybridizer/Year: Olesen 1991
Growth habits: Vigorous, upright, bushy, 20–24″
Foliage: Medium, dark green, glossy, few prickles
Blooms: Velvety, dark red, 15–25 petals, 1½–2¾″, exhibition form
Fragrance: Slight
Comments: This bush produces masses of large clusters of blooms in cycles that repeat rapidly. The

blooms have classic hybrid tea form and hold their color even in hot climates. This bush does equally well in containers and the garden. Rating: 7.8

Scentsational

Type: Miniature
Hybridizer/Year: Saville 1995
Growth habits: Vigorous, upright, bushy, 28″
Foliage: Medium, medium green, semiglossy
Blooms: Light mauve, 17–22 petals, 1½″, exhibition form
Fragrance: Intense

Comments: As its name implies, this miniature has an intense, sweet fragrance. The bushy plant does well in all landscapes. The blooms are edged in pink with a cream reverse and have classic hybrid tea form. They hold their color and form for days and open to display beautiful golden stamens that accent the mauve, reflexed petals. Rating: 7.6

Space Odyssey

Type: Miniature
Hybridizer/Year: Carruth 1999
Growth habits: Medium, vigorous, compact, 1½–2′
Foliage: Small, dark green, glossy, few prickles
Blooms: Red with a white eye and a white reverse, 12–16 petals, 1–1½″, single form
Fragrance: Slight
Comments: This disease-resistant bush presents a novel look in the garden. The velvety red blooms have eyecatching white eyes and white

reverse. The large blooms last and hold their lustrous color for days. The blooms are supported by a mass of deep green, glossy leaves. This plant does well in containers and in the garden. Rating: 8.0

Miniatures and minifloras *(continued)*

Starina

Type: Miniature
Hybridizer/Year: Meilland 1965
Growth habits: Vigorous, upright, dwarf, bushy, 12–18″
Foliage: Medium, dark green, glossy
Blooms: Orange-scarlet, 30–35 petals, 1″, exhibition form
Fragrance: Slight
Awards: Japan Gold Medal 1968, Anerkannte Deutsch Rose 1971, Miniature Rose Hall of Fame 1999
Comments: This has served as a standard-setter for other miniatures. This rose has been popular throughout the world since it was introduced. It is a low-growing bush and a prolific bloomer. The orange-scarlet blooms have classic hybrid tea form and hold their color and form even in the heat. Rating: 8.3

Sun Sprinkles

Type: Miniature
Hybridizer/Year: Walden 2001
Growth habits: Compact, rounded, 15″ tall and wide
Foliage: Small, medium-green, matte
Blooms: Deep yellow blooms, fully double, 30–35 petals

Fragrance: Mild, spicy
Awards: AARS 2001; American Rose Society Award of Excellence 2001
Comments: Outstanding full blooms are borne in huge numbers all summer, with deep yellow color that is nonfading even in heat. Plants are clean, easy to grow, and maintain, and are ideal for containers, edging borders, and walkways. Protect from black spot. Rating: 7.8

Sweet Diana

Type: Miniature
Hybridizer/Year: Saville 2002
Growth habits: Vigorous, upright, bushy, 14–18″
Foliage: Medium, dark green, semiglossy, disease resistant
Blooms: Brilliant daffodil yellow, 20-plus petals, 1¾–2″, exhibition form
Fragrance: None
Awards: American Rose Society Award of Excellence 2002
Comments: This rose was named for the hybridizer's youngest daughter when she was in her first year at Harvard. This disease resistant plant is a prolific bloomer. The blooms have classic hybrid tea form and excellent substance. The medium green, semiglossy foliage accents the yellow blooms perfectly. Rating: 7.8

Tiddly Winks

Type: Miniature
Hybridizer/Year: Carruth 2006
Growth habits: Short, bushy, compact, 1–1½′ tall
Foliage: Small, semiglossy, bright green
Blooms: Yellow blend, petals are glowing yellow in the center, broad orange-pink edging, 1½ ″, semidouble, 15–20 petals, small clusters
Fragrance: None
Comments: Loaded with flowers all summer, this 2008 Weeks Roses introduction is small and compact, perfect for containers, as edging in the front of the border, or massed as a groundcover. Blooms are pointed in bud, opening to reveal electric orange-pink hues with a glowing yellow eye.

Tiffany Lynn

Type: Miniflora
Hybridizer/Year: Jolly 1985
Growth habits: Vigorous, upright, bushy, 36–42″
Foliage: Large, medium green with red edges, semiglossy
Blooms: Light to medium pink blending to white in the center, 21 petals, 2″ or more, exhibition form
Fragrance: Slight
Comments: This is one of the best miniflora roses. It was popular when it was introduced, even before the class of minifloras existed, and it remains popular. The large medium pink and light pink blend blooms have classic hybrid tea form and are great for exhibition and vases. The bush is clothed in large, red-tinged green foliage that contrasts well with the blooms, though prone to mildew. Rating: 8.1

Comments: This disease-resistant plant performs well in all climates. The red-tinged lavender blooms have classic hybrid tea form, hold their color, and open to reveal bright gold stamens. The foliage provides a striking backdrop for the blooms. Rating: 8.2

Valentine's Day

Type: Miniflora, Climbing
Hybridizer/Year: Carruth 2004
Growth habits: Vigorous, upright, bushy, 4–10′
Foliage: Small, dark green, semiglossy, disease resistant
Blooms: Deep velvety red, 25–30 petals, 2–2½″
Fragrance: Slight
Comments: This hardy climber has an abundance of deep velvet red clusters of blooms against dark green, semiglossy foliage. A wonderful addition to the category of miniflora climbers, this is a stunning plant for any garden.

X-Rated

Type: Miniature
Hybridizer/Year: Bennett 1993
Growth habits: Medium, vigorous, bushy, 2–3′
Foliage: Small, medium green, glossy
Blooms: Creamy white edged with soft coral pink, 26–40 petals, 1½″, exhibition form
Fragrance: Moderate
Comments: The well-known hybridizer Dee Bennett set out to hybridize miniature roses and name them alphabetically beginning with A and working to Z. This winner came toward the end of her career as she was down to the letter X. This magnificent plant produces a bounty of blooms. The blooms have classic hybrid tea form and perform as well on the exhibit table as in the garden. This is a consistent performer throughout the country. Rating: 7.9

Winsome

Type: Miniature
Hybridizer/Year: Saville 1984
Growth habits: Vigorous, upright, bushy, 16–24″
Foliage: Medium, dark green, semiglossy
Blooms: Lilac-lavender with red tinge, 40-plus petals, 1½″, exhibition form
Fragrance: None
Awards: American Rose Society Award of Excellence 1985

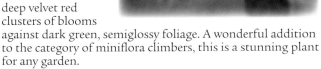

Climbers

Fences, arbors, trellises, walls of buildings, pergolas—structures of all types can be covered with climbing roses to add the beauty of season-long flowers. Climbing roses come in a great number of colors and styles and will enhance nearly any structure they are allowed to climb on. Climbing rose blooms can be of varying sizes, coming on in clusters or singly, but they always grow on vigorous canes that can be attached to whatever structure is nearby.

Defining a climbing rose can be a little tricky. Some roses are clearly climbers, hitting 12 or more feet. Most of these roses have large flowers, hence the name for them: Large-flowered climbers.

Rambler roses are the vertical giants. They usually hit 20 feet and sometimes as much as 50.

Further blurring the definitions are the so-called pillar roses. Some roses have sprawling canes that might hit 10 feet lend themselves to tying to a support. But you allow them to sprawl and grow them like a shrub-type rose.

In recent years, another type of climber has been added: the miniature climber. Growing no more than 6 feet, this downsized rose has tiny foliage and perfectly proportional tiny roses.

Adding to the confusion, too, is the fact that many roses come in two different forms: a shrubby type and a climbing form. Iceberg, for example, is a floribunda that tops out at 4 to 6 feet. In its climbing form, however, it reaches 8 to 15 feet.

Hardiness of climbing and other vertically-climbing roses varies radically. Most are not reliably cold-hardy above Zone 6 and only a handful are cold-hardy above Zone 5. A very few are hardy Zones 4 and above.

See page 29 for more explaination of climbing and other vertical-growing roses.

Alberic Barbier

Type: Rambler (Hybrid Wichuriana)
Hybridizer/Year: Barbier 1900
Growth vv: Vigorous, upright, up to 25′ tall
Foliage: Medium, dark green, glossy
Blooms: Creamy white, yellow center, 35–40 petals, 3½″
Fragrance: Intense, apple
Comments: This rambler was produced by the Barbier Nursery in Orleans, France, which created 23 other popular climbers and ramblers. This once-blooming rose does well in the shade. The blooms are large, and creamy white with a lemon yellow center, and have an apple fragrance. Its thin canes can easily be trained to fit any landscape. Rating: 8.0

All Ablaze

Type: Large-Flowered Climber
Hybridizer/Year: Carruth 1999
Growth habits: Vigorous, upright, tall, 9–12′
Foliage: Large, dark green, semiglossy
Blooms: Medium cherry red, 35 petals, 4″, ruffled
Fragrance: Slight, spice
Comments: This is a robust, hardy, clean plant that readily repeat blooms. The blooms are quite cheery. The large clusters appear to be on fire on the bush. This is a showy addition to any landscape. Rating: 7.4

Aloha

Type: Large-Flowered Climber
Hybridizer/Year: Boerner 1949
Growth habits: Tall, vigorous, bushy, 8–10′
Foliage: Medium, dark green, leathery
Blooms: Rose-pink with a deeper reverse, 58 petals, 3½″, cupped
Fragrance: Moderate
Comments: The large, two-toned blooms of this bush are lighter pink inside and darker pink outside. This upright plant requires warmer temperatures to develop its best color and form. Rating: 8.0

Altissimo

Type: Large-Flowered Climber
Hybridizer/Year: Delbard-Chabert 1966
Growth habits: Vigorous, upright, tall, 8–10 × 5′
Foliage: Large, medium to dark green, semiglossy, serrated
Blooms: Velvety deep red, 5–7 petals, 4½–5″
Fragrance: Slight

Comments: This climber lives up to its name, which means "in the highest." It is a hardy, consistent plant that does well in all climates. The rich, bright scarlet to crimson blooms are saucer shape and have bright golden yellow stamens. The foliage provides a great backdrop for the blooms. This plant is ideal for any climbing landscape project. Rating: 8.5

America

Type: Large-Flowered Climber
Hybridizer/Year: Warriner 1976
Growth habits: Vigorous, upright, tall, bushy, 10–12 × 5–7′
Foliage: Large, medium green, semiglossy
Blooms: Salmon pink with a lighter reverse, 40–45 petals, 3½–4½″
Fragrance: Intense, spicy
Awards: AARS 1976
Comments: This outstanding climber was named and introduced during the U.S. bicentennial. It is a consistent, proven, award-winning performer. The blooms are large and well formed, repeat often, and have an intensely spicy fragrance. The foliage is fairly disease resistant. Rating: 8.3

Awakening

Type: Large-Flowered Climber
Hybridizer/Year: Hortico 1992
Growth habits: Tall, vigorous, bushy, 10 × 8′
Foliage: Medium, light green, glossy
Blooms: Light pink, 26–40 petals, 1½–2¾″, quartered
Fragrance: Moderate
Comments: This is a petal-packed sport of the climber New Dawn. It is very hardy and has excellent foliage. The light pink, full blooms exude a pleasant sweet scent. Rating: 8.0

Berries 'n' Cream

Type: Large-Flowered Climber
Hybridizer/Year: Olesen 1998
Growth habits: Tall, vigorous, 10–12′
Foliage: Large, medium green, glossy, few prickles
Blooms: Swirls of old rose and cream, 26–40, 4–5″, clusters
Fragrance: Moderate, apple

Comments: This clean climber radiates with color. It is vigorous and has a larger growth habit in mild climates. The stunning blooms are a swirl of old rose pink and cream that reflect its name. The disease-resistant foliage contrasts well with the magnificent colors of the blooms. It repeats freely and provides abundant color for any landscape project. Rating: 7.8

Climbers *(continued)*

Blaze Improved

Type: Large-Flowered Climber
Hybridizer/Year: Bohm 1935
Growth habits: Tall, vigorous, 12–14′
Foliage: Medium, dark green, leathery
Blooms: Pure dark red, 20–25 petals, 3″, clusters
Fragrance: Slight
Comments: This plant is one of the most popular climbing roses of all time. It is a hardy, consistent performer in all climates. The pure dark red blooms appear in large abundant clusters. It does equally well in all types of climbing landscape projects.
Rating: 8.9

Blaze of Glory

Type: Large-Flowered Climber
Hybridizer/Year: Jackson & Perkins 2004
Growth habits: 12-14'
Foliage: Glossy dark green
Blooms: 4" pointed ovid blooms, 25 petals
Fragrance: Light musk
Comments: It's hard to find a climber that boasts a gorgeous coral-orange color the way this one does. It produces flowers all summer long in very large clusters.
Rating: 7.6

Candy Land

Type: Large-Flowered Climber
Hybridizer/Year: Carruth 2008
Growth habits: 10-12'
Foliage: Glossy apple green
Blooms: Hybrid-tea shaped, 25 petals
Fragrance: Moderate, applelike
Comments: This is one showy rose. Not only are the flowers striking—pink striped with ivory yellow—but the foliage is extremely lush, glossy, and attractive. It's also highly black-spot resistant. This rose also blooms and reblooms well the very first year.

Don Juan

Type: Large-Flowered Climber
Hybridizer/Year: Malandrone 1958
Growth habits: Vigorous, upright, tall, 12–14 × 6′
Foliage: Large, dark green, glossy, leathery
Blooms: Deep, velvety crimson-red, 30–35 petals, 4″
Fragrance: Intense, rose
Comments: This climber needs a large space. It is one of the best red climbers on the market. The blooms are large and shapely and have an intense rose scent. The foliage is a textural contrast for the petals.
Rating: 8.2

Dr. W. Van Fleet

Type: Large-Flowered Climber
Hybridizer/Year: Van Fleet 1910
Growth habits: Vigorous, upright, bushy, 15–20′
Foliage: Medium, dark green, glossy
Blooms: Cameo pink fading to pink white, 25–30 petals, 3″
Fragrance: Moderate
Comments: This prolific bloomer has sported several other repeat blooming climbers. This is an extremely vigorous grower, however, it blooms only once. It cascades attractively over tall structures. Rating: 8.0

Dream Weaver

Type: Large-Flowered Climber
Hybridizer/Year: Zary 1997
Growth habits: Tall, vigorous, upright, spreading, 10–12′
Foliage: Medium, dark green, glossy, moderate prickles
Blooms: Coral-pink, 26–40 petals, 3–3½″
Fragrance: Slight
Comments: This is a vigorous bush that produces abundant blooms throughout the growing season. The bright coral blooms grow in clusters that always seem to be present. The foliage is relatively disease resistant. Rating: 7.9

Dublin Bay

Type: Large-Flowered Climber
Hybridizer/Year: McGredy 1974
Growth habits: Vigorous, upright, tall, 9–12 × 6–8′
Foliage: Large, rich green, glossy
Blooms: Clear velvety medium red, 25 petals, 4–5″
Fragrance: Moderate
Awards: New Zealand Rose of the Year 1993
Comments: This is one of the best and most popular red climbers on the market. It is a prolific bloomer and repeats quickly. The large clear red blooms do well in all climates and have a pleasant fruity scent. The foliage contrasts well with the petals. This climber will add grace and beauty to any structure in the landscape. Rating: 8.6

Eden

Type: Large-Flowered Climber
Hybridizer/Year: Meilland 1985
Growth habits: Tall, vigorous, spreading, 10–12′
Foliage: Medium, deep green, semiglossy
Blooms: Creamy white suffused with carmine pink, 40–55 petals, 4½–5″, clusters
Fragrance: Slight
Comments: This plant has an old-fashioned rose look with double creamy white blooms with pink and yellow tinges. The foliage is heavy and bushy. This is a good choice to plant near a gazebo or fence.

Climbers *(continued)*

Fourth of July

Type: Large-Flowered Climber
Hybridizer/Year: Carruth 1999
Growth habits: Vigorous, upright, hardy, tall, 10–14'
Foliage: Large, deep green, glossy
Blooms: Velvety red with bright white stripes, ruffled, 10–15 petals, 4–4½"
Fragrance: Moderate, apple and sweet rose
Awards: AARS 1999
Comments: This was the first climber to win an AARS award in 23 years when it was introduced in 1999. The color display of red and white is appropriate to the name. The sprays of long-lasting blooms repeat bloom quickly. The dark green glossy foliage enhances the beauty of this bush. Rating: 8.1

Francois Juranville

Type: Rambler (Hybrid Wichurana)
Hybridizer/Year: Barbier 1906
Growth habits: Vigorous, upright, bushy, 10–15'
Foliage: Small, dark green with bronzy green edges, glossy, few prickles
Blooms: Salmon-pink with a yellow base, 35 petals, 3–4"
Fragrance: Moderate, apple
Comments: This tall rambler produces abundant blooms throughout the growing season. The blooms are large, salmon pink with a yellow base and have quilled petals.

Golden Showers

Type: Large-Flowered Climber
Hybridizer/Year: Lammerts 1956
Growth habits: Tall, vigorous, 6–10'
Foliage: Medium, medium green, glossy
Blooms: Daffodil yellow, 25–28 petals, 4", borne singly and in clusters

Fragrance: Moderate, licorice
Awards: AARS 1957, Portland Gold Medal 1957
Comments: This climber continues to be popular. It is a prolific bloomer that almost always has an abundance of flowers. The bright, cheerful daffodil yellow blooms fade to a softer yellow as they age. The canes have few prickles and are easy to handle when training. Rating: 7.4

Handel

Type: Large-Flowered Climber
Hybridizer/Year: McGredy 1965
Growth habits: Canes grow 10–12' long
Foliage: Dark olive-green
Blooms: Red blend, double, 20–30 petals, white heavily edged in red, borne one to a stem or in small sprays
Fragrance: None
Awards: Portland Gold Medal 1975
Comments: Handel brings a glowing color to the trellis and along a fence. Blooms are strikingly bicolored with pure white petals dramatically edged in red. Best color is achieved in cool climates, which is convenient since it's hardy through Zone 5. It is prone to black spot. Rating: 7.9

High Hopes

Type: Large-Flowered Climber
Hybridizer/Year: Harkness 1994
Growth habits: Canes grow 10–12' long, best grown around a pillar.
Foliage: Glossy, dark green
Blooms: Medium pink, small clusters, elegant pointed buds open to rose-pink, double, 32 petals, high-centered
Fragrance: Spicy, sweet strawberry
Comments: High Hopes provides loads of romantic pink blossoms all summer. While its long canes are perhaps best grown on a pillar, they also perform well on arbors and fences. Although it is generally disease resistant, it is prone to black spot in humid climates. It is hardy through Zone 5.

High Society

Type: Large-Flowered Climber
Hybridizer/Year: Zary 2004
Growth habits: Vigorous, well-branched, canes reach 12–14′ long
Foliage: Large, glossy, dark green
Blooms: Deep pink, 4–5″, classical hybrid tea shape, 26–40 petals
Fragrance: Light, damask
Comments: If you're looking for a vigorous, tall climber with deep magenta-pink blooms, High Society is an excellent choice. Its vigorous canes have no problem climbing an arbor or pergola and covering it with electric color. The nicely fragrant blooms are excellent cut for the vase. Rating: 7.2

Iceberg, Climbing

Type: Large-Flowered Climber
Hybridizer/Year: Cant 1968
Growth habits: Vigorous, upright, 12–14′
Foliage: Medium, light green, glossy
Blooms: Pure white, 20–25 petals, 3″
Fragrance: Slight, honey
Comments: This vigorous climber is a sport of the floribunda Iceberg, one of the world's best landscape roses. This disease-resistant plant is robust and produces an abundance of true white blooms throughout the growing season and over the years has proven itself to be one of the best white climbing roses. Rating: 8.5

Jacob's Robe

Type: Large-Flowered Climber
Hybridizer/Year: Carruth 2006
Growth habits: Canes grow 10 to 12′ long
Foliage: Large glossy leaves are deep green
Blooms: Yellow blend. Blushes and stripes of yellow, pink, and red tones, often on the same blossom. Flowers are large and double (20 to 25 petals), borne in large clusters all summer.
Fragrance: Slight, spicy
Comments: Bred to capture the same great colors as the classic Joseph's Coat, but on a much improved plant, Jacob's Robe was introduced by Weeks Roses in 2008. The multicolored effect is even more dramatic than Joseph's Coat, and plants are much more vigorous, disease-resistant, and hardy, with lush glossy deep green leaves. Free-flowering; blooms on new and old wood.

Joseph's Coat

Type: Large-Flowered Climber
Hybridizer/Year: Armstrong & Swim 1964
Growth habits: Tall, vigorous, 10–12′
Foliage: Medium, dark apple green, glossy
Blooms: Yellow and red, 23–28 petals, 3″
Fragrance: Slight
Awards: Bagatelle Gold Medal 1964
Comments: This is a popular climber, mostly because of its blooms, which provide a profusion of clusters of ever-changing hues throughout the stages of bloom. The blooms open almost flat to show the stamens to their best advantage. Rating: 7.5

Climbers *(continued)*

Lemon Meringue

Type: Large-Flowered Climber
Hybridizer/Year: Radler 2004
Growth habits: Vigorous, upright, 10–12'
Foliage: Medium, medium green, semiglossy
Blooms: Lemon chiffon yellow, 20–25 petals, 3–4"
Fragrance: Intense, spicy and fruity
Comments: This is a sport of Autumn Sunset that has all of its characteristics in a chiffon yellow color. This is a tall, hardy, disease-resistant climber that does well in all climates. The yellow blooms are very fragrant.

New Dawn

Type: Large-Flowered Climber
Hybridizer/Year: Dreer 1930
Growth habits: Vigorous, upright, tall, bushy 18–20 × 6–10'
Foliage: Large, medium dark green, glossy
Blooms: Blush pink, 3½", 35–40 petals
Fragrance: Moderate, sweet, rose
Awards: World Federation of Rose Societies Hall of Fame 1997
Comments: This hardy climber holds the first plant patent issued in the U.S. It needs a lot of space. The large soft pink blooms age to a blush white. The dark glossy foliage provides contrast for the blooms. Rating: 8.6

Night Owl

Type: Large-Flowered Climber
Hybridizer/Year: Carruth 2005
Growth habits: Vigorous, upright, 10–14'
Foliage: Medium, reddish maturing to a grayish green, semiglossy, disease resistant
Blooms: Deep purple, 8–12 petals, 4", ruffled

Fragrance: Moderate, clove and spice
Comments: This disease resistant climber is a must-have for aficionados of dark purple roses. The long-lasting blooms have bright gold stamens and hold their color throughout the stages of bloom.

Paul's Himalayan Musk Rambler

Type: Rambler (Hybrid Musk)
Hybridizer/Year: Paul 1916
Growth habits: Vigorous, upright, bushy, 20'
Foliage: Small, medium green, narrow, matte
Blooms: Blush lilac pink, 25–30 petals, 1½"
Fragrance: Moderate
Comments: This hardy plant has all of the characteristics of the old ramblers. It loves to grow tall and intertwine with a tree. It produces clusters of small lilac-pink flowers surrounded by small, light green foliage. This plant needs plenty of room to expand. It is great for climbing structures. Rating: 7.9

Pearly Gates

Type: Large-Flowered Climber
Hybridizer/Year: Meyer 1999
Growth habits: Vigorous, canes grow 8–14' long
Foliage: Deep green, matte
Blooms: Light pink flowers, double, 35 petals
Fragrance: Strong, sweet, spicy
Comments: While slow to bloom in spring, this sport of the classic climber America rewards with huge, well-formed, symmetrical flowers in pure pastel pink with generous fragrance all summer long. Rating: 7.7

Polka

Type: Large-Flowered Climber
Hybridizer/Year: Meilland 1991
Growth habits: Canes grow 10–12′ long
Foliage: Healthy, dark green
Blooms: Fluffy old-fashioned, 30–35 petals, Copper-salmon and fade to light salmon-pink, deep copper center
Fragrance: Strong, pervading old rose
Comments: Excellent bloom production, good vigor, and good disease resistance make Polka a good choice to cover an arbor or pergola. The rich creamy apricot blooms have delightfully ruffled, old-fashioned effect. Superb fragrance is a lovely bonus. Rating: 7.8

Red Eden *(also known as Eric Tabarly)*

Type: Large-Flowered Climber
Hybridizer/Year: Meilland 2003
Growth habits: Tall, vigorous, upright, 10′ or more
Foliage: Medium, dark reddish green, semiglossy
Blooms: Deep burgundy red, 100–110 petals, 4–5″
Fragrance: Slight
Comments: This rose is from the Romantica series of roses from the royal house of Meilland. Its growth habit, disease resistance, and repeat blooming pattern are similar to that of the popular climber Eden. It is a bushy plant that produces abundant blooms throughout the growing season. The large flowers are many petaled and have the old-fashioned garden rose form.

Rosarium Uetersen

Type: Large-Flowered Climber
Hybridizer/Year: Kordes 1977
Growth habits: Vigorous, upright, tall, 12–14 × 6′
Foliage: Large, profuse, medium green, glossy, dentate
Blooms: Deep pink, 142 petals, 3″, ovoid
Fragrance: Moderate
Comments: This hardy climber is very adaptable and does well in most climates. The large blooms are dark pink aging to a silvery pink and open in an attractive array. They appear more prolifically in the early part of the growing season but continue blooming for the duration. Rating: 8.5

Royal Sunset

Type: Large-Flowered Climber
Hybridizer/Year: Morey 1960
Growth habits: Vigorous, upright, tall, 10–15′
Foliage: Large, dark green, glossy, leathery
Blooms: Large, orange-apricot fading to light peach, 20–25 petals, 5–6″
Fragrance: Intense, fruity
Awards: Portland Gold Medal 1960
Comments: This vigorous plant produces abundant blooms throughout the growing season. The foliage contrasts with the blooms in both color and texture. The bush has its best color and size in cooler temperatures and is popular in the Northwest. Rating: 8.9

Climbers *(continued)*

Scent from Above

Type: Large-Flowered Climber
Hybridizer/Year: Warner 2005
Growth habits: Vigorous, well-branched, canes grow 8–10′ tall
Foliage: Glossy, dark green, medium size
Blooms: Medium yellow, golden yellow in the center fading to cream at the edges, 4–5″, full, 26–40 petals
Fragrance: Mild, licorice

Comments: Golden yellow blossoms that hold their color well even in the heat, and a tantalizing licorice fragrance, are great reasons to grow this fine climbing rose. Use it on arbors and trellises and growing up posts and pillars.

Sky's the Limit

Type: Large-Flowered Climber
Hybridizer/Year: Carruth 2007
Growth habits: Vigorous, upright, tall, 10–12′
Foliage: Medium, dark green, semiglossy
Blooms: Buttery yellow, 20–25 petals, 3–3½″, ruffled
Fragrance: Slight, fruity
Comments: This climber is very hardy, particularly for a yellow rose. It has a tall growth habit and is a prolific bloomer. The dark green, semiglossy foliage provides a backdrop for the bright blooms.

Soaring Spirits

Type: Large-Flowered Climber
Hybridizer/Year: Carruth 2005
Growth habits: Tall, vigorous, 12′ or taller
Foliage: Medium, medium green, glossy
Blooms: Pink and yellow stripes, 5–8 petals, 5″, ruffled
Fragrance: Moderate, apple
Comments: This is one of the roses named in honor of those who perished in the September 11, 2001, tragedy. It was named by families of the victims, and 15 percent of the proceeds are donated to the Remember Me Rose Gardens. The stunning blooms grow in huge clusters of ever-changing colors that beautify any landscape. The glossy leaves start out almost lime green in color.

Social Climber

Type: Large-Flowered Climber
Hybridizer/Year: Zary 2003
Growth habits: Vigorous, upright, bushy, 6′
Foliage: Medium, dark green, glossy
Blooms: Deep pink, 40 petals, 4″
Fragrance: Moderate, spicy
Comments: This rose is one of the better new climbers. The blooms have classic hybrid tea form and a delicious spicy scent. The blooms are produced in abundance throughout the growing season. Rating: 7.9

Sombreuil

Type: Large-Flowered Climber
Year: 1850
Growth habits: Vigorous, upright, 6–12 × 6–8′
Foliage: Medium, medium green, semiglossy
Blooms: Large, creamy white, 60-plus petals, 3″
Fragrance: Intense
Comments: This is an excellent white climber that combines the best of hybrid teas and the old-garden rose look. It does well in any type of landscape. It is superb when mixed with companion plants. The blooms are renditions of the flat quartered old-garden style and are redolent with the old rose fragrance.

Stairway to Heaven

Type: Large-Flowered Climber
Hybridizer/Year: Zary 2002
Growth habits: Vigorous, fast, canes grow 10–12′ long
Foliage: Dark green
Blooms: Medium red, double, 25 petals, 4″ wide, large clusters
Fragrance: Light, sweet

Comments: Rapid growth and vigor make this climber ideal for quickly growing along a fence. It is one of the first climbers to burst into bloom in late spring, and its prodigious repeat blooms that last for weeks keep it continually in color all summer. It is prone to mildew, so spraying should be considered. Rating: 7.5

Summer Wine

Type: Large-Flowered Climber
Hybridizer/Year: Kordes 1985
Growth habits: Vigorous, 12-15′
Foliage: Glossy dark green leaves
Blooms: Deep pink, small clusters, single, 5 petals, coral pink flowers, red stamens, light yellow eye
Fragrance: Sweet but slight
Comments: Summer Wine provides excellent summer-long color with loads of coral blooms. It's also a good cut flower, long-lived in the vase. This is a large rose ideal for training on a pillar, but also good on an arbor or pergola.

Rose resources

The American Rose Society

Gardeners who enjoy growing roses often need help and assistance as well as want to share their experiences. The American Rose Society (ARS) is a national nonprofit organization composed of a network of about 350 local rose societies, located in cities and towns throughout the United States.

Headquartered in Shreveport, Louisiana, the ARS maintains a 118-acre park known as the American Rose Center, which is dedicated to roses.

With more than 15,000 members, the ARS offers many services to promote rose growing:
● Provides access to more than 2,200 local experts who offer personal rose-growing assistance for your area.
● Lists affiliated rose societies in your area.
● Publishes an annual Handbook for Selecting Roses, which rates new roses.
● Publishes a 42-page, full-color monthly magazine, The American Rose.
● Publishes the American Rose Annual, an 84-page, full-color volume containing the latest news and information on roses.
● Publishes four publications on specialized subjects: miniature roses, Old garden roses, rose arrangements, and rose exhibiting.
● Maintains a lending library of books, videos, slides, and Power Point presentations on most rose subjects that can be borrowed.
● Holds annual national conventions and rose shows featuring lectures, garden tours, and a chance to meet with fellow rose growers from all over the nation.

For more information, call 800-637-6534 or write to:

American Rose Society, P.O. Box 30,000, Shreveport, LA 71130- 0300.

Computer-based resources

The following rose societies and organizations have web pages crammed full of color photos, and information on new roses and rose growing:
● All-America Rose Selection (www.rose.org) provides lists and photos of all award winners from 1940 to the present. It also has a search feature that allows visitors to access a list of rose gardens broken down by state.
● American Rose Society (www.ars.org) offers features such as "Rose of the Month," articles by experts on selected topics, links to local rose societies, answers to frequently asked questions, where to buy roses, and much more. It also includes various links to associated websites.
● Canadian Rose Society (www.mirror.org/groups/crs) lists current events and shows, public gardens, instructions on how to plant roses, explorer roses.
● World Federation of Rose Societies (www.worldrose. org) provides a global perspective on roses, plus the Rose Hall of Fame. Site lists "Coming Events" with worldwide conferences and conventions, and editorials from their newsletter, World Rose News. Also includes links to national rose societies.
● Royal National Rose Society (www.roses.co.uk) offers the benefits of membership plus an insight into rose gardens in the United Kingdom, rose care information, events, publications, and more.
● helpmefind.com. This extensive site includes a section devoted to roses, including selecting, buying, breeding, caring for and exhibiting. It has cataloged over 31,000 roses and have more than 60,000 photos along with thousands of rose nurseries, public and private gardens, rose societies, authors, breeders, hybridizers and publications from all over the world.

Roses by Mail

The following are a few of the many mail order companies that carry roses. Most have fairly extensive web sites with growing information.

Edmunds' Roses
6235 S.W. Kahle Rd.
Wilsonville, OR 97070
888/481-7673

Jackson & Perkins
1 Rose Lane
P.O. Box 1028
Medford, OR 97501
800/292-4769

Johnny Becnel Show Roses
8910 Highway 23
Belle Chasse, LA 70037
504/394-6608

Wayside Gardens
1 Garden Lane
Hodges, SC 29695
800/213-0379

Heirloom Roses
24062 N.E. Riverside Dr.
St. Paul, OR 97137
503/538-1576

Pickering Nurseries, Inc.
670 Kingston Rd.
Pickering, Ontario
Canada L1V 1A6
905/753-2155

Vintage Gardens
Antique Roses
2833 Old Gravenstein Hwy S
Sebastopol, CA 95472
707/829-2035

Bridges Roses
2734 Toney Road
Lawndale, NC 28090
704/538-9412

Nor'East Miniature Roses,
902 Zenon Way, PO Box 440
Arroyo Grande, CA 93421
800/426-6485

▲ This Starry Night rose is charming growing through a low picket fence.

Rose gardens to visit

Throughout North America, there are wonderful rose gardens to visit to learn more about roses and just plain enjoy them. June, when roses are at their peak, is always a good time to visit. But also try to visit a rose garden in your region during other less showy times of the year. Visit in August, for example, to see which roses do best over time, can bloom even in the heat and drought of that month, and are still healthy even at the end of the season.

Albuquerque Rose Garden
8205 Apache Ave. NE
Albuquerque, NM 87111

American Rose Center
8877 Jefferson Paige Rd.
Shreveport, LA 71119
318/938-5402 ext. 100

Atlanta Botanical Garden
1345 Piedmont Ave NE
Atlanta, GA 30309
404/876-5859

Bellingrath Gardens
12401 Bellingrath
  Gardens Rd.
Theodore, AL 36582
251/973-2217
800/247-2217

Berkeley Rose Garden
1200 Euclid Ave.
Berkeley, CA 94708
510/981-5150

Biltmore Estate
One Biltmore Estates Drive
Asheville, NC 28803
800/411-3812

Boerner Botanical Gardens
9400 Boerner Drive
Hales Corners, WI 53130
414/525-5650

Brooklyn Botanical Garden
1000 Washington Ave.
Brooklyn, NY 11225
718/623-7241

Cantigny Gardens
1 South 151 Winfield Rd.
Wheaton, IL 60187
630/668-5161

Chicago Botanic Garden
1000 Lake Cook Rd.
Glencoe, IL 60022
847/835-5440

Dubuque Arboretum
3800 Arboretum Road
Dubuque, IA 52001
563/556-2100

Fort Worth Botanic Garden
3220 Botanic Garden Blvd.
Fort Worth, TX 76107
817/871-7686

Hershey Gardens
170 Hotel Rd.
Hershey, PA 17033
717/534-3492

Houston Municipal Rose Garden
1500 Hermann Dr.
Houston, TX 77004
713/284-1986

Huntington Botanical Gardens
1151 Oxford Rd.
San Marino, CA 91108
626/405-2100

Inez Parker Memorial Garden
Information: Balboa Park
Visitor's Center
2525 Park Blvd.
San Diego, CA 92101
619/235-1100

International Rose Test Garden
400 Southwest Kingston Ave.
Portland, OR 97201
503/227-7033

Iowa State University's
Reiman Gardens
1407 Elwood Dr.
Ames, IA 50010
515/294-2710

Jacob L. Loose Memorial Park
51st Sreet and Wornall Rd.
Kansas City, MO 64112
816/561-9710

Longwood Gardens
U S Route 1, Box 501
1001 Longwood Rd.
Kennett Square, PA 19348
610/388-1000

Mabel Davis Rose Garden
Zilker Botanical Garden
2220 Barton Springs Rd.
Austin, TX 78746
512/477-8672

Memphis Botanic Garden
Audubon Park
750 Cherry Rd.
Memphis, TN 38117
901/576-4100

Memorial Park Rose Garden
6005 Underwood Avenue
Omaha, NE 68132
402/444-5955

Missouri Botanical Garden
4344 Shaw Blvd.
St. Louis, MO 63110
314/577-9400

Morris Arboretum
100 E. Northwestern Avenue
Philadelphia, PA 19118
215/247-5777

New York Botanical Garden
Bronx River Parkway at
Fordham Road
Bronx, NY 10458
718/623-7241

Reno Municipal Rose Garden
2055 Idlewild Dr.
Reno, NV 89509
775/334-2260

Rose Hills Memorial Park
3888 South Workman
  Mill Rd.
Whittier, CA 90601
562/699-0921

The State Botanical Garden
2450 South Milledge Ave.
Athens, GA 30605
706/542-1244

United Nations Rose Garden
42nd St. at the East River
New York, NY 10017

Walt Disney World
Lake Buena Vista, FL 32830
407/939-6244

Woodland Park Rose Garden
5500 Phinney Ave. North
Seattle, WA 98103
206/332-9900

Glossary

Acid soil: Sometimes also called sour soil. The opposite of alkaline, sometimes called sweet, soil. Acid soil is a soil with a pH lower than 7.0 is an acid soil. A soil pH higher than 7.0 is alkaline. Neutral soil is in the middle of this range. Some garden plants thrive only in acid soil, others only in alkaline. The vast majority thrive in neutral soil.

Alkaline soil: A soil with a pH higher than 7.0 is defined as an alkaline soil. See also "acid soil."

Balling: Rose flowers that are poorly formed and don't open well because of cool, wet, or humid weather.

Bareroot plants: Plants being sold with all the soil removed from their roots. Usually sold with the tops protruding from boxes or bags and the roots packed in damp sawdust.

Botanical name: The scientific or Latin name of a plant, usually made up on at least one word (the genus) but also often the species (the second word).

Bud: A flower or plant growth (usually a flower or leaf) in its early stage of development.

Bud union: Also called a graft union. The point on a rose, right above the roots, where the top portion of the rose has been grafted onto the roots to produce a superior plant.

Canes: Another name for the main branches of the rose bush. They are thicker and sturdier than mere stems.

Complete fertilizer: A plant food which contains all three of the main elements for plant growth: Nitrogen, phosphorus and potassium.

Compost: The black, crumbly, soil-like material created by decomposing organic matter, such as leaves, weeds, egg shells, clipped grass, and other organic matter.

Deadhead: Pinching or cutting off spent flowers to tidy plants and promote longer bloom.

Dormant: Part of the cycle of a plant when it stops growing. The top of the plant may or may not die back.

Fertilizer: Any material used to feed a plant. May be dry or liquid and different formulations are used for different plants to encourage different processes (foliar growth vs. blooming vs. root development). One function of compost is to fertilize plants.

Floriferious: Heavily flowering over a long period of time.

Foliar feeding: Fertilizer applied in liquid form as a spray so plants can take up the nutrients through their leaves.

Grafting: Attaching a short length of stem of one plant onto the root stock of a different plant. Grafting is usually done to produce a more hardy or otherwise superior plant.

Growing season: The number of days between the last killing frost in spring and the first killing frost in fall. Colder northern regions have shorter growing seasons; warm southern climates have long and even y ear-round growing seasons.

Hardy: Often mistakenly called "hearty." Refers to a plant's ability to withstand cold. Used interchangeably with "cold hardy."

Microclimate: Variations of the climate within a certain area. A microclimate can be as large as a valley or hillside or as small as a portion of your yard.

Micronutrients: Mineral elements that are needed by some plants in very small quantities. If the plants you are growing require specific 'trace elements' and they are not available in the soil, they must be added.

Mulch: A material, either loose or solid, placed over the soil. Most mulch is used to suppress weeds and conserve moisture, but it can also be used, as in the case of plastic, to heat soil.

Own-root roses: An increasingly popular way to sell roses. These are roses without grafts, that is, on their own roots. (See also "rootstock.")

Peat moss: The partially decomposed remains of moss. Peat can come from a bog or fell and can vary in quality. Sphagnum peat moss is harvested from Canadian bogs and is the best quality.

Potting soil: A soil mix used for pots and other containers. Can be blended at home but usually purchased premixed in a bag.

Potting medium: Can also be called growing medium. The material in which plants grow. Can included potting soil (see above), but also soilless potting mixes and barks used to grow things like orchids.

Pruning: Removing plant parts to improve overall plant healthy or shape.

Rootstock: In a grafted rose, the base (roots) onto which the desired variety is grafted. (See also "own-root rose.")

Rose hips: The fleshy fruit of the rose that in late summer and autumn swells and looks like the seedpod.

Sucker: On a grafted rose, the undesirable cane that grows up from the rootstock, below the bud union. It can grow right at the base or might sprout up through the soil a few to several inches out from the bush.

Systemic: A chemical taken up by the entire plant. Can be an herbicide, which kills the whole plant, including the roots, or an insecticide that will kill insects that feed on any part of the plant.

Tender: A term used to describe plants unable to withstand any extreme cold, especially freezing temperatures.

Topsoil: The top layer of soil, usually of a higher quality, in undisturbed ground. Also refers to planting-quality (as opposed to fill dirt) soil sold by landscaping companies.

Winter kill: The damage done to roses by harsh winters. An entire rose can be winter killed or just a portion—usually the ends.

Index

This index is divided into two parts. The first part, the subject index, contains general subjects, such as planting or compost.

The second part, the rose index, contains specific roses, such as Mister Lincoln or Flutterbye.

Page numbers in **boldface type** indicate entries in the Gallery of Roses, which highlights each rose with a photo and information.

Page numbers in *italic type* indicate photographs, illustrations, or information in captions.

Subject index

▲ Good air circulation is critical to healthy roes. Training them along a fence is an excellent way to assure minimal disease problems and the cleanest, most black-spot free foliage.

Subject index (continued)

choosing roses for, 77
rose care calendar, 132–135
Gynoeciums, defined, 11
Gypsum, for clay soils, 66

H
"Handbook for Selecting Roses," 70, 137
Handpainted petal patterns, *14*
Harkness, Philip and Robert, 7
Heat stress
syringing to reduce, 84
varieties tolerant of, 64
See also Hot climates
Heirloom Roses, contact information, 256
Herbicides
how and when to use, 90, 105
preemergent, 105
systemic, 258
Hershey Gardens, contact information, 257
High-centered flowers, classic, *18*
Hips
anatomy, 11
defined, 258
nutritional value, 11
removed by deadheading, 129
for seasonal interest, 74
Hollyhock, as companion plant, 37
Hosta, as companion plant, 36
Hot climates
AHS Heat Tolerance Map, 63, *63*
flowering and, 13
heat stress, 64, 84
hot and dry, 62
hot and humid, 62
microclimates and, *86*
varieties tolerant of, *58*, 59, 62, 71, 72, *77*, 78
Houston Municipal Rose Garden, contact information, 257
Humidity
disease role, 64, 88, 115
roses for humid regions, 64

varieties tolerant of, 62
See also Precipitation; Wet conditions
Huntington Botanical Gardens, contact information, 257
Hydrangea, as companion plant, 37
Hypanthiums, defined, 11

I
Inez Parker Memorial Garden, contact information, 257
Insecticides
for specific pests, 117–119
systemic, 258
when and how to use, 114, *114*, 117, 125, 130
Insect-pest resistance
breeding for, 8
as selection criteria, 110, *110*, 112
top insect-resistant roses, *111*
Insect pests, 117–119
as disease vectors, 117
drought stress and, 103
identifying and controlling, 114, 117, 132–135
pruning and, 125, *125*
spring pruning and cleanup, 130
See also specific pests
Insects, beneficial, 117
Intensity, of sunlight, 84
International Rose Test Garden, contact information, 257
Iris, as companion plant, 37
Irrigation. *See* Watering

J
Jackson & Perkins
contact information, 256
Keith Zary, 7, 137
Jacob L. Loose Memorial Park, contact information, 257
Japanese beetles, 118
See also Insect-pest resistance
Joe-pye weed, as companion

plant, 37
Johnny Becnel Show Roses, contact information, 256
Jones, Steve, 71, *71*

K
Kordes, Wilhelm, 7, 137

L
Lamb's-ears, as companion plant, 37
Lamium, as companion plant, 37
Landscape fabric, 104, *105*
Landscaping. *See* Designing with roses
Lawns
in formal gardens, 48
replacing with roses, 39, *39*
Layering (propagation), 82
Leafhoppers, 117, 118, *118*
Leaf rollers, 118, *118*
Leaky hose irrigation systems, *100*
Leaves
anatomy, 11
as mulch, 104
See also Foliage
Lilac, dwarf, 37
Lim, Ping, 7, 137
Loam soils, characteristics, 66, 67
Longwood Gardens, contact information, 257
Low-maintenance roses
benefits, 7
choosing, 110, 112, *112*
EarthKind, 78, 188
for hedges, 40
for mass plantings, 38
top 16, *113*
Lundberg, Sandy, 80, *80*

M
Mabel Davis Rose Garden, contact information, 257
Macon, Carol, 73, *73*
Maiden grass, as companion plant, 37
Mail-order/online plants
greenhouse-grown, 83
overview, 82, *83*
resources, 256
Martin, Dona and Bob, 72, *72*

Mass plantings, 38–39, *38, 39*
for color, 32–33
groundcover roses for, 44
miniatures and minifloras for, 44
rose hedges, 40–41
Mattia, John, 79, *79*
Maturity, time to reach, 33
Meadow rue, as companion plant, 37
Medicinal uses, 8
Meilland, Alain, 137
Memorial Park Rose Garden, contact information, 257
Memphis Botanic Garden, contact information, 257
Mice, coping with, 121
Microclimates
defined, 258
for sun, 81, *84, 86*
understanding, 86–87, *87*
for wind protection, 73
Micronutrients
defined, 258
in fertilizers, 109
plant growth role, 106
Microsprinklers, *100*
Midwest, Northern
characteristics, 64, 66, 68
choosing roses for, 74, *74*
rose care calendar, 132–135
Midwest, Southern
characteristics, 64, 66, 68
choosing roses for, 75, *75*
rose care calendar, 132–135
Milkweed, as companion plant, 37, *77*
Minnesota tip (trenching), for winter protection, 74, *131*
Missouri Botanical Garden, contact information, 257
Mixed plantings, 36–37
air circulation, *88*
companion plants, 36–37, *77*, 138, 258
for containers, *52*
cottage gardens, 32, *34*
design roles, *32, 33*
groundcover roses for, 44
for hot, dry conditions, 77
mixed hedges, 40, 41
perennials and bulbs for, 37, *37*
trees and shrubs for, 37, *37*

Soil testing
  collecting soil for, 66
  drainage, 93
  pH, 67, 80
Solid petal patterns, *14*
The South
  characteristics, 66, 68, *78*
  choosing roses for, 78
  rose care calendar, 132–135
Southern Coast
  characteristics, 68
  choosing roses for, 80
  rose care calendar, 132–135
Spacing plants
  air circulation and,
    38, 88, *88*
  for mass plantings, 38
Sphagnum peat moss
  defined, 258
  as soil amendment, 67, *91*
Spider mites, 64, 119, *119*
Sprinklers, 101–102, 103
Stamens, defined, 11
The State Botanical Garden,
  contact information, 257
Stem canker, 116, *116*
Stems
  color, 22
  flower, anatomy, 11
  prickles, 22–23, *22*
Stephanadra, as companion
  plant, 37
Striped petal patterns, *14*
Style of garden, 32
  cottage gardens, 32
  formal gardens, 32, 46, *46–*
    47, 48, *48*
Styles (flower part), 11
Subtropical areas, rootstocks
  for, 83
Suckers
  defined, 11, 258
  nonsuckering rootstocks,
    83
Sumac, Tiger Eyes, 37
Sunlight requirements
  flowering and, 13
  fog and, 70
  full sun, 84
  impact on flower color, 14
  microclimates, 81, *84,* 86
  in Pacific Northwest, 69, *69*
  part sun/part shade,
    84–85, *84*

for planter boxes, 53
for rose hedges, 40
as site-selection criteria, 84
See also Shade
Supporting roses, methods,
  43, 246
Syringing, to reduce heat
  stress, 84
Systemic, defined, 258

T

Tarragon, as companion
  plant, 36
Temperature. *See* Climate;
  Cold (winter) hardiness;
  Hot climates
Tender plants, defined, 258
Texas
  characteristics, 68
  choosing roses for,
    76, 76, 78, 188
  rose care calendar, 132–135
Thorns (prickles),
  22–23, *22,* 38, 41
Thrips, 119, *119*
Tile drainage systems, 93
Topsoil
  defined, 258
  as soil amendment, 91
Training roses
  to improve air circulation,
    88, *88, 89*
  support methods, *43,* 246
  See also Pruning
Transplanting, 97, 132–135
  See also Planting
Traps, for animal pests, 121
Trees
  growing near, 37, *37*
  as rose supports, 42, *43*
Trellises. *See* Arbors, trellises,
  and pergolas
Trenching (Minnesota tip),
  for winter protection,
    74, *131*
Tuteurs, *43*

U

United Nations Rose Garden,
  contact information, 257
University of Hawaii
  Botanical Garden, contact
  information, 257
Upright growth habit, *23*

USDA Plant Hardiness
  Zones, 61, *61,* 86

V

Very full flowers, *18*
Viburnum, Blue Muffin, 37
Vierbicky, Connie, 77, *77*
Vigor, defined, 110
Vintage Gardens Antique
  Roses, contact
  information, 256
Virus diseases, 83, 117, *117*
Voles, coping with, 121

W

Walls. *See* Fences and walls
Walt Disney World, contact
  information, 257
War of the Roses, 8, *8*
Washington Park Gardens,
  137
Watering
  container roses,
    52, 55, *99,* 103
  in dry climates, 62, 64, *64*
  in fall, 131
  before fertilizing, 106, 109
  irrigation systems, 100
  methods, 101, *101,* 103
  newly planted roses,
    94, 95, 101
  overwatering, 93, 103
  plant moisture
    requirements, *66,* 100
  rose care calendar, 132–135
  in sandy soils, 67
  in spring, 130
  when to water, 103
  See also specific regions; specific
    roses
Waxbells, as companion
  plant, 37
Wayside Gardens, contact
  information, 256
Weeds
  companion plants as, 37
  herbicides to control,
    90, 105, 258
  mulching to control,
    104, *104,* 105
  prior to planting, 90, *90–91*
  rose care calendar, 132–135
Weeks Roses, 7, 137
Wellan, Marilyn, 78, *78*

Western Mountains,
  choosing roses for, 73
Wet conditions
  characteristics, 65
  container gardens, 52
  moist conditions, 65
  in Pacific Northwest, 69, *69*
  varieties tolerant of,
    58, 59, 65
  See also Humidity
Wind
  protecting plants from,
    73, 79, 80, 131
  varieties tolerant of, 44, *58*
Window boxes, 53, *53*
Winter kill, defined, 258
Winter protection
  mounding soil, 75
  mulching, 75, 131
  for New England, *79*
  for planter boxes, 53
  removing in spring,
    130, *130*
  roses in containers, 50, 98
  snow as insulation, 60
  trenching, 74, *131*
  for Western Mountains, 73
  wrapping plants, *131*
  See also Cold (winter)
    hardiness
Wire cages, to deter animal
  pests, *94,* 120, *120,* 121
Wood chips or bark, as
  mulch, 104, *105*
Woodland Park Rose Garden,
  contact information, 257
World Federation of Rose
  Societies, 137, 256
Wyckoff, Jeff, 69, *69*

Z

Zary, Keith, 7, 137

Rose index

▲ For every purpose, there is just the right rose. To create this effect of a rose weaving lightly through a picket fence, choose a rose with long sprawling canes that grows slightly higher than the fence itself.

Rose index *(continued)*

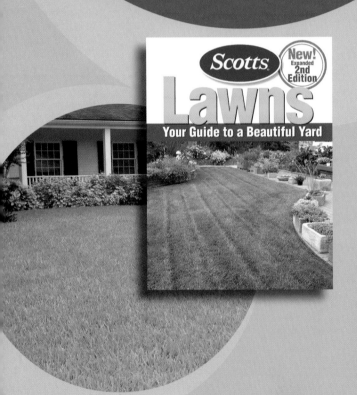